Comparative Law in the 21st Century

W.G. Hart Legal Workshop Series

Comparative Law in the 21st Century

Edited by

Andrew Harding and Esin Örücü

KLUWER ACADEMIC PUBLISHERS
LONDON / THE HAGUE / NEW YORK

Published by:
Kluwer Law International
P.O.Box 85889, 2508 CN The Hague, The Netherlands
sales@kli.wkap.nl
http://www.kluwerlaw.com

Sold and Distributed in North, Central and South America by:
Kluwer Law International
101 Philip Drive, Norwell, MA 02061, USA
kluwerlaw@wkap.com

Sold and Distributed in all other countries by:
Kluwer Law International
Distribution Centre, P.O. Box 322, 3300 AH Dordrecht, The Netherlands

Library of Congress Cataloging-in-Publication Data is available.

Printed on acid-free paper

ISBN 90-411-9875-X

Kluwer Law International incorporates the imprint Martinus Nijhoff Publishers.

CONTENTS

PREFACE

1. Origins and Purposes

This book emanates from the W.G. Hart Legal Workshop, held at the Institute of Advanced Legal Studies, University of London, on 4–6 July 2000 under the title 'Comparative Law in the 21st Century'.[1] This Workshop had itself been conceived following an earlier seminar (December 1997) at the British Institute of International and Comparative Law, at which an interesting discovery was made. The seminar had brought together representatives of what appeared to be two different, even fundamentally opposed, traditions in comparative law: Glasgow University Law School's tradition based largely on comparing civil and common law; and SOAS Law Department's tradition of studying the laws and legal cultures of Asia and Africa.

This encounter, which was more in the nature of a 'friendly' as opposed to a 'cup tie', led those present, and especially the present editors, to think that there was more of a consensus about the new tasks of comparative lawyers and the nature of our subject than we had previously thought; and that what had been taken to be the prevailing orthodoxies had perhaps in fact ceased to prevail. Bearing in mind the impending millennium, and the IALS' need to determine the topics for the W.G. Hart Workshops for the next few years, it seemed an unrivalled opportunity to mark the new millennium by looking at contemporary scholarship, in the UK law schools and more widely, in the context of new tasks or new definitions for comparative law. The W.G. Hart Workshop has always been a forum for the airing of work by younger colleagues in UK law schools, and we felt that there was probably more comparative law actually taking place than had been realised, and we were interested to know how much and of what kind. If comparative law for the next century was in the hands of younger colleagues (as it must be), then the time was clearly ripe for a discussion of comparative law in the 21st century. The year 2000 was also the centenary of the First International Congress of Comparative Law, held in Paris in 1900, which had set the agenda of comparative law for most of the 20th century. To quote from our Call for Papers (1999):

> Although for most of the 20th century it appeared as if the ambitious project of legal unification set out in Paris was retreating from view as the world was torn apart by deep ideological conflicts, the last few years have seen a remarkable turnaround. Not only did the principal object of European legal unification make very significant advances from 1972: global economic and political

[1] For details, see <www.soas.ac.uk/law/wghart>.

> conditions after the end of the Cold War (1945–89) made comparative law more immediately important and more worthwhile globally. The 1990s saw many positive developments in legal science and legal reform on every continent and advances in international norms. As Lord Goff of Chieveley wrote recently: "Comparative law may have been the hobby of yesterday but is destined to become the science of tomorrow".[2]
> These developments have called into question the fundamental orientation and assumptions of comparative law. It seems appropriate at the centenary of the Paris Congress to take a fresh look at the subject and decide where it should be directed during the 21st century. For example, what kind of substantive areas should comparative law research now concern itself with? Should comparative law compare rules, or the contexts or cultures in which rules operate? How 'global' can the subject be? The object of this W.G. Hart Workshop is therefore to reexamine the main propositions of comparative law in a critical perspective in the light of changing socio-legal and other conditions in the world in 2000

Lord Goff, the keynote speaker on the occasion of our Workshop, called comparative law the 'flavour of the next century', but also advocated caution, especially in the comparative study of substantive law, and proposed instead the reform of civil *procedure* by looking at other systems. He did not support European Codes or European Principles or unification by any other means: conversation and marriage, he warned us, are not the same thing. Cross-fertilization however was inevitable and useful.

The Workshop was organised under four consecutive panels, as follows:

(1) *Comparative law and the "religious systems of law"*, convened by Andrew Huxley (SOAS).

Most comparative law textbooks introduce their subject by allocating the world's legal systems into families of law, which typically concentrate on western law and its present influence. Some use a genus 'religious systems' to contain non-European and pre-20th century legal traditions. Asian law is regarded as either wholly western/ modern (Japan, China) or wholly religious/pre-modern (Hindu, Islamic, Jewish, Buddhist). The panel looked at Christianity, Judaism, Hinduism, Buddhism, Roman law, Islamic law, Chinese law and Canon law. Three linked questions were considered: Is it useful to classify the world's legal phenomena into families? If so, should one of the families be labelled 'religious systems'? If so, which of the world's legal cultures should be included here? Not only is it difficult to regard all the presented 'isms' as being of the same genus, but some are not legal systems; 'belief systems' and religious laws are not the same thing. Religious systems do not belong to a family and it is difficult to define a religious legal system. At a time when the theory of legal families is under attack and is not regarded as useful except as a

[2] Lord Goff, 'The Future of the Common Law' (1997) 46 *International and Comparative Law Quarterly* 745, pp. 747–8.

teaching device, comparatists in the 21st Century will no longer talk of a 'religious legal family' and have to recognise the very specialist nature of these studies. Yet the non-black-letter-law approach that is developing among comparatists, will regard religion as part of the underlying deeply seated processes that influence the evolving shape of law.

(2) *Comparative public law*, convened by Andrew Harding (SOAS).

Comparative law in the 20th century omitted almost entirely to deal with public law topics such as constitutional law, administrative law, and even criminal law. Many scholars doubted the possibility of meaningful comparative law scholarship in these areas. This panel examined public law concepts and institutions comparatively in the new climate of a global shift towards democracy and human rights. It was once more pointed out that in the construction of legal systems, especially of the developing world, legal transplants play a very important part and that this is not just a historical, but also a contemporary, phenomenon. This is now most evident in public law. South East Asia and Southern Africa, examples elaborated in the panel, are witness to this. The future of comparative law also involves regional studies and further conversation between regional comparatists, as institutions, rules, the external and internal dynamics and the underlying structures and processes must all be appreciated.

In the area of comparative constitutional law perhaps there is little room for divergences, and hands-on assistance for law reform will prove useful in the coming years, though the importance of differences of legal and political culture have to be kept in mind by comparatists. The comparative approach has a renewed legitimacy. Constitutionalism, human rights and administrative accountability are areas that will attract the attention of comparatists in the years to come.

(3) *Transmigrations and transferability of legal ideas and institutions*, convened by Esin Örücü (Glasgow).

One of the major tasks of comparative law in the 21st century will be to analyse and to aid the transfer of legal ideas and institutions. Reciprocal influence will have a central role in the reshaping of not only evolving systems in transition but all legal systems. The process is not without its problems. This panel contributed to the development of theory in the field and thereby enriched the theoretical matrix by looking at recent examples of transmigration of law, ranging from Hungary to South Africa, and assessing the factors involved in the transferability of law. The relationship between models and recipients and ways of resolving tensions between legal-cultural and/or socio-cultural diversity were also considered through examples. Speakers referred to the works of Watson, Kahn-Freund, the Seidmans, Legrand and Teubner as paradigmatic theories of legal transplantation. New directions in this field were suggested, for example the role of the comparatist for the future was shown to be that of making knowledge available for the growth of legal systems through competition of legal rules as spontaneous orders. It was also pointed out that while the 20th Century looked at similarities between legal systems from the exportation perspective, in the 21st Century we should also look for differences from the importation perspective. The importance of deep-seated epistemic processes was emphasised in assessing why legal transplants succeed or fail. Evolution from within is preferred, nevertheless globalization means that an emerging cosmopolitan elite will have a significant impact on the future of legal systems and the ways in which they develop. Assimilating and fitting of the models into the domestic milieu needs further analysis. Reforming the law will inevitably lead to more transpositions and analysis of contexts.

We were warned against generalizations and asked to test theories and undertake more empirical work to determine instances of anti-transplant or areas of resistance to transplants. Degrees of receptivity and bijurality of laws and legal systems were discussed. Transmigration is however here to stay. It requires both conceptual and analytical refinement – and in many fields hitherto regarded as resistant to transplants.

(4) *Comparative Law: the European Dimension*, convened by Noreen Burrows (Glasgow).

The comparative law method has been adapted to suit the needs of the European Community (Union) both in harmonizing and approximating the economic and commercial laws of its members and in facilitating the countries of Eastern Europe in their modernization programmes, often with the goal of membership of the European Union. This panel assessed the measure of success in the attainment of common laws in Eastern and Western Europe. Individual attempts were viewed in the context of the debate on the possibility and desirability of a new European *ius commune* for the 21st century. Some of the papers reiterated the point that comparative lawyers must work with colleagues from other disciplines and that although there are cultural similarities in the western world, responses to ethical and social issues differ greatly. European experts are working as consultants in Central and Eastern Europe and their crucial role will be enhanced by an understanding of the role of comparative law in such ventures and the realisation that the study of economic and social background should become part of comparative legal studies. Nevertheless Europe is a new market for comparative law studies and comparatists are needed for political processes.

The closing session summed up the comparative law agenda set by the Workshop, reflecting on socio-legal change and the metaphors of legal adaptation. In the following discussion concepts such as eurocentrism, ethnocentrism, fragmentation, legal pluralism, legal anthropology, social engineering, language, channels of transplants, versions of comparative studies and construction of theoretical models, came to the fore. We were left with the questions, are we expecting too much from comparative law? and, more importantly, are we expecting too much from comparative lawyers?

2. Organization of the Book

This book comprises papers from the last three of the four panels and the closing session. The papers from the first panel are published in a parallel volume.[3] They form a nucleus convenient for separate publication.

It was decided not to retain the original order of the papers, but rather to arrange them in such a way as to bring out the narrative or organic progression that they created naturally. Nonetheless they do fall roughly into four sections. The first three papers (Örücü, Nelken and Cotterrell) are general, introductory and also in some ways summatory. The next four (Foster, Raffenne, de Cruz and Thomas) deal with specific examples of comparative study from different areas of law: commercial, private and public – leading to the next four papers (Smits, van Gerven, Banakas, and McDonald), which deal with European legal integration. The last of these, which raises the question of a European constitution, leads seamlessly into a general discussion of public law in the next four papers (Leyland, Bell, Harding, Du Pré) which also range over several geographical regions. The book finishes with a paper (Carey-Miller) that seems to exemplify practically all the themes under discussion in the problematical but promising jurisdiction of South Africa.

It was also decided to introduce each chapter of the book with an editorial linking passage to create a threaded discussion leading the reader through the various themes raised by the authors, and providing continuity of thought.

At the end of the book readers will find a Bibliography, which will hopefully assist in studying and teaching comparative law in the 21st century.

3. Concerning the Scope of Comparative Law

So what is the tenor of current discussion about comparative law against which the contributors have prepared these papers?

Discussions about comparative law tend these days to be concerned less with 'justifying its practical utility', 'making its subject matter manageable', and 'avoiding superficiality',[4] than with emphasizing that it is a 'big tent, encompassing lots of different types of scholarship'[5] or something which 'there seems little point in trying to specify',[6] and which discovers the inadequacy of the discipline's 'tools, classifications and teaching techniques' for 'the analysis of modern legal problems'.[7]

---

3 A. Huxley (ed), *Religion, Law and Tradition: Comparative Studies in Religious Law* (Curzon, Richmond, 2002, forthcoming).

4 W. Twining, 'Comparative Law and Legal Theory: the Country and Western Tradition' in Edge, I.D. (ed), *Comparative Law in Global Context* (2000), p. 51.

5 D. Kennedy, "The Politics and Methods of Comparative Law", in P. Legrand and R. Munday (ed), *Comparative Legal Studies: Traditions and Transitions* (Cambridge, Cambridge University Press, 2002, forthcoming).

6 Roger Cotterrell's piece in this volume.

7 Markesinis (1998), below n. 10, at p. 36.

Twining even says that 'few experienced comparatists compare – and for good reason'.[8]

Many comparatists actually regard the articulation of foreign legal systems in their own particular contexts as the most important task of comparative law. Others again will say that this is insufficient, and that the object is to decide which rule or principle is best. This is all hardly surprising in view of the globalization of, or at least the realisation of the global significance of markets, of the problems of human society, and even culture itself; and in view of increasing knowledge of and interest in, or acceptance of, the way 'the other' organises her affairs. It should be noticed, however, that the new interest in foreign legal systems per se is not exactly a case of reluctance to compare: more accurately, the comparison is simply implicit, and this approach does not obviate the need to have theory, concepts, and methodology, but merely changes their nature.

Comparative law has also become a more significant area for legal research, and for a variety of reasons. As Andrew Harding put it during the sessions, 'some are born comparative lawyers, some achieve comparative law, and some have comparative law thrust upon them: one might add that some merely wander innocently into comparative law, not having had the slightest idea that that was what they were doing.' Esin Örücü reckons that the number of articles and books on the subject has quadrupled in the last ten years:[9] the chapters in this book are merely the tip or at least a rather small segment of a huge iceberg, but are nonetheless indicative of a broad range of comparative law concerns, talents and approaches even just within British scholarship.

Such diversity and popularity are to be welcomed. However, comparative law is not just experiencing the pleasure of the ageing movie star suddenly becoming a cult figure: it is also fraught with internal contradiction, uncertainty, and a sense of mid-life crisis. The new situation raises even more acutely questions that had appeared to be receding in importance, about the nature, aims and purposes of the subject. Who are properly regarded as comparatists, especially if they do not actually compare? What is their actual field of endeavour? What are their motives and agendas? What methods do they, should they, employ? Is comparative law a hobby or a science? How does it differ from other related fields such as international law, socio-legal studies, law-and-development studies, legislative science, and area studies? Does it aim towards legal uniformity and convergence, or diversity and fragmentation?

Örücü notices a quadrupling of effort, but it is also true that a remarkable proportion of these books and articles, compared with other sub-disciplines, are reflexive: these are not comparative-law studies as such but rather angst-ridden

---

8 Twining, above n. 4, at p. 47.

9 'Critical Comparative Law: Considering Paradoxes for Legal Systems in Transition' (2000) 4 *Electronic Journal of Comparative Law* 2.

theses about what comparative law is actually about, or what it is for.[10] This book delves into these questions and provides an indication of the type and scope of comparative law studies at the turn of the millennium.

---

[10] J.S. Bell, 'Comparative Law and Legal Theory' in W. Krawietz et al (ed), *Prescriptive Formality and Normative Rationality in Modern Legal Systems: Festschrift for Robert Summers* (Duncker and Humblot, Berlin, 1995); H. Collins, 'Methods and Aims of Comparative Contract Law' (1991) 11 *Oxford Journal of Legal Studies* 396; I.D. Edge (ed), *Comparative Law in Global Context* (2000); W. Ewald, 'Comparative Jurisprudence I: What was it Like to Try a Rat?' (1995) 143 *Pennsylvania Law Review* 1889; W. Ewald, 'Comparative Jurisprudence II: The Logic of Legal Transplants' (1995) 43 *American Journal of Comparative Law* 489; Fletcher, 'Comparative Law as a Subversive Discipline' (1998) 46 *American Journal of Comparative Law* 683; T. Koopmans, T., 'Comparative Law and the Courts' (1998) 45 *International and Comparative Law Quarterly* 545; P. Legrand and J. H. Merryman 'Comparative Legal Studies: A Dialogue' (1999) 47 *American Journal of Comparative Law* 201; B. Markesinis, 'Comparative Law: a Subject in Search of an Audience' (1990) 53 *Modern Law Review* 1; B. Markesinis (ed), *The Gradual Convergence* (Clarendon Press, Oxford, 1994); B. Markesinis, *Foreign Law and Comparative Methodology* (Hart Publishing, Oxford, 1998); U. Mattei, 'Three Patterns of Law: Taxonomy and Change in the World's Legal Systems' (1997) 45 *American Journal of Comparative Law* P5; .G. Monateri, '"Everybody's Talking": The Future of Comparative Law' (1996) 21 *Hastings International and Comparative Law Review* 825; D. Nelken (ed.), *Comparing Legal Cultures* (Dartmouth, Aldershot, 1997); D. Nelken and J. Feest (eds), *Adapting Legal Cultures* (Hart Publishing, Oxford, 2001); L.A. Obiora, L.A., 'Toward an Auspicious Reconciliation of International and Comparative Analyses' 46 *American Journal of Comparative Law* 669 (1998)'; E. Örücü, 'Critical Comparative Law' (2000) 4 *Electronic Journal of Comparative Law* 2; J.C. Reitz, 'How to do Comparative Law' (1998) 46 *American Journal of Comparative Law* 597; R. Sacco, 'Legal Formants: a Dynamic Approach to Comparative Law' (1991) 39 *American Journal of Comparative Law* 1 and 343; G. Samuel, 'Comparative Law and Jurisprudence' (1998) 47 *International and Comparative Law Quarterly* 817; R.B. Schlesinger, 'The Past and Future of Comparative Law' (1995) 43 *American Journal of Comparative Law* 477; M. van Hoecke and M. Warrington, 'Legal Cultures and Legal Paradigms: Towards a New model for Comparative Law' (1998) 47 *International and Comparative Law Quarterly* 495. And conferences in Michigan (1996), Utah (1996) San Francisco (1997), Chicago (2000); Cambridge (2000) as well as the conference whose papers are published herein (London, 2000). For details of these conferences, see Örücü's chapter in this volume at n. 9.

Chapter 1

UNDE VENIT, QUO TENDIT COMPARATIVE LAW?

*Esin Örücü**

1. *UNDE VENIT* COMPARATIVE LAW?

1.1. Comparative Law as We Know It

> Modern, systematic comparative law is a child of the nineteenth century and an adolescent of the twentieth. During this period, beyond giving the comparative lawyer a free rein and being regarded as interesting, comparative law has provided a seemingly unending pastime for comparatists and others to discuss its true meaning, historical development, dangers, virtues, scope, functions, aims and purposes, uses and misuses, and method, and this even after comparative law had been accepted as part of the undergraduate curriculum in most universities.[1]

Today the subject is regarded as 'strategic', the present century having been heralded as 'the era of comparative law',[2] the time of its majority. Yet there is no decisive definition of what comparative law and comparative method is today. It seems still open to discussion whether this is indeed an independent discipline at all,[3] and comparatists are called upon to re-think their subject.[4] One rather circular and vague definition tells us that: 'the words suggest an intellectual activity with law as its object and comparison as its process'.[5] There is however, an unprecedented growing interest in the subject, and the observation that, 'if comparative law did not exist it

* Professor of Comparative Law, University of Glasgow and Erasmus University Rotterdam.

1 E. Örücü, *Critical Comparative Law: Considering Paradoxes for Legal Systems in Transition* (Kluwer Law International, Deventer, 1999), p. 1.

2 T. Koopmans, 'Comparative Law and the Courts' (1996) 45 *International Comparative Law Quarterly* 545.

3 G. Samuel, 'Comparative Law and Jurisprudence' (1998) 47 *International Comparative Law Quarterly* 817; J. Gordley 'Is Comparative Law a Distinct Discipline?' (1998) 46 *American Journal of Comparative Law* 607.

4 B. Markesinis, 'Comparative Law – A Subject in Search of an Audience' (1990) 53 *Modern Law Review* 1.

5 K. Zweigert and H. Kötz, *An Introduction to Comparative Law* (3rd. edn., Clarendon Press, Oxford, 1998), p. 2.

A. Harding and E. Örücü (eds.),
Comparative Law in the 21st Century, 1–18.

would have to have been invented',[6] is even more pertinent today. Witness the law journals over the last ten years where the number of articles on comparative law has quadrupled.

All comparative law textbooks inform the reader of the 1900 Paris Congress and of the aligning of comparatists as methodologists and social scientists, the aims and purposes of comparative law and how it relates to other branches of law. Comparative law has been categorised as descriptive/ dogmatic/ applied/ contrasting; legislative/ scholarly/ scientific or theoretical; formal/ dogmatic/ historical; comparative nomoscopy/ nomothetics/ nomogenetics; internal/ external; and, macro comparison/ micro comparison. The objectives of comparative law are noted as academic study, law reform and policy development, to provide a tool for research towards a universal theory of law, perspective to students, aid to international practice of the law, international unification and harmonization – common core research, a gap filling device in law courts, and aid to world peace.[7] Whether these uses have been fully taken advantage of and whether the objectives have been realised is open for discussion[8] when taking stock of comparative legal studies as we move into a 'new century for comparative law'.[9]

1.2. Comparative Law at the End of the 20th Century

A number of distinct approaches to comparative law became prominent towards the end of the 20th century. On the one hand these approaches may enhance the prospects of comparative law; on the other, some of them could swallow it up and change its character. Some such distinct trends worth mentioning in comparative law discourse today are comparative law and legal history (historical comparative law or historico-comparative perspective); comparative law and legal philosophy (comparative jurisprudence); comparative law and culture (comparative legal cultures and law and culture studies); comparative law and economics; and comparative law and regions or subjects hitherto not covered. Public law, whether administrative or constitutional, criminal law and human rights demand that comparatists consider these urgently rather than putting all their efforts into private law which has dominated the scene in the past. In addition, attention should be paid to regions

[6] H.J. Ault and M.A. Glendon, 'The Importance of Comparative Law in Legal Education: United States – Goals and Methods of Legal Comparison' in J.N. Hazard, and W.J. Wagner (eds.), *Law in the USA in Social and Technological Revolution* (Bruylant, Brussels, 1974), p. 69.

[7] These objectives are sometimes grouped as practical, sociological, political or pedagogical, and comparative law categorised as 'descriptive', 'applied', 'abstract or speculative'.

[8] See E. Örücü, *Symbiosis between Comparative Law and Theory of law – Limitations of Legal Methodology*, (Erasmus Universiteit Rotterdam, Mededelingen van het Juridisch Instituut Nr. 16, Rotterdam, 1982), pp. 1–25, and citations therein.

[9] Note recent Symposia in the USA and Europe. See for example, New Directions in Comparative Law, Michigan, September 1996 and Hastings College in San Francisco, 1997; New Approaches to Comparative Law, Utah, October 1996; and Centennial World Congress on Comparative Law, New Orleans, November 2000 (see [2001] *Tulane Law Review*).

neglected until recently, and comparatists should not see the world as divided between common law and the civil law traditions only.

1.2.1. Comparative Law and Legal History

The combination of comparative law and legal history is widely used by legal transplant scholars and the 'new *ius commune* seekers'. Legal historians are looking at past legal transplants and transfrontier mobility of ideas and institutions, both in an effort to offer an understanding of, and an explanation for, the development of the law and to help justify future legal development utilizing law reform through the use of foreign models and, in the context of Europe, to rediscover a *ius commune*.

The third thesis of the Trento Manifesto is: 'Comparison turns its attention to various phenomena of legal life operating in the past or the present, considers legal propositions as historical facts including those formulated by legislators, judges and scholars, and so verifies what genuinely occurred. In this sense, comparative law is an historical science'.[10] According to Sacco, 'Comparative law examines the way in which legal institutions are connected, diversified and transplanted from one country to another'.[11] Even the following question has been asked: 'Is comparative law anything more than legal history?'[12]

1.2.2. Comparative Law and Jurisprudence

Its advocates claim that only the combination of comparative law and legal philosophy can reach a true understanding of law. This trend initially saw comparative law as 'just another term for sophisticated legal analysis'.[13] 'A local or national science of law is a contradiction *in adjecto*',[14] and 'in this sense comparative law is another name for legal science'.[15] It has been suggested that 'comparative law should provide the opportunity to study the internal structures of legal knowledge'[16] and contribute to jurisprudence by helping to 'construct a range of different 'ontological' models through the institutional deconstruction and reconstruction of case law and doctrinal analysis from a range of different legal

[10] R. Sacco, 'Legal Formants: A Dynamic Approach to Comparative Law (Instalment I of II)' (1991) 39 *American Journal of Comparative Law* 1, footnote 29, p. 26.

[11] R. Sacco, 'Legal Formants: A Dynamic Approach to Comparative Law (Instalment II of II)' (1991) 39 *American Journal of Comparative Law* 343, p. 388.

[12] D. Roebuck, 'The Past is Another Country: Legal History as Comparative Law' (1994) 2 *Asia Pacific Law Review (Special Issue)*, pp. 9–23

[13] B. Kozolchyk, 'Trends in Comparative Legal Research: Apropos Dainow's the Role of Judicial Decision and Doctrine in Civil Law and Mixed Jurisdictions' (1976) 24 *American Journal of Comparative Law* 100, p. 111.

[14] H. Yntema, 'The American Journal of Comparative Law', (1952) 15 *American Journal of Comparative Law* 1; and L.J. Constantinesco, *Traité de Droit Comparé: La Méthode Comparative*, Tom II, (Libraire Générale de Droit et de Jurisprudence, Paris, 1974), pp. 306–310.

[15] H. Yntema, 'Comparative Legal Research – Some Remarks on Looking out of the Cave' (1956) 54 *Michigan Law Review* 902.

[16] Samuel, n. 3 above, p. 833.

systems'.[17] So here the legal theorist wants to employ the services of comparative law for legal theory, since comparative law 'can go far in testing each system's construction of its perceived social reality'.[18]

Ewald points out that traditional comparative law has failed by paying insufficient attention to context and ignoring the context of ideas,[19] and that 'comparative law, properly pursued, is an essentially philosophical activity'.[20]

To regard comparative law as intertwined with legal theory or jurisprudence is one thing, to utilize comparative legal research exclusively to test theories and see it simply as a helping hand to legal theory is another. In that second sense, comparative law is still not a subject in its own right.[21]

1.2.3. Comparative Law and Culture

In the 1970s, the combination of comparative law and culture took the form of 'law and society studies', and in the 1980s, 'law and popular culture'. At the present time, the main aim is to provide a better understanding of multi-culturalism and integration. There is a growing volume of impressive literature here, with anthropologists and sociologists querying the kinds of complexities and problems arising.

It is among scholars interested in culture that we find the majority of the so-called 'contrarian challenge' supporters. It is they who are most concerned with the clash of cultures surviving under monolithic value systems imposed by legislatures.[22]

By displaying unsuccessful examples, notably those from the colonial period, comparative legal studies can reveal frequent failures and weaknesses of transplants in the past where it was used as a method of law reform and modernization. At the same time, by providing examples of successful transplants, where the recipient has

---

17 Ibid., p. 836. Also see G. Samuel, 'Comparative Law as a core subject' (2001) 21 *Legal Studies* 444.

18 Ibid. Also see along similar lines, W.J. Kamba, 'Comparative Law: A Theoretical Framework' (1976) 23 *International Comparative Law Quarterly* 494.

19 W. Ewald, 'Comparative Jurisprudence (1): What was it like to Try a Rat?' (1995) 143 *Pennsylvania Law Review* 1889, pp. 2111–2112. Also look for a discussion in M. Van Hoecke and M. Warrington, 'Legal Cultures and Legal Paradigms: Towards a New Model for Comparative Law' (1998) 47 *International Comparative Law Quarterly* 495.

20 Ewald n. 19 above, p. 2145.

21 However, Bell claims that legal theory has something to learn from comparative law. See J. Bell, 'Comparative Law and Legal Theory' in W. Krawietz, N. MacCormick and G. Henrik von Wright, (eds.), *Prescriptive Formality and Normative Rationality in Modern Legal Systems: Festschrift for Robert Summers* (Duncker and Humblot, Berlin, 1995), pp. 23–31. On the other hand Ward is worried as he sees macro-comparativism being pursued as an alternative to jurisprudence. See I. Ward, 'The Limits of Comparativism: Lessons from UK-EC Integration' (1995) 2 Maastricht Journal of European and Comparative Law 23, p. 31.

22 See here L.A. Obiora, 'Toward an Auspicious Reconciliation of International and Comparative Analyses' (1998) 46 *American Journal of Comparative Law* 669, emphasising the need to reflect and respect social and cultural diversity while maintaining a universalist claim. Also see G. P. Fletcher, 'Comparative Law as a Subversive Discipline' (1998) 46 *American Journal of Comparative Law* 683, who assesses comparative law as a form of 'cultural criticism'.

used the import to its own benefit through its own creative efforts without alienating the socio-culture, comparative legal studies can also show legal transplanting as the best road towards law reform. Unfortunately, research in this field has not always been impartial.

1.2.4. Comparative Law and Economics

Economists are trying to establish a blue print by which systems can choose the most efficient solution to global problems from the pool of solutions offered by competing systems, as an alternative to harmonization and codification. The belief is that a new *ius commune* in European private law can develop through the competition of legal rules and the eventual emergence of the most efficient or 'best' rule.[23] The prerequisites for achieving harmony will not be necessarily similarity or regularity, but difference and diversity. The comparative law and economics approach aims at building models for efficient legal institutions, and then comparing them with the actual world alternatives provided by different legal systems, offering explanations for the reasons and the mode of the departure.[24]

Comparative law has become the special prey of the 'intellectual imperialism' of the law and economics movement.[25] If this relationship can move beyond 'colonization' into one of co-partnership, then comparative law can only gain and prove to be indispensable.

1.2.5. Critical Comparative Law

I have suggested elsewhere, that comparative lawyers understand comparative law to be a subject in its own right, as the only reliable way of accumulating knowledge of the reality of law, and assessing problems that may arise out of the proposed marriages discussed above, and giving warning signals where need be.[26] One of the tasks is to analyse fully the underlying phenomena addressed, that is, the transfrontier mobility of ideas and institutions and reciprocal influence. Most of the current concerns of comparatists on convergence versus divergence, mismatch in borrowings, and problems for the importer and the exporter of legal ideas and institutions can be constructively approached under the title 'Critical Comparative Law'. In addition, this term is the antithesis of the term 'traditional comparative law', or 'conventional comparative law'.

---

23 See for an interesting variation, J. Smits, 'A European Private Law as a Mixed System' (1998) 5 Maastricht Journal of European and Comparative Law 328. Also see J. Smits, 'How to Take the Road Untravelled? European Private Law in the Making: A Review Essay' (1999) 6 Maastricht Journal of European and Comparative Law 25, especially pp. 40–41.

24 U. Mattei, 'Efficiency in Legal Transplants: An Essay in Comparative Law and Economics' (1994) 14 *International Review of Law and Economics* 3.

25 D. Campbell and S. Picciotto, 'Exploring the Interaction between Law and Economics: the Limits of Formalism' (1998) 18 *Legal Studies* 249.

26 Örücü, n. 1 above.

1.2.6. Comparative Law in Europe Today

Today, comparative law is extensively used within the European Union and its first task is in the 'new *ius commune*' studies where it is asked to facilitate integration and make a case for reciprocal influence as the basis for convergence. Its related task is to find ways of reconciling civil law and common law and furthermore to aid the creation of European Codes. A more general task is to act as a tool for construction in the courts, national and European.

Looking away from home, Europe sees comparative law as a tool for the export of legal ideas and institutions and aiding law reform. Competing models of Western European legal systems are to be put on a convincing display with the help of comparatists.

1.2.7. Comparative Law in the Common Law World

There is renewed interest in research and teaching in comparative common law, and additional concern in the USA that comparative law has grown in the shadow of Europe and that it must develop its own agenda if it is to be taken seriously.[27] There is also the competition of the US with European systems to sell her legal export in preference to any European model, especially in Central and Eastern European States.

A further point is the strong general desire to keep English law intact within the European Union ('EU') by stressing the view that legal systems of our day should remain flexible and realistic and therefore, uncodified. Finally, the attitude of the Privy Council in Britain to legal systems and legal cultures in the Commonwealth and the unity of the common law is changing.[28]

So, at the end of one century and entering the next, comparative law must take stock of some of the most important problematic issues that arise out of the above picture. The shifting and changing horizons for comparative law must be analysed through a critical stance.[29]

1.3. Reciprocal Influence

Reciprocal influence, which has dominated most of the 20th century, will continue to do so in the 21st. This influence today is most prominent within the EU, and transplants from the Western legal traditions to the Eastern and Central European legal systems, in the wider Europe. The result is the birth of systems in transition and

27 M. Reimann, 'Stepping Out of the European Shadow: Why Comparative Law in the United States Must Develop Its Own Agenda' (1998) 46 *American Journal of Comparative Law* 637. Also see, U. Mattei and M. Reimann, 'Introduction' (1998) 46 *American Journal of Comparative Law* 597.

28 See R. Martin, 'Diverging Common Law – Invercargill goes to the Privy Council' (1997) 60 *Modern Law Review* 94; and J. M. M. Chan, 'Hong Kong's Bill of Rights: Its Reception of and Contribution to International and Comparative Jurisprudence' (1998) 47 *International Comparative Law Quarterly* 306.

29 See also E. Örücü, 'Shifting Horizons for Comparative Law in the New Century' (2000) 8 Asia Pacific Law Review 115.

mixing systems, the emergence of new clashes between legal cultures themselves or legal cultures and socio-cultures, and the blurring of the demarcation lines between the generally accepted classification of legal families. These changes are coming about by voluntary reception rather than colonization and imposition, as was the case in the past. Even so, there are still some notable imposed receptions such as is the case in Central and Eastern Europe, which are often termed 'collective colonization by the EU'. There are also distinct differences in the character of the new movements.

It is true that the transplant theory needs some conceptual refinement. Some challenge the 'convergence theses' and 'functional equivalence'; some claim that 'legal transplants are impossible'.[30] Others say that the conceptual refinement needed would 'allow us to analyse institutional transfer in terms different from the simple alternative context versus autonomy'.[31] The term 'legal irritant' is used and defined as an alternative to legal transplants, in that 'when a foreign rule is imposed on a domestic culture ... something else is happening. It is not transplanted into another organism, rather it works as a fundamental irritation which triggers a whole series of new and unexpected events ... it irritates law's "binding arrangements"'.[32]

Classical statements of legal transplants use terms such as transplant, reception, imposed reception, solicited imposition, crypto-reception and inoculation.[33] These terms have been superseded and a colourful vocabulary has been created highlighting nuances in individual instances of such mobility and influence, such as implantation, cross-fertilisation, infiltration, infusion, transposition, emulation, engulfment, grafting, re-potting, cross-pollination, digestion, salad bowl and melting pot; and new bases for analysis are being developed such as contaminants, legal irritants, collective colonization, competition of legal systems, hyphenated-law and layered-law.[34]

1.3.1. Convergence or Non-convergence

There is a significant division of belief among comparatists. On the one hand, it is claimed that only convergent or similar systems can benefit from each other's experience; hence the attempts to enlarge the catchment area of systems covered by the new *ius commune* within the context of a wider Europe. Yet, many systems in transition look at, and are inspired by, systems which are socio-culturally or legal

---

30 P. Legrand, 'The Impossibility of Legal Transplants' (1997) 4 *Maastricht Journal of European and Comparative Law* 111.

31 G. Teubner, 'Legal Irritants: Good Faith in British Law or How Unifying Law Ends Up in New Divergences' (1998) 61 *Modern Law Review* 11, p. 17.

32 Ibid., p. 12.

33 A. Watson, *Legal Transplants: An Approach to Comparative Law* (Scottish Academic Press, Edinburgh, 1974), n. 53, p. 30.

34 See for a more complete list, E. Örücü, 'A Theoretical Framework for Transfrontier Mobility of Law' in R. Jagtenberg, E. Örücü, and A. De Roo (eds.), *Transfrontier Mobility of Law* (Kluwer Law International, The Hague, 1995), p. 5.

culturally different from their own, and legal rules often seem to be equally at home in many places; and 'whatever their historical origins may have been, rules of private law can survive without any close connection to any particular people, any particular period of time or any particular place'.[35] On the other hand, it is claimed that, it is differences that must be stressed for their value in enhancing our understanding of law in society, as it is only by observing differences that we can learn lessons.

Since, to compare means to observe and to explain similarities and differences, the emphasis can be sometimes on differences and at other times on similarities. Schlesinger talks of periods of 'contractive', or 'contrastive' comparison with the emphasis on differences, alternating with periods of what might be called 'integrative' comparison, i.e., comparison placing the main accent on similarities.[36] He concludes that the future belongs to integrative comparative law.[37]

The 'new i*us commune* seekers' in Europe try to integrate legal systems, but look at a legal world that includes 'differents', that is, the UK and Ireland. In the common law world however, the unity of common law is made up of 'similars' as far as legal systems are concerned, though it is now generally accepted that this unity can be enhanced by diversity, and the Privy Council has loosened its hold on the Commonwealth jurisdictions as already mentioned.

Rudolf Jhering gave the conclusive answer to those who object to the foreignness of importations when he said: 'The reception of foreign legal institutions is not a matter of nationality, but of usefulness and need. No one bothers to fetch a thing from afar when he has one as good or better at home, but only a fool would refuse quinine just because it didn't grow in his back garden'.[38] The crucial question must be about how one takes the quinine. For example, within Europe, since there is no room for negotiation on the principle of the acceptance of a rule or solution, such as in the case of putting into practice an EU directive, the obstacle of *mentalité* must be to the structure of what is accepted and the technique of how it is accepted, rather than to what is accepted, that is the quinine.

Is comparative law indeed an instrument of integration and is it the case that 'the last thing we need is "distinctiveness for its own sake"',[39] or, do such strong views defy the virtues of 'distinction' or 'diversity'? Does the 'same-ness and difference debate' dominate most 'theoretical comparativism'? 'Are we identifying difference, and cherishing it, or are we trying to suppress it, by effective same-ness?'[40] At

---

[35] A. Watson, 'Legal Transplants and Law Reform' (1976) 92 *Law Quarterly Review* 79, p. 81. For a thorough analysis of Watson's work see W. Ewald, 'Comparative Jurisprudence (II): The Logic of Legal Transplants' (1995) 43 *American Journal of Comparative Law* 489.

[36] R.B. Schlesinger, 'The Past and Future of Comparative Law' (1995) 43 American *Journal of Comparative Law* 477.

[37] Ibid., p. 481.

[38] Zweigert and Kötz, n. 5 above, p. 17.

[39] E.M. Clive, 'Scottish Family Law' in J. Grant, (ed.), *Independence and Devolution: The Legal Implications for Scotland* (Green, Edinburgh, 1976), p. 173.

[40] Ward, n. 21 above, p. 31.

present, comparative law within Europe is used predominantly 'as a means of effecting same-ness and suppressing difference',[41] and therefore, comparative lawyers are seen as 'powerful players' and not 'neutral observers';[42] and comparativism as a threat with only a limited role to play.[43]

It has been pointed out that between the 16th and the 19th centuries, comparative legal history (the comparative law of the time) was interested in the similarities and not the differences, and it is only with rising nationalism and positivism that comparative law discourse started to stress differences, especially between the civil law and the common law.[44] In the first decades of the 20th century differences between common law and civil law traditions were emphasized, whereas today, within the EU, common elements are sought rather than differences stressed.[45] As legal systems and cultural systems can indeed 'live apart together',[46] is the function of comparative law then, the building of bridges?

When comparing closely related systems, it is usually more rewarding to explain the differences, while in two entirely unrelated systems, it is more rewarding to explain the similarities.[47] In practice, it seems a matter of preference or policy, whether the comparatist highlights the differences or the similarities found.[48] If comparative legal studies were to interest itself seriously in searching for and explaining divergences, especially those between similar systems,[49] not with the 'negative' attitude of stressing 'irreducible differences in *mentalité*' or '*summa differentia*' within the context of a 'contrarian challenge', but rather with a

41 Ibid.

42 Ibid., p. 32.

43 Ward says, referring to Derrida, that by denying difference, but in its very definition, cherishing it, comparativism threatens the differences that characterise post-modern society. Referring to Kant however, Ward suggests that comparativism is in fact too inclined to identify differences, instead of bringing into focus the core-principles within every legal system, jurisprudentially every legal system being at root the same. He says that, in this sense, comparative law has a limited role to play. These are debates about judgment. Ibid., p. 32.

44 L. Moccia, 'Historical Overview on the Origins and Attitudes of Comparative Law' in B. De Witte and C. Forder, (eds.), *The Common Law of Europe and the Future of Legal Education* (Metro, Kluwer Law International, Deventer, 1992), p. 618.

45 Ibid., p. 619.

46 See P.C. Müller-Graff, 'Common Private Law in the European Community' in De Witte and Forder, n. 43 above, p. 254.

47 See M. Bogdan, *Comparative Law* (Kluwer Tano, Göteborg, 1994), p. 18.

48 Any comparatist who wishes his/her subject to play a pivotal role in the 21st century might want to highlight similarities. Yet, in times of animosity, insularity or 'negative nationalism', the choice is the stressing the differences. Today the stress is on the dichotomy between the integrated Western legal culture and the Islamic. Differences are highlighted and the similarities often ignored.

49 Also see in this context, V.G. Curran, 'Dealing in Difference: Comparative Law's Potential for Broadening Legal Perspective' (1998) 46 *American Journal of Comparative Law* 657; and N.V. Demleitner, 'Challenge, Opportunity and Risk: An Era of Change in Comparative Law' (1998) 46 *American Journal of Comparative Law* 647.

constructive attitude in order to develop further a 'critical comparative law', then comparative legal studies could only benefit.

Legal systems in transition look for models that are socio-culturally and/or legal-culturally diverse from their own. History tells us that when the encounter is between legal systems of diverse socio- and/or legal-cultures[50] in the resultant legal system, the diverse elements co-exist. There may be intermingling if, for example, there is no socio-cultural diversity but only a legal-cultural one, so that in time the diverse elements are blended, or one of the elements becomes the dominant element because of political factors, or again, from the very beginning, one of the elements may be systematically erased by the use of the authority of power in its various forms. The outcome however, is often not a matter of choice but a matter of chance, or necessity. For example, the Eastern European systems which are poised to join the EU must somehow prepare themselves to undergo change in 'the desired direction', this desire not necessarily being one of the bottom but of the top, the *élite*, in any of its connotations, and of outside forces.

Some of the terms employed for analysis today, such as 'seepage', 'contaminant', 'irritant', 'underlay', 'overlay', 'cross-fertilization', 'incremental reception', 'competing systems', 'hyphenated' legal systems, layered law, 'chance', 'choice', 'prestige', 'efficiency', '*élite*' and 'historical accident' will be put to the test in the new century.

1.3.2. Contemporary Character of Reciprocal Influence

Ours is not a period of imposition. We no longer see colonial relationships. But, it is not one of voluntary reception either. It is a time of imposed reception, a seemingly voluntary activity of import under circumstances where exporters hold all the cards. In the market, the exporter is packaging his model as the most efficient; the one to be preferred over others. Although it is a buyers' market in that there is such a number of models to choose from, it is, in fact, a sellers' market, since for the importers there is no real choice or freedom to go down any particular path, as market forces tie them to certain of the models only. The process appears to involve the importers more actively than in the past, although it is still assessed from the point of view of the exporter. Most Western academics however, try to guard against the failures of the 'law and development movement' of the 1960s and 1970s.

Past receptions from Civil law and Roman law into English law have been called 'sporadic receptions' or 'injections', with 'civil law based reasoning filtering into common law',[51] ensuring that English law was enriched. However, any rules based on Roman law or the later *ius commune* 'were immediately cut off from their roots', and 'assimilated into the specifically English framework, and given life outside their

[50] E. Örücü, 'Mixed and Mixing Systems: A Conceptual Search' in E. Örücü, E. Attwool, and S. Coyle, (eds.), *Studies in Legal Systems: Mixed and Mixing*, (Kluwer Law International, London, 1996), pp. 344–345.

[51] D.J. Ibbetson, 'A Reply to Professor Zimmermann' in T.G. Watkin, (ed.), *The Europeanization of Law*, (UKNCCL, London, 1998), p. 228.

original context'. The resultant new law 'did not remain in dialogue with the old law from which it derived'; and 'once the borrowings are cut off from their roots they cease to be part of the same culture'.[52] Therefore, the influences were not systematic and the solutions did not remain the same upon import. 'Once the continental ideas were imported into England, the umbilical cord was cut'.[53]

Today, European Law is also regarded by many as an 'irritant', or a 'contaminant' of the common law.[54] However, one should assess the consequences of the encounters within the European Union today as instances of 'reciprocal influence' or 'cross-fertilization', rather than only consider the contamination of common law by the civilian input into EC law. It is true that when English common law co-exists with a jurisdiction that is not codified, it can seep into that other but finds it harder to penetrate into Codes where judges tend to adhere to the wording of the Code itself when deciding cases.[55] According to the 'convergence theories', English law can indeed live with codification of the law, of which there are historical examples.[56] However, 'Divergence theories' are opposed to any involvement of the UK in any pan-European Code.[57]

The understanding of codification as top-down centralist legalism has also led 'law and economics' scholars to propose competition of legal systems in a free legal market as opposed to both codification, which is in effect unification, and direct harmonization. The elements of choice and efficiency here remain the main criteria.[58] Some advocates of the 'new *ius commune*', stressing the need for re-systematization of the law and the development of a European legal doctrine, also claim that this could be done without necessarily a final synthesis and unification.[59]

---

52 Ibid., pp. 229–230.

53 X. Lewis, 'Europeanization of the Common Law' in Jagtenberg et al., n. 34 above, p. 50.

54 N. Grief, 'The Pervasive Influence of European Community Law in the United Kingdom' in Watkin, n. 51 above, p. 110. He asks whether Community law, which he sees as 'habit forming', is 'a corrective (like equity to the common law?) or a contaminant'. Among other serious concerns, Teubner's can be mentioned. See Teubner, n. 31 above, p.11. He regards 'good faith', transplanted into the body of British contract law by the 1994 European Consumer Protection Directive, as an irritant. However, others regard it as a 'healthy infusion'.

55 Although there is the interesting case of 'grafting' common law concepts into the St. Lucia Civil Code; see D. White, 'Some Problems of a Hybrid Legal System: A Case Study of St. Lucia' (1981) 30 *International Comparative Law Quarterly* 879.

56 E.g., Livingston's Draft Criminal Code of 1826 for Louisiana and Macaulay's Indian Penal Code, the draft dating back to 1838, have a lot in common with Continental Codes and markedly with the French code penal of 1810. Stephen's Draft Criminal Code for England of 1878 and Wright's Draft Criminal Code for Jamaica were also influenced, though to a lesser degree, by Continental Criminal Codes. The Louisiana Civil Code and the Louisiana Commercial Codes, both old and new, are also good examples.

57 P. Legrand, 'Against a European Civil Code' (1997) 60 *Modern Law Review* 44.

58 However, also see J. Bell, 'Book review of U. Mattei, Comparative Law and Economics' (1998) 47 *American Journal of Comparative Law* 969.

59 M. van Hoecke and F. Ost, 'Legal doctrine in crisis: towards a European legal science' (1998) 18 *Legal Studies* 197, at. 211–215.

1.3.3. Conceptual Conundrums

'Contaminant', 'irritant' and 'seepage' are very welcome additions to the vocabulary of analysis of reciprocal influence. However, one would be forgiven for thinking that anyone using these words in this context might be a common law lawyer who does not regard it as desirable that civilian concepts and structures should seep into the English legal soil. They seep to contaminate or irritate, not to purify or correct. One would surely be advised therefore, to stand clear of the source of contamination. The term 'contaminant' could be used neutrally as 'leaving a mark', like the dying that takes place when two pieces if cloth of different colours are washed together. Even then, one of the materials may be regarded as the culprit, unless the dying is reciprocal, in which case we have a new colour for both![60] A 'healthy infusion' on the other hand indicates a more subtle, positive and deeply penetrating infiltration. It is obvious that how one assesses the process is entirely related to one's stance in these matters. In the plethora of activities and examples one can always choose illustrations to support one's own position.

The way the term 'legal irritant' has been presented and defined implies the 'production of new and unexpected reactions' that may be side effects of the first 'contamination'. In this sense, it accords with Watson's belief in the power of reception on the imagination of the recipient, and the fact that, 'borrowing is often creative'.[61] In relation to the transplanting of the continental principle of *bona fide* (good faith) directly into the body of British contract law by the European Consumer Protection Directive 1994, it has been suggested that once transplanted, it may either 'be rejected by an immune reaction of the *corpus iuris britannium*' or succeed in interacting productively 'with other elements in the legal organism'.[62] Therefore, it should be regarded not as a 'transplant' but rather as an 'irritant' which can 'trigger whole series of new and unexpected events', as a transfer will always be 'confronted with the idiosyncrasies of the new legal culture'[63] and will face resistance external to the law, a variety of social expectations of highly diverse social environments.[64] A transfer 'cannot be domesticated'.[65] Teubner expects 'repulsion' not 'interaction'. But his metaphor 'irritant', taken in its positive sense, could actually bring about the desired result, and this development could be exactly what is needed. To converge means to accept diversity and not to attempt to create sameness. It is only after this acceptance that there can be a 'healthy infusion', and the transferred norms become 'internalized' and thereby work.

---

60 Of course, one could also think of fugitive colours, which gradually grow fainter and finally disappear! This can happen even before there is time for them to become irritants.

61 A. Watson, 'Aspects of Reception of Law' (1996) 44 *American Journal of Comparative Law* 345.

62 Teubner, n. 31 above, p. 12.

63 Ibid.

64 Among these external forces, Teubner cites markets, organisations, the professions, the health sector, social security, family, culture and religion.

65 Ibid.

Within a framework of 'reciprocal influence', a series of cross currents, rather than one way movements of 'contaminants' or 'irritants' occur, and on the 'reverse seepage' the legal world at large may benefit and be enhanced by the divergences created in different soils. The fact that the identity is fundamentally altered is of no matter if the new species is expertly and creatively handled. Delicious fruit grows on grafted plants, and legal imports survive even with their roots cut, thanks to the 'rooting powder' provided by the 'gardeners'!

1.3.4. Legal Transposition

With the help of outside models chosen from competing systems, many legal systems are experiencing fundamental upheaval as they re-shape themselves. This is so in social, economic and legal terms. Concepts such as 'contamination', 'inoculation', and 'infiltration' are all appropriate terms to describe encounters that are taking place in these regions, and 'transposition', 'imposed and voluntary reception' and 'concerted parallel development', the activities.

The term 'transposition', used as in music where the pitch is changed, is a more appropriate one in these instances,[66] although the term 'legal transplant'[67] is often used to describe this main means of law reform. As no one model is used by any one of the recipients, in fact, a series of 'transpositions' take place. The role of 'tuning' becomes vital in this process.[68]

Needless to say, structure and substance can be transposed with less difficulty than legal culture, itself part of socio-culture. The difficulties are not in the transposition of techniques and forms, but of values and contents. Not only transpositions, but also distortions that will occur here in order to fit the existing traditions, are surely going to have a serious impact on how the structure and substance work. In the twenty-first century, comparatists will have to assess what the transposed irritants produce as anti-bodies, and the health of the systems in transition.

---

66 Each note (legal institution or rule) is sung (introduced and used) at the same place in the scale of the new key (of the recipient) as it did in the original key (of the model); the 'transposition' occurring to suit the particular voice-range (socio-legal culture and needs) of the singer (the recipient). See, E. Örücü, 'Law as Transposition' (2002) 51 *International Comparative Law Quarterly* 205.

67 Monateri claims that the term 'legal transplant' utilised by Watson for 'scholarly purposes' is today taken over by 'purposive practical lawyers' involved in projects of 'exporting their own legal systems'. See, P.G. Monateri, 'The "Weak" Law: Contaminations and Legal Cultures' in *Italian National Reports for the XVth International Congress of Comparative Law, Bristol 1998*, (Guiffre editore, Milano, 1998), p. 83.

68 See for an analytical discussion and examples of transposition and tuning, Örücü, n. 66 above, and E. Örücü, 'A Comparison in Extraordinary Places' (paper prepared for *Comparative Legal Studies: Traditions and Transitions* Conference, University of Cambridge, July 2000, forthcoming), and also Örücü, n. 1 above.

2. *QUO TENDIT* COMPARATIVE LAW?

As newly emerging democracies look to the pool of competing models available in Western Europe and America with the purpose of re-designing and modernizing their legal, economic and social systems, a whole new world of research possibilities is opening up for comparatists. In the present century, comparative law will be tied theoretically and practically to enhanced legal science, convergence and integration as well as an appreciation of diversity, the use of foreign models in law reform, and law and culture studies. New approaches to harmonization, new receptions, mixing systems and re-designing systems, a new European *ius commune*, and emphasis on regional comparative law such as European, Central and Eastern European, Common law, African and Far Eastern will be the occupation of comparatists. Comparative law will also become even more important as an indispensable tool of construction for the European Court of Justice of the Communities, and national courts and law reform bodies.

In the past century we were told that comparative lawyers enjoy privileges to the envy of other colleagues and yet the burdens they bear 'should invoke sympathy',[69] that the subject had 'by common consent the somewhat unusual characteristic that it does not exist',[70] and we were warned that 'the subject-matter, being non-existent, is one which defies definition'.[71] On entering a new century it is astonishing to discover that we have not moved very much further, though the popularity of comparative law has indeed increased.[72] It is important to note here what comparative law is not. It is not simply a way of contrasting and comparing civil law and common law either in an effort to resolve the dichotomy between them, or to stress an impasse. Neither is it merely a sophisticated tool of private lawyers. However, attempts to answer the question 'What is comparative law?' have received a startling range of replies throughout time. As in the past, comparative law will continue to be essentially a 'contested project'.[73]

In the UK, 'Comparative law may have been the hobby of yesterday, but it is destined to become the science of tomorrow. We must welcome, rather than fear, its influence'.[74] On the Continent:

---

69 O. Kahn-Freund, 'Comparative Law as an Academic Subject' (1966) 82 *Law Quarterly Review* 40–41.

70 Ibid.

71 H.C. Gutteridge, *Comparative Law* (2nd edn., Cambridge University Press, London, 1949; reprint, Wildy & Sons, London, 1974), p. 2.

72 See the recent issues of the two prestigious journals of comparative law published in 1999 devoted entirely to articles discussing all aspects of comparative law: (1998) 46(4) *American Journal of Comparative Law* (Symposium: 'New Directions in Comparative law'), and (1998) 21(4) *Hastings International and Comparative Law Review*.

73 The present writer said in 1982 that the combination of all the above observations made her feel 'bewildered', 'interested', 'glad', 'exhilarated', and also 'excited' and 'confident'. Her sentiments are even more pronounced today. Embarras de richesses! Örücü n. 8 above, p. 2.

74 Lord Goff, 'The Future of the Common Law' (1997) 46 *International Comparative Law Quarterly* 745, 748.

> For a long time it looked as though comparative law was a matter for academic research, difficult and, surely, very interesting, beautiful to know something about, but not immediately relevant to the daily life of the law. Over the last ten or fifteen years the legal climate seems to be changing. This evolution may be influenced by the process of European integration; it may also result from the fact that we are living closer together (the 'global village' situation); it may finally be an autonomous process, occasioned by the lawyer's search for fresh perspectives, in particular when completely new legal problems are to be solved[75]

It has been pointed out that 'history' was very much the fashion in the nineteenth century:

> in particular on the Continent, history of the codes, pre-existing Roman law tradition, Poitier on obligations, etc. Our own century discovered society; it wondered how the law works, what its economic context is and how legal decisions can be adjusted to social needs; and it saw the judge as a kind of decision maker, or even a 'social engineer'. The twenty first century may become the era of comparative methods. . . .Our problems in society increase as our certainties in religious, moral and political matters dwindle; and more and more problems are common problems. The search for common solutions is only slowly beginning[76]

Generally, 'It is apt to say that Europe, . . .is currently experiencing a comparative moment . . .ours is the 'age of comparison'. . . .One can be forgiven for thinking that Europe has become a comparatist's paradise. . . .Comparatists . . .should rejoice'.[77]

In our new century, comparative law will be pressed to create blue prints for importers of models for law reform, and to provide better understanding of changing concepts. It will be expected to aid the courts in resolving disputes as one method of construction and interpretation, above all in the field of human rights. Thus comparative law, by providing models and modes of legal reasoning, will supply systems in transition, both within and outside Europe, with the possibility of structured change. Its accepted and well-established role in this field will strengthen. Comparative law cannot be regarded merely as an instrument of integration or an instrument of construction and statutory interpretation, though the knowledge gained through comparative legal studies may be put to such uses. Comparative law is about communication, and, by providing the language of that communication, allows legal scholars to enter into holistic communication.[78] Comparative law research also brings to light how legal institutions are connected, diversified and transposed. Thereby, comparative lawyers can extend their subject beyond the

[75] Koopmans, n. 2 above.
[76] Ibid., p. 555.
[77] P. Legrand, 'How to Compare Now?' (1996) 16 *Legal Studies* 232.
[78] See also Ewald n. 19 above, p. 2149.

traditional areas, both geographic and substantive, placing comparative law in a much wider context, and re-assessing legal systems and legal families. Comparative law now has a broad intellectual agenda, and will remain an essential instrument for legal understanding.[79] Though our new century will be an 'era of comparative method', we must remember however, that comparative law is not the panacea.[80]

The trends discussed earlier which developed on the eve of the new century, will produce tangible results and allow for intellectual vigour to take comparative discourse further.[81] In this way, the market value of comparative lawyers' work will increase as long as comparative law maintains its independent character and is not replaced by 'comparative jurisprudence', 'historical comparative law', 'comparative cultural studies', 'comparative law and economics', or any other kind of 'comparative law and ... ' that may evolve. Comparative law must retain a separateness and distinctiveness in the titles of such perspectives.

Comparatists will be more and more occupied with the question, 'Is similarity a necessity for successful and fruitful cross-fertilization?' We know that socio-cultural and legal-cultural differences are the most serious causes of mismatch. Yet, differences between national rules do not seem to restrict the importation of them, and even the misunderstood can be transplanted. 'When elements from two different interpretive communities combine', 'one drawing its understanding from culture and the other from law' for instance, they may be able to tap into each other and mesh, bringing 'cultural conversation' into a broader narrative.[82] This in fact is the 'fit', and 'transpositions' and creative 'tuning' at the time of transplants are vital for this 'fit'. If communication and conversation are kept moving, then cross-fertilization between the seemingly incompatibles can be facilitated.

The assertion that globalization, the catchword of the new century, will diminish the value of comparative law is mistaken to such an extent that the reverse will prove to be the case. Globalization is already increasing interest in localization. Both the local and those who study the local feel the need to assert it. The trend to integrate

---

79 See Gordley n. 3 above., who claims that comparative law should not be a separate discipline, that all lawyers must work comparatively all the time. See also P.G. Kozyris, 'Comparative Law for the 21st Century: New Horizons and New Technologies' (1994) 69 *Tulane Law Review* 165 who, in spite of seeing comparative law as purely a method, believes that its use and utility will expand and must be taken seriously.

80 Ward, for example, though accepting that at a micro level, proactive comparativism within the EU is methodologically viable and useful, suggests that 'doubts continue with regard to the value of comparativism at the macro-level. ...Comparativism may have a practical bite, but constitutionally, ideologically, philosophically, it is potentially either useless or dangerous, or both': Ward, n. 21 above, p. 30.

81 Mattei says that 'Comparative law has matured from the *common core* approach to *legal transplants*, from *legal formants* to the idea of legal traditions as a phenomenon of *path dependency*, and on to the notion of the *mute* dimension of the law'; U. Mattei, 'An Opportunity Not to be Missed: The Future of Comparative Law in the United States' (1998) 46 *American Journal of Comparative Law* 709 at 715.

82 D.S. Berry, 'Interpreting Rights and Culture: Extending Law's Empire' (1998) IV *Res Publica – A Journal of Legal and Social Philosophy* 1, at 10.

moves the focus to the 'differents' and their value. Thus comparative law will become indispensable in the globalization movement since in the effort to create universalist standards, interest in localised exceptions will flourish. Also, as Twining says: 'processes of globalisation stir up old nationalisms, exacerbate cultural conflict, and encourage post-modern scepticism about the universality of values and ideas'.[83] Comparative law will be needed in the understanding of this diversity to facilitate co-existence and harmony.

How will the 'new *ius commune*' for Europe fare in the 21st century? 'Unity or harmony in diversity' is easier to achieve than 'convergence and integration by eliminating diversity'. The 'new *ius commune*' can be achieved through appreciating differences and 'transpositions', rather than looking for or trying to create 'similars'. Here too a more limited focus and realistic vision must be built upon the 'similarities' between 'differents', and by accommodating 'differents' in harmony. The big question for the comparative law of tomorrow is, can comparative law be the angle from which deformed images may be corrected and distorted perspective, clarified? Comparatists will report at the end of the 21st century.

[83] W. Twining, 'Comparative Law and Legal Theory: The Country and Western Tradition' in I. Edge (ed.), *Comparative Law in Global Perspective* (Transnational, New York, 2000), p. 21.

Chapter 2

LEGAL TRANSPLANTS AND BEYOND: OF DISCIPLINES AND METAPHORS

*David Nelken**

Nelken attempts in this chapter to formulate a theoretical framework for the metaphors of legal transfers. He queries the contribution of legal and sociological scholarship to the discourse on legal transfers and their value and success. Questions such as, what sort of theory is needed to understand such transfers and are the metaphors used as part of the theories, are probed here. The reader can look for answers to two pivotal questions: Has the understanding of legal adaptation been enhanced by legal and sociological scholarship? Is Watson's 'legal transplant' an attack on the very possibility of sociology of law?

Competing approaches to the study of legal transfers – and in this context the contributions of Watson, Ewald and Friedman – are reviewed by Nelken, who uses the metaphor 'legal transfer' for 'legal transplant', the preferred metaphor for many.

Nelken regards any sharp distinction between comparative law and the sociology of law as artificial and he advocates a partnership between comparatists and sociologists, rather than involvement in polemic. Both the sociology of law and comparative law have problems with finding the sort of theory best suited for coming to grips with legal transfers, especially within Europeanization and globalization. There is also a lack of understanding as to how to make successful transplants.

Obviously theoretical developments within the sociology of law itself can throw light on the points raised by comparatists who criticize the transplant theory as presented by Watson. It is indicated that although law does not 'mirror' society, it does change over time in response to social developments, even when it is imported. 'Domestication' or 'adaptation' of imported law is accepted by comparatists, be they sociologically oriented or not, and this includes Watson. Örücü, for example, talks generally of 'transposition' and tuning in her chapter above, and Dupré talks of 'transformations', specifically as related to Hungary, below. However, later we see Smits holding an altogether different view.

---

* Distinguished Professor of Sociology of Law, University of Macerata, Italy, and Distinguished Research Professor of Law, University of Wales, Cardiff. Parts of this chapter were first published in Nelken and Feest (eds.) *Adapting Legal Cultures* (Hart, Oxford, 2001) and in Priban and Nelken (eds.) *Law's New Boundaries* (Dartmouth, 2001).

A. Harding and E. Örücü (eds.),
Comparative Law in the 21st Century, 19–34.

David Nelken

Nelken queries the usefulness of the idea of 'legal transplants' for the purposes of developing a theory of legal transfer. In this context, he considers Teubner's 'legal irritants', asking whether there can be misleading metaphors, and whether metaphors, which he classifies as 'mechanical, organic and discussive', can be altogether avoided.

The conclusion is that rather than avoiding metaphors, we should take them seriously; metaphors should be taken apart and their implications examined. In this thorough analysis of the metaphors of 'legal transplant' and 'legal irritant' by a sociologist of law, it is shown that that all metaphors have their limits.

[A. Harding and E. Örücü]

1. Introduction

What can legal and socio-legal scholarship contribute to the understanding of legal adaptation? And what can the evidence of legal adaptation tell us about the strengths and weaknesses of such scholarship?[1] For many legal scholars, what is striking about law is the extent to which it builds on itself, irrespective of the society in which it finds itself operating. David Ibbetson, for example, claims that:

> the English law of obligations has developed over the last millennium without any major discontinuity. Through this period each generation has built on the laws of its predecessors, manipulating it so as to avoid its more inconvenient consequences and adapting it piecemeal to social and economic changes. Sometimes fragments borrowed from abroad have been incorporated into the fabric of English law; from time to time ideas developed elsewhere have, at least temporarily, imposed a measure of structure on a common law otherwise messy and inherently resistant to any stable ordering[2]

More sociologically inclined scholars, not surprisingly, prefer to emphasise the way society shapes and reshapes law. Thus Lawrence Friedman[3] insists that contemporary legal systems in the economically developed world have much more in common with each other than with their own past legal histories, as can be seen by comparing the extent to which law in present day societies deals with essentially modern institutions and problems such as corporations and transport, and the rights of individuals and consumers.

---

1 For a more comprehensive version of the ideas developed here, see D. Nelken, 'Towards a Sociology of Legal Adaptation' in D. Nelken and J. Feest (eds.), *Adapting Legal Cultures* (Hart Publishing, Oxford, 2001).

2 As summarized in the 1999 Oxford University Press Law Catalogue.

3 L. Friedman, 'Borders: On the Emerging Sociology of Transnational Law' (1996) 32 *Stanford Journal of International Law* 65; 'Comments on Applebaum and Nottage' in J. Feest and V. Gessner (eds.), *The Proceedings of the 2nd Onati Workshop on Changing Legal Cultures* (Onati Institute, Spain, 1998), pp. 139–149.

2. Competing Approaches to the Study of Legal Transfers

At stake in these different ways of relating legal and social change are the competing concerns and pretensions of sociology of law and comparative law. Much discussion of legal transplants was stimulated by Alan Watson's energetic attempts to use the existence of 'legal transplants' as an attack on the very possibility of sociology of law.[4] In a recent paper, William Ewald seeks to reformulate and moderate Watson's arguments, and makes an important distinction between the level of autonomy of private and public law. But, he basically agrees with Watson's view that the frequency of legal transfers – or legal transplants as they both like to describe them – proves the fallacy of seeking to correlate developments in law with the internal evolution of the society in which it is found.

Ewald's argument forms part of a larger broadside, in which he contrasts what he considers the historically and legally informed character of comparative law scholarship, with the allegedly reductionist approach of sociologists of law, who assume that law is no more than an reflection of social structures and relations. But, the claim that sociologists of law are unaware that law travels can hardly be taken seriously. The influential 'law and society' movement in the United States, for example, was pioneered by authors such as Abel, Galanter and Trubek, whose early careers were spent studying law in places heavily affected by transplants such as Africa, India and Latin America, and who played important parts in the 'law and development' movement.[5] The 'law in context' approach in Great Britain, likewise, was pioneered by law professors such as Twining, Atiyah and Wilson, whose exposure to attempts to apply English common law in Africa and elsewhere sharpened their sense of the way the law must be understood, in relation both to the society in which it originates, and in which it operates.

With perhaps more justification, some comparatists accuse sociologists of having too instrumentalist and functionalist an approach to law. Sociologists of law, for their part, however, accuse comparatists of adopting an approach which is often formalistic, microscopic, rule-based and overly concerned with the niceties of private law, rather than the problems of legal regulation and administration. Sometimes apparent disagreements between these two approaches may arise, only because they are asking different questions: for example, why certain legal systems or legal rules

4 See e.g., A. Watson, *Legal Transplants: An Approach to Comparative Law* (Scottish Academic Press, Edinburgh, 1974); *Social and Legal Change* (Scottish Academic Press, Edinburgh, 1977); 'Legal Change: Sources of Law and Legal Culture' (1983) 131 *University of Pennsylvania Law Review* 112; *The Evolution of Law* (Blackwell, Oxford, 1985); *Roman Law and Comparative Law* (University of Georgia Press, Athens, Georgia, 1991); *Legal Transplants: An Approach to Comparative Law* (2nd edn., University of Georgia Press, Athens, Georgia, 1993); *Law out of Context* (University of Georgia Press, Athens, Georgia, 2000).

5 As Feldman points out, 'the idea that law and legal rules are portable and autonomous, and can therefore be transplanted, was a fundamental asumption of those writing on law and development in the 1960's and 1970's': see E. Feldma, "Patients' Rights, Citizens' Movements and Japanese Legal Culture" in D. Nelken (ed.), *Comparing Legal Cultures* (Dartmouth, Aldershot, 1997), p. 219.

are chosen, as compared to what effects rules may have on social change. More often, however, scholars in both camps raise questions for investigation to which their own existing theoretical resources may be insufficient to provide answers.[6] A staple comparatist argument is the claim that English law had limited influence on the Continent, even at the height of England's evident economic and political power 'because of its relatively low degree of "systemization"'. But, the full story here is likely also to involve social and political factors at the time, especially if we consider the otherwise inexplicable growth of influence of just such unsystematized rules and practices of the common law in the current period.

It is likely therefore that both comparatists and sociologists of law would achieve more in partnership than in polemic.[7] For how long can comparative lawyers continue to have the nerve to accuse the sociology of law – which counts Max Weber as one of its founding figures – of the crime of 'reducing' law to social or economic behaviour? On the other side, why are Dezalay and Garth's 'micro stories' about legal transfers celebrated by the same sociologists who have no time for Watson's circumstantial tales of the role of travelling legal scholars in shaping the reception of law? Some rules for an effective division of labour could be, and have been, imagined. It might seem appropriate for comparatists to concentrate on problems of meaning, identity and tradition, and in this way, offer a particular focus on legal discourse. As Merryman says, 'the way lawyers work with the law and reason about it is at the heart of this endeavour'.[8] They would continue to develop their sensitivity to legal history, to the spread of Roman law, or the significance of the 12th century papal revolution, in ways which are not likely to be matched in current sociological work.[9] Sociologists would (or should) concentrate on explaining the 'law in action' or placing the 'law in context'. They would thus be able to demonstrate how even the same legal rules and institutions have widely different consequences, depending on the operation of 'infrastructural' factors which are typically ignored by comparatists (in part, because they require empirical sociological research into the unwritten rules which affect the supply and demand of justice and the way law is or is not used).[10]

On the other hand, any sharp distinction between comparative law and sociology of law is bound to be artificial. There is a direct link between Savigny's discussions of

---

6 Örücü a legal comparatist, asks 'is law producer or product of change', and argues that 'we need a precise and suitable functionalist vocabulary pertinent to individual cases': see E. Örücü, 'A Theoretical Framework for Transfrontier Mobility of Law' in R. Jagtenberg, E. Örücü and A. de Roo (eds.), *Transfrontier Mobility of Law* (The Hague, Kluwer Law International, 1995), p. 6.

7 D. Nelken, 'Studying Criminal Justice Comparatively' in M. Maguire, R. Morgan and R. Reiner (eds.), *The Oxford Handbook of Criminology* (2nd edn., Oxford University Press, Oxford, 1997) 559–576; D. Nelken (ed.), *Contrasting Criminal Justice*, (Dartmouth, Aldershot, 2000).

8 P. Legrand and J.H. Merryman 'Comparative Legal Studies: A Dialogue' (1999) 47 *American Journal of Comparative Law* 201.

9 M. Van Hoecke and M. Warrington, 'Legal Cultures and Legal Paradigms: Towards a New Model for Comparative Law' (1998) 47 *International and Comparative Law Quarterly* 3.

10 E. Blankenburg, 'Civil Litigation Rates as Indicators for Legal Culture' in Nelken, above n. 5, pp. 41–68.

lawyer's law and folk law, and Friedman's ideas about 'external' and 'internal' legal culture.[11] For the great comparatist Otto Kahn Freund, it was essential to appreciate the social and (even more) the political context in which law was shaped in order to avoid rejection of a legal transplant. Zweigert and Kötz, the authors of a leading comparative law textbook, adopt a stronger 'functionalist' approach to legal rules in terms of their capacity to serve social purposes than would be shared by most sociologists of law.[12] Neither sociology of law nor comparative law are anything like homogenous.[13] Leading comparatists are worlds apart on the possibility and desirability of harmonization of law – and relatedly – on the point and purpose of comparative law;[14] and sociologists of law disagree about how far socio-legal behaviour can be explained without respect to the meaning actors attach to their behaviour.[15]

Both sociology of law and comparative law have problems with finding the sort of theory best suited to coming to grips with legal transfers and the way these are affected by interests, mentalities and institutions. Both approaches are struggling to make sense of developments such as Europeanization and globalization which are producing new configurations of the legal, the economic and the political. Harding admits that the comparatists' idea of 'legal families' is of limited use for explanatory purposes because these are now all almost inextricably entangled (their separation being linked to the colonial period).[16] But, sociologists too are asking themselves what is entailed by talking of 'legal culture' and how far the 'nation state' represents a satisfactory unit for research in studying processes of legal transfer.[17] In sharp contrast to Ewald's over confidence, John Henry Merryman, doyen of American comparatists, has recently been quoted as saying 'I do not know of anyone who has done substantial theoretical work addressed to what comparative law is really about', and acknowledges that 'the mainstream which identifies law with legal norms and related texts is an exhausted genre'.[18] His own recommendation is to reconstruct the subject in terms of the study of variability in legal extension, legal penetration, legal culture, legal institutions, legal actors, legal process, secondary rules, and legal experience. All of these variables are crucial for the study of legal transfers and it is

---

11 L. Friedman, *The Legal System: A Social Science Perspective* (Russell Sage, New York, 1975).

12 K. Zweigert and H. Kötz, *An Introduction to Comparative Law* (Oxford University Press, Oxford, 1987).

13 Nelken, 2000, n. 7 above.

14 P. Legrand, *Fragments on Law as Culture* (Tjeenk Willink, Deventer, 1999); B. Markesinis (ed.), *The Gradual Convergence* (Clarendon Press, Oxford, 1994), and *Foreign law and Comparative Methodology* (Hart Publishing, Oxford, 1998).

15 Blankenburg, 1997, n. 10 above; D. Nelken, 'Puzzling out Legal Culture: A Comment on Blankenburg' in Nelken n. 5 above, pp. 58–88.

16 A.J. Harding, 'Comparative Law and Legal Transplantation in South East Asia' in Nelken and Feest, n. 1 above.

17 D. Nelken, 'Disclosing/ Invoking Legal Culture' in D. Nelken (ed.), *Social and Legal Studies, Special Issue: Legal Culture, Diversity and Globalisation* (1995) 4:4, 435–453.

18 Legrand and Merryman, n. 8 above, p. 214.

clear that this is a research agenda which sociologists of law would also find exciting to tackle.

Some comparatists, finding the Watson/Ewald approach sterile, are already accepting the challenge of trying to relate legal thinking to wider institutional and social trends, though the question of the nature of the relationship between them remains relatively under theorised. David Bradley, for example, concludes his recent overview of the variability of family law in Europe by saying that 'legal theory must warrant consideration as a factor influencing the development of legal policy in this sphere, but so also must institutional interests, reinforced by a particular ideology and conditioned by social experience'.[19] Current sociologically oriented legal scholars are bringing fresh theoretical resources to bear. Dezalay and Garth's studies of the making of transnational law rely heavily on the work of the French sociologist, Bourdieu, and in particular, on his notions of 'legal field', 'symbolic capital' and 'praxis'.[20] Teubner has applied Luhmann's system theory and the idea of legal autopoiesis to his study of why attempts at legal harmonization are highly unlikely to produce similar outcomes.[21] The introduction of (new) 'theory' will not resolve the questions of legal transfers – especially the problem of how to make successful transplants. All these theories are in competition with each other – and they may sometimes obscure, as well as reveal.[22] What they can do is help us to reformulate our questions – this too can be progress.

3. The Significance of Legal Transplants

Against this background, Watson and Ewald's discussion of legal transplants could well be regarded as simply too one-sided and polemical to contribute much to any future collaboration between the approaches of comparative law and sociology of law. Many scholars do take this view.[23] Others do see merit in the idea of shifting attention away from 'society' as the major influence on legal change in favour of

19 D. Bradley, 'Convergence in Family Law: Mirrors, Transplants and Political Economy' (1999) 6 *Maastricht Journal of European and Comparative Law* 127–150, at p. 150.

20 Y. Dezalay and B. Garth, *Dealing in Virtue* (University of Chicago Press, Chicago, 1996); 'Law, Lawyers and Social Capital: "Rule of Law" versus Relational Capitalism' (1997) 6 *Social and Legal Studies* 109–143; 'The Import and Export of Law and Legal Institutions: International Strategies in National Palace Wars' in Nelken and Feest n. 1 above.

21 G. Teubner, 'Legal Irritants: Good faith in British Law or How Unifying Law Ends up in New Divergences' (1998) 61 *Modern Law Review* 11–32.

22 Flood, in his review of Dezalay and Garth, 1996, n. 20 above, complains that 'the heavy reliance on Bourdieu, almost to the exclusion of other sociological input, limits the theoretical force of the work. The authors appear to take his concepts uncritically, indeed at times as descriptors rather than techniques to assist analysis': see J. Flood, 'Review of Dezalay and Garth, *Dealing in Virtue*' (1999) 8 *Social and Legal Studies* 601–603, at p. 602.

23 see e.g., R. Cotterrell, 'Is There a Logic of Legal Transplants?' and L. Friedman, 'Some Comments on Roger Cotterrell and Legal Transplants' in Nelken and Feest n. 1 above.

recognising the 'contingencies' of history.[24] If we are to make the best use of Watson and Ewald's evidence, however, it will be necessary to abandon their claim that the existence of legal transplants demonstrates the impossibility of law and society work. I shall seek to show instead that their arguments actually demonstrate the need for such scholarship in as much as even the most telling points raised by these comparatist critics can be better appreciated when read in the light of theoretical developments within sociology of law itself.

Shorn of their polemical excesses, Watson's argument (which it should be remembered was initially directed as much against leading authors in comparative law as at sociologists) is that a large proportion of law in any society is a result of 'legal transplants', transmitted by lawyers, and owing its form and content to its origins in other times and places. Legal rules are often out of step for long periods with the needs and aspirations of society or any particular group or class within it. This includes bodies of law having a great impact on practical life such as contract law or land law. Likewise, major branches of law, for example, conflicts of law, develop with no input from society. Watson also denies that these branches of law are shaped by politics. As he puts it:

> Over most of the field of law, and especially of private law, in most political and economic circumstances, political rulers have no interest in determining what the rules of law are or should be (provided always of course that revenues roll in and that the public peace is kept). It follows ... that usually legal rules are not peculiarly devised for the particular society in which they now operate and also that this is not a matter for great concern[25]

The opposite view, which Watson (and Ewald) believe their argument disproves, they describe as the 'mirror theory of law'. But, while all sociologists of law do seek in some way or another to relate law to society, the evidence that in doing so, they rely on such a crude theory (or metaphor) is much exaggerated.[26] Such an idea can be discovered in the early works of Durkheim,[27] where he argues that law can be treated as an 'index' or mirror of society. But, it is only fair to add that he also saw law as playing an important role in reproducing, and not merely reflecting society. In any case, this part of Durkheim's work has been heavily criticised by sociologists of law on theoretical and empirical grounds; as Cotterrell writes, 'the index thesis, as he explains it, seems to show the worst aspects of the positivist orientation of his

---

24 A. Jettinghoff, 'State Formation and Legal Change: On the Impact of International Politics' in Nelken and Feest n. 1 above.

25 A. Watson, *Roman Law and Comparative Law* (University of Georgia Press, Athens, Georgia, 1991), p. 97.

26 See Cotterrell, n. 23 above. It is another question whether, as Savigny argued, law *should* be a mirror of its society.

27 E. Durkheim, *The Division of Labour in Society*, translated by D. Halls (Macmillan, Hampshire, 1893/ 1984).

sociology'.[28] Nor does the idea turn up in Durkheim's later work, in which he modified his arguments about law as an index of society (for example, finding an independent role for the political),[29] as well as about the relationship between ideas and social practices.

As far as recent sociological writers go, Ewald cites Lawrence Friedman as making the claim in his classic *History of American Law* that 'law is reshaped by change, that nothing is historical accident, nothing is autonomous, every thing is moulded by economics and society'.[30] Even as a sensitising metaphor this formulation may be over strong. But, the basic thesis that Friedman is advancing, for which there is no lack of evidence, is simply that law changes over time in response to social developments. Nor does Friedman assume in his work that law will always faithfully reflect society. Friedman's critics treat as interchangeable the (functionalist) idea that law matches the 'needs' of something we can call 'society' and the (pluralist or conflict theory) claim that law serves as part of the strategies of certain groups in society. Friedman's actual views are that law is an instrument and consequence of group conflict (he sometimes uses the metaphor of 'law as a rope'); his historical research aims to show that, even where it is widely acknowledged to be unsatisfactory, 'law in the books' and, even more, 'the law in action' at any given time, does play a part in constituting, filtering and changing the balance of forces in society. By contrast, Watson's counter argument that law is the special province of lawyers, and that it serves no one's (or no one else's) interest seems highly implausible, especially under modern conditions. To prove this would, in any case, require careful sociological investigation in a form which goes well beyond his celebration of selective examples of apparently useless legal distinctions, his evidence of legal inertia and his general celebration of the 'contingent and unforeseen'.[31]

Paradoxically, polemics apart, progress in this field may be more obstructed by what Watson and Friedman share in common than by what divides them. Watson's own chosen metaphor of legal transplants suggest that transplanting laws should be arduous; certainly medical transplants are not everyday affairs or something one undergoes lightly! But for the purpose of undermining sociology of law, Watson actually uses his many examples of legal transplants to show the *ease and inevitability* of legal transfers. Likewise, Friedman, if he really believed in the idea of 'law as a mirror', would be expected to emphasise the difficulties of importing law from elsewhere. In fact, despite his alleged claims about law's dependence on social evolution, Friedman is as optimistic as Watson concerning the extent to which legal transfers take place successfully. Borrowing other peoples' law is seen as just a method of speeding up the process of finding legal solutions to similar problems – a

[28] R. Cotterrell, *Emile Durkheim. Law in a Moral Domain* (Edinburgh Academic Press, Edinburgh, 1999), p. 33, pp. 70–74.

[29] See E. Durkheim, 'Two Laws of Penal Evolution' in C. Gane (ed.), *The Radical Sociology of Durkheim and Mauss* (Routledge, London, 1900/1992), 21–49, and c.f. Jettinghoff, n. 24 above.

[30] L. Friedman, *History of American Law,* (2nd ed., Simon and Schuster, New York, 1985).

[31] R. Abel, 'Law as Lag: Inertia as a Social Theory of Law' (1982) 80 *Michigan Law Review* 785–809.

process being encouraged all the more by the pressures towards convergence brought about by globalization.

The metaphor of legal transplants implies the need for legal transfers to be somehow 'domesticated' to fit into their new context; otherwise, there is the risk that they may 'fail' by being 'rejected'. Here too, there is no real debate between these authors. Friedman suggests that imported law is normally adapted successfully, and if this does not happen, it merely shows how 'society' can get along without such laws. Watson sometimes claims that he is uninterested in what actually happens to laws once they have been transplanted. But, at other times, he freely acknowledges that what happens next is crucial, and that this depends precisely on those matters of social context which 'law and society' scholars take to be central: 'the insertion of an alien rule into another complex system' Watson concedes, 'may cause it to operate in a fresh way' ... 'the whole context of the rule or concept has to be studied to understand the extent of the transformation'.[32]

There is also not much genuine disagreement about the role of lawyers as mediators. As reformulated by Ewald (in the so called 'weak' and more defensible version of his thesis), Watson's claim is not that law is autonomous or insulated from society, but that it is the values, ideas, intellectual and dogmatic histories and techniques of lawyers which are crucial in the production and reproduction of law. Lawyers frequently neither know or care about possible future consequences; what matters for them is the authority (or authoritativeness) and prestige of the source of law. Friedman and other sociologists of law also give great importance to the role of lawyers, though for them, each of Watson 's blanket assertions would require more careful empirical investigation. Current socio-legal research has much to tell us about the role being played by lawyers and legal scholars.[33] Some writers even argue that the investigation of 'legal ideology' is a more fruitful approach to understanding law's power than the study of legal culture more generally.[34] If anything, Watson and Friedman could be accused of making too sharp a difference between lawyers 'mandarin' concerns and the more practical problems of those who use the law. If Friedman makes much of his distinction between 'internal' and 'external' legal culture, Watson, likewise, insists that the attitudes of businessmen (an example of legal external legal culture) are all in favour of crude harmonization and impatient with academic or judicial concerns about protecting those cultural differences, which are allegedly reflected in different rules and principles.

The real importance of the 'debate' between Friedman and Watson lies elsewhere. What is at stake here is the need to pay more attention to the relationship or 'fit' between law and society, and to develop methods for seeing how this varies culturally. There are likely to be considerable variation in the extent to which law

---

32 Watson, n. 25 above, p. 116.

33 See e.g. Dezalay and Garth, n. 20 above.

34 R. Cotterrell, 'The Concept of Legal Culture' in Nelken, n. 5 above, pp. 13–32.

actually conditions social action or penetrates society as Friedman puts it,[35] or is thought to need to do so, both in the society of origin and that of arrival. This must affect what it means to say, that transplanted law must 'fit' the society to which law is introduced if it is to be 'effective'. One problem with the 'convergence thesis' favoured by Friedman[36] is not so much its assumption that law all over the world is becoming more homogenous, but rather that it fails to explain how far, when and why, law – and even more, any particular model of law – becomes a necessary part of doing things as compared to other forms of securing market certainty, political legitimacy or whatever.

Yet Watson's evidence that law often fails to mirror society does have implications for sociology of law, even if he fails to theorise these implications, preferring to use them to deny the possibility of theory! Sociologists of law have long been aware that law may be out of phase with social change, whether it is behind,[37] or ahead of other developments. Law 'belongs' not only to other places, but also to the past – to a previous social and economic order, to tradition and to history, as much as to the present. It can aim at the future, acting as an index of desired social, political and economic change, what society would like to become, or should like to become. Recent work emanating from the 'law as literature' movement, or 'law as communication' more generally have shown the need to appreciate law as an opportunity for society to authoritatively re-interpret the principles it stands for, rather than merely consider it as an instrument used for the purpose of achieving regulatory goals. Over the last few years, increasing attention has been directed at theorising these aspects of law.[38] Such attempts to rethink the 'law and society' relationship have gone in two, in some ways contradictory, directions. On the one hand, sociological assumptions of a close 'fit' between law and life have, if anything, been strengthened by research into 'law as ideology', 'law in everyday life' or, as some writers would have it, law as 'constitutive' of society.[39] On the other hand, other social theorists have stressed the need to overcome the idea that there is a necessary link between a given social context and a given form of law in favour of stressing law's capacity to transcend and transform social contexts.[40]

A major theoretical challenge to which the study of legal transfers can contribute, is how to reconcile these positions without falling into false dichotomies. As Teubner puts it, 'we need to get beyond juxtaposing cultural dependency and legal insulation

---

35 L. Friedman, n. 3 above.

36 L. Friedman, 'Is there a Modern Legal Culture?' [1994] *Ratio Juris* 117.

37 K. Renner, *The Institutions of Private Law and their Social Functions* (RKP, London, 1949).

38 D. Nelken, 'Beyond the Study of Law and Society' [1986] *American Bar Foundation Journal* 323–338; D. Nelken, 'Changing Paradigms in the Sociology of Law' in G. Teubner (ed.), *Autopoietic Law: A New Approach to Law and Society* (De Gruyter, Berlin, 1987), pp. 191–217.

39 A. Hunt, *Explorations in Law and Society: Towards a Constitutive Theory of Law* (Routledge, London, 1993).

40 R.M. Unger, *False Necessity: Anti-Necessitarian Social Theory in the Service of Radical Democracy* (Cambridge University Press, Cambridge, 1987).

or social context and legal autonomy'.[41] The debate between Watson and Friedman too easily tends to pose the question of how much or how little we need to allow for law's 'relative autonomy' from society. If we are to transcend this way of thinking, we need to find a better route to capture how law both does and does not 'fit' its context.[42] Teubner, for example, seeks to revise our understanding of the relationship between system and environment in modern, highly differentiated societies. He admits, on the one hand, (much as Watson would argue) that 'since contemporary legal rule production is institutionally separate from cultural norm production, large areas of law are only in loose, non systematic contact with social processes'.[43] But, on the other hand, he also insists on what he calls 'law's binding arrangements' to other social subsystems and discourses.

4. Legal Transplants as a Metaphor

What then of the term 'legal transplants'? How far is this a useful idea to use for the purposes of developing a more comprehensive theory of legal transfers? In a recent paper which has attracted considerable interest, Teubner argues that the transplant metaphor is misleading and should be replaced by the idea of 'legal irritants'.[44] But, this then raises a number of wider questions. What is it for a metaphor to be misleading? Can metaphors be avoided? What is the persuasive force of metaphors? Are metaphors just a way of stimulating thought or can they form part of controllable scientific conceptualizations?[45]

Metaphor is defined as 'a figure of speech in which a word or phrase is applied to an object or action that it does not literally denote in order to imply a resemblance'.[46] Given that there will necessarily be limits to this resemblance, it follows that all metaphors will be misleading, at least in some respects. The value of metaphors can only lie in their heuristic possibilities – the way they lead us to think in new and imaginative ways, in the present case, about the processes of legal transfer. But, by the same token, they can sometimes also lead us in the wrong direction, or, in the case of mixed metaphors, send us at the same time in different directions! It is therefore only prudent to pay attention to the implicit assumptions and messages conveyed by different metaphors.

For this purpose, it is interesting to note that we can find a range of mechanical, organic and discursive metaphors applied to the phenomenon of legal transfers.[47] It

41 G. Teubner, n. 21 above, p. 17.

42 D. Nelken, 'Getting the Law "Out of Context"' (1996) 19 *Socio-Legal Newsletter* 12–13.

43 G. Teubner, n. 21 above, p. 17.

44 Ibid.

45 Much of the following discussion is also relevant to the debate over what sense to give to the claim that law is a 'mirror of society', which is of course only another metaphor.

46 Chamber's Dictionary, 1974.

47 c.f. E. Wise, 'The Transplant of Legal Patterns' (1990) 38 (Supplement) *American Journal of Comparative Law* 1.

does not require much effort to work out that each of these types of metaphor reflect and advance different approaches to the relation between law and society. What we could call mechanical metaphors of legal transfer such as 'export and import', 'circulation', 'diffusion' and 'imposition' tend to accompany talking about law in the language of 'impact' and 'penetration' (as in the work of Lawrence Friedman). They reflect a vision of law as a working institution, as an instrument, and as a technique of social engineering. Organic metaphors, on the other hand, speak of 'grafts', of 'viruses' and 'contamination', of 'the double helix' and, of course, of transplants (whether medical or botanical). On this approach, legal transfers, when they succeed, blossom, are fertile and set root; they fail when the body recognises them as 'incompatible'. The use of these metaphors forms part of a functionalist vision of law as an interdependent part of a larger whole. Discursive metaphors, finally, speak about transferring law as a matter of 'translating' and reformulating implicit meanings. They approach law as 'culture', 'communication', 'narrative' and 'myth'. The research agenda within which each of these sets of metaphors are mobilized will be recognizably different. Each approach will have its own way of defining what is meant by 'same' and 'different', what it is for a transfer to 'succeed', and whether this depends on law achieving a given goal, on helping a given type of social order or system to reproduce itself, or conveying on it a well translated meaning.

Of course, we could just try to avoid metaphors. But, the effort to do this in speaking about legal adaptation, or any other matter of importance to socio-legal studies, is almost certainly doomed to failure. Often what we face is the choice of using 'live' or 'dead' metaphors. It is easy enough to find apparently common sense descriptive terms, but such workaday language often only conceals its metaphorical qualities. The advantage of terms such as legal transplants or 'legal irritants' is that their very strangeness means that one is less likely to forget that they are metaphors. Better a striking metaphor which calls attention to its artificiality than one which attempts to pass unobserved!

When we speak, for example, of 'begging, borrowing or stealing' other peoples' laws,[48] or even of 'borrowing, diffusion and imposition',[49] none of these terms denote what actually goes on when laws are transferred. All carry with them from other contexts, questionable implications regarding the manner in which legal adaptation takes place, the means by which it is achieved and its likely results. Can the owner ask for his 'borrowed' legal institution back again? Can the thief be taken to court for theft! Even Friedman is not averse to inventing more elaborate metaphors. In a recent paper he compares the process of legal borrowing to getting clothes 'off the peg', rather than having them made to measure.[50] What he intends to convey here, we may assume, are the advantages of borrowing other people's laws in terms of the gains in time and convenience of not making too much of a fuss about

[48] L. Friedman, n. 3 above.
[49] L. Friedman, n. 23 above.
[50] L. Friedman, n. 3 above.

achieving 'a close fit'. His choice of metaphor implies that borrowing laws is as normal and unproblematic as buying standardized clothes. Perhaps he also seeks to suggest that few can afford the costs of tailor-made!

Friedman does not intend us to take his metaphors as a demonstratation of the truth of such propositions, which are advanced with other arguments, and which will have to be tested in relation to the historical and sociological evidence available. But, all the same, his metaphors do carry these and other question-begging implications. Are laws manufactured like clothes on the basis of abstract and average suitability for all comers? Is this not something which varies by type of law and by time and place? Does it not make all the difference (certainly it does for those advocating competing approaches to legal adaptation) that *laws always already belong to somebody else*? Asking to copy or borrow clothes which someone else was actually wearing might be a better analogy and would suggest a much more complicated transaction, whereby similarity of shape or need to the original owner of the clothes would be all important. Given these problems could it not be Friedman's metaphor itself which has been taken 'off the peg'?

The same applies to other terms such as 'import' and 'export', 'competition', 'borrowing', 'reception', 'transfers' or 'the circulation' of law, to name only some of the currently popular alternatives. Rather than seeking to avoid metaphors, it seems that we will have to take them seriously (which of course does not mean literally). What does it mean to talk about a legal transfer 'failing'? Should we discuss this in terms of 'rejection' of a foreign body by the society or culture, or describe it more in terms of 'resistance' by those groups who oppose it for reasons of interest or ideals? The terms we use will it make a difference. Taking metaphors apart and examining their implications may be the only way to come to grips with their power to shape both scholarship and action.

What are the implications then of the *transplant* metaphor? Those who use this term are often ambiguous as to which transplants are being called to mind – plant and forestry transplanting, the transplantation of people or peoples,[51] or the more recent (but still surprisingly long established) sense of the term used in talking about medical transplants.[52] The variety of referents (and the evident differences in what is involved in such varied types of transplants) can and does lead to confusion. For that matter, some of these meanings may themselves be considered metaphoric variations on the botanical original. In its most general sense, transplant could just mean matter 'out of place'; but once the question becomes what is involved in deliberately

[51] According to the Shorter Oxford Dictionary, 1973/1978, the term transplant, when used as a noun dates back to 1756 in the context of botany, especially in forestry (e.g., to refer to a seedling transferred once or several times). As a verb, it is dated to 1440 (in late Latin) to signify moving a plant from place to place. The term has been used to refer to the moving of people since 1555 (and, since 1813, of nations). The surgical meaning is dated to 1786.

[52] The difficulties and possibilities of which are themselves undergoing rapid change in a period of genetic engineering.

moving foreign laws and institutions, the variety of possible references to such different objects and situations becomes problematic.

Many students of legal transfers are particularly attracted by the medical version of the metaphor. Feldman, for example, finds it suggestive to compare the process of seeking legal transfers to the search for a compatible donor so as to provide hope 'to ailing members of the world community'.[53] The use of the medical model also goes some way in capturing the sense that the recipient wants (or needs) something just because it is different from what he or she already has, but that this difference carries with it the risk of generating problems of 'rejection' afterwards.[54] For both medical and legal transplants to succeed, they must make the new host believe that in some sense they really already belong to it. Feldman notes that there are dangers, both from rejection of the foreign implant, as well as those inherent in the condition of the patient, here conceived as the allegedly ailing legal system.

On the other hand, we do need to be suspicious about some of the implications of thinking about legal transfers with the help of this metaphor. Medical transplants involve a very high level of invasive surgery and even if we know that this in the interest of the body, the body does not. But if we were to take the metaphor too seriously, it would become impossible to see the differences between a society seeking to import foreign ideas and having such adaptation imposed. The very concreteness of the medical example fails to encompass the complexity of legal transfer as a social process, and the importance of subjective factors such as the creation and imposition of meaning (including definitions of 'similarity' and 'success'). Rather than there being an 'objective' contrast between healthy and diseased organs, or between the life and death of the body politic, what we have are claims made by participants or observers, within and without the society concerned, who argue for the 'need' for the society to change in certain directions if it is to stay competitive, be seen as having a legitimate political system etc. Insofar as the difference between what is taken to be normal and what is ailing or outdated is a matter of social choice, the research question becomes how certain features of legal systems succeed in becoming accepted as being universally relevant or as the proper standard to follow.

The legal transplant metaphor does suggest that any given transfer involves moving only a part of a wider legal and general culture. It rightly signals the need to consider the relationship between the part and the whole – on the side of both the giver and receiver. But, even here there may be important differences between the medical or other referent of the metaphor and the legal realities. In case of medical or botanical transplants, the ability of the transplant to become part of its new body or environment may be conditional on it having no further connection with its original source. But, in the case of legal transfers, part of the aim may also be to somehow recreate some aspects of the wider context from which the transplant is taken – as in

[53] Feldman, n. 5 above.

[54] See T. Tanase, 'The Empty Space of the Modern in Japanese Law Discourse' in Nelken and Feest, n. 1 above.

current attempts to transplant western legal institutions into former Communist regimes.[55] There are also many other matters which the metaphor does not serve to highlight. Often, the problem of legal transplants has to do not with the compatibility of places or societies, but the compatibility of interests or language between intermediaries. The way legal transplants are typically taken from places of prestige, where lawyers or politicians happened to have studied, also finds no real parallel in medical and botanical transplants.

No metaphor is likely to be perfect, but can we do better? And how are we to decide? An alternative metaphor, that of 'legal irritants' has been recently put forward by Teubner in a paper which applies autopoietic theory to the problem of legal transfers.[56] Teubner's argument – the details of which will not be described here – concerns the likely fate of applying a European Union Directive a doctrine of 'good faith', most at home in the context of German law and society, throughout the countries which make up the Union. He claims that the transplants metaphor – which he sees as dominating academic debate – is misleading in two respects here. Firstly, because it suggests that the result of transferring legal rules and institutions is either an outright success or failure, when it is more likely to be mixed. Talking instead of 'legal irritants' will allow us to get over what he calls 'the false dichotomy of repulsion or interaction which is a result of thinking with this metaphor'. Secondly, his new metaphor is recommended as being superior because it suggests that what happens is not that a new rule or institution is transplanted into an existing organism, but instead that it triggers off a set of new and unexpected events.

Much of the interest of Teubner's proposal, as a step in advance of the idea of legal transplants, comes from the way his metaphor forms part of a fundamental attempt to rethink the relationship between law and society. But it is not so clear how radical Teubner wants his claims to be considered. On the one hand, when describing how commercial law does and should 'fit' the different production regimes in different European societies, Teubner's arguments seem to be well within the tradition of 'law in context'. He criticises the assumption that we can, or should, expect legal rules or institutions to have the same effects when torn from their original context, and appears to share the sociological conventional wisdom that the more law is 'congruent' or 'compatible' with its new environment, the more likely it is to transfer effectively. Correspondence is all. On the other hand, in drawing on the theory of autopoiesis, Teubner also argues that under modern conditions, law is bound to other social discourses as much by 'difference' as similarity. Hence, he asserts, (useful) change is best achieved by seeking to ensure that transferred law

[55] Admittedly much of this may be unrealistic, a species of 'sympathetic magic', but, it is still important to note the extent to which the goal here is to use what is borrowed as a step towards becoming more like the source of the borrowing.

[56] G. Teubner, n. 21 above, p. 17; D. Nelken, 'Beyond the Metaphor of Legal Transplants? Some Consequences of Autopoiesis Theory for the Study of Cross Cultural Legal Adaptation' in J. Priban and D. Nelken (eds.), *The Consequences of Autopoeisis* (Dartmouth, Aldershot, 2001).

works as a 'strong irritant', which will trigger reaction just because it does *not* correspond to current conditions in the society in which it is introduced.

The place which Teubner's metaphor occupies within a new theory of law and society, however, could also be considered a weakness, as much as a strength. The metaphor of legal transplants is certainly under-theorised, in the case of Watson's use of it, deliberately so. But, the idea of legal irritants may suffer the opposite problem. It is far from clear whether 'legal irritation' is intended to be a metaphor used heuristically for highlighting only certain aspects of legal transfers, or whether instead, it must be taken as a 'term of art' within autopoiesis theory, whose meaning is to be determined by consulting Luhmann's writings about the possibility of communication between functionally differentiated social systems.[57] In the end, the criticism of the idea of transplants is not so much that it represents a misleading metaphor, but that it does not belong within the concepts of Luhmann's system theory.

Like any metaphor, the idea of 'legal irritation' has its limits. It tells us little about when transfers are made, where they are taken from, or why they are introduced. In this way it distracts attention, quite as much as the transplants metaphor from the 'palace wars' which Dezalay and Garth[58] tell us lie behind the decisions in the originating and receiving societies whether or not to transfer one or other aspect of law. In any case, any *one* metaphor is unlikely to enable us to capture all that is important about different types of legal transfers, or the situations in which they occur. Attempts at legal harmonization raise different issues from other processes of legal transfer – globalization, for example, can have divergent as well as convergent effects.[59] The metaphor of 'legal irritation' will also be less helpful for investigating periods of revolutionary and post revolutionary nation-building, cases where legal institutions are re-formed (e.g. in Australia or Canada), cases where borrowing aims at a radical break (e.g. Japan or Turkey), or, where the object of legal transfer is to go back to previous traditions as with some fundamentalist states, or, in different respects, some post-communist regimes. A metaphor which belongs in a theory, which presupposes a high level of modern sub-system differentiation in the receiving society, will not be appropriate for analysing transfers from first world nations to economically or politically 'less developed' countries (including those of the 'third world'). But, all these are important examples of situations in which the prospects for legal transplants come to be debated.

57 Nelken, ibid.

58 Y. Dezalay and B. Garth, n. 20 above.

59 D. Nelken, 'The Globalization of Crime and Criminal Justice: Prospects and Problems' in M. Freeman (ed.), *Law and Opinion at the End of the 20th Century* (Oxford University Press, Oxford, 1997) pp. 251–279.

Chapter 3

SEEKING SIMILARITY, APPRECIATING DIFFERENCE: COMPARATIVE LAW AND COMMUNITIES

*Roger Cotterrell**

This is a call for more theory for comparative law. Re-understanding society as community, and the relationship of comparative law and sociology, are the main themes here. Accepting that comparative law is many different things, and comparative legal studies covers a broad range of subject matters, Cotterrell points to the two theoretical problems of comparative law: Why compare? And, what can be compared? This contribution analyses the relationship between comparative law and sociology and links them through legal interpretation. The view is that integrity and consistency in interpretation is more important than identifying difference. Cotterrell argues that determining the balance between 'achieving integration' and 'delineating boundaries' is 'one of comparative law's hardest but most important current practical tasks'. The focus of comparative law must take account of the dynamics of social change represented by the conflict of globalization and localization: that is, seeking similarity and appreciating difference; and the changing environment of contemporary law makes comparative law especially appropriate as a method and outlook.

Here, the claim is that comparative law's relationship with legal sociology should be exploited and developed to enable it to observe and interpret this changing environment. However, contemporary developments, especially in Europe, mean that comparative law is not any more on neutral ground between appreciation of difference and search for similarity. Rather, comparative law is driven by the urge to unify. Cotterrell claims that its assigned task is to be a facilitator of globalization and its object is to make legal adjustment as needed. He indicates that in legal interpretation today, there is a 'search for unity, integrity or consistency of meaning', 'over the identification of difference'. Difference is only admitted upon failure in finding similarities. Nevertheless many contemporary comparatists see the main purpose of comparative law as being the appreciation of difference. The author states that, although difference should be

* Professor of Legal Theory, Queen Mary and Westfield College, University of London.

A. Harding and E. Örücü (eds.),
Comparative Law in the 21st Century, 35–54.

appreciated, it is important to find out in what circumstances is difference 'important, inevitable or even desirable'.

'What makes comparatists' search for uniform law or harmonization of law or their welcome of legal "convergence", appropriate?' 'What is it that makes diverse legal solutions – the appreciation of difference – appropriate?' This is the context in which we see a discussion of 'regulatory efficiency' and 'legal culture'.

It is argued that in the area of human rights however, appreciation of difference alongside seeking for uniformity is recognized as a necessity. Here is a field where seeking universality is challenged by cultural relativism. As Dupre also shows below, difference is not failure.

We are reminded that, if comparative law is to set its own agenda, it needs theory. The most important starting point could be 'to break down the idea of culture' into several distinct components, as neither 'law' nor 'society' are monolithic entities. Communities are classified and analyzed by Cotterrell here and the role of comparative law in these communities is highlighted. 'Rights to options', and 'rights to roots' put forth by Santos also seem to support the search for both similarity and difference; a new global-local dynamic is indicated. Cotterrell tells us that, comparative law can do this 'if it understands systematically the nature of the social', and this only if comparative law is armed with appropriate theoretical resources. Comparatists in the 21st century will have to address this challenge.

[A. Harding and E. Örücü]

1. Introduction

Comparative legal studies now cover a vast range of subject matter and have very diverse aims. These aims and the means of pursuing them are themselves discussed in a large literature. Today, there seems little point in trying to specify what comparative law should be, because it already is many different things. Its importance is clear and growing, a fact illustrated by its use in many practical current contexts. These include mapping the future of European legal integration, aiding and analysing the legal transformation of post-communist economies, developing transnational law and legal practice in many fields, exploring legal consequences of the interactions of religious and other belief systems, and plotting parallels in legal reform in different countries or regions.

Despite this importance, two theoretical problems haunt comparative law. The first is an epistemological problem: why compare? What is the nature of the knowledge that comparison gives? What is its status as knowledge? Knowledge for what, and subject to what conditions? The other is an ontological problem: What can properly be compared – legal rules, principles, cultures, systems, families, functions, styles? Or should comparison be of legal responses to social needs, interests or problems? What ensures that the entities chosen for comparison really are comparable? In other words, what is the necessary subject matter of comparative law?

These problems are closely related. It has often been suggested that their existence makes comparative law a different kind of research enterprise from the analysis of law in a single legal system.[1] The problems seem sufficiently serious to some writers to make them argue that comparative law should give up comparison altogether: its aim should be to study adaptation and development in particular legal systems. The comparative element, in what would otherwise be an inquiry into legal history or jurisprudence, is given by a focus on the way legal systems borrow rules or institutions from other systems.[2]

Other writers accept that purely technical comparison of rules unrelated to a wider context may be of limited or indeterminate value and so comparison must usually be of socio-legal phenomena including, but extending, beyond legal rules. They advocate alliance with social science, or see comparative law as a social science itself.[3] Thus, Konrad Zweigert and Hein Kötz claim that comparative law and sociology of law 'use much the same methods'.[4] Clearly this cannot be said generally of doctrinal studies limited to a single legal system. Although socio-legal studies have made great headway, especially in English-speaking countries, they have not influenced doctrinal legal studies to such an extent that most jurists can be said to use much the same methods as legal sociologists. The dimension of 'internationalism'[5] is said to make the difference as regards the methods of comparative law. And undoubtedly, for some comparatists, the attraction of comparative legal study is that it is a means of 'putting legal science on a sure and realistic basis'[6] because it demands the study of law in a broad context. On one view, while comparative law is a social science, the study of national law is an 'interpretive human science',[7] or not even a science at all because its subject-matter is limited arbitrarily on a territorial basis.[8]

---

1 K. Zweigert, 'Quelques Réflexions sur les Relations entre la Sociologie Juridique et le Droit Comparé' in Cassin, R. et al., *Aspects Nouveau de la Pensée Juridique: Recueil d'Etudes en Hommage à Marc Ancel* (Pedone, Paris, 1975), p. 84; P. Legrand, *Fragments on Law as Culture* (Tjeenk Willink, Deventer, 1999), pp. 11–12.

2 A. Watson, *Legal Transplants: An Approach to Comparative Law* (2nd edn., University of Georgia Press, Athens, Georgia, 1993); and see W. Ewald, 'Comparative Jurisprudence II: The Logic of Legal Transplants' (1995) 43 *American Journal of Comparative Law* 489.

3 K. Zweigert and H. Kötz, *An Introduction to Comparative Law* (3rd edn., T. Weir translated, Clarendon Press, Oxford, 1998) p. 45; and see generally J. Hall, *Comparative Law and Social Theory* (Louisiana State University Press, Baton Rouge, 1963).

4 Zweigert and Kötz, ibid., p. 10.

5 Ibid., p. 2.

6 Ibid., p. 33.

7 Zweigert, n. 1 above, p. 84.

8 Zweigert and Kötz, n. 3 above, p. 15.

2. Comparative Law and Legal Interpretation

But matters are more complex than this. The assertion of a close link between legal sociology and comparative law has often presupposed (wrongly in my view) the continuing dominance of positivist methods in both – the positivist aim being to describe and explain law as social fact in some sense.[9] Explaining law as a social phenomenon that presents itself in different ways in different national contexts may seem significantly different from municipal lawyers' efforts to interpret law in their own legal system. But, if comparative law's task is seen as not only to describe positivistically, but also to interpret law on a comparative basis, to seek the most appropriate legal ideas or understandings in particular contexts, its close relationship with other doctrinal legal studies seems reaffirmed. All such studies involve comparison[10] – the linking or contrasting of rules, the creative comparison of their wording and meanings, and the effort to relate them or distinguish them. For Vivian Curran, comparative legal analysis is 'a paradigm for legal analysis in general, and is distinguishable from general legal analysis more in name than in substance'.[11] Like some other contemporary comparatists, Curran sees the main purpose of comparison as being appreciation of *difference*.[12] But this can, of course, only be a matter of emphasis. The identification of likeness and difference go together in legal interpretation generally: jurists order and integrate doctrine by making distinctions in it, and general categories indicate necessary distinctions.

In all modern legal interpretation, however, the search for unity, integrity or consistency of meaning is usually privileged, in certain ways, over the identification of difference.[13] For example, common law lawyers usually try hard to reconcile precedents, and only on failure do they admit the existence of judicial disagreements or differences of interpretation. Certainly it is not satisfactory to declare too often

---

9 This presupposition is certainly not necessary: see R. Cotterrell, 'Comparatists and Sociology', paper prepared for 'Comparative Legal Studies: Traditions and Transitions' Conference, University of Cambridge, July 2000, arguing that comparative law and legal sociology can be closely interrelated as interpretive practices.

10 V.G. Curran, 'Cultural Immersion, Difference and Categories in US Comparative Law' (1998) 46 *American Journal of Comparative Law* 43, at 45.

11 Ibid.

12 Curran, n. 10 above, p. 44: Comparative law 'is the one field which by definition has always dealt with and analysed the *other*, the different'; Legrand, n. 1 above, pp. 11, 13: comparatists should 'cherish difference' and have an 'empathy for alterity' rather than 'obstinately pursue similarity and consensus as if confined to a groove'.

13 Another way of putting this is in terms of the balance of the systematic and the empirical in legal interpretation. See R. Cotterrell, 'Why Must Legal Ideas Be Interpreted Sociologically?' (1998) 25 *Journal of Law and Society* 171. If all legal interpretation involves balancing a need to systematize doctrine, on the one hand, and to address it empirically to particular cases, on the other, modern approaches to legal interpretation ultimately always tilt in favour of systematization. Every effort is made to justify particular decisions in terms of legal principles, or at least explain how they relate to these. A legal decision, however just it seems on the facts, appears legally unsatisfactory if it cannot be rationally linked to what lawyers see as broader patterns of legal doctrine governing its field.

that a past decision must be confined to its own unique facts (to recognise that it does not fit other cases, that it represents an irreconcilably different view). The task is to decide how past decisions can best be generalised to play their part in a larger body of legal doctrine. Where legal rules relate without referring to each other and appear to conflict, interpretive effort often aims to show how their interrelation gives new subtleties of meaning in their application together as a doctrinal unity. This is different from (and perhaps more highly prized than) the often unavoidable task of merely recognising conflict between rules, or seeing one rule as derogating from another.

Similarly in comparative law, it is certainly important to stress the value of appreciating difference between legal rules, solutions, styles, cultures, systems, etc. through comparative study and to ask in what circumstances difference is important, inevitable or even desirable. But this strong emphasis is valuable, partly because historically so much effort has been devoted by comparatists to projects of *integrating* or *unifying* law.[14] In this traditional emphasis, comparatists have been no different from other modern lawyers in typically preferring to seek unity and consistency of legal meaning, rather than contrast and differentiation.[15] Where this unity and consistency is elusive, comparatists have often seen their task as that of trying to build it in programmes of transnational 'uniform law', just as jurists of municipal legal systems have tended in modern times to see the task of expounding law as being to construct order from, or superimpose it on, the varied doctrinal detail given by legislation, case law or other sources. To write of the lawyers' preference here is not to imply that this exists independently of powerful client pressures (for example, from governmental and commercial interests) as well as lawyers' own need to legitimize their professional knowledge and practice.[16] A range of considerations of regulatory efficiency and legitimation no doubt gives comparatists a powerful impetus to work towards uniform law, just as it powerfully promotes lawyers' efforts to build system and unity in the doctrine of modern state legal systems.

Seeking similarity, appreciating difference: we could speak also of 'achieving integration' contrasted with 'delineating boundaries'. I want to argue in this paper that determining the balance between these is one of comparative law's hardest, but most important current practical tasks, and that this task must be understood in relation to the activity of legal interpretation more generally.

In legal interpretation, delineating boundaries can refer to the fixing of boundaries of meaning (for example, the meaning of one rule limited by that of another, or of a word or phrase in a statute, or of an entire style of thought or way of understanding that informs law). Equally, it can refer to the extent of the authority

---

14 See R.H. Graveson, *One Law: On Jurisprudence and the Unification of Law: Selected Essays Volume II.* (North-Holland, Amsterdam, 1977); H.C. Gutteridge, *Comparative Law*, (2nd edn., Wildy reprint, London, 1971), chs 11 and 12.

15 Legrand, n. 1 above, pp. 12–13.

16 R. Cotterrell, *The Politics of Jurisprudence: A Critical Introduction to Legal Philosophy* (Butterworths, London, 1989), pp. 9–13.

of law (limits of jurisdiction), whether this concerns a specific rule, a set of procedures (such as those of a particular court or administrative agency) or a legal system. And it can be a matter of defining spheres of devolved or federal regulatory authority within a state legal system, or marking jurisdictional relations between systems.

Integration of law involves removing contradictions between rules or other elements of legal doctrine. This can be done by fiat (for example, a superior court declaring invalid an inconsistent rule laid down by a lower court). Here, law's politically guaranteed authority determines matters conclusively.[17] Or, it can be done by persuasion as where a community of legal interpreters (for example, lawyers drafting a code, a panel of judges hearing a case, juristic commentators) reaches agreement on the best meaning to give to particular elements of legal doctrine or the most appropriate rule to apply in a particular context. Integration can also involve establishing uniform legal authority by merging jurisdictions or setting a uniform legal regime over a diversity of others (as with the creation of a supranational European legal order or various transnational regimes of trade regulation or human rights). Thus, integration and differentiation of law involve a continuum of comparisons that, in their essential nature, concern comparatists and municipal lawyers alike.

If the activity of comparing as such does not fundamentally distinguish comparative law from other legal studies, what does? Legal interpretation of rules or judicial decisions usually assumes a single structure of legal authority to which all these materials can be related: a structure explicable theoretically by using, for example, ideas of sovereignty, rule of recognition or basic norm, which identify its apex or centre. By contrast, comparative law involves comparisons *not limited* within any single system of established legal authority (such as that of the legal system of a nation state).

The absence of a common structure of legal authority embracing the elements to be compared produces the epistemological and ontological problems of comparative law referred to earlier. In legal interpretation related to a single legal system, the answer to the question 'why compare?' is usually simply: to expound and clarify what is at a certain time valid law in that legal system (perhaps as a prelude to evaluating it). The answer to the question 'what is to be compared?' is: whatever can be recognised, according to established understandings within the relevant legal professional community, as legal rules, principles or concepts co-existing in the system. The task of comparison is to integrate and differentiate these various legal materials so as to establish plausible conclusions about the legal position in relation to a particular regulatory field or problem. Of course, this in no way suggests that

[17] Strictly speaking, integration of meaning by fiat is suppression (not integration) of contrary meanings. See R. Cover, 'The Supreme Court 1982, Foreword: *Nomos* and Narrative' (1983–4) 97 *Harvard Law Review* 4, at 40: courts exist 'to suppress law, to choose between two or more laws, to impose upon law a hierarchy'.

comparison is itself simple. Nevertheless, it is usually limited and directed by settled juristic criteria and practices in a way that does not apply in the same way in comparative law.

In most legal interpretation, law's politically guaranteed authority or *voluntas* (for example, the authority of a sovereign legislature or a superior court over an inferior one) limits debates on the rational meaning of legal doctrine (what can be called law's *ratio*) and structures their relevance at all times.[18] And debates on *ratio* are given urgency and point by the assumption that the meanings of legal doctrine arrived at will represent valid law. But in comparative law, no common legal authority exists to produce these effects. So comparatists' elaborations of law's *ratio* on a transnational basis, as in efforts at creating uniform law, are often persuasive rather than authoritative,[19] though they may be adopted by international agreement.[20]

What then makes for good interpretation of legal doctrine in comparative law? For example, in 'seeking similarity' what makes similarity worth seeking? In 'appreciating difference' what makes difference worth appreciating? When and under what conditions? What is to be compared? And what is comparison for?

3. The Authority of Comparative Law

To set these questions, as has been done here, in the context of a discussion of general legal interpretation emphasizes how crucial 'authority' is in determining answers to them. What makes comparatists' search for uniform law or harmonization of law, or their welcome of legal 'convergence', appropriate? The answer may be greater regulatory efficiency (for example, economic utility) as often claimed for projects of unifying commercial laws. Or, it may be that law is thereby made to represent, symbolize or give effect to shared values or beliefs, as in the claim that uniform human rights laws express universal civilized values associated with respect for the autonomy or dignity of all human beings. Again, the answer may lie in the simplicity, predictability or security of a uniform law, as where the same rules (whatever they may be) are applied consistently across a certain geographical area (or in a region of shared language, traditions or historical experience). Finally, a uniform legal solution might be appropriate because it seems congruent with, or a public expression of, widely shared feelings. One of the best known theoretical arguments for uniform law on this basis is Savigny's invocation of the 'spirit of the

18 For the concepts of *voluntas* and *ratio* see F.L. Neumann, 'The Change in the Function of Law in Modern Society' in E.W.E. Scheuermann (ed.), *The Rule of Law under Siege: Selected Essays of Franz L. Neumann and Otto Kirchheimer* (University of California Press, Berkeley, 1996).

19 M.J. Bonell, 'The UNIDROIT Principles of International Commercial Contracts' in R. Cotterrell (ed.), *Process and Substance: Butterworth Lectures 1994* (Butterworths, London, 1995), pp. 73–74.

20 Gutteridge, n. 14 above, ch. 13.

people' (*Volksgeist*) as the source of law[21] – an impenetrable and mystical idea and therefore dangerous, but powerful in some circumstances (as in the politically disunited Germany of Savigny's era). More recently, the fear of extreme nationalist feelings and the wish to marginalize them and prevent future war has been a spur to efforts to harmonize or unify law on a transnational basis, especially in Europe.

These criteria of appropriateness might pragmatically influence international agreements or the decisions of particular states. In any case, they serve as potential substitutes, in comparative law, for a settled (legal) authority (*voluntas*) that can put an end to the debate about law's *ratio*: that is, about its principled justification and appropriate meaning.

Conversely, what is it that makes diverse legal solutions – the appreciation of difference – appropriate? Comparatists have recently tended to answer this question by explicitly invoking conceptions of 'legal culture',[22] or urging a very broad recognition of cultural differences underlying different legal styles or systems. These are identified mainly in lawyers' outlook, practices and traditions but they, in turn, are often seen as 'intimately linked to our civilization and ways of thinking'.[23] What constitutes cultural difference here is usually mysterious but the claim is sometimes that cultural 'features of the law... can only be changed at the slow rhythm at which the civilisation of the country itself, the sense of justice of its citizens, its economic structure, language and social manners themselves are changed'.[24]

The cultural authority invoked to justify difference is often ambiguous and undifferentiated.[25] If we try to separate its elements, they might include ultimate values or beliefs (such as those that underpin the distinctiveness of religious legal systems). They might also include different traditions (for example, common language or historical experience). The traditions that some comparatists see as most powerful in determining differences between legal systems, styles or cultures are those of professional legal elites,[26] rather than of the wider society. Otherwise, a justification for legal difference may lie in distinctive collective interests (for example, national economic interests) that require special legal protection. Finally, what remains as a potential 'cultural' justification of difference is the difficult idea of collective sentiments (feelings, for example, about the 'nation' or the 'people' and its character or destiny – the hard-to-analyse but often very powerful sense of

21 F.C. Von Savigny, *Of the Vocation of Our Age for Legislation and Jurisprudence*, (A. Hayward, translated, Arno reprint, New York, 1975).

22 See e.g. Legrand, n. 1 above; Curran, n. 12 above; A. Watson, *Legal Origins and Legal Change* (Hambledon Press, London, 1991), pp. 100–102.

23 R. David and J.E.C. Brierley, *Major Legal Systems in the World Today*, (3rd edn., Stevens, London, 1985), p. 19.

24 Ibid.

25 R. Cotterrell, 'The Concept of Legal Culture' in D. Nelken (ed.), *Comparing Legal Cultures* (Dartmouth, Aldershot, 1997).

26 See e.g. A. Watson, *The Evolution of Law* (Blackwell, Oxford, 1985).

patriotism, nationalism or group identification).[27] The authority of culture as a criterion guiding comparative law is thus a compendium of diverse elements (beliefs, traditions, interests, sentiments), some of which cannot be defined in any conclusive way.

These ideas merely illustrate the kinds of authority that comparative law typically invokes to justify, underpin or explain its legal interpretations. This is not a matter of the legal authority of *voluntas* but of the persuasive 'authority' of instrumental utility, appeal to shared beliefs or ultimate values, tradition or shared sentiment. These kinds of authority point towards a logic of socio-legal analysis that, I shall argue, makes comparative law specially appropriate in methods and outlook to confront the changing environment of contemporary law.

What is most important about this changing environment? The general forces of change in it that are most significant for present purposes are indicated by concepts of 'globalization' and 'localization'. These much used terms have many diverse and often contradictory meanings. Here, I take globalization simply to mean tendencies (however interpreted) towards transnational uniformity in economic or social arrangements, institutions and values. Localization is taken here to refer to counter-tendencies (of whatever kind) towards protection, assertion or facilitation of diversity, difference, independence, separation or autonomy of groups, nations or territories, most often in matters of government or common values or traditions. Without referring to the extensive debates about these tendencies, it can at least be said that, in social life beyond its specifically legal aspects, the tension between seeking similarity and appreciating difference clearly exists, writ large in major social movements that are still imperfectly understood. Globalization seems pre-eminently to be about seeking similarity by unifying social, economic and often legal arrangements. Localization seems to be about appreciating difference by creating, preserving or rediscovering conditions in which difference (for example, political or cultural) can flourish and be respected.

Because the focus of comparative law is not restricted to the law of any particular nation state, it is better fitted than other doctrinal legal studies to take full account of the dynamics of social change represented by the conflicts of globalization and localization. Comparative law's long-professed but ultimately still inchoate relationship with legal sociology can be exploited and developed to enable it to observe and interpret the changing economic and social contexts of regulation. Certainly, the epistemological and ontological problems of comparative law should force it, in seeking to solve them, to take account of these contexts in pursuing many, though not all, of its aims. Comparative law's commonly adopted focus on legal and social 'functions', 'problems' or 'interests'[28] as bases of comparison ought to point it towards serious concern with analysis of the social environments in relation to which legal doctrine must establish its meaning. For example, comparatists have long

27 Gutteridge, n. 14 above, p. 158.

28 See e.g. Zweigert and Kötz, n. 3 above, p. 10.

recognized that power relations between nation states can strongly affect legal change[29] and legal sociologists have begun to demonstrate some mechanisms of this influence.[30] Indeed, power relations in and between regulated groups, and communities more generally, should be a major focus of attention.

On the other hand, comparatists have understandably not wished to become sociologists or to see their focus on legal comparison dissolve away into sociological inquiries.[31] So they have held back from exploring some implications of comparative law's inevitable dependence on social criteria of legal interpretation (discussed above in terms of instrumental efficiency, shared values or beliefs, traditions and affective considerations). To explore these criteria more rigorously and to understand their interaction in relation to comparative law's tasks of seeking similarity and appreciating difference, much more co-operation between comparatists and legal sociologists is needed.

A further difficulty is more serious because solving it may not be merely a matter of productive academic alliances. In an important sense, the most important contemporary agenda of comparative law is obviously not set by comparatists. It is determined particularly by those engaged in, and seeking to benefit from, projects of European integration, the opening of trade and commerce on an ever-wider transnational basis, the development of international banking and financial systems, the world-wide control and exploitation of intellectual property, the development of the internet, and the control of transnational crime of many kinds. All of these projects are seen to require, for their efficient pursuit, significant harmonization of the laws of nation states, or the creation of new transnational regulatory regimes.[32] Viewed in these contexts, the great recent resurgence of interest and activity in comparative law is in no way neutrally situated between the appreciation of difference and the search for similarity. Comparative law is powerfully driven now, as through much of its history, by the urge to unify or harmonize law. Recognizing difference does not, in these contexts, lead to its celebration, but to devising means of removing it.

To this extent, the co-ordination of law by unification or harmonization that comparative law has always sporadically pursued[33] has now become for some major interest groups, an urgent priority. The question is not 'whether or when?', but 'how and on what model?' The predominantly economic process of globalization is like a whirlwind carrying comparative law along. 'It is... the mechanism of the market which now takes upon itself the role of the judge, the opinion-maker, the verifier of

---

29 Gutteridge, n. 14 above, p. 160.

30 Y. Dezalay and B. Garth, *Dealing in Virtue: International Commercial Arbitration and the Construction of a Transnational Legal Order* (University of Chicago Press, Chicago, 1996).

31 See Z. Péteri, 'Some Aspects of the Sociological Approach in Comparative Law' in Z. Péteri (ed.), *Hungarian Law – Comparative Law: Essays for the 8th International Congress of Comparative Law* (Académiai Kiadó, Budapest, 1970), especially at pp. 90–93.

32 J. Wiener, *Globalization and the Harmonization of Law* (Pinter, London, 1999).

33 Gutteridge, n. 14 above, ch. 11.

values. Intellectuals have been expropriated again'.[34] Comparative law's task is apparently to aid processes of unstoppable change, to identify sources of friction (perhaps embedded in some way in what is taken to be culture) and to find the most efficient means of removing or bypassing them. Perhaps it can ease the pain of transition by inventively smoothing out legal differences, creatively interpreting legal change to those who must accept it, or preserving familiar forms, concepts and styles of legal practice and thought while adjusting their effects to meet transnational requirements.

With transnational organization of economic activity in many fields, some see a 'retreat of the state'[35] so that law's *voluntas* in many areas of regulation is slowly being detached from its dependence on the political guarantee that the state provides. Nevertheless, for the present, much harmonization of law is still accomplished by adjusting the private and public law regimes of nation states.[36] Hence a huge scope for comparative law opens up. Yet, strictly speaking, the task assigned to it as a facilitator of globalization in these contexts will be neither to appreciate difference nor even to seek similarity between the legal systems, styles or cultures of nation states. Instead, the object will be to make legal adjustments, as needed, to avoid tension and friction in governance systems that seek as far as possible to free themselves from significant moorings in or dependency on the law of any particular nation state.

In one area – at least that of human rights, appreciation of difference alongside a search for uniformity seems widely recognized as a continuing necessity. While the drive to universalize human rights is as powerful in many respects as the whirlwind of economic globalization (and in some respects promoted by it), the dynamics of legal development are clearly different. Economic globalization serves primarily instrumental aims. In the terms I have sketched earlier, the persuasive authority for unifying or harmonizing law is that of greater efficiency in commercial or related activities (though this can have major consequences on wider fronts). By contrast, the universalization of human rights is a matter of the export, reception or transplanting of fundamental values or beliefs (for example, about the essential nature of humanity) in legal form. These values can be variously interpreted, or confronted by opposing values, in certain settings. Hence the drive for universalism, seeking similarity in human rights jurisdictions, is challenged by so-called cultural relativism that demands the appreciation of difference.[37] Nonetheless, the drive for legal uniformity is very strong given that the universality of the values to be represented in human rights law is powerfully championed. So, respect for human

[34] Z. Bauman, *Legislators and Interpreters: On Modernity, Post-modernity and Intellectuals* (Polity, Cambridge, 1987), p. 124.

[35] S. Strange, *The Retreat of the State: The Diffusion of Power in the World Economy* (Cambridge University Press, Cambridge, 1996).

[36] See generally, Wiener, n. 32 above.

[37] H.J. Steiner and P. Alston, *International Human Rights in Context: Law, Politics, Morals* (2nd edn, Clarendon Press, Oxford, 2000), pp. 366–402.

rights is said to be 'the only regulative principle of state organisation which unites every country, race and creed in the world ... the ideology at the "end of history"'.[38]

4. Comparative Law and the Regions of the Social

If comparative law is to set its own agenda of finding appropriate balances between the search for similarity and the appreciation of difference in legal phenomena, it will need powerful theoretical resources to help with this. In their absence, the residual assumption is likely to be that the aim of all contemporary comparative scholarship must be to facilitate legal uniformity on the widest possible scale. The reason is that, while it is now widely accepted that national economic survival and success depends on transnational regulatory harmonization, other kinds of persuasive authority, for or against harmonizing or unifying different areas of law remain insufficiently analysed. In such circumstances, most legal differences are likely to be judged negatively: as failures of or challenges to harmonization, or as occasions for ranking so that one legal solution is necessarily seen as worse or better than another, or simply incomprehensible.

But law can be, for example, a means of protecting or symbolizing collective identity in various ways. It must serve the needs not only of economic communities, but of other kinds too, and it can serve, in some respects, as a normative expression of the nature of these communities. It can provide what Boaventura De Sousa Santos has called 'rights to roots' that give groundings of identity and solidarity, as well as 'rights to options' that allow the greatest scope for free personal initiative and choice.[39] Thus, interests in harmonizing or unifying law can be confronted with other interests that require that law express or preserve difference.

Debates around cultural relativism in human rights show that in some contemporary circumstances, this kind of confrontation is recognised and the invocation of culture as a powerful marker of difference is surely significant in these debates. In a very different context from the human rights debates, the idea of culture has also been invoked to focus attention of the appreciation of difference generally in comparative law. Recent efforts to develop a sophisticated concept of legal culture as *mentalité* – the entire law-related outlook of a community – represent an attempt to work towards theoretical conceptions of difference that might be powerful enough to confront assumptions about the significance and even

38 C. Douzinas 'Justice and Human Rights in Postmodernity' in C. Gearty and A. Tomkins (eds.), *Understanding Human Rights* (Pinter, London, 1996), p. 115.

39 B.D.S. Santos *Toward a New Common Sense: Law, Science and Politics in the Paradigmatic Transition* (Routledge, London, 1995), p. 262.

inevitability of convergence, harmonization or unification, especially in European law.[40]

But, I have suggested earlier (and elsewhere)[41] why it is important to break down the idea of culture in comparative law scholarship into several distinct components. It is difficult to invoke 'culture' or 'legal culture' as a reason for appreciating, rather than condemning or dismissing difference, because these terms refer to an indeterminate number of variables, mostly undifferentiated so that their relative importance cannot be gauged in specific contexts of regulation. We need, instead, clearly to distinguish the different kinds of social relationships or types of community that law regulates. We need to identify different aspects or regions of the social – that is, the environment in which legal doctrine finds its meaning and to which it refers and relates.[42] In this way, the potentially most important components of culture can be examined systematically.

A way to do this is to recognise that today, the social to which law relates can no longer be thought of as 'society' – an undifferentiated entity of some sort. It is no longer adequate to speak of law's functions in relation to society as though 'law' and 'society' are two monolithic entities confronting each other. Different kinds or areas of law relate to different *types of community*, by which I mean the different types of bonding that can exist between individuals and draw them together in relations of trust. These types of community, in turn, find expression in complex combination, in the innumerable kinds of group life that actually exist in any society.[43]

Thus, we can think of *instrumental* community as the kind of social relationships that are based on common or convergent purposes – especially, but not necessarily, economic purposes. It is clear that much pressure for harmonization of law has always arisen through perceptions of law's role in regulating this kind of community life. But, it is only one kind, and if law serves it exclusively at the expense of protecting and promoting the well-being of other kinds of social bonds, other types of community, it fails to meet some important demands. The law of instrumental community (most obviously, for example, contract, commercial, financial, corporate and much other recently burgeoning regulation) is *powerful* because it can be tailored to serve precise instrumental objectives. But it serves social groups (especially commercial enterprises, trade networks and economic interest groups) that mutate rapidly as national and international markets alter. These are weak patterns of community. Law serves them mainly by providing rights to options in Santos' sense – that is, patterns of regulation geared to flexibility, growth and change, and to facilitating innumerable convergent deals, bringing people together in relationships

---

40 Legrand, n. 1 above; P. Legrand, 'European Legal Systems Are Not Converging' (1996) 45 *International and Comparative Law Quarterly* 52; P. Legrand, 'The Impossibility of "Legal Transplants"' (1997) 4 *Maastricht Journal of European and Comparative Law* 111. See also Curran, n. 10 above.

41 Cotterrell, n. 25 above.

42 R. Cotterrell, 'Law and Community: A New Relationship?' (1998) 51 *Current Legal Problems* 367.

43 R. Cotterrell, 'A Legal Concept of Community' (1997) 12 *Canadian Journal of Law and Society* 75.

of a relatively transient character or otherwise specifically focused on limited but shared or congruent objectives.

The grand historical ideal of unifying law, now most likely to be pursued by articulating convergences and strategies of harmonization, is skewed and partial if it serves relations of community subsisting only in these limited, loose social groupings. So, comparative law, in alliance with legal sociology, needs to pay special attention to law's contributions to other types of community that tend to be marginalized in the whirlwind of globalization. These correspond to other types of justifications, referred to earlier, for seeking similarity and appreciating difference through comparative law. They are communities of *tradition* (for example, based solely on co-existence in the same territory, or sharing the same language or historical experiences), of *beliefs or values*, and of *affect* (shared or mutual sentiment). As suggested earlier, these traditional, belief-based or affective kinds of community life do not necessarily demand either that their legal protection and promotion be increasingly 'globalized' on the one hand, or resolutely 'localized', on the other. They do not inevitably point the law that serves them towards the search for similarity by unifying or harmonizing law across boundaries of jurisdiction, or towards the appreciation of difference and the positive evaluation of legal particularity and distinctiveness. But they raise these issues in quite different ways from the way they are raised (and usually resolved with little theoretical discussion) in many of comparative law's projects of uniform law or harmonization to serve the needs of instrumental community.

5. Regulating Non-instrumental Relations of Community

5.1. Community of Values or Beliefs

Take, for example, law's role in expressing shared ultimate *values or beliefs*. Specifically belief-based community life is usually strong. People cling to ultimate values they recognise as their own. It is painful to discard them or see them fundamentally challenged. But because values are often ambiguous in their implications when translated into specific regulatory demands, law, seen as the expression of fundamental values or beliefs is typically weak and problematic law. Thus, human rights as legal ideas are not, to use Bentham's term, 'nonsense upon stilts',[44] but they can have very different practical meanings in different contexts and be subject to controversial interpretation. It is not difficult for them to be subordinated or adapted to the regulatory requirements of instrumental community, which give rise to clearer, more specific law that defines freedom of action in economically related fields. And because community of belief is often a strong kind of bonding when present in group life, harmonization or unification of the law expressing it is often difficult or impossible between groups whose values or beliefs

[44] See generally e.g. H.L.A. Hart, *Essays on Bentham* (Clarendon Press, Oxford, 1982), ch. 4.

are claimed to differ. This is why comparatists and legal sociologists have long recognised that, in many cases, law seen as expressing fundamental values or beliefs (for example, with strong religious overtones) is hard to replace effectively with law transplanted from environments where beliefs or values are significantly different.[45]

Even in societies strongly wedded, as regards official pronouncements at least, to legal protection of the dignity and autonomy of individual human life, considerable differences in the interpretation of these values in legal form exist. For example, many Americans are strongly wedded to the maintenance of capital punishment within the framework of a belief system that strongly enshrines the values of individual autonomy. But, as I write this, newspaper reports tell of 'disgust' popularly expressed in several European countries against this stance, which is said to have damaged 'America's image as a bastion of freedom'.[46] This is, of course, not only a transnational issue which makes appreciating differences between national legal systems necessary, but an intranational one, because in many individual European countries and particular states of the United States, significant value-conflict around it exists. The same, of course, can be said of many other issues that arise in interpreting values of human dignity and autonomy, for example issues relating to abortion, euthanasia or genetic research.

These considerations highlight the important point that the choice between seeking similarity and appreciating difference is not only a matter to be considered in regard to different national conditions taken as unities. A focus on law's relation to community, rather than political society treated as a single entity, requires that full account be taken of the complex interrelations of different kinds of community life within the territory of state legal systems. People have allegiances, with varying degrees of transience or permanence, at different times and in different ways, and often simultaneously, to different groups and social relations involving intricate overlapping of the different types of community life – instrumental, traditional, belief-based and affective. Sometimes law, faced with impenetrable complexity (especially, perhaps, in the interplay of values and beliefs), steps aside and regulates in the most limited, neutral, locally pragmatic way possible, or not at all. For comparatists, the task in relation to these legal areas may sometimes be neither to seek similarity nor to appreciate difference, but only to recognize the appropriateness of leaving well alone.

---

45 E. Levy, 'The Reception of Highly Developed Legal Systems by Peoples of Different Cultures' (1950) 25 *Washington Law Review* 233; G. Massell, 'Law as an Instrument of Revolutionary Change in a Traditional Milieu: The Case of Soviet Central Asia' (1968) 2 *Law and Society Review* 179; J. Starr, 'The Impact of a Legal Revolution in Rural Turkey' (1973–4) 8 *Law and Society Review* 533.

46 M. Kettle, 'Dead Certainties' 29 May 2000, The Guardian, p. 18.

5.2. Traditional Community

Relationships founded on what I have termed *traditional* community are limited ones arising from mere proximity: not necessarily physical proximity, as in the case of co-existence in a particular territory, but also, for example, the proximity of shared language or common historical experience. They are often, but not always, weak bonds getting weaker in the era of globalization.[47] Santos' 'rights to options' may be, above all, the right to move freely from place to place and seize opportunities wherever they arise. Hence the most powerful drives towards economic development on a transnational base weaken the significance of territorial roots for many people (who merely follow the job, the project or the enterprise to whatever location is most appropriate). Instrumental community, although limited and transient as a basis of group life, undermines traditional community.

Language, from this standpoint, becomes an obstacle to be overcome rather than a basis of group allegiance. English is pragmatically adopted most often as the transnational language through which 'rights to options' are realised. But instrumental community life is not always or even mainly realised in transnational groups and relations, and traditional community, while attenuated and instrumentally transformed for some people, remains powerfully significant in its own right for many others. These include, most obviously, individuals who do not move their place of residence or work frequently, if ever, and have no second language that frees them from the ties of their native language group. It also includes others who deliberately affirm tradition as a basis of community, for example by reviving and nurturing the previously neglected distinctive language or customs of their group.

Law's relations with traditional community are focused on providing basic conditions for co-existence (rather than facilitating the pursuit of projects or expressing shared ultimate values or beliefs). We might see the law of tort or delict and much basic criminal law as central to these regulatory aims, although it is impossible exactly to link categories of law and types of community life. Crime obviously threatens the co-existence of individuals and groups. Its control is a prerequisite for any stable community life. Thus, although traditional community is socially weak in many and perhaps an increasing range of conditions, the law that protects it most fundamentally is typically strong and must be so. It deals primarily only with a bare social minimum – basic requirements of peaceful co-existence – and this minimum is likely to be similar in societies having broadly similar levels of social complexity. For these reasons the regulation of traditional community is often similar in different legal systems. So comparatists understandably and appropriately tend to seek similarity, rather than to appreciate difference, in this field of legal regulation.

[47] But the dynamics are complex. As local territorial settings seem less important bases of social relations, global, or at least transnational ones (recognised, for example, in international environmental legal concerns) achieve more prominence. The recognition of needs for global co-existence is providing new foci of traditional community.

To the extent that instrumental community life expresses itself increasingly in transnational relationships and groups, the requirements of basic co-existence also acquire an increasingly strong transnational dimension. Hence the special importance and urgency of current efforts to develop transnational criminal law. Modern legal regulation for co-existence also increasingly covers health and safety, hygiene and the environment – at least there are strong demands that it should. But it is in these areas that some instrumental economic relations tend to conflict most obviously with regulatory demands of traditional community, as where interpretations of transnational trade laws or agreements hamper national health-related controls on food products, or in other ways frustrate or deter local environmental regulation, or where transnational demands for environmental or health regulation impose restrictions on local industries or even national economies.

As has been widely recognised by comparatists, lawyers as a group, operating in different legal systems, themselves show many characteristics of traditional community. Tradition shows itself in the persistence of distinctive styles of practice and legal thought, purely because these are familiar and close at hand. The tendency in comparative law scholarship has been to attach much significance to tradition in this sense, as a condition to be taken into account in considering legal transplantation,[48] or perhaps as a key element in legal culture that might cause special problems for convergence or harmonization of law.[49] From a perspective of legal sociology seeking to aid comparative law, it is hard to generalize about the significance of tradition in this kind of context. But the dynamics of change may be similar to those of traditional community more generally. In other words, tradition, despite some appearances, is often a relatively weak basis of community. The admittedly transient and fluid bonds of instrumental community tend to transform or weaken the bonds of tradition. Hence, instrumental need can bring about remarkable transitions in traditional allegiances and practices,[50] especially when transnational groups and relationships cut across all boundaries of local tradition. Hence, as lawyers travel and practise transnationally, it seems highly likely that traditions of practice and styles of work and thought will be radically transformed.

5.3. Affective Community

For many reasons, *affectively* based community life is particularly hard to interpret in legal terms.[51] For Max Weber, affective action was clearly irrational, by which he meant not governed by any consciously recognised principles.[52] Similarly, the

---

48 Watson, n. 26 above.

49 Legrand (1997); Legrand (1996), n. 40 above.

50 See e.g. Dezalay and Garth, n. 30 above.

51 R. Cotterrell, 'Is There a Logic of Legal Transplants?' in D. Nelken and J. Feest (eds.), *Adapting Legal Cultures* (Hart Publishing, Oxford, 2001).

52 M. Weber, *Economy and Society: An Outline of Interpretive Sociology*, (E. Fischoff et al., translated, University of California Press, Berkeley, 1978), pp. 24–26.

Volksgeist idea, associated most strongly in legal theory with Savigny's work, has often been condemned as irrational. Certainly, affective bonds have an unpredictability and analytical impenetrability that makes it hard to frame or recognise them with any real precision in law. But these bonds are often strong: people may be prepared to die for family, friends or nation when love ties them to these groups or relationships. I think comparatists have always clearly recognised the significance of affective community in connection with prospects for unifying law. Usually, national feeling has been judged negatively as a dangerous or regrettable barrier to legal unity, since it has so often led not to transnational co-operation but to tension, conflict and war.

If, however, we take seriously Santos' idea that individuals in contemporary conditions seek from law both rights to options and rights to roots, it is easy to see that the notion of roots can have strongly emotional connotations. A place or group may be just a site of co-existence (as with traditional community), a setting for current projects (as with instrumental community), or more prominent in consciousness as an environment, where people think like me and believe what I believe' (as in community of belief). But it may also be a setting of sentimental attachment which gives powerful, if intangible and ultimately unanalyzable bases of security, identity or meaningful existence. National identity may be a combination of traditional attachments (such as to locality, language and literature, or shared historical experience), collective pursuit of economic well-being (measured, for example, in gross national product) and adherence to values or beliefs ('we hold these truths to be self-evident...'). But these elements can be overlaid by purely sentimental national pride or patriotism. And this can substitute for any of them.

Nationalism clearly remains significant. While it has in the past sometimes inspired legal unification, today it is usually a powerful force for localisation (taken in this setting as the promotion through law of specific national interests and prerogatives) in opposition to globalisation. Because of its history as a begetter of wars and its frequent inclusion of an apparently purely emotional component, it is an morally and intellectually inadequate opponent of globalisation, even if a powerful affective focus. Indeed, often it allies itself with globalisation in so far as transnational economic objectives or the spread of certain fundamental values are seen to support national interests.

6. Conclusion

If, however, comparative law's necessary concern with the social is taken as a concern with the interrelation of types of community, as this paper has tried to do, a different view of the global-local dynamic is possible. Comparative law's central orientation today, I suggest, should be to balance the promotion of similarity in legal arrangements between legal systems, on the one hand, and the defence of differences in legal arrangements, styles, outlooks and ideas. But it can do this only if it understands systematically the nature of the social.

The positive valuation of legal difference may be, as some comparatists have long affirmed,[53] at least as important in some circumstances as unification or harmonisation. But there is no point in simply defending, in generalised, abstract terms, either the promotion of legal harmonisation or the protection of legal difference in distinctive legal cultures. Seeking similarity and appreciating difference make sense as aims only in relation to specific, differentiated categories of social relationships and purposes of regulation. It follows that comparative law can solve its epistemological and ontological problems in general terms only if it confronts the social armed with appropriate theoretical resources.

In a world of globalizing tendencies, it is necessary to distinguish carefully different components of law's social environment. Specifying different bases of community life is a step towards this. It allows us to begin to conceptualise the complexity of law's tasks in regulating social relationships and groups and to give proper attention theoretically to social relations that are other or more than instrumental. This is particularly necessary today when the importance of instrumental economic relations is so strongly emphasised politically, and legal analysis seems impelled towards a similar emphasis rather than towards giving equal prominence to studying conditions for legally expressing and protecting other kinds of relations.

I have focused here on aspects of comparative law's concerns that might bring comparatists and legal sociologists closer together in their research objectives. Through the elaboration of the legal concept of community, legal sociology can serve comparative law. In turn, comparative law can address, rigorously and systematically, practical issues of regulating community life. Comparative lawyers may indeed be better fitted to achieve success in this than other legal interpreters because they are well used to legal analysis unbounded by the specific controls of structures of state legal authority. They should be able to appreciate ways in which types of community are expressed in social relationships that are often limited within state boundaries, but increasingly extend beyond them. So, techniques of unifying and harmonising law that comparatists have long worked with can be used to solve transnational regulatory problems of community in these contexts.

But the slow liberation of legal analysis from its 'imprisonment' within the boundaries of nation state jurisdiction,[54] a liberation comparatists have usually welcomed and promoted, should also lead to a radical rethinking of possibilities for legal localisation. The nation state will surely remain for the foreseeable future the single focus of much legal regulation. But comparatists and legal sociologists should be able to combine to explore needs for regulatory localisation *within* the state, or *irrespective* of it (in special jurisdictions not confined within states). Again, I suggest that the guiding concept in this enterprise should be that of community (and its

[53] Gutteridge, n. 14 above, pp. 156–157.

[54] Cf. F.H. Lawson, *The Comparison: Selected Essays, Volume II.* (North-Holland, Amsterdam, 1977) p. 73, noting that, for the lawyer, comparative legal study is 'like escaping from prison into the open air'.

fourfold typology), which is an aid towards understanding, for regulatory purposes, contemporary patterns of social relations in all their fluidity and variety. It is time to escape the limits of the familiar but now largely empty rhetoric of 'law and society' or even 'law in society', a rhetoric that obscures the sheer complexity and frequent indeterminacy of what society means today as the environment of legal regulation.

Chapter 4

TRANSMIGRATION AND TRANSFERABILITY OF COMMERCIAL LAW IN A GLOBALIZED WORLD

*Nicholas Foster**

In the following contribution, transplant theories are tested, this time through the example of commercial law comparisons. The piece belongs with the papers on the theory of transplants, and therefore, the theory of comparative law, and also commercial law.

The worldwide movement towards harmonization of commercial law makes it pertinent to question how legal transplants can or will function in this field. Commercial law transplants are 'extremely common', and 'many hopes are pinned on them'; but can transplant theories be used to predict whether these transplants will work?

This contribution analyses the current debate on legal transplants by dividing modern literature into 'culturalist' and 'transferist', and considers the recent attempts to move on from this debate. In this, it looks at the works of Watson, Legrand, Seidman, Kahn-Freund, Ewald and Teubner, as do many of the other contributions. Foster, however, tests these approaches in the field of commercial law, specifically as related to universal security in England, France and Quebec, to find out whether commercial law is 'closely linked' to social processes or divorced from culture. In doing this, he looks at the English 'floating charge' and the opposite positions in England and France, which he then analyses in the example of Quebec, 'an island of civilian law in a sea of common law'.

In looking at the French example the conclusion is, that the culturalists are right, but when looking at Quebec, that the transferists are right. Does the 'social processes' idea provide a better answer? In order to refine the search, Foster looks at commercial law

* Lecturer, Law Department, School of Oriental and African Studies. This version of the paper is substantially revised from that given at the W.G. Hart Legal Workshop 2000. The author is grateful to the participants in the Workshop for comments and discussions. These include (with apologies for omissions) Frédérique Dahan, Andrew Harding, Andrew Huxley, David Nelken and Esin Örücü. The usual disclaimer applies. The idea of looking at universal security and Quebec came from M.C. Sabourin, 'Legal Transplants: The Quebec Floating Hypothec: A Case Study' (Unpublished SOAS LL.M dissertation, 1999). Translations are the author's, apart from those of the Quebec legislation, where the official version is used.

A. Harding and E. Örücü (eds.),
Comparative Law in the 21st Century, 55–74.

and culture. We are led into mental gymnastics, by considering various possibilities, to show, for example, that probably one of the theories of legal transplant may be correct but that we have insufficient information to prove that. Are we leaving out from our equation one of the dimensions of analysis: culture, society, economy, history, politics or legal logic? If there are misunderstandings surrounding Watson's legal transplant theory, is it possible to consider Ewald and Teubner as corrections, or, is there something wrong in the methods used?

As far as commercial lawyers are concerned, we are told that they want an answer to the question, 'How will this transplanted law work?' Can there be predictions? If not, can transplant theory be a theory at all, or, is it really just a hypothesis? Foster contends that transplants vary so much that broad generalizations cannot be offered and therefore there cannot be a Grand Transplant Theory. The conclusion may have to be that, not only is there no one thing called a 'legal transplant', but neither is there only one meaning attached to the word 'work' in the question, 'do legal transplants work?' The reader may be interested in comparing the concept 'work' used by Foster, with the concept 'successful' used by Smits and Nelken, and rethink the whole field of transplants and metaphors after reading this chapter.

We can only be aware of the complexity and try to reformulate our research questions. Foster suggests a move from simplicity to complexity, admits that no predictive answers can be given to commercial lawyers, and demonstrates amply that the comparative law venture seeking explanations for 'the true function of comparative law', is full of pitfalls. The problems will only get more intense with globalization.

[A. Harding and E. Örücü]

1. INTRODUCTION

Commerce is by its nature international, and there is therefore no field in which there is more harmonisation than commercial law, with numerous transplants. This has always been the case, but ever since the fall of the Berlin Wall and the collapse of the Soviet Union, globalization has resulted in a greatly increased range, pace and sheer number of commercial law transplants, together with an increase in the number and diversity of host jurisdictions. Globalization is itself largely a commercial phenomenon.

This huge movement towards harmonization of commercial law worldwide presents a contrast to the move away from Western influences that many colleagues in the SOAS law department see in their fields. From the perspective of a commercial comparatist, 1979 is a major date in comparative law, not so much because the Iranian Revolution symbolized this new independence, but rather because the election of Margaret Thatcher marked the start of the profound ideological change which drives the forces of commercial law harmonization.

In this situation, the question of whether legal transplants will function as expected is of considerable practical importance.

This chapter will examine the concept of a universal security, i.e. one in which all the assets of a person are given as security, consider the possibilities of a successful transplant of universal security into two jurisdictions, France and Quebec, and compare the results. The intention is to investigate the possibility of making successful commercial law transplants, and to draw some conclusions about legal transplant writing.

2. Harmonization

Before 1989, there was a considerable degree of commercial law harmonization. One well-known example is the Vienna Convention on International Sales of 1980 ('the Vienna Convention'), adopted in numerous countries.[1] Generally, however, such harmonization concerned international trade in goods, and had little effect on domestic legal systems.

After 1989, the picture changed dramatically. Massive worldwide transplantation took place, affecting the domestic law of many legal systems.[2]

Various harmonization processes exist. They can be categorised as: institutionally organised; customary, market-based; and pressure to conform/inter-jurisdictional competition.

Institutionally organized harmonization is expressly designed in the context of an institution. Such institutions vary in type: many are governmental or public in some way (such as UNCITRAL, UNIDROIT, the World Bank or the EBRD); others are non-governmental (such as the ICC).[3]

Types of harmonization effected by these institutions vary greatly, and include such projects as the Vienna Convention, the UNCITRAL Model Law on International Commercial Arbitration of 1985,[4] UNIDROIT's Principles of

---

1 See the UNCITRAL website at <www.uncitral.org> and R. Goode, *Commercial Law* (Penguin, Harmondsworth, 1995) ch. 33, pp. 925–937.

2 See for example 'Law in transition', <www.ebrd.org/english/public/index.htm>, which refers to 'the promotion of legal reform as a core dimension of [the European Bank for Reconstruction and Development ('EBRD')'s] work'.

3 UNCITRAL: United Nations Commission on International Trade Law, <www.uncitral.org>; UNIDROIT: International Institute for the Unification of Private Law, <www.unidroit.org>; World Bank: International Bank for Reconstruction and Development, together with its affiliate organisations known as the World Bank Group, <www.worldbank.org>; EBRD, <www.ebrd.org>; ICC: International Chamber of Commerce, <www.iccwbo.org>.

4 Also available on the UNCITRAL website, ibid.

International Commercial Contracts,[5] the EBRD's Secured Transactions Project[6] and the ICC's Uniform Customs and Practice for Documentary Credits.

Customary/market based harmonization is another broad category, in which harmonization processes arise out of international transactions. They are not consciously planned, and *a fortiori* are not conceived within any institution. They divide into: (i) transactions standardized by uniform legal practice and documentation, based on the use of one municipal law as the transaction's governing law (e.g. international financial transactions governed by English law); and (ii) transactions new to the host jurisdiction (e.g. leasing in France).

The common factor in the third category is a general pressure on states to conform to 'international legal standards' in order to compete with other states. Factors leading to this inter-jurisdictional competition include the necessity to attract inward investment, the desire to make trading entities of that state internationally competitive, the need to comply with World Bank requirements in order to qualify for financial assistance, and the wish to qualify for membership of the World Trade Organisation.

Manifestations of harmonization as changes in municipal law (i.e. transplants) also fall into three categories, with some degree of relationship between the categories of harmonization process and the types of manifestation. The three categories are: (i) legislation; (ii) new transaction types; and (iii) conflict of laws cases.

The category most often discussed is that of legislation, but new transaction types (governed by the law of the host jurisdiction) are also very significant, as are transactions governed by the law of the donor jurisdiction, manifested as a transplant through conflict of law cases in the forum of the host.

The last of these can almost be regarded as a type of legal pluralism, where the 'unofficial' law is the governing law of the transaction, and, upon enforcement of some aspect of the transaction, is assessed by reference to the 'official' law, the law of the forum.

3. Transplant Theories

Let us say then, that we have to deal with our transplant of a commercial law mechanism effected by any one of the processes just described. According to the transplant theorists, what result should we expect?

Academic debate on legal transplants is venerable. Montesquieu's famous passage that transplants constitute '*un grand hazard*' is often quoted in isolation, but it

5 See the aims of the Principles at <www.unidroit.org/english/principles/pr-pres.htm>.

6 The aim is that the Model Law should serve: 'as a catalyst for defining the essential requirements of a collateral law in a modern market economy. It is not intended as detailed legislation for direct incorporation into local legal systems but has been widely used by the Bank and others to support reform projects' (<www.ebrd.org/english/index.htm >, visited 16 February 2001).

formed part of an important debate at that time and later. In recent years, the topic has been revived, with strong opinions being voiced in favour of, and against, the effectiveness of transplants. One can roughly divide the modern literature into: (i) the debate between 'culturalists' and 'transferists'; and (ii) more recent attempts to move on from this debate.

To caricature the positions of the principal protagonists in the culturalist/transferist debate (or more accurately, their positions as often represented,[7] we have on one side those, represented notably by Watson, who believe that: 'legal rules may be very successfully borrowed where the relevant social, economic, geographical and political circumstances of the recipient are very different from those of the donor system'.[8]

He also says that borrowed rules are the major source of legal change, and that the legal profession has a significant role to play in this process.

On the other side, we have those represented notably by Legrand[9] and the Seidmans, who believe that law is a culturally determined artefact, which cannot be transplanted. The Seidmans have even formulated a 'Law of non-transferability of law'.[10]

Here the claim is that: 'in introducing foreign legal and political norms into any society, those norms will become effective and take root only if they incorporate also a part at least of the norms and philosophy of the native society'.[11]

In a somewhat similar vein, Kahn-Freund's opinion was that some areas of law are more closely linked to society than others (which are more 'organic'), and that the success of transplants of more organic areas of law depends primarily on the political system.[12]

---

7 Others include: A. Allott, *The Limits of Law* (Butterworths, London, 1980), pp. 109–120; W. Ewald, 'Comparative Jurisprudence (II): the Logic of Legal Transplants' (1995) 43 *American Journal of Comparative Law* 489; J.A. Gardiner, *Legal Imperialism: American Lawyers and Foreign Aid in Latin America* (University of Wisconsin Press, Madison, 1980); U. Mattei, 'Efficiency in Legal Transplants: an Essay in Comparative Law and Economics' (1994) 14 *International Review of Law and Economics* 3; E. Örücü, 'Critical Comparative Law: Considering Paradoxes for Legal Systems in Transition' [2000] *Electronic Journal of Comparative Law* <www.law.kub.nl/ejcl/41/art41–1.html>; R. Sacco, 'Legal Formants: a Dynamic Approach to Comparative law' (1991) 39 *American Journal of Comparative Law* 1, 343.

8 A. Watson, 'Legal Transplants and Law Reform' (1976) 92 *Law Quarterly Review* 79, 80. A list of Watson's writings is contained in Ewald n. 7 above, p. 489; A. Watson, *Legal Transplants: An Approach to Comparative Law* (2nd edn., University of Georgia Press, Athens, 1993) is one of the best known.

9 See P. Legrand, 'Against a European Civil Code' (1997) 60 *Modern Law Review* 44; P. Legrand, 'European Legal Systems are not Converging' (1996) 45 *International and Comparative Law Quarterly* 52; P. Legrand, 'The Impossibility of "Legal Transplants"' (1997) 4 *Maastricht Journal of European and Comparative Law* 111.

10 See A. Seidman and R.B. Seidman, *State and Law in the Development Process: Problem Solving and Institutional Change in the Third World* (Macmillan, Basingstoke, 1994), pp. 44–46.

11 F.S.C. Northrop, quoted in Legrand (1997), n. 9 above, at 118, n. 22.

12 O. Kahn-Freund, 'Uses and Misuses of Comparative Law' (1974) 37 *Modern Law Review* 1 at 5–6.

The debate has been discussed by Ewald in a detailed analysis of Watson's work, in which he distinguishes 'Weak Watson' from 'Strong Watson'. According to Ewald, both Watsons maintain that law is not a mirror of society. 'Weak Watson' does so cautiously, 'Strong Watson' does so 'recklessly'.[13] Ewald also reminds us that there is a range of 'mirror theories'.

Teubner builds on the work of both sides, as well as on Ewald's work, and further contributes to the debate by arguing that some areas of law are more or less strongly 'coupled' to 'social processes', and that the degree of success of a transplant depends on the degree of coupling. He also claims that the transplant interacts with the host to produce 'new divergences', thus rendering true harmonization impossible:[14]

> While in the loosely coupled areas of law a transfer is comparably easy to accomplish, the resistance to change is high when law is tightly coupled in binding arrangements to other social processes[15]

A notable recent work, which may well indicate a change in the type of literature being written, is the Seidmans' article on China, recounting the lessons learnt by their participation in assisting in the drafting of an enormous range of Chinese legislation.[16]

So what is the significance of all this for commercial law transplants? If the transferists are right, there should be no problem in transplanting commercial law. If the culturalists are right, then the answer will depend on whether commercial law is culture-neutral or culture-specific: if it is culture-neutral, there is no problem; if it is culture-specific, it is not possible. If the Teubner variation of the mirror theory is correct, the answer will depend on how 'closely linked' it is to social processes. So we need to investigate the relationship of commercial law to culture.

Most people (including academic, non-commercial lawyers) say that commercial law is culture-neutral. Kahn-Freund, for example, refers to the obstacles to transplants being 'least formidable in all that relates to trade and transport, and most potent in all that is closest to people's lives'.[17]

Let us look at the case study to see if it can provide any assistance.

---

13 Ewald, n. 7 above, p. 491. Also see R.L. Abel, 'Law as Lag: Inertia as a Social Theory of Law' (1982) 80 *Michigan Law Review* 785, particularly 793 et seq.; Watson replied in A. Watson, 'Legal Change: Sources of Law and Legal Culture' (1983) 131 *University of Pennsylvania Law Review* 1121, 1136 et seq.

14 G. Teubner, 'Legal Irritants: Good Faith in British Law or How Unifying Law Ends Up in New Divergences' (1998) 61 *Modern Law Review* 11.

15 Ibid., at 19.

16 A. Seidman and R.B. Seidman, 'Drafting Legislation for Development: Lessons from a Chinese Project' (1995) 44 *American Journal of Comparative Law* 1.

17 Kahn-Freund, n. 12 above, 10. See also de Cruz in this volume.

4. UNIVERSAL SECURITY IN ENGLAND, FRANCE AND QUEBEC

As an example of a transplant, universal security is of particular interest in the light of the 1994 EBRD model law and the growth in international secured financing. It is typical of common-law attitudes towards security and commercial law in general.

In English law, a charge is the grant of rights[18] to B by A over A's property in order to secure the performance of an obligation owed (usually by A) to B. The principal rights are: the right to take possession of the asset; the right to have it sold; and the right to be reimbursed out of the proceeds of sale.

The charge can be fixed or floating. The main difference between the two types is the degree of control exercised over the assets by the chargee. In the fixed charge the chargor (company) must ask permission before disposing of any charged asset. A fixed charge over stock-in-trade is therefore impossible (since the debtor would have to ask for permission to sell each item), as is a fixed charge over all of the assets of a trading chargor. In the floating charge the chargor does not have to ask for this permission, so long as it sells in the ordinary course of business. A floating charge over stock-in-trade is therefore possible, as is security over all of the assets of the debtor – a universal security.[19]

The ability of a company to grant security over all its property is seen as an advantage, enabling the provision of more credit, and this, together with other perceived virtues, has led to it becoming an integral part of English security law.

The floating charge evolved out of commercial practice, and was then recognised by the courts, following a well known English commercial law tradition of judges facilitating and recognising business transactions whenever possible. It exemplifies the importance of the combination of freedom of contract with enforceability of obligations in English commercial law, as well as the willingness of the courts to circumvent inconvenient principles, such as the previous impossibility of granting future property as security.[20]

In France, however, universal security is regarded with suspicion.[21] One reason is the principle of 'no priority without legislative authority'. A security mechanism

---

[18] This distinguishes it from a mortgage (transfer of legal title) and a pledge (transfer of possession). Confusingly, 'charge' is also used to mean 'security mechanism'. See W.J. Gough, *Company Charges* (2nd edn., Butterworths, London, 1996), pp. 18–21 (nature); pp. 28–32 (history); pp. 38–39 (nature of proprietary interest). Its validity was first recognised in *Brown v Bateman* (1867) LR 2 CP 272.

[19] See ibid., 102–108 (history), 109 et seq. (characteristics). Its validity was first recognised in *Re Panama, New Zealand and Australian Royal Mail Co* (1870) 5 Ch. App 318. The most commonly cited description was given by Romer LJ in *Re Yorkshire Woolcombers' Association Ltd* [1903] 2 Ch. 284, 295. Note Gough's comment: 'The transmission from specific assignment of future property to floating security was assisted by a spirit of innovation on the part of the judges to create a workable and convenient commercial security, clearly evident in the critical cases of the 1870s': ibid., p. 107.

[20] *Holroyd v Marshall* (1862) 10 HL Cas 191 established the founding principle of the floating charge that all present and future property could be assigned.

[21] On civil law generally, see J. Auger, 'Problèmes Actuels de Sûretés Réelles' (1997) 31 *Revue Juridique Thémis* 619. On French security, see M. Gdanski, 'France' in Norton Rose, *Norton Rose on Cross-*

must derive from (statute) law, in default of which it is invalid.[22] Contractual, practice-based mechanisms tend classically (although, the modern view tends to be more flexible) to be regarded at best as '*montages*', a word with pejorative undertones.

Another is the principle of 'speciality'. This has two limbs: the first being a disapproval of security granted in respect of all present and future obligation; the second a disapproval of security granted over all present and future property of the grantor.[23]

Linked to the principle of speciality is the view of universal security as 'very harmful to the future credit of the debtor company'.[24] The sentiment is often expressed in terms of repugnance to the idea of a single bank for a business (it is morally wrong to give such power to a moneylender over any person, whether natural or legal): '[T]he floating charge possesses an inherent vice... the exclusivity of the chargee bank. The principle of the sole bank does not belong to French culture ...'.[25]

There is therefore no equivalent to the floating charge in French law. Mestre, Putman and Billiau conclude their discussion of the floating charge by saying that: '[W]hat is practical and obvious in one legal tradition of security can be a doubtful stratagem in another: legal cultures are not easily reconcilable'.[26] In the light of the French attitude, what of Quebec?

Quebec is an island of civilian law in a sea of common law, with a long history of resistance to cultural imperialism, in which one can sense 'a strong sense of nationalism to fight against perceived dangers of assimilation'.[27] The civil (as opposed to public) law is predominantly French based.

In such an environment, what result might one expect from an attempt to introduce a universal security into Quebec? One could easily be forgiven for expecting an outright rejection of anything so redolent of Anglo-Saxon legal imperialism.

Border Security (Butterworths, London, 2000), p. 67, particularly pp. 78–79. On French attitudes to universal security, see J. Mestre, E. Putman, and M. Billiau, *Traité de Droit Civil: Droit Commun des Sûretés Réelles* (LGDJ, Paris, 1996), p. 180 (floating charge discussed at some length), and pp. 237–238.

22 In French: 'Pas de privilège sans texte'. See ibid. at p. 237. Compare their description of the judiciary as 'disciplined sentinels' guarding this principle with Gough's description above of the English judges' attitude.

23 See Auger, n. 21 above, p. 639. The second limb is the opposite of the principle in *Holroyd v Marshall* (1862) 10 HL Cas 191, but should not be exaggerated: Mestre et al., n. 21 above, at p. 321.

24 Mestre et al., n. 21 above, at p. 180.

25 F. Dahan, 'La *Floating Charge*: Reconnaissance en France d'une Sûreté Anglaise' (1996) 123 *Journal du Droit International* 381, at 403–404. See also P. Simler, and P. Delebecque, *Droit civil: Les Sûretés, La Publicité Foncière*, (2nd edn., Dalloz, Paris, 1995) p. 258.

26 Mestre et al., n. 21 above, at 180.

27 Sabourin, n.* above.

However, this does not seem to be the case. A universal security, called the 'floating hypothec' ('*hypothèque ouverte*') broadly based on Art. 9 United States Uniform Commercial Code ('UCC')) has been introduced.[28]

5. Predicting the Outcomes of Transplants

As we have seen above, commercial law transplants are extremely common. They are also important: many hopes are pinned on them in many countries, where commercial law reform (read as transplantation) is seen, rightly or wrongly, as a vital part of the modernization of the economy.[29]

It would be very valuable, therefore, if we could predict whether those transplants were going to work or not. Can we use the legal transplant theories to do this?

If we use the 'culturalist/transferist' arguments, the initial impression is that we have a picture of French repugnance and Quebec acceptance.

The French example, our 'anti-transplant', looks simple. Universal security derives from English culture. French and English cultures are different, so universal security is not accepted in France. In the debate between the culturalists and the transferists, the culturalists are right, and the transferists are wrong ('Conclusion A'). In predictive terms, transferism did not predict the French repugnance. As regards the link of commercial law to culture, we have a clear answer: this part of commercial law at least is culture-specific.

The Quebec example spoils this picture. Using the results of our French experiment, we could have concluded that the culturalists are right, and that, since Quebec civil law has its roots in French ideas, and exists in a broader social environment openly hostile to Anglo-Saxon assimilation, Quebec would not receive such a typically Anglo-Saxon mechanism as universal security, or at least would resist it stoutly. But this does not seem to be true. A transplant has occurred, and has been a valuable source of legal change in that jurisdiction. The transferists are right and the culturalists are wrong ('Conclusion B'). In predictive terms, culturalism did

[28] Art. 2666 (hypothec of a universality). Book Six, Title 3, Section V Civil Code of Quebec ('CCQ'), Art. 2715 et seq. (floating hypothec). On the CCQ see G. Remillard, 'Présentation du Projet de Code Civil du Québec' (1991) 22 *Revue Générale de Droit* 5 (history, at 8–13); P.G. Jobin, 'La Modernité du Droit Commun des Contrats dans le Code Civil du Québec: Quelle Modernité?' [2000] *Revue Internationale de Droit Comparé* 49. On Canadian security law see J. Farley, 'Canada' in Norton Rose, n. 21 above, p. 23 (Quebec discussed at p. 43 et seq.). On the Quebec reforms see R.A. Macdonald, 'Change of Terminology? Change of Law? An Overall Assessment of the Provisions of the Civil Code of Québec Relating to Prior Claims and Hypothecs' (1992) 23 *Revue Générale de Droit* 357, and other contributions in that volume.

[29] The difficulties associated with legal instrumentalism are well known. On commercial law see R. Cranston, 'The Transplant of Commercial Law: Security Law in Sri Lanka' (1991) 19 *Canadian Business Law Journal* 296, 317: 'Yet it is still the case that our knowledge of the role of commercial law in facilitating economic activity is rudimentary'. Cranston puts forward (at 308) an intriguing suggestion for the low usage of the floating charge in Sri Lanka: 'Because there are no receiverships, there are no experienced receivers, and hence a reluctance to use the device'.

not predict the Quebec acceptance. As regards the link of commercial law to culture, it may well be that this part of commercial law, if not all commercial law, is culture-neutral.

The social processes idea might provide a better answer. We could explain the results in terms of this idea by saying that this area of law is closely linked in each jurisdiction to social processes; the French repugnance arises because there is a significant difference between the relevant French and English social processes; and the Quebec acceptance arises because there is sufficient similarity between the Quebec and English social processes. This presupposes that this part of commercial law is culture-specific.

However, the idea does not tell us how closely an area of law is linked to a social process. We have to find this out for ourselves. This is not a failing of the idea itself, but it does mean that we have to investigate carefully the link between the relevant transplant and the social processes in both jurisdictions.

So the case study appears, on first impression, to show up some problems with some of the theories (this impression is reinforced when we consider the degree of difference and disagreement among many of the eminent colleagues involved) and a need for some more guidance in applying them (particularly regarding the link between commercial law and culture/social processes).

Various issues are discussed below. For the purpose of exposition, each is examined separately, but it may well be that a combination of some or all of them is significant.

5.1. Misunderstandings

As regards the culturalist/transferist debate, it may be that all the protagonists have something valuable to say, and that much of the controversy arises from misunderstanding. Watson himself writes: 'If I am correct then to a large extent [Legrand] and I are talking at cross-purposes, using the word "transplant" in different senses',[30] and 'from early days I have argued that a rule once transplanted is different in its new home'.[31]

If this possibility is correct, then Ewald and Teubner's attempts to synthesise the best of both sides' work, and thereby eliminate the misunderstandings, is a significant step forward.

[30] A. Watson, 'Legal Transplants and European Private Law' (December 2000) Vol. 4.4 *Electronic Journal of Comparative Law*, <www.law.kub.nl.ejcl/44/44-2.html>, 9, in which Watson states that Legrand 'grossly' caricatured his position (at 8) and assesses two pieces of Legrand's as having 'no substance' (2, 3, footnote 8).

[31] Ibid., at 2; see also Watson (1983), n. 13 above, at 1141 and 1152. Ewald stresses the complexity of Watson's arguments, and argues that this adds to the risk of them being misunderstood: Ewald (1995), n. 7 above, pp. 502–503.

5.2. Ignorance

Or, maybe one of the theories is correct, and the problems derive from insufficient information. If this is true, we simply have to find those answers in order to apply the theories correctly.[32] This applies particularly to the social processes idea, where we need guidance on how to establish the strength of the link between law and social processes.

The principle is easily comprehensible, but the practice is difficult.[33] Take the case study, for example. The possible answers here include: the French hostility is imaginary; Quebec's legal culture is more receptive to Anglo-Saxon ideas than France; and commercial law is actually easily transferable.

To take the first possibility, perhaps we are misinterpreting the French situation and the transferists are actually right. Conclusion A above relies on the assumption that the French attitude is both real and significant, and that it is unchanging. Maybe one or more of these assumptions is false, and the French 'repugnance' is an out-of-date myth perpetuated by French lawyers.

Dahan recently considered the floating charge in some detail and came to the conclusion that it might be capable of adoption, so long as it was limited to 'small and medium enterprises'.[34]

The second possibility is that we are misinterpreting the Quebec situation, and the culturalists are actually right. Conclusion B above relies on the assumption that France and Quebec are very similar. One could argue that this assumption is false because the French legal system has kept itself isolated, so preserving its hostility to universal security, whereas a duality of sources in Quebec, its 'bijurality' ('*mixité*'), allows easier reception of Anglo-Saxon legal concepts.[35] Brierley has written in this regard that bijurality '... has opened the way for an effort to be made to adapt the

---

[32] One can also wonder whether it is legitimate to compare France, where a transplant has not (yet?) been introduced with Quebec, where it has. So long as one is aware of the limitations of such a comparison, there should be some benefit in the exercise.

[33] Collins has written that: '... no-one ever succeeds in pursuing this method satisfactorily, for the budding comparatist always leaves out one of the dimensions of culture, society, economy, history, politics, and legal logic': H. Collins, 'Methods and Aims of Comparative Contract Law' (1991) 11 *Oxford Journal of Legal Studies* 396, 398, cited in W. Twining, 'Comparative Law and Legal Theory: The Country and Western Tradition' in I. Edge (ed.), *Comparative Law in Global Perspective* (Transnational, New York, 2000).

[34] Dahan, n. 6 above, 403–404. At the Workshop she indicated that, as a result of the changes in thinking effected by globalization, if the legislature attempted to introduce the floating charge now, there would be little or no resistance. See also Simler et al., n. 26 above, p. 258.

[35] See J.E.C. Brierley, 'The reception of English law in the Canadian province of Québec' in M. Doucet and J. Vanderlinden (eds.), *La Réception des Systèmes Juridiques: Implantation et Destin* (Bruylant, Brussels, 1994), p. 103, 136. Or was bijurality strong enough to override the social process difference? Compare the presence of the trust in Quebec law (pp. 135–136) with the failure to introduce it into France (see Rafenne in this volume).

genius of those private law institutions, drawn from other legal cultures, within a residual legal environment often thought hostile to such elements'.[36]

In the commercial field, Brierley points to special considerations of Canadian federal harmonization, which have resulted in a predominance of common law input into commercial law generally.[37] If this is correct, the results of the case study are a surprise only as a result of the previous ignorance of bijurality.

Bijurality is not a sufficient explanation in itself, though. The introduction of the floating hypothec did not take place in isolation; it was part of the reform of the Quebec system of security, conducted against the background of the harmonization of this area of law in Canada. The reform was also part of a decade long process of the recodification of the civil law of Quebec, culminating in the Civil Code of Quebec ('CCQ'), brought into force on 1 January 1994.[38] It may be that, as the amount of non-civil law input into the process as a whole was not very great, the idea of universal security was more easily accepted.[39]

The length of time taken by the reform is also significant. As noted above, although discussions of culture sometimes seem to assume that it is unchanging over time, this is not the case. Attitudes to common law borrowings into Quebec have changed over the years, and those changes have been well documented.[40] It is not enough to look at a 'society'; one must look at that society at the time when the reception took place.

Consider also the method of reception. At the beginning of the process, the wholesale adoption of Art. 9 UCC was considered, but quickly rejected. Caron recounted the reaction of Quebec lawyers in measured terms, which seems to screen a reaction of some disbelief and horror.[41] He put political impossibility at the top of the list,[42] followed closely by Art. 9's obscure, and (although he is too polite to say so) primitive common law language, its lack of principles and its failure to reach the status of a code in the civilian sense of the word. He did stress, however, that the content aroused great interest. This content was therefore put into an acceptable form:

36 Ibid., p. 136. See also P.-G. Jobin, 'Le Droit Comparé dans la Réforme du Code civil du Québec et sa Première Interprétation' (1997) 38 *Les Cahiers de Droit* 477, who points out (at 482) that some of the law was 'home-grown'.

37 Brierley, n. 35 above, pp. 108–109.

38 See J.E.C. Brierley, 'The Renewal of Quebec's Distinct Legal Culture: The New Civil Code of Quebec' (1992) 42 *University of Toronto Law Journal* 848.

39 On foreign influences on the CCQ, see Jobin, nn. 8 and 36 above.

40 Jobin n. 36 above, pp. 482–484.

41 Caron, 'L'article 9 du Code Uniforme de Commerce, Peut-il être Exporté? Point de Vue d'un Juriste Québécois" in J.S. Ziegel and W.F. Foster (eds.), *Aspects of Comparative Commercial Law* (Oceana Publications, New York, 1969) p. 374 at 376. Compare the linguistic simplicity of the EBRD Model Law with Art. 9. On the old law, see R.A. Macdonald, 'The Counter-Reformation of Secured Transactions Law in Quebec' (1991) 19 *Canadian Business Law Journal* 239, 255 et seq., and 379.

42 The article appeared in 1969.

> The various proposals ... clearly reveal that the intention of the government was to modernize the law of security on property along the general functionalist lines of the Article 9 of the U.C.C., but to retain as an overarching framework the existing civil law approach to the subject[43]

Art. 2644 CCQ[44] provides one example of the civil law framework. This article confirms the general civilian principle of the necessity for statutory authority, the complete opposite of the freedom given by the common law to the business community to invent mechanisms. The registration/court-based enforcement mechanisms, which present a striking contrast to the English system, provide another.[45]

In addition to this obviously 'cultural' aspect, the general climate of opinion in Quebec at the time also played an important role. Macdonald, who participated in the law reform process, attributes this to Art. 9 being 'seen to respond to the goals of modernization and harmonization of commercial law, both powerful themes in post-Quiet Revolution Quebec'.[46] He adds, 'subsidiarily, it was also because the conceptual elegance of its rationalizing motif appealed to the instincts of those nurtured on the merits of systematic codification'.[47] He also claims that the general structure of Art. 9 was borrowed from the civil law and so was 'not disruptive to the overall conceptual structure of the civil law'.[48] So the 'cultural' side was certainly important, but was only one factor in a complex situation.[49] Glenn provides a further twist.[50] He argues that our idea of 'legal system' is in fact a product of nationalist movements, before which law was not jurisdictionally based. In this conception, Quebec kept the European tradition, derived from *ius commune* thinking, of plurijurality of sources – an idea that may come back into its own as a result of globalization – in the face of 'legal and political nationalism' in Quebec.[51]

---

43 Macdonald n. 28 above, 359–360.

44 A re-enactment of Art. 1983 Civil Code of Lower Canada, which provides: 'Hypothecation may take place only on the conditions and according to the formalities authorized by law'.

45 Under Art. 2755 CCQ: 'The holder of a floating hypothec may not exercise his hypothecary rights until after registration of notice of crystallization'.

46 Macdonald n. 28 above, p. 266. He also maintains (at 285–287) that the hypothec was not properly integrated into the CCQ.

47 Ibid., p. 266 (emphasis added).

48 Ibid., 292 (footnote 72), 296.

49 Macdonald suggests that many Quebec lawyers were indifferent to the cultural protection aspect: ibid., 266–267.

50 H.P. Glenn, 'Droit Comparé et Droit Québécois' (1990) 24 *Revue Juridique Thémis* 342. See also Örücü, n. 7 above, where she refers (at 21) to the 'exceptional developments in Quebec, which is no longer the "mixed jurisdiction" it once was, but may be a new one' and to the former role of the Privy Council in preserving the uniformity of the common law in the Commonwealth.

51 Glenn, ibid., 348. See also Sacco, n. 7 above, at 395.

If this is correct, universal security is not a transplant at all – it derives from a legitimate source of Quebec law.[52]

5.3. Commercial Law as Culture

Here too there are no easy answers. We saw above that the generally held belief is that commercial law is culture-neutral. But the case study indicates that, in one area of commercial law (universal security), in one jurisdiction (France), this belief should, at the least, be carefully considered. Although initially the Quebec example seemed to point the other way, on closer examination it provided some evidence of the culture-specificity of universal security, in that the legislature did respect the civil law sub-stratum in the way it introduced and circumscribed the mechanism.

Looking beyond the confines of the universal security idea to the broader field of the Canadian security law reform experience, we see more evidence of the culture-specificity of security law, for even in the most 'technical' areas, provinces differed in their attitude (large lenders are more favoured in Ontario, but farmers are more protected in Saskatchewan, for instance).[53]

One suggested explanation for the difference between easily transferable and less easily transferable commercial law is that the less easily transferable parts are property-based mechanisms, such as security, and the more easily transferable parts are those which are not related to property (this category would include international trade law, where the pressures are greater to have a more uniform legal regime). This distinction could certainly be significant, but it does not explain all instances, such as the United Kingdom's reluctance to ratify the Vienna Convention.

Perhaps the germ of an answer is contained in the nineteenth century transplant of English commercial law into Scotland. On the surface, this is comparable to the introduction of universal security into Quebec, but in that instance, Scottish industrial magnates not only accepted the new law wholesale, but were 'insistent that the law ... should be modern and should help them trade in the larger English and Empire markets. They were practical men rather than romantic supporters of a native legal system of whose doctrines they would usually be entirely ignorant'.[54]

In terms of the relationship of commercial law to culture, one could conclude from this, *inter alia*, that: commercial law was not part of Scottish culture at that

---

[52] And are we justified in regarding the mechanism as being transplanted, when so much effort was put into reforming the law by the Quebec authorities? Are we in fact ever justified in using this term, except in the case of the wholesale adoption or imposition of someone else's statute? Note also the concept of 'maturity': Jobin, n. 36 above, pp. 493, 500: 'even if a transplant does take place, the Quebec legal system is "mature" enough to develop the relevant branch of the law without reference to the donor jurisdiction'.

[53] Macdonald n. 41 above, p. 276. He remarks (at 292) that 'the notion of objective rationalization underlying Article 9 is shot through with fundamental substantive choices ...'.

[54] A. Rodger, 'The Codification of Commercial Law in Victorian Britain' (1992) 108 *Law Quarterly Review* 570, 571–572.

time; or commercial law was not part of the culture of the Scottish magnates at that time; or commercial law was part of Scottish culture and the culture of the Scottish magnates at that time, but another consideration (making more money) was more important; or culture is only culture if people care about it.

There may be a grain of truth in all of these statements. Examining them in depth would go beyond the scope of this paper, but they could indicate that the reply to our particular question is that it is the wrong question. The Quebec and Scottish examples may indicate that commercial law is not necessarily bound to, or dissociated from, culture (or 'social processes'). In these jurisdictions, at least, and maybe in others (how generally this idea is applicable is a difficult question), whether or not it is 'culture-specific' depends on the attitude towards it of those in a position to influence the success of the reception. In the Quebec example, the decisive factor was the attitude of the Quebec legal profession, for whom certain principles and traditions were important to the extent that they were only prepared to accept the idea of universal security, but only so long as it was dressed up in civilian garb. In the Scottish example, the decisive factor was the attitude of the magnates, for whom legal tradition had no importance (and therefore, in one sense, was not 'culture') compared to commercial efficiency. Accordingly, what we really need to ask could be questions such as: Which people will influence the reception? How much do they care about commercial law as a cultural artefact?

5.4. Predictions, Commercial Lawyers and the Academy

Another possibility is that some perceived problems lie in the nature of the literature, or in methods used in it. One such problem might be that commercial lawyers want specific, predictive answers to their questions (in this instance, they want an answer to the question: how will this transplanted law work?), but it is unreasonable to expect the academy to produce such answers, because transplant theories, like historical or social science studies, cannot be predictive.

Consider the following definition of 'theory': 'A generalized statement which has been tested by making sufficient predictions about verifiable outcomes to justify its level of generality'.[55]

One can argue that a transplant 'theory' cannot be a theory in this sense. It cannot be tested (with so many variables, predictions are not possible), nor, even if they were to be made, are the outcomes verifiable (they cannot be measured). If true, academic writers cannot predict the fate of transplants any more than a historian can predict the future. In view of the complexities, this is a serious possibility.

On the assumption that this is correct, there is nothing wrong with authors putting forward 'theories' about transplants, even though they are in fact, and can

[55] The author's definition.

never be more than hypotheses.[56] It may be, indeed, that the real difficulty arises from the fact that our hypothetical commercial lawyer is simply unused to the unspoken conventions of academic writing, one of which could be that there is no intention to produce theories in the sense defined above.

It would be helpful though, especially given the present wider audience for this literature, if its aims and assumptions were to be more clearly stated.

Even if one accepts both these arguments, two issues remain: conclusions often being phrased in terms more general than are justified by the evidence; and conclusions, even if correct, being very broad and needing elaboration.

As regards over-generalization, Ewald writes of Watson: 'Watson's focus has been almost exclusively on the rules of private law in western Europe, and he is not entitled, on this slender evidential basis, to draw conclusions about law in general'.[57]

As regards the need for elaboration, Watson in one article gives various examples and then concludes that '[T]he lesson *must be* that ... lawmakers rely heavily on foreign law for their own changes, whether as legislators, judges or jurists'.[58]

One cannot quibble with the conclusion *per se*: many lawmakers do use foreign law. To cite only one example, we have seen Quebec using foreign models for its security law reform. But it needs to be expanded – we have also seen that to say that Quebec used foreign law is only the start of a discussion of a long and complex process.[59] Can we say whether or not it was used 'heavily' or not? What does this mean precisely? Much more work needs to be done on the many different ways in which foreign law is used.[60]

The foundations having been laid by the authors in their writings to date, a more cautious and qualified approach which takes account of these two issues, an approach in which the limited nature of the evidence is reflected in the wording of the conclusions, and more account is taken of the differences between situations, would be helpful to move the discussion forward. Some authors seem to be thinking along these lines already.[61]

---

56 The Oxford Paperback Dictionary, 1990 defines a hypothesis as: 'A supposition or guess put forward to account for certain facts and used as a basis for further investigation by which it may be proved or disproved'.

57 Ewald n. 7 above, at 509. Both examples concern Watson, but there is no intention to single him out, all the writing follows this pattern.

58 Watson n. 30 above, at 5 (emphasis added).

59 See Twining n. 35 above, at 53: 'a picture of law-making which depicts law reformers choosing the "best solution" from a range of foreign models seems like a naïve caricature of actual law reform processes. And ... the practical significance of the few examples of explicit reference to foreign "solutions" in legal argument can easily be overstated'.

60 And the apparent, although perhaps unintentional, equivalence of the use of foreign law by legislators and judges simplifies a complex issue. See, in the Quebec context, Jobin n. 38 above, pp. 493–495.

61 Note the practical base of Seidman, n. 16 above, especially 37–40 (and note the use of the word 'hypotheses').

5.5. The Complexity of Transplants

The final possibility was implied in the categorization above of the different types of harmonization and the different types of commercial law transplants that result therefrom. Transplants vary immensely.[62] The factors of variation include:

i The factors leading to the transplant (WTO membership? international competition between stock markets?).

ii The factors determining the choice of donor jurisdiction; the type of donor jurisdiction; the type of transplant object (a law? a concept? a mechanism? an institution? something else?).

iii The legal subdivision of the transplant object (and it is not enough just to draw distinctions between broad categories like 'commercial law' and 'family law' – we must be much more precise).

iv The type of host jurisdiction (what is its history? is it bijural? which people will be involved in the process and what are their attitudes to the particular type of law, which we are proposing to transplant? what are the needs of the host jurisdiction?).

v The political and economic climate in the host jurisdiction at the time of the reception.

vi The type of transplant process (imposed? voluntary? something in between? something else entirely?).

And so on and so forth.[63]

Given this complexity, it may be that different types of transplant differ so much from each other that very few broad generalizations are definite enough to be useful, and that any search for a Grand Transplant Theory, even using the word 'theory' in its historical/social science sense, is a wild goose chase. In this event, we will have to be content with hypotheses of different levels of generality, which vary according to the context, plus, on a more general level, broad guidelines only.

In order to reach such hypotheses and guidelines we need to examine more transplants in more detail. A new technique for this research would be helpful. At the

62 The terminology involved does not contribute greatly to clarity. Örücü, for example, who has done considerable work on the terminology (Örücü, n. 7 above, p. 68), prefers 'transposition' to 'transplant'. Nor is it particularly helpful that 'transplant' can refer to the overall event of incorporating the 'transplant object' (for want of a better expression including statute law, judicial decisions, concepts, etc.), the process by which it is incorporated and the transplant object itself.

63 On different types of transplant, see Gardiner, n. 7 above, at p. 22. Sacco, n. 7 above, 398–400; C. Bontems, 'La Coutume Kabyle et l'Implantation des Systèmes Etrangers' in Doucet and Vanderlinden, n. 35 above, p. 76; A. Huxley, 'The Reception of Buddhist Law in S.E. Asia 200 B.C.E. – 1860 C.E.', ibid. p. 139; Örücü, n. 7 above, at 7.3.

moment, in accordance with our wish to find a Grand Transplant Theory, we seem to be using a very general base question: Do legal transplants work?

This presupposes that there is one thing called a 'legal transplant' (not true – see above) and that there is one meaning attached to the word 'work' (not true either).[64]

We could try to accommodate the variation among transplants and among the ways in which they 'work' by formulating the base questions for additional research along these lines:

What sort of effectiveness (X) of a transplant object of type A will result from its incorporation by a transplant process of type B pursuant to factors of type C from a jurisdiction of type D into a jurisdiction of type E?

Answering questions formulated in this way will not be easy. But at least the questions will carry in their formulation an awareness of the complexity involved.

And if a Grand Transplant Theory is possible, we can slowly and cautiously attempt to formulate it, progressively generalizing from the principles and guidelines we have accumulated, using the answers to the questions formulated in this way.

In either case, it is not likely, as we have seen, that we will ever reach physical science-type predictability. In particular, any Grand Transplant Theory will probably never attain the status of a theory as defined above. However, the answers to questions formulated as suggested could assist us in an attempt to approach that asymptotic, unattainable ideal.

6. Conclusion

The main theme of this chapter has been a move from simplicity to complexity, from broad theories, naïve expectations and caricatures of academic positions, to possibilities related to geographically, chronologically and subject-based specifics, difficult and impressionistic suggestions, and complex arguments. We have even been led to question whether an apparent transplant (universal security into Quebec) is a transplant at all, and to wonder whether it is better viewed as an expression of a plurijural tradition.

We should not really expect anything else. It is a commonplace that comparative law is complex and full of pitfalls for the unwary, but at least some of the literature seems to indicate a need for us to be reminded of this in the context of transplant writing. This lesson of complexity is amply demonstrated in the contrast between the crude, initial conclusions[65] drawn from the case study and the complex issues briefly examined in the later sections.

Given this complexity, it is hardly surprising that the literature has not given (and maybe cannot give) commercial and other lawyers all the answers they would like.

[64] Unless we mean that the transplant will have exactly the same effect in the host as in the donor jurisdiction, and the authors are agreed that this will not happen.

[65] It is perhaps worth pointing out that someone who knew Quebec was a 'mixed jurisdiction' might have concluded that it would easily receive universal security – this too would have been mistaken.

However, we cannot ignore the fact, even while acknowledging with gratitude the considerable progress made in transplant literature in recent years, that globalization poses new challenges for transplant theory. This may seem depressing; but the realisation of reality is itself useful knowledge. By more consciously appreciating the complexity of transplants and the limitations of our techniques, we can start to move forward to the next stage of research.

There are some indications that this is already happening; it is hoped that some of the suggestions herein will be of value in that progression.

On a more general level, what are the consequences of what has been said in this paper for comparative law in the 21st century? As we have seen, predicting the result of even one legal transplant is fraught with complexities. Predicting the future of comparative law is impossible. Who in 1900 could have foreseen the Treaty of Rome or the Iranian Revolution? But in order to hazard some thoughts, rather than predictions, let us return to another of the (methodological) themes of this paper, that good research tool – surprise: the surprise that a commercial lawyer should be so concerned with theory.

It is fair to ask why someone whose day-to-day activity concerns a practical, down-to-earth subject should take such an interest in abstract matters. We have become accustomed to, and expect, a great divide between the people who do things and the people who think about them. The answer to this question lies in commercial practicality itself. The divide is highly inefficient on both sides, for theory (even historical/social science theory) must be grounded in reality, and practice without sound theory amounts to, in the commercial field, the mortal sin of inefficiency leading to a waste of money. Some people on both sides of the divide (those theoreticians who wish to live in a safe ivory tower, and those 'practical' people who are irritated by abstract thinking) dislike such sentiments, but history is peppered with examples of the dangers of one side ignoring the other. Kelsen surely never dreamt that his 'pure theory' would be used as a justification for tyranny, nor, one presumes from the nasty shocks they received, did the 'practical' Roman generals consult the works of Archimedes before laying siege to Syracuse.

In the globalized world of 2001 the result of this reasoning is that, if our world continues on the path laid down in 1979, transplant theorists and commercial lawyers will, despite all the difficulties of such cooperation, be obliged to work closely together. Only in this manner will either side produce results sufficient for the needs of the next few years (and maybe longer) of this new millennium.

Chapter 5

WHY (STILL) NO TRUST IN FRENCH LAW?

*Coralie Raffenne**

In the following piece Raffenne looks at the institution of trust and discusses why it has not entered French law. As most comparatists writing in the English language look at the impact of the civilian tradition on common law, this is a valuable and insightful departure. The author says: '[t]he Fiducie *confirms the fact that the trust's dual ownership structure cannot be transplanted into French law; the trust had to be processed, modified and cleansed of its fragmented proprietary essence.' This study analyses this processing. To make the 'alien institution' legitimate, the trust had to be handled within the parameters of the French epistemic tradition and be regulated and transformed into* Fiducie. *The French drafter gave* Fiducie *a contractual structure to clearly distinguish it from the trust. The piece discusses the concept of* Fiducie, *the absolute ownership of the civilian tradition, the French epistemic tradition, the French* mentalité *and the dynamics of French legal culture.*

We are offered a comprehensive analysis of the failed 1992 Bill, a first attempt to introduce the institution of trust into French law, by initially looking into the genesis of the Bill. Ensuring the Frenchness of the new device and its uniformity with the traditions of the Napoleonic codification was foremost in the minds of the drafters. Yet in spite of this, and also the absence of real opposition to the Bill, it was dropped from the agenda of Parliament in late 1994, without ever having been discussed. Was the reason for the failure the attempt to fit the trust into the 'existing legal system'?

However, Raffenne suggests that, despite the lack of a regulated status, a new conceptual element has been added to French law. A pragmatic recourse to fiduciary devices emerged and it has become a 'widely used conceptual tool', although Fiducie *cannot be considered as a transposition of the trust into French law.*

Within the French epistemic tradition, is the peculiarity of 'absolute ownership' related to the logical structures and mythological images of the French 'epistemic imaginary'? Obviously, the enduring significance of the symbolism of 'absolute ownership' obstructed the transfer of the trust into the French legal framework. This persistent significance is shown by Raffenne to be mainly epistemic and symbolic. The author claims that, nevertheless, this absolute right is subject to 'the contradictory ethos

* PhD, School of Law, University of Warwick.

A. Harding and E. Örücü (eds.),
Comparative Law in the 21st Century, 75–100.

of state surveillance of ownership'. This is the revelation of 'governmentality', existing on another epistemic plane, 'deeply ingrained in French legal culture'.

The trust also conflicted with the basic premises of French succession laws and challenged the concept of 'unitary patrimony', which, according to Raffenne, creates an 'examinable economic subject' in France.

If the trust cannot be transplanted into French law, with which it is seen to be incompatible, why is there still such an interest in it? One explanation offered is that the epistemic resistance is now overcome. Raffenne suggests that this is due to changes within the legal profession linked to the rhetoric and reality of globalization. The emerging global legal elite in France, shaped by the Anglo-American model of lawyering, acts as broker of the rules. Fiducie, *an early illustration of the impact of globalization, is seen as 'a microcosmic expression' of 'two-tiered competition' by these brokers.* Fiducie *was not a competitor to the trust, which might have gained more support from legal and financial experts.* Fiducie, *made a useless device by the Bill, may nevertheless develop through lawyers' international practice.*

The study shows that the epistemic tradition underlying French law is symbolically powerful, even though not anchored in economic power, and yet the restructuring of legal training and doctrinal research, especially as regards commercial law, helps to erode this mythology of the state. How far does this example show the strength of epistemic structures in the process of transmigration of legal institutions? Does the transmigration of a commercial and business device depend on the practice of local experts and stakes raised at national and global levels? One can look back to Foster and ahead to Carey-Miller.

[A. Harding and E. Örücü]

In a 1953 article, V. Bolgàr was already posing the question 'Why no trusts in the civil law?' noting that '[i]n the field of property, the trust furnishes a striking antinomy between the common law and the civil law'.[1] Indeed, there is still no concept of trust in French law, despite an attempt in the early 1990s to introduce a Bill that would have incorporated into the Civil Code a 'trust-like' device, named *Fiducie*.

The Bill was laid before the French Parliament on 20 February 1992.[2] This was the first attempt to introduce the trust into French law, which had and still has no comparable device, as the Bill was never debated in Parliament and finally withdrawn in late 1994.

---

1 V. Bolgàr, 'Why No Trusts in the Civil Law' (1953) 2 *American Journal of Comparative law* 204.

2 The Bill will be referred to as 'the 1992 Bill'. Its documentary reference is Doc. Ass. Nat. 2583.

Prior to the 1789 Revolution and the 1804 codification of private law, there were a few institutions and practices that resembled the trust. The substitution, for instance served purposes similar to that of dynastic trusts, and for this reason was expressly prohibited in the new Civil Code. Other practices such as the pre-revolutionary *Fiducie*, which were not expressly prohibited in the new codified law, did not survive the demise of the *Ancien Régime*.

From a comparative perspective, the *Fiducie* is particularly interesting as it gives concrete expression to the antinomy mentioned above. This confrontation of French law with the trust, resulting in the *Fiducie*, reveals and exacerbates the particularity of a certain civilian way of understanding, articulating and regulating ownership. The *Fiducie* confirms the fact that the trust's 'dual ownership structure' cannot be transplanted into French law: the trust had to be processed, modified and cleansed of its fragmented proprietary essence. It is this processing which will be explored here. This processing is epistemic, that is, it relates to the workings and discursive dynamics of French legal knowledge, and dual. Its two objects are legitimization and regulation.

As regards the first aspect of this epistemic processing of the trust, this alien institution had to be made legitimate and understandable within the parameters laid down by the French epistemic tradition. One such parameter is the sanctity of absolute ownership. The power of absolute ownership prevented the reception of the trust's splitting of proprietary prerogatives. This power is symbolic, and stems from the enduring epistemic function of absolute ownership as a representation of man's natural power over things and of the modern rejection of a fragmented feudal past. Absolute ownership in the French epistemic tradition will be explored in section 2 below.

The second aspect of this processing relates to the way in which the trust was regulated, and thereby transformed into the *Fiducie*, following the ethos of surveillance of ownership, which permeates both the Civil Code and administrative (fiscal) regulation. The absence of a trust-like device in French law and its processing into the *Fiducie* can be explained in terms of the paradoxical combination of doctrinal and theoretical reverence to the principle of absolute ownership on the one hand, and the actual limitations imposed on proprietary prerogatives and freedom, notably through succession laws on the other. The French impulse to regulate and control ownership will be explored in section 3 below, as the second level of our argument as to why the trust cannot be transplanted as it is, into French law.

French law displays a deep-seated epistemic resistance to the trust. Why then has the introduction of the trust, albeit in an altered state, become, in the early nineties, a project viable enough to warrant the drafting of a Bill? Is this evolution towards an acceptance of the trust purely due to epistemic changes? To answer this, it will be necessary in the last section of this paper to understand the more general context of the 1992 Bill, and in particular, globalization, its meaning and effects as regards the societal and professional stakes of which the *Fiducie* is one illustration.

1. An Outline of the *Fiducie*

The genesis of the Bill is to be found in the interplay of three types of factors: (i) a persuasive doctrinal challenge to the orthodox view, which established the incompatibility of the trust with French law;[3] (ii) the 1985 Hague Convention on the law applicable to trusts and on the recognition of trusts in 'non-trust' countries; and (iii) in the late eighties, a proposal by professional organisations to integrate into French law fiduciary techniques under the generic term of *affidation*.[4]

A doctoral thesis in the early 1980s provided a definition of a new institution, the *Fiducie*, which was to be progressively introduced into French law through practice and its eventual acceptance by the courts.[5] But the 1985 Hague Convention's definition was sufficiently precise to be included in a statute, and did not contain any reference to the division of ownership into legal title and beneficial title. The aim of this private international law convention is to ensure the worldwide recognition of trusts, even in countries that do not have and may not wish to introduce this institution. The drafters of the Convention wanted to make it possible for civil lawyers to understand and think of the trust without the obstacle of fragmented titles and equitable rights. Their 'translation' of the trust inspired the drafters of the 1992 Bill.[6] The definition proposed in the 1992 Bill is the following:

> The *Fiducie* is a contract by virtue of which a settlor transfers all or part of his assets and rights to a fiduciary (*fiduciaire*) who, holding the same separate from his personal estate (*patrimoine*), deals therewith for a specific purpose benefiting one or more beneficiaries in accordance with the provisions therein contained. The settlor himself may be a beneficiary[7]

The third factor in the genesis of the 1992 Bill was to be found in an initiative of the *Association Française des Entreprises Privées* (A.F.E.P). This body representing private businesses in France issued a draft legislative text proposing the introduction

3 The thesis of C. Witz, '*La Fiducie en Droit Privé Français*' (Economica, Paris, 1981) on the *Fiducie* which was published in 1981 and widely praised for its persuasive, thoroughly researched and grounded arguments, is an important landmark in the genesis of the *Fiducie*. The drafters have referred to Witz's work to ground their proposal. The thesis of Witz subtly undermines the three-decade reign of the orthodox doctrinal view, established in 1948 by H. Motulsky in '*De l'Impossibilité Juridique de Constituer un Trust Anglo-Saxon sous l'Empire de la Loi Française*' [1948] *Revue Critique de Droit International Privé* 451, according to which the trust is incompatible with French law.

4 The term '*affidation*' has the same Latin root as the *Fiducie*, that is, '*fides*', which means 'trust'.

5 Witz defines the *Fiducie* as: 'a legal act by which a person, the fiduciary, who has become the holder of a property right, is restricted in the exercise of that right by a number of duties, amongst which there generally is a duty to transfer his right after a certain period has lapsed, to either the settlor or a third party beneficiary' (my translation of '*La fiducie est un acte juridique par lequel une personne, le fiduciaire, rendue titulaire d'un droit patrimonial, voit l'exercice de son droit limité par une série d'obligations, parmi lesquelles figure généralement celle de transférer le droit au bout d'une certaine période soit au fiduciant, soit à un tiers bénéficiaire*', in Witz above n. 3, at p. 15.

6 See ibid., p. 27.

7 Definition in the proposed new Art. 2062, Civil Code.

of an institution similar to the trust and named 'affidation'. This text was not adopted. Another text, proposed by the C.S.N, the National Council of Notaries, also failed. Nevertheless, the pressure from the representatives of branches of business and of the legal profession was evident and increasing. As a result of these initiatives, a proposal for a new Bill was then issued by the French Ministry of Justice and presented by their drafters in December 1989, at a professional symposium organised by 'Legal Studies and Services Limited' and chaired by a renowned practitioner.[8] This proposal was then formulated as a Bill and, after three years of discussions between the Ministry of Justice and the fiscal administration, the Bill was laid before the French Parliament in 1992.[9]

The drafters of the Bill, J. de Guillenchmidt and A. Chapelle of the Commercial law section of the Civil Affairs Department in the Ministry of Justice, clearly set out their aims and methodology in a presentation and commentary of the Bill for the benefit of practitioners and the business world.[10] The part of the Bill dealing with the fiscal regulation of the *Fiducie* was drafted separately and anonymously by the French Inland Revenue.

The drafters justified their proposal by referring to the implications of developments in the international context; the ratification of the 1985 Convention would allow an even easier recourse to common law trust techniques, which would have to be recognised as valid by French courts. There would be an even greater incentive to export business transactions to trust countries. Thus, a French trust would respond to the emerging needs of international legal practice in France in the face of the pressures on regulatory competition, that is, of competition to attract businesses on the basis of favourable legal and fiscal rules. It would also fit into a more general evolution of property and the use of full ownership as a security in commercial transactions.

The term *Fiducie* was preferred both to the English word 'trust' and to 'affidation' suggested by the world of practice. The word *Fiducie* has no pejorative undertone and suggests a connection with the Roman law institution named 'Fiducia'. The single notion of *Fiducie* would cover a wide range of applications in the area of finance and banking, in labour relations and in most family situations, including the specific case of the transfer of a business unit from one generation to the next. The use of the *Fiducie* for charitable and public interest purposes would offer more flexible solutions than the foundation. The aim was to provide a general framework for this variety of possible applications, as opposed to a specific regulation envisaging all possible uses. The drafters asserted that they wanted to stand against

8 This information stems from the drafters themselves, see A. Chapelle and J. de Guillenchmidt 'Trusts, business trusts *et Fiducie*', *Les Petites Affiches*, n. 76, 25 June 1990, 4.

9 See *Le Monde*, 19 Feb. 1992.

10 See A. Chapelle and J. de Guillenchmidt, above n. 8; see also an interview with J. de Guillenchmidt in dissertation by T. Clay, '*La Fiducie au regard du Trust*' (D.E.A., *Université Paris II*, Paris, 1993).

the contemporary tendency of the Legislator to provide a plethora of specific regulations.

The drafters reasserted the impossibility of transplanting the trust. In their view, this would have been impossible, given the importance for the trust of equitable rights, the existence of specific means of enforcement in Common law courts and of an organised body of professional trustees. The *Fiducie* had to be formulated as a French institution, fitting into its legal context. In particular, the *Fiducie* was constructed independently from the trust so as to respect fundamental principles in French law. The *Fiducie* was also to be required to fit into the general spirit and text of the Civil Code.

This aim to ensure the 'Frenchness' of the new device and its conformity with the tradition of the Napoleonic codification has had a major impact on the legal profile and framework of the *Fiducie*. The consequences are three-fold.

First and foremost, the *Fiducie* does not reproduce the equitable/legal division of ownership operated by the trust. It was defined simply as a transfer of full ownership by the settlor to the fiduciary who must thereby act according to a specified aim or for a public interest purpose. The fiduciary would have received full ownership rights and the settlor and beneficiary would have only *rights in personam* against the fiduciary.

The drafters chose to be more specific than the 1985 Convention in one important aspect: they preferred the notion of transfer of rights and assets, rather than just the legally unspecific idea of 'control and powers' of the trustee over the trust fund. Under article 2 of the Convention, assets are placed under the control of the trustee who has 'the power and the duty' to manage the fund. The drafters preferred to specify that a transfer of property rights determines the legal origin and nature of the fiduciary's rights. The fiduciary is the owner, although his rights are limited by a general contractual duty of management of the assets transferred.

Secondly, the protection of the beneficiary is not ensured through the definition of their rights as proprietary, but through the formation of an autonomous fiduciary fund or patrimony within the beneficiary's control.[11]

The fiduciary would have had two patrimonies and would have been obliged to clearly separate his/her own assets from those of the *Fiducie*. Even if the full ownership of the assets was transferred to the fiduciary, his/her prerogatives over the assets were to be limited by a number of duties and obligations defined in the instrument. The beneficiary's rights stemmed from these duties, which were to be enforceable and controllable by the courts. The constitution of an autonomous fund was intended to protect the beneficiary against the fiduciary's personal creditors. Furthermore, the autonomous fiduciary fund could not be part of the estate of the deceased trustee. The drafters did not go any further in the protection of the beneficiary, especially as regards the issue of third parties with notice of the beneficial

[11] A patrimony is the totality of assets, rights and also liabilities and debts that a legal subject accumulates during his/her lifetime.

entitlement. Such entitlements were not defined as a property right. It is unclear what rights a beneficiary could have had against a third party with notice to whom the trust property was fraudulently transferred.[12]

Thirdly, the drafters underlined that the aim was to avoid a heavy and detailed regulation of the fiduciary contract. Following the tradition of codification, the *Fiducie* was to be a flexible and barely regulated contractual structure.[13] The contractual nature of the *Fiducie* would have clearly set it apart from the trust. It was left mainly to the courts to provide ad hoc rules regarding the regulation of the fiduciary's duties and liabilities.

The aims of the creators of the *Fiducie* were frustrated by the French fiscal administration. Part III of the Bill contains the fiscal regulation of the *Fiducie* and is by far the lengthiest and most complex part of the Bill. Through this section, the French fiscal administration wanted to avoid any situation of opacity as regards ownership of assets, thereby preventing tax avoidance and evasion.[14]

The Bill, which was initiated by the French Department of Justice, was never debated in Parliament and was finally dropped from the legislative agenda in Autumn 1994. Despite some concern about the effect of the *Fiducie* on entrenched inheritance rights, there was no real opposition to the Bill, which was simply not perceived as a legislative priority and, eventually, forgotten. Nevertheless, the *Fiducie* remains a topic of discussion in professional and doctrinal literature, as well as in Parliament.[15] Professional symposia are still organised on the subject. Since 1994, the bar has been ready to recognise the function of trustee. Articles 3–26 of the Internal Regulation of the Bar of Paris allow *avocats* to undertake duties as a trustee or a *Fiduciaire*.[16] At the level of practice, a process of re-conceptualization of well-established legal forms is emerging. Institutions which were not previously named as *Fiducies* are now being identified as fiduciary devices.[17] As regards new fiduciary practices, it has been argued that there have been new discoveries in a variety of fields.[18]

---

[12] The proposed legislation did not envisage the issue of tracing as a possible remedy for the beneficiary although the '*droit de suite*' of secured creditors could have provided an equivalent solution.

[13] See interview above n. 10.

[14] See '*Fiducie et Fiscalité*', *La Semaine Juridique* (JCP, *Edition Enterprise*, 1991), n. 13, p. 150.

[15] In 1996, a parliamentary report, known as the *Rapport Marini*, proposed a general reform of company law. The introduction of the *Fiducie* was included as part of a general framework of legislative reform and modernization. The primary objective would be to provide a piece of legislation ensuring the competitiveness of French law in years to come. A recent thesis has referred to the *Fiducie* to demonstrate the current evolution of the notion of ownership towards a recognition of its economic, as opposed to strictly legal, dimension; G. Blanluet, '*Essai sur la Notion de Propriété Economique en Droit Privé Français-Recherches au Confluent du Droit Fiscal et du Droit Civil*' (Thesis, *Université Paris II*, Paris, 1998).

[16] *Droit et Patrimoine Hebdo*, 20 Dec. 1994.

[17] See A. Gobin, '*Fiducies sans la Fiducie*' *La Semaine Juridique* (JCP, *Edition Notariale*, 1994), nn. 44–45, p. 315.

[18] Ibid.

The Bill has widened the perspective of French legal analysis by adding to law a new conceptual element, a new way of analysing legal relations, despite its lack of regulated status. This could also indicate a pragmatic recourse to fiduciary devices despite the lack of a regulatory framework for the *Fiducie*.[19] *Although the Bill failed, the* Fiducie *has become a more widely used conceptual tool in French legal knowledge. But, this hardly amounts to a transposition of the trust into French law.*

2. THE *FIDUCIE*, ABSOLUTE OWNERSHIP AND THE FRENCH EPISTEMIC TRADITION

The failure of the Bill can partly be attributed to the fact that the creators of the *Fiducie* explicitly sought to ensure the 'Frenchness' of the proposed institution. In their own words the device should have fitted in the 'existing legal system'. The acceptability and legitimacy of the proposed device depended on its complying with fundamental principles of French law, and in particular, with the principle of absolute ownership enshrined in article 544 of the Civil Code. The *Fiducie* is therefore both based on the trust and the product of the epistemic weight of doctrinal principles in French law. Hence, it is argued that the *Fiducie* results from the epistemic processing of the trust according to the fundamental premises of French doctrinal tradition. A notable outcome of this processing was the fact that the *Fiducie* did not reproduce the trust's characteristic ownership structure. This is an important feature as it illustrates the impossibility to transplant the split ownership of the trust, and it is argued that this impossibility is the result of processes that characterise the French epistemic tradition.

The particular legal profile of the *Fiducie* and the fact that it fails to reproduce the trust's advantageous divided ownership, cannot satisfactorily be explained by referring solely to the conceptual divergences between the common law and French law. The particular conceptual apparatus of French property law, and the central role of absolute ownership is itself the product of deeper knowledge processes, what Michel Foucault might have called the *savoir* of French law.[20] The following analysis examines the deep-level structures of French legal knowledge, to go beyond a textual or conceptual analysis of principles such as absolute ownership. We are looking for the unspoken, unconscious framework that dictates not only the meaning of the principle, but its importance and its role in the functioning of legal knowledge. The latter constitutes a surface-level body of knowledge a – what Foucault might have called the *connaissances* or discipline. The characteristics of French epistemic tradition are to be found, not at the surface level of concepts, but in the discursive processes that underlie them.

---

19 See also J. Lucas, *Le Droit des Sociétés et le Droit des Contrats à l'Epreuve des Transferts Temporaires de Valeurs Immobilières* (Thesis, *Université Paris II*, Paris, 1995).

20 The term '*savoir*', meaning knowledge, is opposed to '*connaissance*', another word for knowledge, in M. Foucault, *The Archaeology of Knowledge* (Tavistock, London, 1972). For a definition of '*savoir*' as pre-knowledge, see G. Gutting, *Michel Foucault's Archaeology of Scientific Reason* (Cambridge University Press, Cambridge, 1989).

French legal epistemic tradition is usually perceived as highly principled, hierarchical, doctrinal and abstract. As Weber might have put it, it is dominated by the formal rationality of University Professors and their reverence to abstract legal logic. It constitutes the knowledge of the 'Keepers of the Temple' of law.[21] In other words, it is a knowledge attached to the function of legitimization of law destined to secure obedience to juridical authority.

But recent scholarship, based on the work of French legal theorist P. Legendre, has demonstrated how the legal logic characterizing the French epistemic tradition, is in fact subordinated to a mythology.[22] The myth to which legal logic is subsumed is that of the unity and transparency of a gapless Law, echoing the characteristics of the power of its mystical Originator – once God, the King, and in the modern era, the Legislator, or Man. The intermingling of myth and logic is inherited from the mediaeval roots of legal scholarship and its confusion of the sacred and the secular, the cross-fertilization between canon law and the revived Roman *Corpus Iuris Civilis*.

The discursive base of French law's epistemic tradition, therefore, mixes logical structures and mythological images, which together form an epistemic imaginary. It is argued here that absolute ownership is one of these images or icons essential to the workings of French law *qua* knowledge. It is an operative part of a mythical mode of representation, the purpose of which is to communicate the existence and legitimacy of an idealized creator. The symbolic image thereby created is not a representation of a specific power-holder – the King, God, or the Enlightened Man or Legislator – but of a form of power. The representation reflects the characteristics of sovereign juridical power rather than a character exercising power.[23] Hence, the legitimacy of the Legal Order is reflected through the power that can be wielded by the Sovereign subject, the Sovereign Assembly or any other legitimate power-holder. As a consequence, the characteristics of sovereign juridical power – unity, unidirectionality – have a regulative role in the production of legal knowledge.

The weight of absolute ownership as a principle of French law will thus be explained on the basis of its part in the ritualistic representation of power that underlies French epistemic tradition. Absolute ownership is more than a conceptual particularity; it is an epistemic icon of juridical power. Its essential task of legitimization of power is performed symbolically, through the ritualized representation of unitary juridical power. What is being represented is both the absolute power of Man over things, and the unity of the post-revolutionary legal order.

Indeed, as regards the latter, French legal doctrine portrays absolute ownership as a symbol of unity of a new order, opposed to the multiplicity and fragmentation of

---

[21] This expression is borrowed and translated from Y. Dezalay, *Marchands de Droit* (Fayard, Paris, 1992).

[22] See notion of mytho-logic as developed by Ost and Lenoble in F. Ost and Y. Lenoble, *Droit, Mythe et Raison – Essai sur la Dérive Mytho-logique de la Rationalité Juridique* (Publications St-Louis, Brussels, 1980).

[23] 'Juridical' power is understood in the Foucauldian sense. See V. Tadros, 'Between Governance and Discipline: The Law and Michel Foucault' (1998) 18 *Oxford Journal of Legal Studies* 75.

the *Ancien Régime*. The structure of ownership of the *Ancien Régime* is constructed as characterised by a multiplicity of estates and rights over land. It is also described as centered on the distinction between *dominium utile* and *dominium directum*, 'which manifestly resembles the legal and equitable ownership of the common law'.[24] The *dominium utile* was a form of ownership granting solely enjoyment of the land and was ultimately derived from *dominium directum* of the sovereign. Thus, in the pre-revolutionary customary law:

> ownership was divided into two rights over two separate aspects of the property. These rights could, then, be called ownership rights as customary law did not understand ownership as the totality of prerogatives over a thing, including the abusus. Indeed, in customary land law, the right to the enjoyment of the property is the essential element of ownership as . . .the land belongs to God who only grants man the use of the soil through the King[25]

Absolute ownership symbolizes a rupture with the feudal past and its fragmented and limited property prerogatives. Indeed, article 544 of the Civil Code declares: 'Ownership (la propriété) is the right to enjoy and dispose of things in the most absolute manner, insofar as it is not used in a way prohibited by the law'. Man's power over things is thus comparable to God's all-mightiness and power over His Domain.

There is indeed an epistemic link between the modern concept of absolute ownership and mediaeval theological thought:[26]

> The idea that man, by his very essence, has a natural right to appropriate all things for his own use and enjoyment, implemented by the definition in article 544, owes its existence and part of its meaning to the efforts of the scholars of the Church to understand the legitimacy . . . of human property over a world of which the Scriptures say that God, its creator, is the only master, the *solus dominu*[27]

The modern juridical notion of absolute ownership stems from natural law theories; however, the latter are inscribed in an older, intellectual tradition, arching back to the theological and juridical reflections of scholars on the Christian Scriptures and Roman law. Mediaeval scholasticism is 'the theological prehistory of the so-called modern vision of ownership'.[28]

The theological vision of human *dominium*, which founds Man's right to property, is organised around two key ideas: *dominium* over things can only belong to God and God has allowed humans to participate in his *dominium*. God is both the origin and

[24] V. Bolgàr, above n. 1, at p. 207.

[25] P. Croq, 'Propriété et Garantie' (Thesis, *Université Paris II*, Paris, 1992) at p. 266 (my translation).

[26] Doctoral study by M.-F. Renoux Zagame, summarised in the article '*Du Droit de Dieu au Droit de l'Homme: sur les Origines Théologiques du Concept Moderne de Propriété*' (1985) I *Droits* 17.

[27] Ibid, at pp. 17–18, my translation.

[28] Ibid, at p. 19, '*propriété*' is translated as ownership and '*domaine*' as property or *dominium.*

model of human *dominium*. The term *dominium* refers both to God's power over His Creation and to the human exercise of property prerogatives. The term is borrowed from Roman law's vocabulary as a result of the mediaeval cross-fertilization of juridical theories and Christian thought. 'The progress of the term *dominium* therefore translates a slow evolution leading the theologians to perceive divine *dominium* as a type of right, and then to confuse *dominium*, law and the divine ... this evolution is crucial ... as it could be that the notion of subjective right is rooted therein'.[29]

Divine *dominium*, the model and basis of human *dominium*, is interpreted as the site of divine sovereignty and expression of God's unlimited power of creation and ordering. Man's submission to God allows human participation in the divine dominium. The *dominium* of Man over things was thus interpreted as a way by which God allows humans to participate in His action, to share part of his power for the purposes He has assigned. According to the theologians, human *dominium* is confused with God's power and mission. In natural law theories, the role of God has been confined to the explanation of the origins of human *dominium*; the latter was no longer confused with God's own *dominium*. Accordingly, Man, in his worldly endeavours, was no longer constrained by God's will. *Dominium* was inscribed in human nature and man was born free. However, Man's natural right to property, expressed in absolute ownership, had the same content as its theological ancestor. 'Freed from its ties with God ... the moving divine *dominium* of theological thought became in a way a human right'.[30]

The theological human *dominium* resembles the absolute power of the King; in both cases, submission to God is the basis and the limit of these two types of power. Moreover, absolute ownership, grounded in the human/divine *dominium*, 'could have been better named right of God, as it was modelled on the divine for Man conceived as the agent of God on earth'.[31]

The modern concept of absolute ownership originates in theological reflections about God's power. It seems that, to express the all-mightiness of Man, absolute ownership had to crystallize the attributes of divine and monotheistic power: unity, sovereignty, and unidirectionality. Absolute ownership is part of the enduring epistemic imaginary rooted in theological reflections on power and producing legal conceptualizations focused on sovereign power.

Understanding absolute ownership's epistemic function and symbolism allows us to explain its enduring significance in French law. The power of this principle is such that it was able to defeat the transmigration of the trust. This surely cannot be the result of the operation of absolute ownership as the legal expression of the political importance of individual property. Collective ownership and power form part of French political and economic culture. But this does not lead us to the conclusion

---

[29] Ibid., at p. 20.
[30] Ibid., at p. 30.
[31] Ibid., at p. 31.

that the role of absolute ownership is simply ideological, masking the reality of fragmented rights, corporate power and the magnitude of state regulation of ownership, which will be explored in the next section. The concepts of 'imaginary' and 'ideology' are not synonymous.[32] The persistent significance of absolute ownership in French law is mainly epistemic and symbolic. It is specific to the imaginary of French – and other jurisdictions based on the *Code Napoléon* – epistemic tradition;[33] absolute ownership's discursive role is quite independent from the non-discursive significance of individual property.

3. Surveillance of Ownership, Governmentality and the Problem of Trust in French Law

It could legitimately be expected that the practical implication of absolute ownership would be the possibility to fragment and dispose of any proprietary prerogative for the purpose of a flexible management of property. However, the principle co-exists with another logic underlying French legal knowledge, one based on surveillance and restricting the freedom of the absolute owner. Indeed, absolute ownership is countered by the contradictory ethos of state surveillance of ownership inherited from the Revolutionary and Napoleonic vision of government. The epistemic processing of the trust into the *Fiducie* illustrates the potency of the impulse to control property through surveillance, reflected in particular, in the 1992 Bill's fiscal provisions. Such ethos is deeply ingrained in French legal culture, rather than a mere

[32] Ost and Lenoble's concept of imaginary is distinct from the Marxist notion of ideology. 'These notes on the imaginary allow us to begin a debate with the concept of *ideology*. This confrontation is necessary if we are clearly to distinguish our own hypotheses from those analyses, from now on classical, of legal discourse that are proposed in terms of critique of ideologies'. For further details see F. Ost and Y. Lenoble, 'Founding Myths in Legal Rationality' (1986) 47 *Modern Law Review* at 537–538.

[33] The role of absolute ownership as epistemic icon is further argued by focusing on in its enduring importance in jurisdictions which have based their private law system on Napoleonic codification, but which also have been considerably influenced by the common law. Quebec and Louisiana have both consecrated absolute ownership in their nineteenth century codification. They both have adopted their own equivalent of the trust through statutory reform. In both jurisdictions, absolute ownership has been the focus of doctrinal and judicial debates and analyses on the legal definition of the imported institution. Absolute ownership is also an epistemic symbol of identity in these jurisdictions. Unlike French doctrine, legal knowledge in these jurisdictions has been considerably influenced, or at least exposed to, common law concepts. However, the epistemic unity and uniqueness of Quebec's and Louisiana's legal identity seems to depend on reverence to the epistemic icons consecrated by Napoleonic codification. Absolute ownership in Quebec and Louisiana does not merely translate the conceptual particularity of a system of property law based on Roman law. It subsists, in the face of adversity, as a symbol of the law's identity. In Quebec and Louisiana, unlike in French legal doctrine, the issue of legal identity is at the forefront of legal discourse and is formulated as a clash between legal traditions. In all three cases, legal discourse maintains its sense of identity and unity through the epistemic icons. See K.V. Lorio, '*Le Trust en Louisiane: l'Expérience du Trust par une Juridiction Civiliste*' [1990] *Revue Juridique et Politique* 240; J. Brierley, '*De la Fiducie*' in J. Brierley (ed.), *La Réforme du Code Civil: Textes Réunis* (Tome I, Press Université de Laval, 1991).

ad hoc policy reaction to the trust. It exists on another epistemic plane than that of the principle of absolute ownership, but interacts with it. This epistemic plane is concerned with the definition of the proper object, goals and techniques of government and has been defined by Foucault as 'governmentality'.[34]

The proposed introduction of a trust-like device and its regulation through legislation has brought to the fore a particular way of thinking and understanding ownership, which can be perceived in terms of the specific 'governmentality' shaping French law. In particular, in legal debates about the trust and its adaptation as the *Fiducie*, the possibility of using the device as a screen to conceal ownership, seemed particularly problematic. It is argued here that this is because the trust conflicts with French governmentality's vision of governable society and the individual as transparent entities, subsumed to the gaze of the state. This notion of governmentality will be first examined before illustrating how the legal analysis and regulation regarding the *Fiducie* reflect it.

French mentality of government is influenced by techniques of government inherited from Napoleonic rule and enshrined in law through codification. In particular, modern governmentality has developed techniques of surveillance, also called 'panoptic techniques'. The French Revolution dreamed up this new form of power, panoptic power, 'exercised by virtue of the mere fact of things being known and people seen... [the Panopticon] provided ... the formula for [this] "power through transparency", subjection by "illumination"'.[35] Investment in panoptic power 'climax[ed] in the regime of Napoleon, who wished to arrange around him a mechanism of power that would enable him to see the smallest event that occurred in the state he governed'.[36] A number of codified institutions and legal principles that still inform French law illustrate the enduring relevance of the surveillance of ownership. The goal of surveillance of ownership is two-fold: it allows state control over assets, and it ensures the disciplining of the economic subject.

As regards the first objective, a detailed regulation of successions compromising freedom of disposition was deemed necessary to ensure the state's control over its property-owning subjects. The codifiers based the regulation of successions on the belief that:

---

[34] 'Governmentality', which combines the words mentality and government, is a neologism that refers to a mentality of rule or government. As such, it determines the rationalizations and techniques of government that are reflected in law. This concept was invented and explained by Michel Foucault in 'Governmentality', a lecture given in 1978 and published in D. Burchell, C. Gordon and P. Miller (eds.), *The Foucault Effect: Studies in Governmentality* (Harvester Weatsheaf, England, 1991).

[35] M. Foucault, 'The Eye of Power' in C. Gordon (ed.), *Power/Knowledge* (Harvester Wheatsheaf, England, 1980) at p. 154. The Panopticon is an architectural structure, in the form of a tower, devised by Bentham. It aimed to secure discipline through the sole feeling and awareness of being watched. The primary application of this panoptic structure would have been the prison, although its utility in civil society was envisaged by Bentham. See M. Foucault, *Discipline and Punish* (Penguin Books, London, 1977).

[36] C. Gordon, 'Foucault, Governmentality and Subjectivity', in B. Smart (ed.), *Michel Foucault: Critical Assessment*, vol iv (2) (Routledge, London, 1995), at p. 437.

> The law must intervene to shape society and constitute a large class of small property holders, as they are 'the most stable support for the State's safety and tranquillity', and as a corollary, reduce 'the numbers forming the proletarian class', that is the most dangerous class, without running the risk of reconstituting the large hereditary estates characterizing the *Ancien Régime*, which are economically inefficient and politically damaging for the State[37]

Hence, the trust potentially conflicted with a basic premise of French succession laws and the *Fiducie* had to be formulated to comply with this imperative. In particular, it had to comply with the rules governing the legitimate, a statutory encumbrance on all estates, creating entrenched inheritance rights for surviving descendants. It is in effect, a statutory trust restricting the powers of free disposition by testament or donation to a fraction of the testator's fortune. This fraction is called the *quotité disponible*. The purpose of the *quotité disponible* was to maintain paternal authority and to preserve the economic integrity and efficiency of landholdings as cohesive production units. The intention was indeed to dismantle large dynastic holdings but without reducing these to a barely exploitable fragmented multitude.

The freedom of disposition tied with absolute ownership is therefore both carefully monitored and instrumentalized for the purpose of government. The State is to exercise its oversight primarily through the regulation of successions. Napoleonic governmentality included a concern for the distribution of wealth in the State's and the population's best interest. This goal is tied to a vision of the State as capable of overseeing and controlling the inter-generational movement of assets. An institution like the trust, which, according to Maitland,[38] originated as a weapon against restrictions on freedom of testation, would clearly conflict with an essential aspect of Napoleonic governmentality.

This aspect of Napoleonic rule has endured as the only possible political grounds for the parliamentary opposition to the *Fiducie*; the drafters of the Bill feared that the Bill would be opposed because of its threat to the *réserve*. It was therefore decided that a *Fiducie* could only transfer assets that are part of the disposable fraction – *quotité disponible*. The Bill provided that where the transfer of assets in *Fiducie* is of a value over and above that of the disposable share, the court would order a reduction of the value of the assets, but not necessarily a return to the bulk of the estate of specific assets.[39]

The imperative of state surveillance of ownership is even more evident in the attempt to legislate against the possibilities of tax evasion/avoidance that a trust-like device would entail. The French *Ministère de l'Economie et des Finances*, in charge of

37 J.F. Niort, '*Droit, Economie et Liberalisme dans l'Esprit du Code Napoléon*', *Archives de Philosophie du Droit*, *Tome* 37 (Sirey, 1992), at p. 109.

38 *Collected Papers, vol. iii* (edited by A.L. Fisher, Cambridge University Press, 1911), at p. 311.

39 Arts. 2070–2073 to 2070–2075. Where the assets in *Fiducie* form a business unit worth more than the disposable share, the reduction to the value of the share will be in value by payment of a sum of money, as opposed to the return of some of the business assets.

the drafting of the fiscal provisions of the Bill on the *Fiducie*, was primarily concerned to prevent the constitution of such unclear situations through the use of the trust's opacity, which, if introduced into French law, would generate a 'black hole' for fiscal resources. In order to avoid this, the fiscal regulation of the new *Fiducie* was to reflect the two central principles of transparency and neutrality.

Transparency entails that, for the purposes of determining tax liability, the fiduciary device would have been ignored, and the *fiduciaire* could not have been a subject of taxation. Hence, in the eyes of the fiscal administration, economic reality would have been privileged over legal form and the fiduciary, constituted in the rest of the Bill as the only owner and the main element of the new device, would be from the fiscal point of view, non-existent.[40] The fiscal construction of the *Fiducie* reflects concerns connected with the imperative of surveillance, such as the simplification of legal forms into a decipherable economic reality; the intermediary level occupied by the fiduciary was ignored and the focus was on the traditional dyad, owner-thing.

The *Fiducie* would not have been allowed to be used as an instrument obstructing surveillance. The possible use of the *Fiducie* as a discretionary trust was perceived as particularly problematic and specifically targeted. Hence, section 23, Part III of the Bill states that where the beneficiaries cannot be identified, the fiduciary will have to pay income tax at its highest rate, on their behalf. Moreover, the names of the beneficiaries could not be changed (article 2064) and one condition of validity of the fiduciary contract was the existence of named beneficiaries or of clear rules determining their designation (article 2062).

The transparency of the *Fiducie* was to be ensured through legally required accounts, and the role of the fiduciary in drawing up and communicating such information. Section 33, Part III of the Bill would have introduced an obligation on the *fiduciaire* to provide the Inland Revenue with the names and activities of the beneficiaries, the nature and value of the assets and the value and distribution of the income of a *Fiducie*.

The principle of neutrality was also applied. Its meaning, in French doctrine and in the Bill itself, overlaps with the notion of transparency. Indeed, the neutrality of the proposed new device was declared in the preamble of the 1992 Bill. The application of this principle comprised two aspects: the transparency of the device for the purpose of determining tax liability, and the lack of particular fiscal advantages connected with the use of a *Fiducie*. Hence, the constitution of a *Fiducie* would not have entailed inheritance or gift tax exemptions. The fiscal regulation of the *Fiducie* was not perceived as an instrument of public policy and a means of encouraging certain aspects of private activity. However, nor were the fiscal rules seen as a way of redressing inequalities and market distortions resulting from the advantages of the *Fiducie* over a simple transfer of ownership. The transparency of the device, that is the invisibility of the *Fiducie* and *fiduciaire* in the eyes of the fiscal administration, would have posed problems in dealing with practices equivalent to

[40] Except, where the beneficiaries cannot be identified.

the accumulation or discretionary trust, where the advantages of the interposition of a fiduciary would have had to be ignored.[41]

One of the main aims of the fiscal administration was to encompass foreign trusts involving economic subjects outside the State's jurisdiction, but at least partly enforced in France. The recognition of trusts in accordance with the 1985 international convention would have entailed, thanks to the 1992 Bill, further revenues for the Public purse.[42]

The fiscal policing of the new device and the consequent application of the imperative of surveillance prevented the constitution of the *Fiducie* as a flexible instrument. Whilst the English 'public law of taxation has conventionally been adapted to the private ordering of property law', the private freedom granted under the auspices of the *Fiducie* was structured and policed by the public imperative of surveillance.[43] Hence, the mentality of rule behind fiscal regulation still remains unaffected by the practices of French private lawyers, who, unlike their English counterparts, do not have the necessary epistemological and political space to structure the relationship between taxpayers and the fiscal administration.

It seems therefore that to rule, the modern French state has established a requirement and a vision of economic subjects as transparent units. Moreover, this perception, shared by the economic agent him/herself, would induce self-discipline on the marketplace and therefore, trust in the security of economic transactions. Economic agents are required to display a truthful appearance of solvency in order to obtain credit, which means, both trustworthiness in business and the loaning of money.[44] It is expected that, by acting as a guardian of the truthfulness of such appearances, and providing legal sanctions in case of dishonesty, the state, and the Code, will promote the self-discipline of the economic agent.[45]

This paradigm informs fundamental concepts of private law such as the notion of patrimony, unknown to the common law, and central to the argument that the trust is incompatible with French law.[46] A patrimony is intrinsic to personality – every legal subject has one – and is the totality formed by potential and actual property rights and obligations. It is a virtual balance sheet attached to the individual and passed on after his/her death. It is comparable to the notion of estate but is more abstract notion as it is detached from actual possessions.

One important characteristic of patrimony is its unity. This notion and its implications were established by two nineteenth century treatise writers; Aubry and Rau, basing their reflection on German law, devised the theory of unity of

[41] See G. Moffat, *Trusts Law* (2nd edn., Butterworth, London, 1994), at pp. 294–311 and n. 14 above.

[42] Ibid.

[43] G. Moffat, n. 40 above, at p. 311.

[44] Treilhard, one of the Code's drafters said: 'Credit is constituted by the opinion one has of the morality and wealth of a citizen': cited in Niort, above n. 37.

[45] See two doctrines raised in analyses of the *Fiducie*: the sham or simulation theory of apparent solvency. See Witz, n. 3 above, pp. 211–258.

[46] See Motulsky, n. 3 above.

patrimony.[47] The theory has three main propositions; first, only persons (natural or legal) can have a patrimony. Secondly, every person has a patrimony, whether or not he/she has any possessions. Finally, a person can only have one patrimony.

This fundamental theory and conception of patrimony is problematic as regards the reception of the trust and the formulation of the *Fiducie*. The trust is regarded as operating a division of the unitary patrimony, as the fiduciary would have at least two patrimonies, his/her own personal one, and that created for the purpose of the *Fiducie*.[48] The drafters of the 1992 Bill were concerned that the *Fiducie* should, as far as practicable, respect the rule of unity.[49] Hence, it was decided that the *Fiducie* should be understood as constituting an autonomous patrimony, reserved for a specific purpose, but comprised in the patrimony of the *Fiduciaire*. This inclusion of an autonomous fund within the trustee's patrimony has been described as highly artificial and as a way of complying in appearance to the idea of unity.[50]

But how is patrimonial theory connected to surveillance? The theory of unity of patrimony based on articles 732 and 2092 of the Civil Code, implements general objective of protection of creditors.[51] This goal would be achieved by ensuring that debtors cannot divide their patrimony, thereby protecting some of their assets by the creation of secret funds. The division of patrimony is equated with the creation of a situation of opacity, in which the assets of the debtor become invisible to the creditors. Economic agents are required to display the reality of their patrimonial situation and the conformity thereof with appearances. This general principle of transparency, and the legitimacy and fluidity of surveillance should ensure the disciplining of the economic actor. Trust and security in transactions is ensured by

---

47 The Civil Code only rarely refers to the notion of patrimony and does not state any definition or theory of patrimony. See C.B. Gray, 'Patrimony' (1981) 22 *Cahiers de Droit* 81.

48 Quebec's solution of the patrimony by appropriation, according to which a *Fiducie* creates an ownerless patrimony connected only to its purpose is equally contrary to the unity of patrimony.

49 See the report on the rule of the unity of patrimony and the *Fiducie*, commissioned by the Ministry of Justice and drafted by a research unit at *Université Paris II*: '*Sociologie juridique du Patrimoine; La Réalité de la Règle de l'Unicité du Patrimoine (dans la perspective de la Fiducie)*' 1992.

50 See M. Grimaldi, '*La Fiducie: Reflexions sur l'Institution et sur l'Avant-projet de Loi qui la Consacre*' (JCP *Edition Notariale*, 1991), p. 897. The *fiduciaire* only has one patrimony within which one or more fiduciary funds operate. This aspect of the Bill differs from the definition of the trust proposed in the 1985 international convention, according to which the trust fund is totally autonomous and does not form part of the trustee's patrimony. This is the solution adopted in the new Quebec Civil Code, which defines the *Fiducie* as an ownerless patrimony reserved for a specific purpose.

51 In these provisions, there is 'not an allusion to the institution of a cohesive patrimony, but only an intention to exclude the arbitrary withdrawal of some types of goods. That is, instead of pointing to the uniqueness of patrimony as a common pledge as against the multiplicity of creditors, what is stressed is the additive character of their pledge: every new item acquired feeds into them': C. Gray (1981), above n. 47, p. 97.

the enforcement through law, of the obligation to reveal and display the reality of one's assets.[52]

Patrimonial theory also expresses another imperative relating to the relationship between the State and the individual. The individual must offer himself/herself as a readable unit, controllable by a centralised gaze. Their patrimony, representing them in simple accounting terms, constitute this readability. No screen-like device should be allowed to affect this decipherability. The corporation was historically perceived as suspicious, as it contravenes the principle of unity of patrimony by allowing the multiplication of patrimonies and the constitution of intermediary bodies with their own patrimony.[53] Legal personality was invented to allow the fragmentation of patrimonies entailed by the constitution of a corporation, whilst maintaining the apparent integrity of the unity of patrimony. Although the constitution of a legal person fragments and multiplies the patrimonies of the natural persons involved, the various patrimonies are fused into one, that of the legal person, which itself is understood to have a unique patrimony.

Like legal personality, patrimony is a fiction. This fictitious role is to ensure continuity and identity to the 'organic individuality' of groups. Legal fictions give unity to this data by 'representing' it.[54] In other words, patrimony and legal personality are used to give legal reality and a governable status to groups, by constructing them as single juridical subjects. Moreover, through the notion of patrimony, the subject is represented in examinable accounting terms as a balance sheet, a statement of account.

The notion of patrimony is at the heart of the juridical conceptualization of the economic subject, be it individual or group. 'Patrimony is the emanation of personality in the economic domain'.[55]

> ... Patrimony – which was no more than a type of *image*-would be considered as the attribute of the subject's personality... As the emanation of personhood, patrimony was in a circular relation to the person supporting it; it also signified this very personhood: it *materialized*, actualized and designated personhood, to

[52] Credit was understood by the drafters of the Civil Code as having two complementary meanings: first, as the loaning of money between economic agents, and secondly, as the trustworthiness and reputation of the citizen; 'Credit is constituted by the opinion one has of the morality and wealth of a citizen' (one of the drafters, Treilhard, cited in n. 37 above, at p. 103).

[53] Maitland refers to the French attitude towards corporations as a 'pulverizing, macadamizing tendency in all its glory, working from century to century, reducing to impotence, and then to nullity, all that intervenes between Man and State... the work of the monarchy issues in the work of the revolutionary assemblies. It issues in the famous declaration of August 18, 1792: "A State that is truly free ought not to suffer within its bosom any corporation ... " That was one of the mottoes of modern absolutism: the absolute State faced the absolute individual': see Maitland, above n. 38, at p. 311.

[54] Ibid. (my translation).

[55] '*Patrimoine et Vie Privée*' in n. 51 above (my translation).

the extent that an author wrote 'behind the mysteries of its components and management, a way of being is to be discovered'[56]

Hence, patrimony is the legal representation of the economic subject. This representation is given in the static and accounting terms of assets and liabilities.[57] The notion of patrimony contributes to the constitution of the examinable economic subject. Hence, the imperative of unity, with its correlated restrictions on the creation of autonomous and fragmented funds, is connected to the objective of surveillance in governmentality. The Trust and the *Fiducie* constitute a challenge to surveillance because they are intermediary bodies that do not fit into the grid of visibility of legal personality. They are not recognised as transparent and governable subjects. Indeed, Maitland noted that the trust form was preferred to the corporate form because it allowed more autonomy and freedom from the State.[58] This echoes my argument that the corporation is a legally subjected form of association, whereas the trust remains a fluid entity.

The rejection of the trust and its reformulation as the *Fiducie* have thus, been understood here, as determined by the underlying imperative of surveillance in French mentality of rule. 'Panoptic' surveillance may not be the most prevalent technology of power in French legal culture, but it seems to be particularly relevant to the issue of reception of the trust in the shape of the *Fiducie*. It may be that the trust poses a similar problem in the common law culture, which has also been concerned with the protection of creditors' rights and the policing of such enigmatic creatures as the purpose trust. However, it would seem that surveillance imperatives in French law have been strong enough to subsume practices and lawyers' devices proposing to foster opacity. Lawyers' practices, such as the trust, which may conflict with imperatives of transparency required for the efficient exercise of administrative power, were not allowed to flourish. They may have found a more favourable climate in the international arena.

Hence, the introduction of the *Fiducie* would have implied a compromise as regards the traditional vision of state economic sovereignty and surveillance. Such compromise was based and justified on a contradictory premise: that of the limits of the state rule in the face of internationalization, or as it would be formulated today, globalization.

---

56 Ibid., p. 14 (my translation).

57 Ibid. The static notion of patrimony in civil law is contrasted with the focus on movements of funds in the financial culture. This reflects the legal emphasis on the localization of assets and the financial understanding of patrimony as a fluctuating entity for the purpose of investment.

58 Above n. 38.

4. Wider Horizons: Globalization, Professional Opportunities and the *Fiducie*

Through the *Fiducie*, the limits of government are touched upon and acknowledged. French law has to compete with other jurisdictions to attract through its regulation, businesses and capital. Governmental rationality is assumed powerless before the pressures of the 'internationalized' economy. The paradox of the Bill lies in its unformulated assumptions about, on the one hand, French economy as a governable entity, and on the other, the international sphere as both a constraint, and a renewed challenge for government. Hence, the *Fiducie* indicated both, the limits of government as an activity and a rationality confined to the nation, and put at the forefront of the problematic of government, the almost mythical and non-governable entity, global society.[59]

The *Fiducie* has revealed the epistemic and regulative difficulties and tensions that are raised by the attempt to introduce the trust into French law. These tensions are tangible at the level of legal discourse, but cannot be explained adequately by referring exclusively to the internal workings of knowledge and discourse. Hence, it is argued that the workings of French legal knowledge and discourse are inscribed in material practices and struggles.

Indeed, 'discursive relations become associated with non-discursive milieus, which are not in themselves situated either inside or outside the group of statements but form... the specific horizon without which these objects could neither appear nor be assigned a place in the statement itself'.[60] The *Fiducie* is thus also the product of changes in the non-discursive horizons within which agents are constructed by discourse and interact within legal culture. Indeed, legal culture is not only a discursive site, but also a field of struggles.

The issue addressed here is the following: if the trust cannot be transplanted into French law, and indeed was once deemed incompatible with it, why has its introduction, albeit in the form of the *Fiducie*, become more acceptable? The 1992 Bill indicates that the epistemic resistance to the trust has, to a limited extent, been overcome. What has enabled this? Is this evolution of French legal knowledge in its understanding and acceptance of the trust a purely epistemic phenomenon that is solely linked to the internal evolution of French legal knowledge? I wish to argue that this change can only be accounted for through an analysis of changes within the legal profession linked to the emerging rhetoric and reality of globalization. The *Fiducie* is not only the product of epistemic processes; it is also the outcome of agent strategies in the domestic and global context.[61]

59 This is so although there is no specific reference in the Bill or related literature, to globalization. This is arguably due to the fact that in the early 1990s, the notion had not yet penetrated the juridical field to any significant extent.

60 G. Deleuze, *Foucault*, (University of Minnesota Press, Minneapolis, 1996) p. 43.

61 According to French sociologist P. Bourdieu, a field is a dynamic structure defined at any specific moment in time by a particular configuration of relations of power or distribution of capital: 'In

The *Fiducie* is the result of unformulated strategy of professional self-promotion of an emerging global legal elite in the French field of law. The role of the elite as brokers of rule as been persuasively illustrated by French sociologist Yves Dezalay.[62] According to him, the emergence of this new cosmopolitan elite shaped by the Anglo-American model of lawyering has entailed turf wars and competition at the national level with the established French state technocracy. This competition opposes these experts as producers of rule, the technologies they support, and also the representations and symbolic constructions upon which their regulatory models are built. The argument here is that the *Fiducie* is a microcosmic expression of such two-tiered competition.

The legal form of the *Fiducie* is illustrative of the struggle and professional stakes in the field of legal expertise and knowledge. In the first place, the Bill is characterised by a tension between two regulatory models. A facilitative framework should have allowed the *Fiducie* to develop with little regulatory control through lawyers' international practices. This is what was hoped by the professionals and granted, to a certain extent, by the commercial law section of the Ministry of Justice in the first part of the Bill. However, the fiscal administration disappointed the hopes for a lightweight framework for the *Fiducie*. The heavy fiscal regulation of the device and its general incidence on the economy of the Bill has meant that the proposed *Fiducie* was perceived amongst practitioners as a useless device. The technocratic aims and regulatory model hampered the more practitioner-led contractarian approach to the *Fiducie*. This conflict in visions is paralleled by a competition between experts in the field of regulation. The legal experts at the interstice of law and the market, of the national and the global threaten the monopoly of the state technocrat in the regulatory arena.

The impact of globalization, of which the *Fiducie* seems to be one of the early illustrations, entails changes in the way society is constructed and therefore also in the way the role of law is envisaged. International legal experts are very much implicated in this construction of new regulatory models to deal with the phenomenon of globalization. These models threaten the legitimacy of state technocrats in the regulation of economic power. This will be demonstrated next with regard to the *Fiducie*.

---

analytic terms, a field may be defined as a network ... of objective relations between positions. These positions are objectively defined, in their existence and in the determination they impose upon their occupants, agents or institutions, by their present and potential situation (*situs*) in the structure of the distribution of species of power (or capital) whose possession commands access to the specific profits that are at stake in the field, as well as by their objective relation to other positions ... ': Bourdieu, interview with L. Wacquant in *An Invitation to Reflexive Sociology* (Polity Press, Cambridge, 1992), at p. 97 (original emphasis).

62 Y. Dezalay, *Marchands de Droit* (Fayard, Paris, 1992); 'Between the State, Law, and the Market: The Social and Professional Stakes in the Construction and Definition of a Regulatory Arena' in W. Bratton et al. (eds.), *International Regulatory Competition and Coordination* (Clarendon Press, Oxford, 1996).

One important impetus for the drafting of the 1992 Bill was the planned ratification of the 1985 Hague Convention on the recognition of Trusts. The impact of this Convention was two-fold: first, it offered an opportunity to push for the adoption of a trust-like device which would allow lawyers based in France to compete on the global market for legal services. Secondly, this convention proposed a definition of the trust which, it will be argued, reflects the practice of the global/off-shore trust and provided a blueprint of such trusts for the *Fiducie*.

As regards our first point, it is important to remember that the 1985 Convention did not attempt to impose the trust as a new institution on all ratifying countries' domestic law. The Convention purported only to unify conflict of laws principles by making sure, firstly, that a trust would be recognizable according to any private international laws, even those of non-trust countries. Secondly, the rule determining which law is applicable to a trust would be the same in every ratifying state. The ratification of the Convention does not necessitate the adoption of the trust by non-trust countries.[63] But it was seized as an opportunity by professionals based in France dealing with the financial operations of their international clientele. They sought to add the trust to their array of financial and tax-planning devices. Thus, the globalizing effects of the Convention are not inherent to this effort of harmonization, but also dependent on more local strategic needs of competing elites.

In order for the trust to become an acceptable category of private international law in non-trust countries, the drafters attempted to provide an uncontroversial definition of the trust – that is, a definition that avoids any reference to the legal/equitable division of ownership.[64] The trust model provided in article 2 of the Convention is characterised by its shapeless, almost invisible, ownership structure.[65]

63 Special Commission on the proposed Convention, report cited by A. Dyer, Deputy Secretary General of the Hague Conference on Private International Law, in a paper 'Creation and Progress of the Hague Convention on Trusts', presented at the Conference *Hot Topics In the World of Trusts*, Nov. 1994. For an account of The Hague Convention see D. Hayton, 'The Hague Convention on the Law Applicable to Trusts and on their Recognition' (1987) 36 *International and Comparative Law Quarterly* 260; P. Gaillard and S. Trautman, 'Trusts in Non-Trust Countries: Conflict of Laws and the Hague Convention on Trusts' (1987) 35 *American Journal of Comparative Law* 307; C. Jauffret-Spinosi, '*La Convention de la Haye Relative à la Loi Applicable au Trust et à sa Reconnaissance* (1 *Juillet* 1985), vol. i *Clunet* 27. For the text of the Convention see J. Underhill and D. Hayton, *The Law Relating to Trusts and Trustees* (15th edn., Butterworth, London, 1995) pp. 939–956; and J. Glasson (ed.), *International Trust Laws* (London, Chancery, 1992), Appendix 50. The conflict of laws rule would be: the law applicable to all international trusts is the law chosen by the settlor.

64 See Dyer, n. 63 above.

65 'For the purposes of this Convention, the term "trust" refers to the legal relationships created – *inter vivos* or on death – by a person, the settlor, when assets have been placed under the control of a trustee for the benefit of a beneficiary or for a specified purpose. A trust has the following characteristics: (a) the assets constitute a separate fund and are not a part of the trustee's own estate; (b) title to the trust assets stands in the name of the trustee or in the name of another person on behalf of the trustee; (c) the trustee has the power and the duty, in respect of which he is accountable, to manage, employ or dispose of the assets in accordance with the terms of the trust and the special duties imposed upon him by law' (Art. 2).

We wish to argue that this definition is based on international trust practice, and for this reason, influenced the legal construction of the *Fiducie*.

Hayton reminds us that the Convention, besides its general and theoretical aim to unify private international law, aims to facilitate the mobility and delocalization of assets.

> It is a fact of life that, with the increasing mobility of capital and persons, more and more trust assets, beneficiaries and trustees, are to be found in non-trust States. Currently, different non-trust States deal very differently with trust problems arising in their jurisdictions. ... Inevitably, a common lawyer from a trust State finds it very difficult to predict for a client what may happen if some aspect of a trust comes to involve a non-trust State ... [T]rustees ... have particular cause to be concerned over investing in non-trust States since, if they lose control of or diminish the value of the trust assets as a result of detrimentally subjecting them to some foreign law, they may be personally liable for breach of trust. It is in the best interests of States to adopt the Convention and harmonize their approach to trust issues, so ... producing greater legal certainty and greater protection for property rights[66]

Hayton seems to suggest that, despite the apparent unilateral benefit for common law practitioners and their clients in the (almost) worldwide recognition of trust, non-trust countries will derive some benefit from the promotion of certainty and the protection of property rights. According to this author, trustees and other fund managers will be encouraged to invest in the countries, recently 'civilized' to the virtues of the trust. However, the influence of offshore trust practices on the Convention's aims and the resulting 'shapeless trust' has not been addressed by the drafters or doctrinal writers. We will have to take examples from offshore trust practice to illustrate the similarities between these, the Convention's trust, and the *Fiducie*.

The non-charitable purpose trust is a fine example of recent developments in offshore trust practice.[67] There seems to be converging characteristics between the latter, the Convention's shapeless trust and the *Fiducie*. The trick of the purpose trust is to make beneficial ownership disappear. It does rely on the traditional division of ownership between the trustee and the beneficiary, but:

> the characteristic of the true non-charitable purpose trust is that it has no beneficiaries ... the property the subject of the trust cannot, in strict law, be said to belong beneficially to *anyone*. Now there are estate-planning exercises and commercial transactions that can make good use of this phenomenon[68]

---

66 Hayton, n. 63 above, at pp. 260–261.

67 See D. Oakley (ed.), *Contemporary Trends in Trust Law* (Clarendon Press, Oxford, 1996).

68 R. Matthews, 'Non-Charitable Purpose Trusts', ibid. at 19.

We have noted the Convention's and the 1992 Bill's fuzziness regarding the precise entitlement of the beneficiary. *The Fiducie* altogether avoids any formulation of beneficial ownership. This is probably due to the fact that the beneficiary's rights have no equivalent in French law. However, what is significant is the lack of concern for this missing element. Beneficial ownership was easily sacrificed as the definitional priority focused on the contractual characterization of the relationship between the *constituant*/settlor and the fiduciary. The perceived importance of this relationship echoes offshore trust practice and its emphasis on the protection of the settlor's interest and the lack of third party beneficiary.

The definition of the *Fiducie* also focused on the fact that the settlor would create a separate and autonomous fund albeit owned by the fiduciary. As we have seen, the constitution of a separate fund within the fiduciary's patrimony is inconsistent with the principle of unity of patrimony. The fiduciary's ownership is of course everything but beneficial and is, in strict legal terms, artificial, as a legal subject is only entitled to one patrimony. It could well be argued that the French *Fiducie* is almost an ownerless patrimony.

The offshore purpose trust could be said to epitomize the ownerless fund. The function of this device, as statutorily introduced and regulated in most offshore jurisdictions, is to provide a flexible and autonomous structure for asset management and protection.[69]

This may be a coincidence, but the drafters of the 1992 Bill have arguably overestimated the ability of French courts to deal with issues relating to fiduciary administration. According to nineteenth century contractual theory, the principle of freedom of contract requires the non-intervention of the judge in the life of a contract. Thus, traditionally, French judges have not been encouraged to police contractual relations, except where a statute specifically provides for such an intervention. The 1992 Bill envisaged the role of the court in determining the standard of fiduciary duty, or the usual content of a *Fiducie* contract. It seems that, intentionally or not, the drafters had granted prominence to the judge in the life of the *Fiducie*. This contrasts with the non-interventionist ethos of French courts in contractual matters.[70] Could it be that, on the basis of current international trust practice, much litigation was not anticipated? Was it simply hoped that the *Fiducie* would run itself as autonomously as the settlor wishes? After all the *Fiducie* was to be a contract and should have provided for its own administration – in the French tradition – independently of courts.

The *Fiducie* is a contractual structure. The drafters opted for this qualification in the second draft of the Bill. The reason given was that the *Fiducie* would thereby be clearly distinguished from the trust. This seems to contradict judicial authority,

[69] The autonomy of the purpose trust has been furthered by the emergence of a new figure: the Protector. See M. Waters, 'The Protector: New Wine in Old Bottles?' in Dyer (1984), n. 61 above.

[70] See C. Witz, '*Rapport Introductif – Les Traits Essentiels de la Fiducie et du Trust en Europe*' [1991] *Bulletin Joly* 9–20.

according to which the trust is a contract.[71] However, it was observed by a Luxembourg court that the reason why the trust has been interpreted as a contract by French courts is that the type of trusts involved in conflict of laws litigation are international business trusts, and this type of trust can adequately be described as a contract.[72] Hence, the contractual qualification of the *Fiducie* echoes the French legal conceptualization of the offshore trust.

This conceptual analysis of the *Fiducie*, as compared to the purpose trust and the shapeless trust supports our argument that the stakes here are the opportunities of local, i.e. French practitioners, to reinforce their position as global elite mastering offshore techniques, with the support of their national law. This particular political stake is reflected in both the Convention's and the Bill's embracing of the only globalizable element of trust law: offshore trust practice.[73]

The local exploitation of opportunities opened up by globalization is not limited to the competition between regulatory models and technologies. There are also struggles over the symbolic force and imagery of law. The reception of the trust, albeit in a modified form, became possible because doctrinal knowledge became more open to it. And doctrinal knowledge opened up because the way in which it is produced is changing with an intensification of the role of practitioners in the production of doctrine. The restructuring of legal training and doctrinal research, particularly as regards commercial law, around the biggest, often Anglo-American law firms, has been documented.[74] It would be inaccurate to argue that doctrinal knowledge has ever been totally independent from a more practice based form of legal knowledge. However, such independence is part of the mythology in the French epistemic tradition. This myth has been eroded and the *Fiducie* is both a consequence and an illustration of such erosion.

However, the *Fiducie* also illustrates the strength of epistemic structures and icons such as that of the principle of absolute ownership. No matter how influent the global financial technostructure may have become, the epistemic tradition that underlies French law remains symbolically powerful despite its lack of anchoring in economic power and because of its inherent and persisting association with the mythology of the state and juridical power.

---

71 Court of Appeal case *Courtois c. de Ganay*, Paris, 10 *Janvier* 1970, Rev. crit. 1971, 518.

72 *Tribunal de Luxembourg, jugement du* 21 *Janvier* 1971, Rev. crit. 1973, p. 51.

73 The 1992 Bill excludes judicially implied trusts and statutory imputed trusts.

74 P. Jestaz, '*Déclin de la Doctrine?*' (1994) 20 *Droits* 85; Y. Bancaud and Y. Dezalay, '*Des "Grands Prêtres" du Droit au Marché de l'Expertise Juridique – Transformations Morphologiques et Recomposition du Champ des Producteurs de Doctrine en Droit des Affaires*' (*Juin* 1994) vol. 12, n. 2 *Revue Politiques et Management Public* 203. See in particular the role of *avocats-agrégés* who combine the authority linked to an academic post with knowledge sensitive to commercial practice.

5. Conclusion

The failure of the 1992 Bill on the *Fiducie* is double; it is a failure to transpose the essential proprietary traits of the trust. Linked to this is the unnoticed vanishing of the Bill from the legislative agenda. The *Fiducie*'s limitations, particularly as regards tax planning, meant that few perceived it as a credible rival for the trust. The first aspect of the Bill's shortcomings illustrates the power and impact of local cultural and epistemic structures in the process of transmigration of legal institutions. This seems to indicate that the will of policy-makers or legislators might not suffice to ensure the reception of alien legal ideas and devices. On the other hand, the transmigration of commercial and business devices, such as the *Fiducie*, very much depends on the practices of local experts and the stakes that are raised at the national and global levels. As regards the second aspect of the Bill's failure, the *Fiducie* lacked the support of professional organisations of legal and financial experts, who probably would have been more willing to push for the introduction of a device capable of competing with the trust. The *Fiducie* reveals the complexity of the dynamics of French legal culture as a variable space of power struggles and epistemic tensions.

Chapter 6

LEGAL TRANSPLANTS: PRINCIPLES AND PRAGMATISM IN COMPARATIVE FAMILY LAW

*Peter de Cruz**

Looking into the nature of legal transplants, the circumstances under which transplanted rules take root in the new soil, and specifically legal transplants in family law, de Cruz proposes a 'pragmatic' approach to legal transplants, and in the specific area under consideration, this is the 'best interests' of the child.

Here, the measure of success is seen as the rooting of a transplant. This view should be compared to others presented in previous chapters. De Cruz first discusses the concept 'legal transplant' through the works of Watson, Kahn-Freund, Grossfeld and Glendon. Glendon's work is especially important since the test bed of the piece is family law. De Cruz tells us that in family law, the pragmatic approach works well to produce 'principles which have been adapted to reflect the changing social, religious and economic conditions of the host country'. The author argues that as court cases assume greater authority both in the common law and civil law jurisdictions, similarities will be created by transplants, irrespective of legislative intervention. In the field under consideration, there is also the impact of Conventions.

To assess the pragmatic approach to legal transplant theory, de Cruz deals particularly with one area in family law, that is, childcare law, the 'best interests of the child' test, and factors affecting 'child custody' in a number of common law and civil law jurisdictions. The 'best interests' test is increasingly used in several jurisdictions and has transcended the common law/civil law divide, showing that such transmigration can embed itself in very different environments. The chosen systems are France, Germany, Sweden, the United States, England and Wales, Australia, New Zealand, the Far East, Sri Lanka and India. Because of this wide field of reference, the research remains rather superficial; however, as the discussion revolves around the reasons for receptivity of legal transplants, it is necessary to look at a number of diverse systems.

The study shows that several historical, religious and political factors, all receptive to the 'best interests' principle, override the established values such as patriarchal dominance, and this principle has helped in the formulation of certain legal values which protect interests hitherto violated by traditions with social legitimacy. The 'suitable receptive environment' in the host country is of primary importance in the success of transplants. In addition, it is claimed that in the field of family law some of the

* Ph.D, Professor of Law, Staffordshire University, England, United Kingdom.

A. Harding and E. Örücü (eds.),
Comparative Law in the 21st Century, 101–120.

cornerstone principles have universality and therefore transferability, and in the case of many of these principles, the reasons for their adoption have been pragmatic. This finding defies earlier assumptions by comparatists that legal transplants do not work well in areas such as family law.

[A. Harding and E. Örücü]

'In most places at most times borrowing is the most fruitful source of legal change'

Alan Watson[1]

1. Introduction

This paper begins by exploring two preliminary points: firstly, what is the nature of legal transplants and secondly, in what circumstances might these principles or ideas have been borrowed from one country or jurisdiction to another and then taken root? It then considers examples of such transplants in the field of family law which have occurred in selected common law and civil law jurisdictions, before evaluating the impact of a 'pragmatic' approach on the development of law in various jurisdictions, with particular reference to the 'best interests' principle in child law.

2. The Concept of Legal Transplants[2] in Comparative Legal Studies

In their most basic form, the term 'legal transplants' connotes the notion of the 'legal borrowing' of a principle or concept; thus Professor Alan Watson describes 'legal transplants' as 'the moving of a rule [. . .] from one country to another, or from one people to another'.[3] Watson argued that when looking at a foreign system, a law reformer should look for an *idea* that could be transformed into part of the law of his country. He appeared to be referring primarily to statutory rules. However, he also made it clear that he believed that in the modern world, legal rules deeply embedded in their political context, may be successfully transplanted to a country with very different traditions, citing the example of Japan in the 19th century, where French law served as the model for the Japanese Penal Code and Code of Criminal

1 A. Watson, 'Aspects of Reception of Law' (1996) 44 *American Journal of Comparative Law* 335.

2 The term 'transplants' as used in this paper may refer to both the *process of transplantation* and the *principles/ideas* themselves that have been borrowed, depending on the context of the discussion.

3 A. Watson, *Legal Transplants: An Approach to Comparative Law* (Scottish Academic Press, Edinburgh, 1974), p. 21.

Procedure, which were enacted in 1882. He also argued that legal rules live and in some cases, even outlast changes in a particular society.

The late Professor Kahn–Freund,[4] however, argued that the degree to which to which any rule can be borrowed depends on how closely it is linked with the foreign power structure. This view is echoed by some modern writers, but is by no means universal.

2.1. The Terminological/Jurisprudential Debate

There is also a terminological or jurisprudential debate on what it is that has been 'transplanted' or precisely, what it is which can be so borrowed or transferred from one jurisdiction to another. Are laws or legal principles which are thus transplanted purely rules (i.e. *ex facie* written statutory rules) or do these principles also represent cultures, traditions and a number of social, political and economic mores which might not necessarily be easily 'received' by the 'host' legal system? The first of these approaches has been called the 'law as rules' approach and the second is the 'law as culture' approach that can accommodate both the 'law as rules' and 'law as an instrument of integration' approaches in comparative law.[5]

In his monograph *The Strength and Weakness of Comparative Law*[6] Grossfeld declares that while he does not agree with Watson's view, he concedes that '[C]omparatists keep coming across the same or similar legal ideas and institutions, perhaps with a different twist' and that the 'recurrence of legal forms is a familiar phenomenon'.[7] But, he does not accept Watson's view that a legal rule may be easily transplanted from one foreign jurisdiction into another irrespective of the host jurisdiction's social and cultural environment. Other writers have talked about the 'impossibility of legal transplants'[8] and the need for 'cultural immersion' into the political, historical, economic and linguistic contexts that moulded the legal system being examined as a prerequisite for effective comparative analysis,[9] which suggests that transplants might not be integrated into a particular *milieu* unless certain conditions exist which facilitate receptivity. It would be simplistic and superficial to believe that legal transplantation, even at a basic statutory level, has simply taken place in a vacuum, somehow divorced from the cultural, political, economic, linguistic and historical heritage of either jurisdiction.

4 O. Kahn-Freund, 'On Uses and Misuses of Comparative Law' (1974) 37 *Modern Law Review* 1.

5 See Van Hoecke and M. Warrington, 'Legal Cultures, Legal Paradigms and Legal Doctrine: Towards a New Model for Comparative Law' (1998) 47 *International Comparative Law Quarterly* 495.

6 See B. Grossfeld, *The Strength and Weakness of Comparative Law* (Clarendon Press, Oxford, 1990).

7 See Grossfeld, ibid., at p. 43 citing Mayer-Maly.

8 See P. Legrand, 'The Impossibility of Legal Transplants' [1997] *Maastricht Journal of European and Comparative Law* 111.

9 V.G. Curran, 'Cultural Immersion, Difference and Categories in US Comparative Law' (1998) 46 *American Journal of Comparative Law* 43.

In the words of Professor Mary Ann Glendon, an eminent comparatist whose work has had a seminal effect on comparative studies for over twenty years, '[I]n any comparative legal study, the hazards can be summed up in one word: *context*. To understand a legal rule in any system, one must have some understanding of its social and economic background and its practical consequences in operation'.[10] In any such enterprise, she stresses, one has to compare not just the rules themselves, 'but their social context and the manner in which they actually operate within their surrounding legal systems'. She also asks: '[T]o what extent do procedural rules or general social norms make it practically difficult for a clearly expressed legal sanction to be applied?'[11]

As far as developed countries are concerned, Kahn Freund identified four factors that indicate that there may well be fewer obstacles than previously thought for valid family law comparisons to be made.

The first factor is *gradual cultural assimilation* (i.e. people in London, Hamburg, New York and Paris read the same kind of newspapers and weekly news magazines, watch similar (or the same, only dubbed) television programmes and follow the exploits of the same popular celebrities. In contemporary times, this obviously applies to the so-called superstar footballers, who have a following all over the world. The newspapers in different parts of the globe all have a slightly different slant or approach or focus, but the main world news being reported often contain the same items that have been selected all over the world as a headline: the genome is a recent example where the scientists have, on both sides of the Atlantic, completed the first draft of the human genetic blueprint, the DNA.

The second factor is *gradual economic assimilation*, in the sense that people in developed countries earn their living in ways almost indistinguishable from one country to another, doing the same kinds of jobs, so that their manner of spending their earnings follow similar patterns owing to the evolution of trade, mass production and advertising.

The third factor is the *mobility of persons*, and the ease with which people move from place to place, so there is great familiarity between countries about each other's lifestyles, conduct and value systems. The fourth factor is the *emergence of similar legal problems* with respect to employment and housing.

There is certainly a great deal of credibility in all these factors and Glendon[12] adds the following three points: the declining influence of formal religion; the increase in family disorganisation and dysfunctionality; and the roles of women in developed countries like France, England and the USA tend to be similar in relation to their family roles and relationships (and, it might be added, their economic independence).

---

[10] M.A. Glendon, *State, Law and Famliy: Family Law in Transition in the United States and Western Europe* (North–Holland, New York, 1977), pp. 17–18.

[11] Ibid.

[12] Ibid., at p. 19.

In short, the world is becoming smaller and some form of globalization,[13] in the sense of a commonality of practices, beliefs, ideologies, values and icons, is taking place across the world. This phenomenon has been current for over a decade and a half. Professor Twining, for example, defines globalization as 'those processes which tend to create and consolidate a unified world economy, a single ecological system, and a complex network of communications that covers the whole globe, even if it does not penetrate to every part of the world'.[14]

Glendon has also pointed out that 'among the factors that facilitate comparison and render it increasingly useful, is the remarkable degree to which the family law of many systems has become open to foreign influences'.[15] For instance, she notes that in Germany, England, France and the USA, legislatures and law revision committees have examined foreign law 'in order to adjust their own law to social change which they perceive as being shared by other countries'.[16] These four countries have generated a vast amount of generally accessible case and statutory law. Glendon also observes that it appears to be coincidental that 'similar legal developments were produced at about the same time in the various legal systems apparently independently of each other'.[17]

Historically, there are many examples of jurisdictions which have received legal ideas and concepts as a result of colonization, annexation or secession from the time of the Roman and British empire, and in more recent times, many jurisdictions have adapted legal ideas to suit local conditions (e.g. Hong Kong, parts of the Far East and the British Commonwealth). Hence, some form of 'reception of law' has taken place since at least the time of the 'movement' of Roman law into Western Europe. Indeed, as Levy puts it, '[T]he reception of legal ideas of one people by another is a universal phenomenon in world history'.[18] Reception of law has been distinguished

---

13 For the past 16 years or so, there has been extensive literature on globalization; for its particular relevance to Comparative Law, see W. Twining, 'Globalization and Comparative Law' (1999) 6 *Maastricht Journal of European and Comparative Law* 217; 'Comparative Law and Legal Theory: The Country and Western Tradition' in I. Edge (ed.), *Comparative Law in Global Perspective* (Transnational Publishers, New York, 2000), p. 21; and W. Twining, *Globalization and Legal Theory* (Butterworths, London, 2000), where he defines globalization as 'those processes which tend to create and consolidate a unified world economy, a single ecological system, and a complex network of communications that covers the whole globe, even if it does not penetrate to every part of the world'. Twining observes, ibid., at p. 24, that 'we are living in rapidly changing and increasingly interdependent world [and] the trend towards globalization and fragmentation are complex and do not point in a single direction'.

14 Ibid., at p. 4.

15 Glendon, n. 10 above, at p. 19.

16 Ibid.

17 Ibid.

18 Levy, 'The Reception of Highly Developed Legal Systems by Peoples of Different Cultures' (1950) 25 *Washington Law Review* 233.

from transplantation by writers like Rheinstein,[19] and words like 'infiltration' and 'inoculation' have been used to describe this process.[20]

This paper argues that despite differing interpretations, terminological issues and cultural ambiguities, legal transplantation of some kind, and at some level, has frequently occurred between jurisdictions and will continue to do so; thus, it remains instructive from a legal reformist and comparatist's point of view to evaluate the impact of such 'transplants' (however defined and interpreted) as they have occurred in various jurisdictions. For present purposes, examples will be cited from family law, a field where a pragmatic approach has worked particularly well with 'transplanted' concepts to produce principles that have been adapted to reflect the changing social, religious and economic conditions of the host country.

2.2. Conditions under which Legal Transplants take Place

As Watson stated in his earlier writing, '[V]ery different social, political and economic circumstances may nonetheless be conducive to the creation of the same legal rule ... [this] can also be found in instances of independent development'.[21] Indeed, in his view, the transplanting of legal rules is 'the most fertile source of development',[22] but he emphasized that jurists may well exaggerate the extent of transplantation if the rule already existed in the host country; but even in this instance, the mere use of the terminology would tend to ensure the continuing influence of the imported principle. He placed the phenomenon of 'voluntary' major legal transplants, when either an entire legal system or a large portion of it is moved to a new sphere, into three main categories: When people move into a different territory where there is *no* comparable civilization and takes their law with them; when people move into a different territory where there *is* a comparable civilization, and takes their law with them; and when people voluntarily accept a large part of the system of other people or peoples.[23]

Clearly, therefore, reception of legal ideas takes place in many different circumstances and, as history has shown, over many centuries, dominions and transformations of societies. Watson[24] also highlighted other reasons for legal transplantation or borrowing that included extreme practical utility, chance, the absence of a clear principle and the need for legal authority (or authoritative legal source) to support the rule that is being invoked. As he puts it, '[A]ll lawmaking, apart from legislating, desperately needs authority'. This principle is accepted and practiced by doctrinal writers and judges alike.

---

19 M. Rheinstein, 'Types of Reception' (1956) 6 *Annales de la Faculté de Droit d'Istanbul* 34.

20 R.W. Lee, 'Roman Law in the British Empire, Particularly in the Union of South Africa' (1934–1935) 2 *Atti Congresso Internaz Dritto Romano* 251.

21 A. Watson, *Society and Legal Change* (Scottish Academic Press, Edinburgh, 1977), at p. 106.

22 A. Watson, above n. 3, at p. 95.

23 Ibid., at pp. 29–30.

24 A. Watson, 'Aspects of Reception of Law' (1996) 44 *American Journal Comparative Law* 335.

3. Family Law in Comparative Perspective: Pragmatism, Legal Transplants and Legal Reform

Family law in various common law jurisdictions provides a rich source of material, which may be tilled to identify legal ideas and concepts which originated from English law, but which were borrowed by other jurisdictions, in accordance with their changing social needs, and which reflect the *zeitgeist* of the particular jurisdiction. In 1997, Lord Goff reflected on the future of the common law and identified 'working from case to case' as the classic common law methodology, distinguishing this from the typical continental practice of working from abstract generalizations (of authoritative principle) contained in definitive Codes. He regarded the typical pragmatic common law approach as epitomized in the phrase 'common lawyers' worship at the shrine of the working hypothesis'.[25]

In several common law and civil law jurisdictions, many examples of legal transplants can be found in: statutory divorce grounds; judicial decisions on matrimonial and marital property; judicial decisions and legislation on rights of cohabitants; and childcare law.

The so-called common law methodology, dubbed 'argument by analogy', has apparently been seeping into parts of the European continental system, for example, to fill a gap in a Civil Law Code, and even in judgments of the European Court of Justice.[26] There has also been greater reliance on case law in Germany, although their style of judgment tends to be markedly different from the typical common law style of judgment[27] and there is no doctrine of precedent *a la* English law. Even in France, where *stricto sensu*, judges are forbidden to lay down rules of conduct as rules of law on an equal footing with codified regulations, there may be a consistent line of cases affirming a single authoritative principle (*la jurisprudence constante*) which French courts might decide to follow, albeit only as illustrations of a general principle. The point that emerges is that if cases begin to assume greater significance in a non-common law jurisdiction, then this clearly impacts on the development of law in that jurisdiction and legal transplants may consequently begin to take root (by sheer repeated and consistent usage), irrespective of legislative intervention.

This chapter considers (below) examples of some legal transplants of principles in family laws that have thrived in the countries of reception.

3.1. Divorce: Common Grounds and the Concept of Fault

'Fault' as a ground for divorce appears to have been transplanted from England to common law countries such as the USA, Australia and also the Far East. Adultery may be identified as the common denominator in various jurisdictions: the

[25] Lord Goff, 'The Future of the Common Law' (1997) 45 *International Comparative Law Quarterly* 745.

[26] K. Lagenbucher, 'Argument by Analogy in European Law' (1998) 57 *Cambridge Law Journal* 481.

[27] B. Markesinis, 'Conceptualism, Pragmatism and Courage: A Common Lawyer Looks at Some Judgments of the German Federal Court' (1986) 34 *American Journal Comparative Law* 349.

provenance of this ground stems from ecclesiastical law – in other words, because of the monogamy requirement under canon law, hence the influence of the Church continues.

As societies in the West and westernized societies in other parts of the world became more liberal in their attitudes towards sex, marriage and fidelity, this eventually led to the introduction in statutory form of 'no-fault grounds' i.e. separation for a certain period of years which has been made a ground irrespective of the (mis)conduct of the parties to the marriage.

Attempts at introducing mediation and dispensing with fault altogether have so far, not proved very successful in England, even though it has been widely believed that this is the sign of the future, namely, heralding a complete absence of fault grounds so that divorce becomes a purely administrative procedure, with delays being countenanced only for safeguarding of the welfare of children under 16. A combination of fault and no-fault grounds still exists in current English divorce law as of mid-2001,[28] French law and Belgian law,[29] although Germany opted in 1977 for 'breakdown' as the sole ground for divorce, abolishing fault-based grounds altogether.[30]

3.2. Matrimonial Property

The 'community property' regime in certain American jurisdictions such as California, appears to have originated in Spain around the time of the Visigoths and this law was taken to the New World, including California, which in 1850, affirmed that the law of community property would continue to be the governing law.

3.3. Criteria used in Determining Child Custody

Some of the criteria used by domestic courts also provide examples of legal transplants, for example, parental fitness to care for the child, and the child's wishes and feelings in the light of her age and understanding.

The weight attached to spousal (mis)conduct (i.e. if a spouse was proved to be 'unfit' in some way to have responsibility for caring for the child), would be taken into account so that the person with the unsatisfactory history of misconduct might be denied parental responsibility for the child. Was it ever thus? No, because in the era before the advent of the Children Act 1989, English case law shows that if the child happened to be very young and female, then the so-called 'maternal preference'

[28] Matrimonial Causes Act 1973 (as amended), s. 1 (UK).
[29] See Belgium Civil Code, Arts. 229, 231–233.
[30] See BGB, Arts. 1565–1566.

or 'presumption' would apply in about 86% of all cases,[31] although the English courts made statements to the effect that there was no actual rule of law to this effect, but that in some cases, this is what 'nature had ordained'.[32] Under the 1989 Act, (i.e. since October 1991), the court must now consider how capable each of the child's parents is of meeting the child's needs.

Under the UK Children Act 1989, when a court determines any question with respect to the upbringing of a child, section 1 requires a court to ascertain, *inter alia*, the child's wishes and feelings (in the light of his age and understanding).[33] This has been the unwritten practice for English courts since at least the latter part of the twentieth century, but the advent of the *Gillick*[34] principle and its enshrinement in the Children Act 1989 has meant that courts will assess the maturity of each child according to whether that child has 'sufficient age and understanding'.[35] There is a growing trend for civil law jurisdictions to also require that courts ascertain the child's wishes and feelings, for example, in Germany.

However, this chapter will focus on one legal transplant, namely, the 'welfare principle' or 'best interests of the child' test in common law *and* civil law jurisdictions; and its relationship to the list of factors which affect the disposition of 'child custody' as it is still called in many jurisdictions (though no longer in England and Wales since October 1991 with the implementation of the Children Act 1989), noting the similarities and modifications between the various jurisdictions. In the international context, it will then evaluate the impact on various jurisdictions of the United Nations Convention on the Rights of the Child 1989, particularly Article 3(1) thereof, which appears to give the 'best interests test' a central position in international children's rights law.

3.4. The 'Welfare Principle' or 'Best Interests of the Child Test' in Family Law

Children's rights have been called a 'slogan in search of a definition'[36] but the notion of 'the best interests of the child', whilst accepted as the guiding principle in so many jurisdictions, may also be described in the same way. This is because of its indeterminacy or chameleon-like qualities; every child is different, so, adults and courts have to decide in every case what is 'best' for that particular child in those particular circumstances that present themselves. Clearly, the 'best' course of action has become whatever a court says it is, and its content will vary from case to case.

---

[31] See J. Priest and J. Whybrow, *Custody Law in Practice in the Divorce and Domestic Courts* (HMSO, London, 1986) and see also *Re B* [1962] 1 All ER 872; *Re S* [1958] 1 All ER 783; *Re O* [1971] Ch 748.

[32] See *M v M* [1978] 1 FLR 77.

[33] See Children Act 1989, s. 1(3)(a) (UK).

[34] i.e. under *Gillick v Wisbech and West Norfolk AHA* [1985] 2 All ER 402 (House of Lords).

[35] See, e.g., ss. 43(8), 44(7), 39, Children Act 1989.

[36] In the oft-quoted words of Hillary Rodham, (later Hillary Clinton) in H. Rodham, 'Children under the Law' [1973] *Harvard Educational Review* 487.

Yet the principle has been called 'the most important principle in child law'[37] and in many situations where the child's future welfare and upbringing are in issue, it certainly is.[38] This makes its migration to many different jurisdictions all the more significant, particularly where the indigenous law and customs do not *prima facie* have such a rule.

3.4.1. Best Interests' Standards: Child's Welfare the Paramount/Primary and First Consideration

Parker[39] points out that rather than just one 'best interests' standard, there are at least *three* 'best interests' standards that can be found in various jurisdictions. By this, Parker seems to be highlighting the different levels of rigour with which the 'best interests' principle seems to be applied in different contexts. The standard that applies in custody, guardianship and contact cases in Western legal systems expects the best interests of the child to be the paramount consideration whenever a decision is made. This is the standard that applies under the UK Children Act 1989, and in relation to Australian law for custody, welfare of, and access to, a child.[40] However, the next, 'weaker' level is that used by the current s.6 of the UK Adoption Act 1976 where in reaching any decision relating to the adoption of a child, a court or adoption agency shall have regard to all the circumstances, first consideration being given to the need to safeguard and promote the welfare of the child throughout his childhood.[41] The third, and least rigorous version is that under Article 3(1) of the United Nations Convention on the Rights of the Child, where 'in all actions concerning children, whether undertaken by public or private social welfare institutions, courts of law, administrative authorities or legislative bodies, the best interests of the child shall be a primary consideration'. The fact remains that this criterion, albeit at different levels, is the yardstick that has been and is increasingly being used to govern decisions relating to children in several jurisdictions around the world, and has even transcended the common law/civil law divide. Given its early origins in English law, it bears testimony to the transmigration of a general legal concept that has embedded itself in these very different environments and jurisdictions.

---

37 See K. Kurki-Suonio, 'Joint Custody as an Interpretation of the Best interests of the Child in Critical and Comparative Perspective' (2000) *International Journal of Law, Policy and the Family* at p. 183.

38 i.e. under the Children Act 1989, see s. 1.

39 See S. Parker, 'The Best Interests of the Child – Principles and Problems' [1992] *International Journal of Law and the Family* 27.

40 i.e. under s. 64(1)(a), Family Law Act 1975 (Australia).

41 The reason for this 'first consideration' principle being used here is usually said to be because there are several competing interests in an adoption case and while the child's welfare must be considered first, there are other competing interests which might mean that the child's interests might not be 'paramount'. The Adoption Act 1976 is due to be repealed and the paramountcy of the child's interests is due to be restored as the guiding principle.

Below, I shall attempt to trace the evolution, indeterminacy and statutory development of the 'best interests' principle in various jurisdictions.

i *France*

As far as civil law countries are concerned, in France, the 'best interests' principle has been a dominant influence in French law since the early nineteenth century. It was called 'a general principle in law' and has long been present in both codified law[42] and case-law, although the original version of the principle was that of best interests of childhood rather than of the child, 'perceived as serving the general interests of society'[43] and this was apparently the impetus for nineteenth century laws to be devised to protect children from exploitation by child labour, apprenticeship contracts, control of wet-nurses and to provide for compulsory schooling.[44] It applies when the court is deciding any question relating to guardianship, custody or the upbringing of a child. In the nineteenth century, the child came to be perceived as an individual, and when the law of 24 July 1889 allowed courts to deprive a father of his paternal power, Rubellin-Devichi argues that this has been 'unanimously interpreted' as a measure to protect the child and not as a form of removing a parent's power.[45] The 'best interests' test is also the basis of educative assistance, so if a child's health, safety or morality are in danger, a judge may be consulted.

ii *Germany*

In Germany, it appears that since the very early 1960s, the psychological dimensions of the 'best interest' standard were being emphasized in child psychiatric and psychological publications. The attitude that the child's perspective should be taken into account was already being expressed when determining custodial arrangements.[46] Kaltenborn and Lempp[47] observe that in the Germany of the 1980s, joint custody and the child's 'attachments' were seen as a 'concrete expression of the best interest standard' in accordance with paragraph 1671 II BGB, (German Civil Code) for custodial arrangements. Custody of young children after parental divorce is regulated in accordance with paragraph 1671 BGB (Civil Code). This paragraph designates the child's

42 The French Civil Code of 1804 enshrined paternal power as a discretionary prerogative entrusted to the father, but commentators like Malaurie and Demolombe took the view that paternal power was to be exercised in the best interests of the child: see P. Malaurie *Cours de Droit Civil, La Famille* (Cujas, Paris, 1989), n. 789; and C. Demolombe, *Cours de Code Napoleon* (2nd edn., Auguste Durand, 1860), t.VI, *de la Puissance Paternelle*, n. 266.

43 See J. Rubellin-Devichi, 'The Best Interests Principle in French Law and Practice' [1992] *International Journal of Law and the Family* at p. 260.

44 Ibid., at p. 261.

45 Ibid., at p. 260.

46 See K. Kaltenborn and R. Lempp, 'The Welfare of the Child in Custody Disputes after Parental Separation or Divorce' [1998] *International Journal of Law, Policy and the Family* 75.

47 Ibid.

welfare as the paramount consideration for determining custodial arrangements after the divorce of the parents.

iii *Sweden*
In Sweden, the 'best interests of the child' is also the guiding principle for the court when deciding on issues of custody and access.[48]

iv *United States*
The 'best interests' test features prominently in cases on child custody in American jurisdictions. Each state has its own laws on child custody. For example, California's Civil Code states that custody is granted 'according to the best interests of the child' (paragraph 4600 Californian Civil Code). Other states have specific criteria listed in their statutes that are similar to the UK Children Act 1989 checklist and give prominence to the ascertainment of the child's wishes and feelings in determining what is best for the child. In view of the English common law heritage, this development may not appear surprising but it needs to be borne in mind that the United States is, in many ways, 'separated by its common language' (George Bernard Shaw) and has moved away from its early English legal origins, and the multiplicity of its influences, which includes French and Spanish 'receptions' of law, customs and language, might well have led to a composite set of criteria to decide child custody cases, which might have been a synthesis of its many influences. However, the 'best interests' test, used both to decide on medical treatment for a child as well child custody cases, has been transplanted primarily, it is submitted, to fulfil a need for a flexible guideline which could be used for a variety of situations.

v *Different Contexts of the Application of the 'Best Interests'/ Welfare Principle in English Family Law*
There are at least four areas in which the welfare principle has been utilised as the guiding principle: i) In the context of the proposed medical treatment of a child, for example in the case of anorexic teenagers[49] or a child in need of a heart transplant,[50] where the court has usually ignored the wishes of the child stating it would not be in the child's best interests to accede to these because of their life-threatening consequences; ii) in relation to the proposed sterilization of a mentally disabled child[51] or adult;[52] iii) in disputes over

48 See A. Saldeen, 'Family Law in Sweden' in C. Hamilton and K, Standley (eds.), *Family Law in Europe* (Butterworths, London, 1995).

49 E.g. in *Re W (A Minor) (Medical Treatment)* [1992] 4 All ER 627.

50 See *Re M (A Minor) (Medical Treatment)* LTL 15/7/99 (Lawtel).

51 As in *Re B (A Minor) (Wardship: Sterilization)* [1988] AC 199.

52 As in *Re F (Mental Patient: Sterilization)* [1990] 2 AC 1.

child custody;[53] and iv) in the ascertainment of a child's wishes, especially for an older child, when a court is seeking to decide on alternative courses of action for that child.[54]

The welfare principle made its first appearance in a statute in 1925 in the English Guardianship of Minors Act of that year. However, it had been used for many years by English judges, and is traceable to at least 1857.[55] The principle evolved through the English courts of equity as a way of protecting the property of children in a legal environment where the predominant ethos was the enforcement of patriarchal authority, rather than to support childcare.[56] Researchers like Susan Maidment argue that the history of the child welfare principle should also be linked to the Women's Movement of the nineteenth and early twentieth centuries and she argues that the 1886 and 1925 Guardianship of Infants Acts were, at least, in part, a means of deflecting the debate about women's rights from the public to the domestic sphere by adopting a more official stance which admitted the importance of women to children.[57] English judges have generally espoused it throughout the twentieth century,[58] and since 1991,[59] it has been enshrined in the Children Act 1989, section 1 of which states: 'when a court determines any question with respect to the upbringing of a child or the administration of a child's property or the application of any income arising from it, the *child's welfare shall be the court's paramount consideration*'. There is a 'welfare checklist' provided in s. 1(3) of the Act which includes the statement that 'a court shall have regard in particular to (a) the ascertainable wishes and feelings of the child concerned (considered in the light of his age and understanding)'.

---

53 There is a checklist under Children Act 1989, s. 1(3) (UK), of factors to be taken into account by the courts when making a decision about a child, bearing in mind that the child's best interests is the 'paramount' consideration (s. 1(1)). The term 'custody' no longer exists in English law but is still used in other jurisdictions, such as the USA.

54 Which is the first factor under the checklist in Children Act 1989, s. 1(3).

55 In 1857, by virtue of the implementation of the Divorce Reform Act of that year, there was a transfer of jurisdiction over divorce from the ecclesiastic to the secular courts, which created a need for guidelines in dealing with dependents of broken marriages which had not previously existed, since divorce had previously been restricted to the very few who could afford to pay for a divorce by a private Act of Parliament.

56 See the study by S. Maidment, *Child Custody and Divorce* (Croom Helm, London, 1984).

57 See Maidment, ibid. *Passim.*

58 Although there are family law cases even in the early 1960s where there is no mention of a child's best interests by even as prescient a judge as Lord Denning; see *Re L* [1962] 1 WLR 886. However, in 1977, Ormrod LJ, in a dispute about children, did assert categorically that the question was not what the 'essential justice of the case requires' but 'what was in the best interests of the children': see *S(BD) v S(D)* [1977] 1 All ER 656. These points are made in M. Freeman, 'Disputing Children' in J. Eekelaar et al. (ed.), *Cross Currents. Family Law and Policy in the United States and England* (New York, Oxford University Press, 2000), at p. 441 et seq.

59 i.e. from 14 October 1991,when the Children Act 1989 came into force in England and Wales.

vi *Australia and New Zealand*

Common law countries such as Australia and New Zealand have adopted some form of the 'best interests' test, which was borrowed from the British settlers who had emigrated there and who, once they were established and presided over the local courts in these territories, began to implement (and thus 'transplant') the case law which they had 'received' from their 'mother country', which was England. The law reports in these countries indicate that this reception and transplantation was then extended to further developments in family law in the context of children.

vii *Sri Lanka*

Asian countries, however, found English law to be a value base when these countries experienced British colonial rule. Countries like Sri Lanka, although a British Colony at the time also experienced the reception of Roman-Dutch law. This law, while accepting the husband's marital power over his wife and marital children, also accepted the overriding responsibility of the courts to act as *parens patriae* in order to safeguard the interests of children. As Goonesekere[60] points out, this meant that the Courts, acting as 'upper Guardian of minors' could deprive the father of any or all of the incidences of parental power and, as was the case in France, this was seen as being done in the best interests of the children. Dutch jurists have claimed that the courts are the guardians of minors so that they could deprive a parent of all or any of the components of parental power if necessary. Goonesekere[61] stresses that '[A] comparison of the received and indigenous legal heritage in South Asia shows that indigenous systems reflected some child-centred concerns that were not found in the early English Common Law and Roman-Dutch law'. The 'best interests test' therefore entered Sri Lankan law through the combined influence of Roman-Dutch law and English law, but certain elements of indigenous customs and the political *mores* of the time were also receptive to this test. However, the 'best interests' concept and its permutations also conflict with certain norms and practices of those indigenous systems that do not reflect contemporary social standards of behaviour. The modern-day Sri Lanka still sees 'sweeping paternal authority, exploitation of girl children, child marriage and infanticide'.[62] Nevertheless, the child's best interests are identified with 'the personal rights of the father or mother and the concept have been developed entirely by the judiciary without any legislative intervention'.[63] Its endurance as a guiding principle in the face of local custom, religious and cultural

[60] S. Goonesekere, 'The Best Interests of the Child: A South Asian Perspective' [1994] *International Journal of Law and the Family* at p. 120.

[61] Ibid., at p. 124.

[62] Ibid.

[63] Ibid., at p. 131.

conditions, is remarkable in itself but also shows the pervading influence a legal transplant can have.

viii *India*

India is a particularly significant example of a jurisdiction where transplantation has taken place in spite of a pluralism of cultures and religions, because of British colonization. The received colonial laws partly coincided and partly differed from the indigenous laws of the region. However, in order to introduce uniformity, the 'best interests' test was adopted and this undermined the cultural and religious pluralism of the region. The 'best interests' concept derives from the colonial legal heritage. The Guardianship and Wards Act 1890 requires a court to determine custody according to the 'welfare' of the minor child.[64] Section 17 of the 1890 Act lists guidelines for determining whether an order is in the best interests of the child. The court must have regard to the age, sex and religion of the child and the character and nearness of kin to the child. As has been pointed out, these guidelines have encouraged courts to 'give weight to factors such as kinship relationship of wider family members, and the "morals" of a parent, particularly of the mother'.[65] This provision has influenced law and policy in the post-independence period and established child-centred standards, despite reflecting the English law of the time, by declaring the superior parental right of the father which would prevail unless he were 'unfit' to be a guardian. Although Indian courts have continued to give preferential status to the father, there are certainly sufficient precedents to support awarding custody to the mother where this has been in the child's best interests.[66] This law still applies to Bangladesh and Pakistan. Today, this uniformity of approach is in danger of itself being weakened by an increase in religious and ethnic awareness. Indeed, there is sweeping paternal authority, exploitation of female children, child marriage and infanticide. Infanticide and child abandonment are regularly reported in the Indian press, and child marriage is one area where notions of the child's welfare have not been invoked to either declare such marriages void or to even modify personal laws. However, all the countries which belong to the South Asian region have ratified the UN Convention on the Rights of the Child, signifying their commitment to upholding this standard in their home jurisdictions.

64 Indian Guardianship and Wards Act 1890, s. 19(b), ss. 7, 17.
65 Goonesekere, above n. 60, at p. 127.
66 Ibid.

3.4.2. Reasons for Receptivity of Legal Transplants

A common rationale can be identified in all these jurisdictions. Over the years, the welfare principle has served a need – an authoritative general legal principle that could be invoked to guide and support a decision on a child's future, which could also resolve a dispute; in some jurisdictions, it was inherited from a colonial past or through a more widespread reception of English law. There were also certain elements in the indigenous cultures of these jurisdictions that were sufficiently receptive to such a criterion. Indeed, as we shall see, it was the pluralism of certain cultures whose religious norms and patriarchy were interpreted as child-centred and encouraged the adoption of the 'best interests' approach.

This is partly explainable by the increasing westernization of countries outside Western Europe, which has also led to principles such as equality of treatment of spouses and greater regard for children's welfare begin to take root in societies where the notion of 'male dominance' has traditionally been the norm, where, for example, property was usually put into the male partners' sole names as the male partners were assumed to be the ones who had the legal and beneficial right to the property and fathers were usually assigned the role of legal guardian for their children, giving them the ultimate power to decide the future of their children.

The remarkable feature of this 'best interests' test, therefore, is the universality of its reception in both common law and civil law countries and its successful transplantation in those jurisdictions, despite different legal traditions and cultures and different methods of reacting to changing social conditions. The 'best interests' test is arguably a 'child of its time' reflecting the *zeitgeist* of an era, an era where an international Convention on the Rights of the Child has now been signed by over 200 countries and in which this principle has become predominant, however each country wishes to interpret and apply it. How is it that despite patriarchal and parental dominance, religious, cultural and economic conditions prevalent in several Asian countries, a child-centred approach has begun to apply globally, at least on paper, or more accurately, in statute? In Sri Lanka, it appears that 'a strong social welfarism which originated with the British colonial administration, linked with egalitarian Buddhist values and a populist political and trade union movement, introduced child-oriented measures in health and education'.[67] Hence, there were several historical, religious and political factors that were receptive to the 'best interests' principle being transplanted and developed by the Sri Lankan judiciary. Even more remarkably, the 'best interests' principle has been used to formulate legal values that are designed to protect female children from exploitation in marriage, 'even where there has been a tradition of social and legal legitimacy for child marriage'.[68] In addition, the 'best interests' approach appears to have filled the need for an authoritative and all-encompassing principle, which typifies the pragmatic aspect of family law.

67 Ibid., at p. 144.
68 Ibid., at p. 135.

3.4.3. The 'Best Interests' Principle in International or Regional Treaties

i *United Nations Convention on the Rights of the Child 1989*

In the United Nations Convention on the Rights of the Child, Article 3(1) states that 'in all actions concerning children, whether undertaken by courts, legislatures, administrative bodies or welfare agencies, 'the best interests of the child shall be a primary consideration'. The treaty gives no further indication of guidance to resolve the indeterminacy of the principle. How did the principle get into this international treaty? Quite simply, the drafters of this Article were so familiar with the extensive usage of the 'best interests' phrase in the domestic legislation of so many countries that there was a consensus that it should be the universal test.[69] Unfortunately, the drafters obviously did not see any need to elaborate on the principle's application, or to supplement it with more specific guidelines on its interpretation.

ii *African Charter on the Rights and Welfare of the Child*

Similarly, the African Charter on the Rights and Welfare of the Child, Article IV thereof, also provides: '[I]n all actions concerning the child undertaken by any person or authority the best interests of the child shall be the primary consideration'. Although the Executive Committee of the United Nations High Commission for Refugees has stated that 'all action taken on behalf of refugees children must be guided by the principle of the best interests of the child as well as by the principle of family unity', again, there is no definitive guidance on criteria for deciding what is in a particular child's 'best interests'.

Given these problems, is it justifiable to assess the relative success of the transferability and integration of such a test in different jurisdictions across the globe? In comparative law terms, it depends on certain prerequisites. In certain jurisdictions it would be fairly straightforward and simple to do so, for example, where there is similarity of cultural, economic, political and social conditions despite apparent differences. A case in point would be Germany and France, very different in so many respects but possessing sufficiently similar characteristics for meaningful comparisons to be made of the provenance of common and transferable concepts. In other jurisdictions, a more detailed understanding of local cultures, religions and political environment may be required before a valid comparative analysis and evaluation of its transferability and integration could be undertaken.[70]

---

[69] See P. Alston, 'The Best Interests Principle: Towards a Reconciliation of Culture and Human Rights' [1992] *International Journal of Law and the Family* 11.

[70] For a fuller discussion of a method of comparison with detailed steps that might be taken, see P. de Cruz, *Comparative Law in a Changing World* (2nd edn., Cavendish, London, 1999), especially pp. 235–239.

4. Theoretical, Cultural and Jurisprudential Perspectives

We began this paper with a remark from Alan Watson. In that same source, he also said that to build up a theory of borrowing seems to be 'an extremely complex matter'.[71] Nevertheless, comparison is vital to ensure progress and to be an active member of the wider community of nations. However, any meaningful comparison has to bear in mind the particular socio-political, socio-economic, religious, and ideological conditions of the host country. Legal transplants can be merely the borrowing of legal rules, but in order to be successfully embedded in a new jurisdiction and to thrive, there has to be a suitably receptive environment. Of course, the mode of thought, methods of law-making (codes as opposed to cases decided by the judiciary), foreign influences and the unique cultural conditions of the host country must be carefully entered into the melting pot of comparison. In this sense, therefore, law is always more than simply rules but constitutes a culture *sui generis* which interacts with local conditions.

5. Conclusion: Back to the Future?

What value may legal transplants have for the future? In the light of the foregoing discussion, the following conclusions mentioned below may be drawn.

Some form of legal transplantation has taken place for centuries, traceable to Roman times and indeed to the observations of Greek philosophers like Cicero and Aristotle. Legal transplantation has also taken place because of wars, colonization, annexation, globalization and other factors such as practical utility, chance and the need for some authoritative legal principle which could be used as a general guideline for practically all cases that required judicial resolution.

The field of family law provides several examples of such transplants, primarily because of the universality and 'transferability' of some of its cornerstone principles. Hence, rules governing legal unions such as the formation of marriage, the grounds for divorce, methods of allocating financial provision after divorce, methods for dealing with marital property upon separation of the spouses and/or divorce, approaches to dealing with disputes over children, and guiding principles such as the 'best interests' test, have all been borrowed in one way or another by many common law and civil law jurisdictions around the world. This so-called test operates at different levels of abstraction and with varying degrees of rigour depending on the context, but the child-centred focus remains the starting point for decisions and disputes relating to children, even in jurisdictions where patriarchal dominance has been the overriding ethos. It has clearly made its mark both domestically and internationally, in national and international legislation. In other family law contexts, commonality of concepts such as the 'no-fault' principle or 'community property' rule have been borrowed from English law or from early sources as remote

[71] A. Watson, 'Aspects of Reception of Law' (1996) 44 *American Journal of Comparative Law* 335.

as the Visigoths! In the case of many of these concepts, the impetus for the adoption of a general principle has frequently been pragmatism, or the need to utilize a principle that can fit a wide range of situations and has both practicality and accessibility.

Various issues have to be resolved in any critical evaluation of the success of these transplants: the comparability and currency of these transplants; the degree of integration into local cultural and religious conditions which has taken place; the influence of 'pragmatism'; the accessibility and the durability of these concepts in social, cultural, religious and political terms – factors which might explain both their appeal, transferability and longevity in various jurisdictions.

If, as Francis Fukuyama[72] has argued, the world is coming closer together, and a global village will one day be a reality, at least in the convergence of certain central ideas and values, then it becomes even more important to perceive not just the differences, but also the similarities between jurisdictions. Reformers then have to decide what are the things that can be adapted, the things that can never change, and perhaps, most of all, the things they would like to change. The task for the law reformer is thus to decide how best to utilize the comparative methodology to recognise and select transferable, flexible ideas with a proven pedigree for dispute resolution to deal with common problems and situations which would adapt to a fast-changing world. The adaptation and integration of legal transplants into various common law and civil jurisdictions may well play a vital role in expediting law reform.

Comparative law in the 21st century remains an extremely useful and challenging enterprise that provides the methodological basis for identifying, interpreting and evaluating legal transplants; it thereby provides a vital step towards a deeper and more informed understanding of the cross-fertilization of ideas across different jurisdictions, legal systems and cultures. In this way, legal comparatists from all over the world may continue to maintain some degree of concordance with the wider community of nations.

[72] See F. Fukuyama, *The End of History and the Last Man* (Routledge, London, 1992).

Chapter 7

CONTINENTAL PRINCIPLES IN ENGLISH PUBLIC LAW

*Robert Thomas**

Much is made in comparative law discourse of the common law/civil law distinction. While it is often accepted that legal outcomes are not wholly dissimilar in these two systems, it is also said that the legal methods employed are so different that the two systems cannot really address each other. In the context of the development of public law, Thomas' chapter indicates that these two assumptions may not be correct. In considering the gradual absorption of the concepts of legitimate expectation and proportionality from civil law via European law into English law, he points out ways in which they raise for English public lawyers constitutional obstacles which do not exist in civilian systems. In particular they create obligations on judges effectively to substitute their policy judgment for that of the administration in some circumstances. However, these obstacles appear to have been overcome, but only because the distinction between substance and procedure in English law is in any event breaking down as judicial review of administrative action expands ineluctably. The study indicates that even in public law, where constitutional differences were thought to preclude practical or applied comparative law, the kinds of problem discovered are not so very different in kind or difficulty from those we find in private law. In any event English public law has been enriched by its European encounters.

[A. Harding and E. Örücü]

1. INTRODUCTION

In 1977 Lord Diplock noted that for the purpose of developing standards against which to review the abuse of power, the European Court of Justice (ECJ) had looked to the more progressive doctrines from the national legal systems.[1] In particular, the

* Lecturer, School of Law, University of Manchester.

1 Hansard HL Deb. vol. 379 col. 993 3 February 1977.

A. Harding and E. Örücü (eds.),
Comparative Law in the 21st Century, 121–136.

ECJ had incorporated two principles, legitimate expectations and proportionality, which had not then been applied by the English courts. Furthermore, Lord Diplock intimated that although these two principles had not yet been accepted as part of English law, he had them 'in mind particularly as doctrines which... [are]... only just beginning to be assimilated in this country'.[2] Since this statement was made the principles of legitimate expectations and proportionality have, on the whole, come to be accepted as part of English public law. English courts are frequently invited to review public decisions on the basis that they infringed the legitimate expectations of the claimant or that they constituted a disproportionate way of achieving the desired objective and that the administrator could have used a less restrictive alternative instead. The development of the two principles has been viewed as a triumph for the subtle and incremental development of the common law by the judges. Indeed, the inclusion of both principles in the most recent edition of *The Judge Over Your Shoulder*, the British Government's guide to judicial review for administrators, is recognition that both principles are now accepted by the administration as established legal norms and that officials need to be aware of their practical implications.[3]

This paper will examine the development of these two principles in English public law by comparing their recognition in the common law with that in the case – law of the ECJ. The integration of the principles will be then be set against the different notions of public law that exist between English and Continental legal systems. The suggestion made in this paper is that English judges have managed to integrate the two principles, despite the differences in legal culture.

2. Legitimate Expectations

The principle of legitimate expectations encapsulates the notion of trust in public administration. The citizen should be able to place confidence in the future activities of the administration in order to enable him to plan his life with both certainty and predictability. Put at its most simple form, the principle means that if a public authority induces an expectation that it intends to act in a certain manner in the future, then it should fulfil such expectations unless the public interest requires otherwise. A citizen who acts in reliance on an expectation concerning the future conduct of the administration deserves a legal remedy if such trust is then disappointed without good reason. This principle would appear to have received its earliest articulation by the German administrative courts that held that actions of the state should be governed by the concept of *Vertrauensschutz*, the protection of trust.[4]

---

2 Hansard HL Deb. vol. 379 col. 994 3 February 1977.

3 *The Judge Over Your Shoulder: A Guide to Judicial Review for UK Government Administrators* (3rd edn., Treasury Solicitor's Office, London, 2000), paras. 2.44–2.48, 2.58–2.69.

4 F. Ossenbühl, 'Vertrauensschutz im Sozialen Rechtsstaat' (1972) 25 *Die Öffentliche Verwaltung* 25.

From German public law the principle was adopted by the ECJ in the 1970s and is not accepted as a general principle of European Union law.[5]

The principle has proved to be of particular importance to individuals when the administration has decided to change policy without adopting transitional provisions to safeguard the position of individuals who have been caught between the two policies. For instance, the changes in Community policy considered necessary to reduce the milk surplus during the 1980s prompted the ECJ to use the principle of legitimate expectation to protect individuals as exemplified in the *Mulder* litigation.[6]

In 1977 the European Commission introduced a scheme to reduce the milk surplus throughout the Community. The key aspect of the policy was to encourage milk farmers to agree to a non-marketing agreement whereby they would receive a premium for ceasing milk production for a five-year period. Many milk producers, including Mulder, agreed to a non-marketing agreement. While this policy may have made some headway in reducing the milk surplus, it was not by itself sufficient. The Commission therefore decided in 1984 to introduce a quota based scheme by which the amount of milk produced in each farm in the Community would be regulated; every milk producer was allocated a production quota that they could not exceed. The level of each quota was to be determined by reference to the quantity of milk produced in a given reference year. The problem for Mulder and for other producers who had agreed not to produce milk for five years was that the quota scheme effectively excluded them from returning to the milk market because they had not produced any milk in the relevant reference year and had therefore been refused a milk quota. The introduction of the milk quota scheme was challenged before the ECJ on the basis that it violated the legitimate expectations on producers in the position of Mulder in that it had failed to introduce transitional provisions in order to safeguard their position. In response it was argued that those producers who had agreed to a non-marketing undertaking could not expect to return to the market on the same terms as which they had left it. While the ECJ accepted this point it, also recognised that producers such as Mulder held a legitimate expectation that their position as milk farmers would not be specifically affected precisely because they had availed themselves of the possibilities offered to them by the Community such as the non-marketing undertaking. The new quota scheme had failed to take account of their special position as producers who had in effect been prevented from returning to the market, specifically because they had been previously encouraged by the Community to suspend their production for a limited period. When Mulder and other producers had originally agreed the non-marketing undertaking, they had not expected to then be subject to subsequent measures, which would then exclude them from the market altogether.

5 J.A. Usher, *General Principles of EC Law* (Longman, London, 1998), ch. 4.

6 Case 120/86, *Mulder v Minister van Laudbouw en Visserij* [1988] ECR 2321.

Given the need for administrative agencies to adapt and modify policy, the principle of legitimate expectations is a useful mechanism to ensure that agencies take into account the special position of individuals, such as Mulder, who have proceeded on the basis of one policy, only then to find their position threatened by a change in policy. How have the English courts applied this principle? The first point to note is that the English courts have felt more comfortable applying the principle in relation to matters of administrative procedure rather than the implementation of policy. For instance, the courts have held that a past practice of consultation between the Government and the representatives of civil service unions over changes in employment conditions created an expectation that future changes would also be preceded by similar consultations.[7] Also, a direct statement by an official that a number of people will have their cases decided on their own individual merits created an expectation that the administration would afford an opportunity for each person to be heard before a decision was made.[8]

While the English courts have developed the principle of legitimate expectations in relation to matters of procedure, they have been reluctant to apply the principle of legitimate expectations to matters of policy as in *Mulder*. This scepticism towards the extension of the principle derives from a fear of the courts becoming entangled in examining questions of policy and the exercise of administrative discretion. The customary approach of the English courts to question of policy has been that they will only step in if the public decision is so unreasonable or irrational that no sensible decision-maker could every have arrived at it, the so-called *Wednesbury* unreasonableness test.[9] As the courts have traditionally refused to deal with issues concerning the implementation of policy, they have drawn a line between legitimate expectations concerning procedural matters and those concerning substantive or policy matters. It has been stressed that there is a crucial constitutional distinction between matters of procedure and substance which impacts upon the role of the judiciary in this regard.[10] The English courts can assess whether it would be fair for a public authority to disappoint an expectation that a certain procedure would be adopted in the decision-making process. However, it has been argued that as regards substantive expectations relating to policy that the only legitimate role for the courts is to examine whether the failure to take account of the individual's expectations was unreasonable in the *Wednesbury* sense.[11] Should the courts examine whether the administrator could in fact have fulfilled the individual's expectations without harming the achievement of the public interest, then they would be undermining the separation of powers and inevitably end up replacing the administrator's assessment of the needs of public policy with their own assessment. The English courts have then

7 *Council of Civil Service Unions v Minister for the Civil Service* [1985] AC 374.

8 *Attorney-General of Hong Kong v Ng Yuen Shiu* [1983] 2 AC 629.

9 *Associated Provincial Picture Houses Ltd v Wednesbury Corporation* [1948] 1 KB 223.

10 Lord Irvine of Lairg QC, 'Judges and Decision-Makers: The Theory and Practice of *Wednesbury* Review' [1996] Public Law 59, 70–72.

11 *R v Secretary of State for Transport ex parte Richmond LBC* [1994] 1 All ER 577.

adopted a positivistic distinction between procedural and substantive expectations that is unparalleled in the case law of the ECJ.

Despite this scepticism of some English judges towards the protection of expectations concerning policy, in recent years a series of judgments has confirmed that English law will protect such expectations. In *Hamble*, a case concerning a change of policy in the transfer of fishing licences, Sedley J. held that the principle of legitimate expectations would extend to matters of substance.[12] The judge reasoned that the real question was one of fairness in public administration. If it is unfair for an administrator to frustrate a legitimate expectation that the individual would be listened to before a decision was made, then it was difficult to understand why it was any the less unfair to frustrate a legitimate expectation that something will or will not be done by the administrator. The distinction between substantive and procedural expectations was unreal because the underlying issue was one of fairness in public administration. Such a doctrine was not in danger of unduly limiting the proper exercise of discretionary power because no one could reasonably expect administrative discretion to be fettered.

To an extent the reasoning of Sedley J. had been intimated some years earlier by the Court of Appeal.[13] However, what is significant for present purposes is that in his reasoning the judge drew extensively from the case law of the ECJ and academic commentary.[14] By explicitly referring to the approach of the ECJ, Sedley J. sought to clarify the scope of the principle in English law and to develop a consistent approach to the principle between European and domestic law. While the reasoning of Sedley J. has confirmed the possibility of protecting expectations concerning policy, a more contentious issue has been the appropriate standard of review that the court should adopt in order to test whether it was permissible for the administration to override the individual's expectations.

The approach toward this question by the ECJ is exemplified by its ruling in the *Spagl* case which concerned the position of milk farmers following the *Mulder* case.[15] After *Mulder* the Commission was faced the issue of how the reconcile two competing aims. First, the milk quota scheme had been found to be contrary to the legitimate expectations of those producers who had made the non-marketing undertaking. A revised scheme would need to take account of the position of such producers. Secondly, the milk surplus still needed to be reduced. If the class of producers refused re-entry to the market were to be each allocated a quota, then this would inevitably increase the overall production of milk. The Commission therefore decided to introduce a revised quota scheme whereby those producers who had made the non-marketing undertaking would receive a quota but that it would only be 60%

---

12 *R v Ministry of Agriculture, Fisheries and Food ex parte Hamble (Offshore) Fisheries* [1995] 2 All ER 714.

13 *R v Secretary of State for the Home Department ex parte Khan* [1985] 1 All ER 40.

14 Sedley J referred to a number of cases decided by the ECJ including *Mulder* and also J. Schwarze, *European Administrative Law* (Sweet and Maxwell, London, 1992).

15 Case C-189/89, *Spagl v Hauptzollamt Rosenheim* [1990] ECR I-4539.

of what they would otherwise have received. It had been estimated that the volume of milk covered by these producers was one million tons and that the largest additional quantity of milk that could be produced would be limited to 600,000 tones in order to achieve the overall aim of the quota scheme that was to reduce the surplus. This revised scheme – the 60% rule – was held by the ECJ to have infringed the legitimate expectations of the milk producers who had voluntarily left the market. The ECJ reasoned that the expectations of such producers had again been specifically affected precisely because they had made the non-marketing undertaking. Instead of placing a burden directly on these producers the Community institutions could have spread the burden more evenly by reducing the milk quota of all producers proportionately by a corresponding amount in order to allow for larger quotas for the producers in the special class.

In effect the ECJ had identified an alternative way of reconciling the competing interests that were at stake. It ruled that the Commission and Council could have implemented a revised scheme in a way which took more account of the expectations of such producers but which did not affect the overall aim of reducing the surplus. The ECJ conceived of its role as supplying the solution to this administrative problem by seeking out the optimal way of reconciling the individual's expectations with the desired policy objective.

If we return to the approach of the English courts it can be seen that the issue of exactly who decides whether an expectation should be overridden or limited has provoked disagreement and uncertainty. In *Hamble* Sedley J. stated that it was for the court to undertake an examination of how the administration had balanced the competing interests. The court was not restricted to inquire whether or not the balance struck was unreasonable; instead the court had to examine whether the reconciliation was fair and proportionate. In effect Sedley J. was stating that English courts should adopt the same approach as the ECJ. The court should seek out the most optimal solution and examine whether the administrator could have achieved its objective by adopting an alternative measure that afforded better protection to the individual's expectations.

However, this proposal soon met with sharp criticism. Lord Irvine described it as 'no more than judicial irredentism'.[16] The approach in *Hamble* was simply an attempt to allocate more power to the court to interfere in the merits of public decision-making that was improper. In a subsequent case the Court of Appeal overruled the *Hamble* decision on this point. To suggest that the court undertake a balancing exercise on matters of substance (as opposed to procedure) was heresy and wrong in principle; only *Wednesbury* unreasonableness provided the correct test.[17]

Despite such strong criticism of the *Hamble* approach, it was subsequently approved by the Court of Appeal in *Coughlan*.[18] In this case the court explained that

[16] Lord Irvine, n. 10 above, at p. 72.

[17] *R v Secretary of State for the Home Department ex parte Hargreaves* [1997] 1 All ER 397.

[18] *R v North and East Devon Health Authority ex parte Coughlan* [2000] 3 All ER 850.

the role of the court in protecting legitimate expectations was not to examine the merits of a proposed policy change. It was for the court to reconcile the continuing need for public authorities to develop policy with the legitimate interests and expectations of individuals who have come to rely on a current policy or practice. This would involve the court examining whether the administrator had struck the fairest balance between the competing interests and in making a decision concerning the implementation of administrative policy.

While the judgment in *Coughlan* has clarified the role of the court in determining the legitimacy of an expectation, it is apparent that some judges feel an acute unease in their position when called upon to examine whether a public authority could have adopted an alternative measure in order to secure better protection for the expectations of affected individuals. For the court to decide how else the administrator could have organised its policy programme in order to take into account such legitimate expectations requires an institutional confidence on the behalf of the court and an ability to handle the same information and data that was before the administrator. While it is apparent that some English judges wish to undertake the balancing of public and private interests, other judges feel distinctly uncomfortable and uncertain over such a role.

3. PROPORTIONALITY

Proportionality is a central principle of French, German, European Union and European Convention law.[19] The principle concerns the relationship between the ends of public action and the means used to attain them. Proportionality gives the court the scope to examine whether the administration could have adopted an alternative way of securing its objectives by suggesting alternative measures that could have utilised. If the administrator could have used an alternative course of action that imposed less of a restriction on the affected private interests, but was equally effective in terms of achieving the desired aim, then the court may invalidate the measure. Examination of the proportionality of a public decision clearly envisages the strongest form of substantive review. The court is able to tell the administration that the measure it adopted was wrong because the court can think of a better measure, one that would also achieve the desired objective but with less cost to private interests.

An example of the application of proportionality can be found in the skimmed-milk case decided by the ECJ.[20] In order to reduce the quantity of skimmed milk in the Community market, the Council decided to increase the use of this product in animal feed. Producers of animal feed would have to use skimmed milk in their products and purchase it as a price that was three times its market value. The ECJ

[19] See generally N. Emiliou, *The Principle of Proportionality in European Law: A Comparative Study* (Kluwer Law International, London, 1996).

[20] Case 114/76, *Bela-Mühle Josef Bergmann KG v Grows-Farm GmbH & Co KG* [1977] ECR 1211.

struck the measure down on the basis that it was both disproportionate and discriminatory. In the opinion of Advocate General Capotorti, the objective of reducing the skimmed-milk surplus could have been more evenly distributed if the burden had been spread throughout the whole of the Community indirectly via the budget. Rather than impose such a heavy burden upon a single class of producer, the Council could have adopted an alternative measure that distributed the burden more evenly.

Proportionality review clearly affords the court a wide degree of discretion in its framework of intervention in public decisions. If applied too strenuously, the court could exercise a *de novo* review of the merits of administrative action. However, in practice the application of proportionality is constrained. The ECJ, for instance, is aware that proportionality has to be applied through a variable framework of review that takes into account the nature of the measure before it and the context in which it was made. When the ECJ is faced with a challenge to an economic policy measure, it has stated that it will only invalidate the measure if it can be shown that it was manifestly disproportionate.[21] However, when the court is faced with a challenge to a measure that affects one of the fundamental freedoms of Community law, such as the free movement of goods, the ECJ has tended to undertake a close scrutiny of the measure to ensure that it does not restrict the freedom any more than is necessary.[22]

A number of reasons may be identified to explain the variable application of proportionality. First, all courts are to varying degrees limited in their knowledge of administrative processes. Questions of economic policy may, for instance, change in scale and complexity over a relatively short period. Such issues are typically polycentric in that their determination will inevitably have both direct and indirect consequences in other areas and for other interests that may not be represented before the court.[23] Modern bureaucracy is simply too complex for many specialist administrators to retain some overall knowledge of the administrative system quite apart from a court whose experience may be far from representative from the mass of cases. Courts should be reluctant to strike down administrative action in a particular area if they are unaware of the possible consequences or lack the necessary knowledge to suggest alternative courses of action. Courts are also aware that in order to achieve a desired objective, some burdens will simply have to borne by someone or some class of persons. For the court to announce that it was willing to review public measures merely on the basis that they impose some burden or cost would be to invite all individuals affected by an administrative measure in some way to launch legal challenges. Courts are also conscious that administrators may need to make quick decisions concerning a fast changing situation or an emergency. While such decisions may not appear to have struck the most proportionate balance in

[21] Case C-331/88, *R v Minister for Agriculture, Fisheries and Food ex parte Fedesa* [1990] ECR I-4023.

[22] See de G. Búrca, 'The Principle of Proportionality and its Application in EC Law' (1993) 13 *Yearbook of European Law* 105, 126–146.

[23] See L.L. Fuller, 'The Forms and Limits of Adjudication' (1978) 92 *Harvard LR* 353, 394.

retrospect, for the court to intervene in such circumstances would impose an unrealistically high burden on administrators and amount to a *de facto* correction of the measures that were taken. Furthermore, policy-making may in reality be far from the classical analysis whereby a problem is identified, an objective determined, and appropriate measures adopted. Policy-making may involve a variety of different objectives and may be constrained by limited time and resources. Far from being the methodical application of a rational administrative logic to a pre-determined factual scenario and the selection of optimal measures, policy-making may be intuitive, incremental and appear to be more like 'muddling through'.[24]

While the ECJ will adopt a variable framework of review through which proportionality is applied, it will be prepared to review a measure, even one involving choices of economic policy if it can be shown that the Community institutions made a manifestly disproportionate decision which could have been avoided. At the same time the ECJ has used proportionality to ensure that restrictions upon the fundamental freedoms are justified by sound policy reasons and do not limit or restrict those interests any more than is strictly necessary.

English judges have in the past proved to be highly sceptical of arguments that they should examine the proportionality of administrative action.[25] They have treated such arguments as invitations to investigate the merits of the decision and therefore as a step beyond the legitimate scope of judicial review. English judges have also stressed that they lack the necessary policy expertise to suggest alternative courses of action to the administrator that would be equally effective in terms of securing the desired objective but would impose less of a burden on affected individuals. Such an inquiry would require the court positively to seek out alternative means of implementing the social purpose for which the measure was adopted. As English judges typically lack the necessary knowledge and expertise in governmental processes, they have been reluctant to embrace proportionality as an independent principle of judicial review. Instead, the judges have proclaimed that proportionality would involve the courts in crossing the jurisdictional boundary between merits and legality. In this way the courts have stressed this positivistic distinction in order to preserve the exercise of their subjective judgment through the doctrine of *Wednesbury* unreasonableness.

However, this received wisdom has been questioned in recent years through a combination of three interrelated pressures. First, the test of *Wednesbury* unreasonableness has come to be perceived as an inadequate form of substantive review.[26] This anti-rationalist test indicative of the common law tradition of artificial

[24] See C. Lindblom, 'The Science of "Muddling Through"' (1959) 19 *Public Administration Review* 79.

[25] See, e.g., *R v Secretary of State for the Home Department ex parte Brind* [1991] 1 AC 969; Lord Hoffmann, 'A Sense of Proportion' (1997) 32 *Irish Jurist* 49 and 'The Influence of the European Principle of Proportionality upon UK Law' in E. Ellis, (ed.), *The Principle of Proportionality in the Laws of Europe* (Hart Publishing, Oxford, 1999), p. 107.

[26] J. Jowell, and A. Lester, 'Beyond *Wednesbury*: Substantive Principles of Administrative Law' [1987] Public Law 368.

reasoning by the judges has been criticised as unrealistic and for not providing any constructive guidance as to how administrators should pursue their goals. Invocation of the 'admonitory circumlocution' of *Wednesbury* unreasonableness breeds the suspicion that the court is in reality dissatisfied with the merits of the decision in question.[27] English judges have increasingly come to recognise that if they consider there to be something wrong in the substantive legality of an administrative measure, then proportionality can provide a more legitimate basis of intervention than the *Wednesbury* test.

Secondly, *Wednesbury* unreasonableness has been subject to criticism on the basis that it provides limited protection for human rights. For human rights to receive adequate protection the courts need to apply proportionality rather than require applicants to surmount the high threshold of irrationality. For example, in the *Smith* case where the Court of Appeal was faced with a challenge to the policy of the Ministry of Defence to prohibit homosexuals from membership of the armed forces, it was stated that although the case raised human rights concerns, the applicants still had to demonstrate that the policy was irrational. While the court would require more by way of justification before it was satisfied that a decision was reasonable, the court also had to exercise caution when reviewing matters with a high policy content. Applying this test the court felt bound to conclude that the policy was not unreasonable.[28] In contrast when the same policy was challenged before the European Court of Human Rights it was struck down on the basis that it constituted a disproportionate infringement of the right to private life.[29] The court found that instead of operating a blanket policy that discriminated against homosexuals, the Ministry of Defence should have adopted a conduct-based code in order to meet concerns relating to the operational effectiveness of the armed services. The British Government had not shown that a conduct based code could not adequately deal with the behavioural issues arising from the presence of homosexuals in the armed services, and therefore the blanket policy was struck down as disproportionate.[30] Furthermore, the European Court of Human Rights also held that the threshold of review adopted by the English judges was placed so high that it effectively excluded any consideration of the question of whether the interference with the applicants' rights was proportionate. This failure of the English courts to examine the legality of the policy beyond the limits of the *Wednesbury* test constituted a violation of the right to an effective remedy for the protection of the Convention rights. Following the coming into force of the Human Rights Act 1998, the courts must now recognise

[27] *R v Chief Constable of Sussex ex parte International Trader's Ferry Ltd.* [1998] 3 WLR 1260, 1289 *per* Lord Cooke of Thorndon.

[28] *R v Ministry of Defence ex parte Smith* [1996] 1 All ER 257.

[29] *Smith and Grady v United Kingdom* (2000) 29 EHRR 493; *Lustig-Prean and Beckett v United Kingdom* (2000) 29 EHRR 548.

[30] Following the judgment of the European Court of Human Rights the Government responded by withdrawing the blanket policy and introducing a code of conduct, see Hansard HC Deb. Vol. 342 col. 287 12 January 2000 (Geoff Hoon MP).

that *Wednesbury* review is largely inapplicable in their new jurisdiction to examine whether or not administrative action infringes a Convention right.

Thirdly, the duty placed on English courts to apply proportionality as a matter of European Union law has prompted them to reconsider whether they should restrict themselves to *Wednesbury* review when faced with a legal challenge on purely domestic law. It has been recognised that while unreasonableness and proportionality are both models of the same concept, the imposition of legal standards on decision-makers necessary to secure the repudiation of arbitrary power, the former is somewhat looser than the latter.[31] If the courts are to insist upon the strict division of legal tests between challenges based on European Union law and those based on domestic law, then an apparent difference in the legal protection for the individual is created which is difficult to justify. Indeed, Lord Slynn has commented that it would be undesirable for the court to maintain such a strict division.[32] In order to provide consistent legal protection for the individual, European Union law has therefore been acting as a pressure on English judges to develop proportionality as a principle in English law and thereby close the gap between domestic and European law.[33]

It may take some time for the precise role of proportionality to become settled, especially in relation to its application outside the Human Rights Act 1998. However, it is apparent that the both internal and external pressures on the English courts point towards the explicit recognition of proportionality as an independent head of English public law.

Despite such pressures for adopting proportionality, the concern remains that English courts lack the institutional ability to operate proportionality review effectively. Proportionality clearly requires the court to engage in assessments of questions of policy and administration. As Sir Thomas Bingham has noted, when a court is examining the proportionality of a measure it is 'perhaps beginning to enter the administrator's mind rather than simply reviewing the process by which the decision was reached'.[34] Speaking in 1987, Lord Scarman noted that the application of proportionality makes sense when there is a blending of judicial and administrative roles as it requires 'administrative skill and experience' in the context of a specific legal dispute.[35] However, Lord Scarman went on to express 'grave doubts ... [whether] ... outside the field of protection of fundamental rights ... the

[31] See the comments of Laws J in *R v Ministry of Agriculture, Fisheries and Food ex parte First City Trading Ltd.* [1997] 1 *Common Market Law Review* 250, 279.

[32] Lord Slynn, 'European Law and the National Judge', in *Butterworths Lectures 1991–1992* (Butterworths, London, 1993), pp. 27–28.

[33] Another example of such 'levelling up' is the availability of interim injunctions against the Crown, see *Factortame Ltd. v Secretary of State for Transport* [1990] 2 AC 85; *R v Secretary of State for Transport ex parte Factortame Ltd. (No 2)* [1991] 1 AC 603; *M v Home Office* [1994] 1 AC 377.

[34] T. Bingham, '"There Is a World Elsewhere": Changing Perspectives on English Law' (1992) 41 *International Comparative Law Quarterly* 513, 524.

[35] Annual Members Conference, *Judicial Review of Administrative Action* (Justice, London, 1987), p. 17.

principle of proportionality could ever be really developed by British judges'.[36] Much of the current attention is focused on the role of proportionality in relation to the Human Rights Act. But whether the courts will apply proportionality as a generally applicable principle of judicial review remains to be seen. The growth in expertise in public law litigation as evidenced by the establishment of the Administrative Court could provide the necessary basis upon which judges evaluate and compare the effectiveness of alternative measures and decide whether the public authority could have chosen an option that had the less impact on the individual. Alternatively, the courts could state that proportionality is not generally applicable, even if it was to be applied through a variable framework of review similar to that adopted by the ECJ. Whatever approach the courts decide to take will be indicative of what they consider to be the limits of their institutional ability to review administrative action.

4. Towards an Explanation

The English courts have made great strides towards the integration of legitimate expectations and proportionality in English public law. Nevertheless it is apparent that this process has, in certain fundamental respects, been problematic. The suggestion made here is that the explanation for the difficulties encountered by the English courts is to be found in the different cultures and traditions of public law between Continental Europe and England. Furthermore, it is suggested that such differences in legal culture have not presented insurmountable difficulties to the effective adoption of the principles in English law.

When considering the integration of legitimate expectations and proportionality into English law, the starting point must be the different legal traditions of public law that exist between Continental Europe and England. Legitimate expectations and proportionality originally developed with Continental systems of public law and particularly within German public law. In such systems law is viewed as an integral aspect of public administration and state action. Public law forms a discrete branch of the legal system concerned with the exercise of public functions. There is a strong concern for the formalization of public power through legal processes. Separate administrative courts staffed by specialist administrative judges exist to resolve disputes between individuals and the state. By contrast, the common law is an informal and customary tradition that places reliance not upon formal principles but on the artificial reason of the common law. For instance, the *Wednesbury* unreasonableness test exemplifies the anti-rationalist culture of the common law. This test is not susceptible to rational explanation or justification but the courts have insisted that it provides the appropriate standard against which to review public decisions. The common law has also traditionally been based on the notion that public authorities are subject to the same laws as private

[36] Ibid.

individuals.[37] The integration of principles such as legitimate expectations and proportionality into this culture has raised difficulties precisely because the common law has traditionally eschewed the existence of distinct legal principles concerning the exercise of public power.

The difference in legal cultures is reinforced when one turns to the differences in political culture, and in particular, the importance of a legal conception of the state for the development of public law. In Continental legal systems such as France and Germany, there exist strong traditions of understanding the state as a distinct entity.[38] The significance of this is that those countries with a state tradition tend to exhibit a consciousness of public institutions, which reflects the strength of legalism and codification within the political culture and reveals itself in formal organisations and their detailed constitutions. As the state is conceived of as a unique legal institution that acts to achieve the public interest, distinct rules and principles are needed to control and regulate its activities. By contrast, if we turn to the United Kingdom it can be seen that it lacks a tradition of understanding political authority in terms of 'the state'. The concept of the state has typically been considered inappropriate to describe the empirical, historical and evolutionary character of government. The significance of the absence of a state tradition in England is apparent. Without a distinct legal concept of the state to which distinct principles could be attached, English law has experienced a proliferation of statute law complemented by the empirical development of the common law from accumulated precedents and the artificial reasoning of the judges. English law therefore has no tradition whereby distinct legal principles are created specifically for the purpose of structuring and regulating the achievement of public objectives.

This difference in cultural orientation is reflected in the institutional forums in which public law issues are handled. In Continental states, the existence of administrative courts has provided the institutional forum in which distinct principles of public law have been developed. The emphasis in each state, of course, differs. In France, the *Conseil d'Etat* is staffed with administrative judges who receive an administrative training. The intermingling of administrative and judicial functions is perceived to be beneficial as it allows the administrative judge to keep in contact with the realities of public administration.[39] In Germany, the primary focus of public law has been the emphasis on the control of administrative discretion and the protection of the rights guaranteed under the basic law. By contrast, the development of an administrative jurisdiction in England has been achieved from within the common law. One implication of this is that the English judges still tend to consider law as separate from administration.

[37] See A.V. Dicey, *An Introduction to the Study of the Law of the Constitution* (10th edn. by E.C.S. Wade, Macmillan, London, 1959), pp. 193–195.

[38] See generally K.H.F. Dyson, *The State Tradition in Western Europe: A Study of an Idea and Institution* (Martin Robertson, Oxford, 1980).

[39] See R. Odent, quoted in L.N. Brown, and J. Bell, *French Administrative Law* (Clarendon Press, 1998, Oxford), p. 288.

A further point may be made here. While the common law is a customary and rhetorical tradition dependent on the practical experience of the judges, it has come to be understood through the language of analytical positivism. This change, initiated by Dicey, has permeated the whole of English public law and is most noticeable in the insistence on the conflicting ideas of Parliamentary sovereignty and the Rule of Law in providing the foundations of the British constitution. In relation to legitimate expectations and proportionality it can be noted that barriers have been erected to the integration of the principles by maintaining that fundamental positivistic distinctions such as procedure and substance, legality and merits and administration and adjudication prevent the integration of the principles into English law.

The basic argument developed here is that the difficulties faced by the English courts when handling the principles of legitimate expectations and proportionality stem from the different legal traditions concerning the role of law in government. In Continental states public law has been constructed as a distinct set of rules relating to the exercise of public functions. Separate administrative courts have provided the institutional forums in which distinct principles have been developed and applied by specialist administrative judges. By contrast, the common law has been based on the tradition that there is no separate system of public law. Instead, it is for the ordinary courts to enforce the intention of Parliament subject to certain common law presumptions that public authorities will act fairly and reasonably. The common law tradition has therefore inhibited the development of special public law principles.

However, despite the different understanding of public law, it is clear that English law has, to a large extent, proved itself capable of adopting legitimate expectations and proportionality as principles that control and structure the exercise of public functions. How have the courts been able to overcome the difficulties associated with these principles? The explanation for the success of the English courts in grafting the principles into English law, I would suggest, is to be found in the desire of the courts to respond to the nature of the modern administrative state and a willingness to look elsewhere for solutions to similar problems.

The growth in the scale and complexity of the modern administrative state has presented a challenge to the legal systems of most modernized countries and in particular the need to control the exercise of discretionary powers exercised by public administrators. In England the administrative state has developed through the twin concepts of executive discretion and ministerial accountability. So long as Ministers were accountable to Parliament, then a balanced constitution could be maintained. However, the demands placed on government by the electorate have required the establishment of a vast and complex bureaucratic structure composed of officials, who in reality exercise the wide discretionary powers conferred on Ministers. With the extension of state activities it has largely come to be accepted that accountability through a Parliament sharply divided on party political lines is an inadequate mechanism for securing the fair exercise of administrative power. Indeed legislative accountability may be ineffective because the administration has now taken on an autonomy of its own and may in practice be far from the control of its political leaders. The response of the courts to the growth in bureaucratic power has been to fashion distinct public law principles to regulate the exercise of public power. As Lord Mustill has put it, 'to avoid a vacuum in which the citizen would be left without protection against a misuse of executive powers, the courts have had no option but to occupy the dead ground in a manner, and in areas of public life, which could not have been foreseen 30 years ago'.[40] This development has been reflected in the growing specialisation and expertise in public law litigation in the Crown Office List, recently renamed the Administrative Court.[41] Indeed the result of such changes has turned Dicey's view, that the existence of administrative courts undermined the rule of law, on its head. Now it is accepted that bureaucratic power can only be controlled and regulated by channelling cases to a specialist administrative jurisdiction that applies distinctive public law principles.

An essential part of this whole process has been the willingness of the English courts to look elsewhere for guidance. In order to give themselves the conceptual tools to protect the individual in their dealings with the administration, the courts have looked to European law and the progressive principles selected by the ECJ. In particular, it would appear that Lord Diplock, who exercised an important influence on the development of public law, was in favour of the courts adopting principles from European law both in order to develop English law and to show that it would provide protection of the individual equivalent to that in other legal systems.[42] With the growth in public law litigation and the growing influence of European Union law, the willingness to learn from elsewhere has demonstrated an ability of English judges to set aside deep rooted common law concerns over the validity of using doctrines developed in Continental systems of public law. The comment of Lord Goff, that English law 'should welcome rather than reject these new ideas', exemplifies the change in judicial attitude.[43]

5. Conclusion

No attempt will be made to summarize the entirety of the above arguments. Instead, some comments will be made on the role of comparative law. Public law has traditionally been viewed as an area of law which least lends itself towards comparison. As the activities of the state have been primarily located at the national level, therefore the law applicable to such activities was primarily a national

---

40 *R v Secretary of State for the Home Department ex parte Fire Brigades Union* [1995] 2 All ER 244, 268.

41 *Review of the Crown Office List: A Report to the Lord Chancellor* (The Bowman Report), London: Lord Chancellor's Department, March 2000; Practice Direction: Administrative Court [2000] 1 WLR 1654.

42 See R. Thomas, *Legitimate Expectations and Proportionality in Administrative Law* (Hart Publishing, Oxford, 2000), pp. 25–33.

43 Lord Goff, 'The Future of the Common Law' (1997) 46 *International Comparative Law Quarterly* 745, 747.

phenomenon. It is now apparent that such a focus can no longer provide an adequate form of inquiry for comparative law. Governance is no longer located solely at the national level. The effective application of European Union law requires national courts to engage positively with new principles and concepts. It has required the English courts to handle comparative law materials in order to understand the novel tasks that they are required to perform. In other words, the growth in public power exercised at the European level has motivated an exchange in legal principles and an interest in comparative public law.

Furthermore, while the institutional setting of public law is located at the national level, it will increasingly look elsewhere for solutions to problems that exist within the national legal system. As John Bell suggests in his paper, public law concerns the organisation, legitimation and control of government, and involves realising sets of principles through organisational structures and procedures which constitute the environment in which common functions are implemented.[44] Countries with complex and powerful bureaucratic structures recognise that functions such as the protection of an individual's expectations in government and ensuring that public action is proportionate are important objectives that ensure that the individual is treated fairly. Comparative law has not in itself motivated the integration of the principles of legitimate expectations and proportionality into English law. However, it has proved to be a highly useful tool to select the legal principles suited to the fulfilment of such common functions by the courts.

[44] See Bell's Chapter in this volume.

Chapter 8

ON SUCCESSFUL LEGAL TRANSPLANTS IN A FUTURE *IUS COMMUNE EUROPAEUM*

*Jan Smits**

The success of a transplant is measured by what it achieves, and this for Smits is uniformity. For Smits, the aim is to establish a new private law for Europe and the main role for comparative law is in the supplying of an answer as to how to establish this, which he sees as the main methodological question of European private law. This piece makes the claim that uniformity can be achieved in an organic bottom-up way by the competition of legal rules, transplanting rules through a 'market of legal culture', for which national courts should be responsible. According to Smits success is in organic growth. He challenges those who claim that legal transplants do not lead to uniformity, and assesses the internal and external factors influencing legal transplants. Like Nelken and Örücü, and also Foster and de Cruz, Smits discusses, compares and contrasts the views of Watson, Legrand and Teubner. The author claims that the use of legal transplants is the most promising way to build a European ius commune *if national courts are allowed to choose the most suitable rules. However, diversity of law will remain in Europe and any centralist imposition will strangle diversity. This piece also paves the way for van Gerven's contribution.*

Smits is not so much interested in the process of, or the reason for, transplants, as in their results. He claims that past transplants have been successful and have led to uniform law and the future European ius commune *will largely use legal transplants, which will again lead to uniform law. The contribution presents a programmatic approach to European private law and empirical evidence, through the areas of contract and property (trust), of successful legal transplants. Unlike Nelken and Örücü above, Smits' criterion for assessing the success of a transplant is the creation of some degree of uniformity between the laws of the importing and exporting countries. Mixed legal systems, for Smits, present the answer, a 'mix of national mentality and European uniformity'.*

He tests his ideas through commercial contract law and property law in Europe because transplants were successful, and no uniformity is seen in property law because there is a lack of successful legal transplants in this field. The acceptance of trust-like arrangements in civil law countries in recent years is, according to Smits, one result of

---

* Professor of European Private Law at Maastricht University.

A. Harding and E. Örücü (eds.),
Comparative Law in the 21st Century, 137–154.

the increasing globalization of world trade. This is also shown as an unsuccessful transplant, since the institution of the trust changed while it moved into the civil law countries from its common law environment. Here the reader might also like to consider the contribution by Rafenne. According to Smits, what is important, then, is the environment of the transplanted rule, international or national. He looks at South Africa and suggests that the transplanted law should be seen by the legal elite as suitable to the environment of the importing country.

The environment into which the foreign legal rule is imported is the external factor. The internal factors are approached through the concept of 'path dependence'. The socio-economic environment (that is, the external factor) may favour legal transplants, but the type of rules (that is, the internal factor) may prevent the uniform law from materializing and vice versa.

In this contribution legal transplantation is seen as the most promising way of establishing a European ius commune *and the test of success is seen as uniformity, any tension to be resolved by national courts. We must accept that diversity will remain. But is this indeed 'just as good as uniformity'?*

[A. Harding and E. Örücü]

1. INTRODUCTION

In the now very alive discipline of European private law, one of the main methodological questions is *how* to establish a common law for Europe. Given the desirability of a uniform private law, various methods have been proposed as to its realisation in a European context.[1] In this paper, it is investigated to what extent the specific method of using legal transplants (or, the borrowing of law) may contribute to the emergence of this *ius commune Europaeum*. In doing so, I will focus not so much on *the way* legal transplants take place[2] or *why* these take place,[3] but on *what they lead to*. This seems to be an appropriate subject for a contribution to a volume devoted to aspects of 'Comparative Law in the 21st Century' for two different reasons. First of all, the success of legal transplants has been huge in the past and if we must believe Alan Watson, it is even so that 'most changes in most systems are the result of borrowing'.[4] If this is true, the development of European *ius commune* in

[1] For an overview of the debate cf. J. Smits, *Europees Privaatrecht in Wording*, (Intersentia, Antwerpen-Apeldoorn-Oxford, 1999), 51 et seq., and C.U. Schmid, 'The Emergence of a Transnational Legal Science in European Private Law' (1999) 10 *Oxford Journal of Legal Studies* 673.

[2] Cf. A. Watson, *Legal Transplants* (2nd. edn., The University of Georgia Press, Athens, Georgia, 1993), 30: 'imposed reception, solicited imposition, penetration, infiltration . . . '.

[3] This question is addressed by U. Mattei, 'Efficiency in Legal Transplants' (1994) 14 *International Review of Law and Economics* 3.

[4] Watson, n. 2 above, p. 95.

the near future could, to a large extent, also be directed by the use of legal transplants. Secondly, despite the presence of so much historical evidence for legal transplants in the past, a recent discussion of a more theoretical nature has been launched as to the extent to which legal transplants really *did* lead to uniform law in the past and *will* lead to uniform law in the future. The main argument against transplants is that they tend to lead to a disintegration of national legal systems and not to any uniformity at all. According to me, this argument overlooks some essential features of the whole European enterprise and I will elaborate on this by looking at, *inter alia*, the mixed legal systems. I thus hope to contribute to the development of theory in the field of transfer of legal ideas and institutions, in particular to the assessment of factors involved in the transferability of law.

This paper is a mixture of a programmatic contention about the future of European private law and a presentation of empirical evidence of what legal transplants lead to. In paragraph 2, it is explained what we should consider to be a legal transplant and why transplants are important for the development of European legal uniformity. In paragraph 3, some objections against the use of legal transplants for this purpose are discussed. Paragraph 4 and 5 provide the reader with some evidence of how uniformity through legal transplants may come about and try to assess the factors that favour or hamper this process. Finally, paragraph 6 offers a general outlook on the future of European *ius commune* through legal transplants, mixing the programme and the findings of the other paragraphs.

2. IUS COMMUNE AND LEGAL TRANSPLANTS: TOWARD A MIX OF NATIONAL MENTALITY AND EUROPEAN UNIFORMITY

At the outset, we need to have some idea of what is meant with legal borrowing or legal transplanting. In a very broad definition of these concepts, one can indeed[5] maintain that practically all legal change is the result of the transplanting of law from one legal system to another. The inspiration Justinian drew from the classical Roman law sources, the reception of Roman law in later times, the making of the *Code Civil* out of different types of materials (custom, scholarly literature, case law, *etc.*), the enactment of the *Code Civil* in other countries than France, the interaction of English law and Scots law in the United Kingdom,[6] even the very development of a legal institution on the basis of arguments derived from other legal sources than the legal system itself, all these are examples of borrowing legal rules or ideas from a different time period or a different legal system. This borrowing could take place by both the legislature and the courts and could be imposed from the above because of reasons of political power (as in the case of the enactment of a Civil Code) or be

[5] As Alan Watson does. See, e.g., ibid.; A. Watson 'Aspects of Reception of Law' (1996) 44 *American Journal of Comparative Law* 335.

[6] Cf. recently R. Evans-Jones, 'Roman Law in Scotland and England and the Development of one Law for Britain' (1999) 115 *Law Quarterly Review 1999* 605.

much more driven by a need to find better law than one has in one's own legal system. Some examples of legal borrowing from more recent times include the inspiration that Eastern European countries drew from American and Western European sources in transforming their economies,[7] and the use of Anglo-American legal institutions (like trust, lease, franchising, swaps and netting) in the European continent.[8]

To use such a broad definition of legal borrowing is, however, not very insightful. Watson deliberately abstains from elaborating a classification of different types of borrowing, as he abstains from developing any theory of legal borrowing what so ever.[9] To him, as a legal historian, the providing of real evidence of legal transplants that took place in the past, is enough. Any need to critically assess the transplants from the perspective of what they led to or why they took place, can then be absent. However, as this paper is concerned with the extent to which legal transplants may be of use for the emergence of a *ius commune*, there is a need for some criterion to critically evaluate these transplants. In the following, I simply assess legal transplants as successful if they create some degree of uniformity between the laws of the importing and the exporting country, and as unsuccessful if they do not lead to any uniformity at all or, even worse, pose a threat to the consistency of the importing system. In the latter case, the system would even be worse off than it was before the transplant.

As I have defended before,[10] the use of legal transplants in this narrow sense is one of the most promising ways of establishing a uniform private law in Europe. Uniformity of law in most of the cases cannot be created by just imposing rules through public policy considerations. Private law is – at least partly that is – *more* than rules and may, in this respect and in some cases, be considered as (legal) *culture*;[11] in those cases, public policy consequently cannot have a serious influence on private law, and uniformity thus will not follow automatically from the famous

---

[7] On which E. Örücü, *Critical Comparative Law: Considering Paradoxes for Legal Systems in Transition* (Kluwer, Deventer, 1999) 118 et seq.; G. Ajani, 'By Chance and Prestige: Legal Transplants in Russia and Eastern Europe' (1995) 43 *American Journal of Comparative Law* 93.

[8] On which W. Wiegand, 'The Reception of American Law in Europe' (1991) 39 *American Journal of Comparative Law* 229; U. Mattei, 'Why the Wind Changed: Intellectual Leadership in Western Law' (1994) 42 *American Journal of Comparative Law* 195.

[9] Watson, n. 2 above, pp. 13, 30; cf. A. Watson, *The Evolution of Law* (Blackwell, Oxford, 1985), ix. Cf. however W. Ewald, 'Comparative Jurisprudence (II): The Logic of Legal Transplants' (1995) 43 *American Journal of Comparative Law* 489, 504.

[10] J.M. Smits, *The Good Samaritan in European Private Law; on the Perils of Principles without a Programme and a Programme for the Future* (Kluwer, Deventer, 2000); Smits, n. 1 above, 19 et seq.; J.M. Smits, 'A European Private Law as a Mixed Legal System' (1998) 5 *Maastricht Journal of European and Comparative Law* 328; J.M. Smits, 'How to Take the Road Untravelled? European Private Law in the Making' (1999) 6 *Maastricht Journal of European and Comparative Law* 25.

[11] For the most outspoken defense of this thesis see P. Legrand, *Le Droit Comparé* (PUF, Paris, 1999).

'berichtigende Worte des Gesetzgebers'.[12] The two different claims that are immanent in this presupposition still need some elaboration.

The first claim is that the mere drafting and enacting of Principles of European Private Law[13] or the mere searching for a common core[14] does not in itself lead to uniformity. Private law is to a certain extent harmonization-resistant, even when confronted with centrally imposed rules. To which extent this is the case (is it true for all areas of private law and for all types of legal rules?), is a question that may be answered by looking at legal transplants and the uniformity already created by these. The contention of Pierre Legrand that 'legal systems (. . .) have not been converging, are not converging and will not be converging'[15] appears to be too radical. His idea of law as *entirely* embedded in the society and culture of a specific country has not been recognised as insightful.[16] Moreover, many comparative lawyers would not identify Legrand's idea of comparative law as falling within the limits of that discipline at all. Lawson, for example, once stated that comparative law in itself 'is bound to be superficial' and linking law to other societal and cultural phenomena of a specific country would be impossible.[17] But Legrand is right, up to a certain point: there are areas of law where the morality of the civil law and the common law are indeed too divergent to reach uniformity. The problem of how to establish where this is precisely the case, leads me to the second claim.

The second claim I want to make is that a greater extent of legal uniformity than exists right now *is* possible, but this should come about, to a large extent, in an *organic* way, by proceeding bottom-up instead of top-down. The best way of attaining this would be through the competition of legal rules.[18] In transplanting legal rules from one country to another on a 'market of legal culture',[19] the best European legal rule may survive. This does not automatically imply that *any* rule glorifies or that uniformity does indeed evolve in the end: in some instances, diversity of law may be just as good as uniformity, as long as there is this free movement of

---

12 J. Kirchmann, *Die Wertlosigkeit der Jurisprudenz als Wissenschaft* (Manutius Verlag, Berlin, 1848).

13 Like O. Lando and H. Beale (eds.) *Principles of European Contract Law, Parts I and II Combined and Revised* (Kluwer Law International, The Hague, 2000); D.J. Hayton, S.C.J.J. Kortmann and H.L.E. Verhagen (eds.), *Principles of European Trust Law* (Kluwer, The Hague, 1999).

14 On common core projects such as the Trento Project see M. Bussani and U. Mattei, 'The Common Core Approach to European Private Law' [1997–1998] *Columbia Journal of European Law* 339.

15 P. Legrand, 'European Legal Systems are not Converging' (1996) 45 *International and Comparative Law Quarterly* 52, 61–62.

16 Although Legrand has some illustrious predecessors. I refer to F.C. Von Savigny's idea of the *Volksgeist* and of civil law as characteristic for the people of a country: F.C. Von Savigny, *Vom Beruf unsrer Zeit für Gesetzgebung und Rechtswissenschaft* (reprint, Olm, Hildesheim, 1814/1967); and to Lord Cooper of Culross, 'The Scottish Legal Tradition' in *Selected Papers*, (Edinburgh, 1957), p. 199 (cited in Watson (1993), n. 2 above, p. 22: 'law is the reflection of the spirit of a people, and so long as the Scots are conscious that they are a people, they must preserve their law'.

17 F.H. Lawson, 'The Field of Comparative Law' (1949) LXI *Juridical Review* 16.

18 Smits (1998), n. 10 above, p. 328.

19 Cf. U. Mattei, 'Efficiency in Legal Transplants: An Essay in Comparative Law and Economics' (1994) 14 *International Review of Law and Economics* 3.

legal rules, at least creating the *possibility* of legal change toward uniformity. Although several different legal actors may play a role in this borrowing process, pride of place should, in my opinion, be given to the national courts. These can be considered to be best able to judge which areas of the law are so invaded with national morality that it is impossible to reach uniformity in these areas.[20] As long as national courts do not consider it appropriate to deviate from their national rules – having taken into account the different solutions in other countries – there is obviously some national mentality that stands in the way of borrowing another rule. What will result in the end is thus not just uniformity through the imposing of principles or no uniformity at all because of differing national mentalities, but a mix of the two: as much uniformity as is possible, given the differing mentalities, to be judged by the national courts.

This theory also explains the fact why this paper is mainly about the *voluntary* borrowing of law by national courts in Europe. I feel this is appropriate since an imposed transplant (for example, in the case of legislation of an exporting country imposed upon an importing country) is fundamentally different from a voluntary one. The true essence of an imposed transplant is that its success (the extent to which it creates uniformity) is artificially created by the exporting country through the use of mere force. The example of the French Civil Code is paradigmatic: its success can only be understood from the point of view of political power. Uniformity of private law in Europe can, in my view, however, only be successful if it comes about in an *organic* way, in a bottom up approach in which the courts play a primordial role. Examples of what I typically see as legal borrowing in Europe include the transfer of the doctrine of offer and acceptance from the European continent to English law in the nineteenth century,[21] the incorporation of the German *Verwirkung* doctrine in Spanish law in the 1980s[22] and the incorporation of the French distinction between *obligations de moyen* and *obligations de résultat* in Belgian and Dutch case law.[23]

It is this programmatic assertion that is taken as a starting point for the rest of this paper. First, we must deal with the argument of those who contest that legal transplants lead to uniformity of law at all (paragraph 3). Then, it is apt to discover the factors that influence legal transplants taking place in a successful way. If these factors are assessed well, we are able to explain why there is already uniformity in some areas of the law, divergence in others. I believe that two different sorts of factors are at work here. First, there are *external* factors related to the environment in which the transplanted legal rules have to try to survive (paragraph 4). Second,

---

20 Smits (2000), n. 10 above, p. 45.

21 See A.W.B. Simpson, 'Innovation in Nineteenth Century Contract Law' (1975) 91 *Law Quarterly Review* 247; and more generally, M. Reimann (ed.), *The Reception of Continental Ideas in the Common Law World 1820–1920* (Duncker and Humblot, Berlin, 1993).

22 See A. Vaquer, 'Importing Foreign Doctrines: Yet Another Approach to the Unification of European Private Law? Incorporation of the *Verwirkung* Doctrine into Spanish Case Law' (2000) 8 *Zeitschrift für Europäisches Privatrecht* 301.

23 Cf. Smits, n. 10 above, p. 93.

there are also *internal* factors, concerned with the transplanted rules themselves (paragraph 5).

3. Legal Borrowing and the Consistency of a Legal System

Any theory that tries to assess the success of legal transplants should take into account the extent to which law is tied to its social, economic and cultural environment.[24] It is after all this environment that is decisive for the extent to which uniformity will arise. If the legal rule that is transplanted has a wholly different meaning within its new environment, only a terminological and not a true uniformity arises. Two opposite views as to the interaction of a transplanted rule and its environment have actually been held in the scholarly literature.

The one extreme view we have seen already is held by Alan Watson: legal evolution (including the borrowing from other legal systems) takes place more or less insulated from the environment the legal rules are part of. That Watson regards legal transplants as having been so successful in the past is of course caused by this view of law, most of the time *not* being the mirror of society: if legal rules can be transported from society to society and do not change under pressure of their environment, law is relatively autonomous and not related to some *Volksgeist* or *mentalité*. Borrowing law could then never infringe upon a national system's consistency or legal culture. This view is however not evidenced by all legal transplants. Sometimes, there is indeed uniformity coming about, but more often, the legal rule that is borrowed from another country obtains a whole new meaning within the importing legal system.[25] This is the reason why some authors have disputed the usefulness of speaking of a transplant, a word that seems to imply that the transferred rule remains identical, playing the same role in its new environment.[26]

The most outspoken dissenter in this respect is Pierre Legrand. He is at the other end of the spectrum, emphasising that all legal rules are embedded in a national environment.[27] While Watson says that 'the recipient system does not require any real knowledge of the social, economic, geographical and political context of the origin and growth of the original rule',[28] Legrand emphasises that legal transplants are actually impossible because of the always differing meaning a rule begets in another legal system. The mere fact that the rule is imported into that other system

[24] Cf. E. Örücü, 'Mixed and Mixing Systems: a Conceptual Search' in E. Örücü, E. Attwool and S. Coyle (eds.), *Studies in Legal Systems: Mixed and Mixing* (Kluwer, The Hague, 1996), p. 335 (and Table II, appearing on p. 343).

[25] Think of the very different interpretation of art. 1384 *Code Civil* in Dutch law (art. 1402 *Burgerlijk Wetboek*).

[26] G. Teubner, 'Legal Irritants: Good Faith in British Law or How Unifying Law Ends Up in New Divergences' (1998) 61 *Modern Law Review* 11.

[27] P. Legrand, 'The Impossibility of Legal Transplants' (1997) 4 *Maastricht Journal of European and Comparative Law* 111.

[28] A. Watson, 'Legal Transplants and Law Reform' (1976) 92 *Law Quarterly Review* 79, 81.

makes it a different rule: its local meaning is an inevitable part of that rule.[29] For this reason, rules cannot travel from one system to another.

The point Legrand is making is important: from a standpoint of what legal transplants lead to, regard should be had to both the exporting and the importing environment. Without looking at the way the transplant is received in the importing country, one cannot judge to what extent the transplant has been successful. Here, I will not argue that a lot of the criticism of Legrand against Watson's argument stems from a different understanding of what a legal transplant actually is (Watson not being concerned with its effect, Legrand on the other hand emphasising it).[30] Legrand's argument, should however be supplemented in two other ways. In the first place, Legrand – who does not deny that legal borrowing in Watson's sense has taken place extensively – does not show what the fact of borrowing leads to, other than that it does *not* lead to uniform law. Does it, for example, lead to inconsistencies within the importing system, or is there a smooth adaptation of the imported rule? Secondly, Legrand seems to go too far in asserting that *the whole* of the law is tied to *the whole* of society ('a social totality').[31] Why could it not be that the environment in which a national rule is operating is identical to the environment in another country? This refers to a point recently made by Gunther Teubner.

Teubner, standing midway between Watson's insulation thesis and Legrand's contextual thesis, maintains with Legrand that to speak of a legal transplant is in itself misleading.[32] To speak of a transplant suggests that the transferred rule or institution 'will remain identical with itself playing its old role in the new organism' (i.e. the legal system into which it is imported). Teubner would then rather not speak of a legal transplant, but of a legal 'irritant': if some rule is imported into another legal system, what happens is that a series of new and unexpected events takes place within that system. The 'binding arrangements' of the law are irritated, having the result that not only the rules of the importing legal system have to be reconstructed, but also the alien element itself is altered.[33] The introduction of good faith in English contract law as a result of the implementation of the European Directive on Unfair Terms in Consumer Contracts[34] does, for example, not mean that after a careful implantation and cultivation in its new environment, good faith – or the English legal system – will still be the same as they were *before* the implantation. Both English contract law *and* good faith are irritated until evolution leads to a new 'binding arrangement'. In maintaining this thesis, Teubner stresses that law does not operate in a vacuum, but is closely connected with its socio-economic environment. The delicate equilibrium within the legal system as reflecting that environment is

29 Legrand, n. 27 above, p. 117.
30 Cf. A. Watson, *Legal Transplants Again*, Ius Commune Lectures on European Private Law (Research School Ius Commune, Maastricht, 2000).
31 Legrand, n. 27 above, p. 122.
32 Teubner, n. 26 above, p. 11.
33 Teubner, n. 26 above, p. 12.
34 Directive 93/13.

perturbed by the transplant, leading to new divergences. Teubner thus offers what is missing in Legrand's thesis: a notion of what legal transplants do cause in their new environment.

But the extent to which there is irritation of the national legal system may differ – and here it is that Teubner takes side with Watson. Building upon the work of Kahn-Freund,[35] Teubner states that not all legal institutions are culturally embedded; some are insulated from culture and society. In the latter case, legal institutions are more or less 'mechanical' and transfer is easier than in the former case, where law is much more 'organic' and transfer more difficult.[36] Teubner thus sees law as tied to 'social fragments': the degree to which a legal institution is tied to a social system (be it a political, economic, cultural, scientific or technological one) is decisive for the success of transplanting that institution. As the English production regime, characterised by an 'unmediated interplay of market forces[37] and external governmental regulation, is for example, quite different from the German one, in which good faith came up as a way of enforcing legal cooperation duties in an economy, allowing a high degree of autonomy to the different economic agents, the transplanting of good faith to English law cannot be expected to be successful.

To what extent is Teubner right in answering the two questions I just raised? The great benefit of his analysis is that it is a *differentiated* one: not the entire legal system is tied to the economic, social and cultural environment of a country, but parts of it are less 'national'. Although Teubner does not pay much attention to the case where law in different legal systems is tied to a similar 'social fragment' (being mainly concerned with cases where this is *not* so), it follows from his analysis that this could very well be the case. Any 'irritation' of the importing system could not occur. The very important question of where these identical social fragments are now present, may show us where uniformity through legal transplants may be reached. Moreover, it should be noted that Teubner's argument against legal transplants is based upon the example of a European Directive, which is essentially a form of law that is imposed upon the European member states.[38] As far as voluntary borrowing by national courts is concerned, it is – at least in the theory I just proposed – impossible that a court decides to borrow a foreign legal rule that it considers inconsistent with its own legal system or socio-economic environment.

It is thus, very well possible that legal transplants have led to uniformity in the past and will lead to uniformity in the future, as long as there is a similar environment in both the exporting and the importing country. In that case, the emergence of uniformity among several legal systems does not create inconsistencies in the present national systems. In the next paragraph, I hope to show how

[35] O. Kahn-Freund, 'On Uses and Misuses of Comparative Law' in O. Kahn-Freund, *Selected Writings* (Stevens, London, 1978).

[36] Teubner, n. 26 above, p. 17.

[37] Teubner, n. 26 above, p. 26.

[38] On the character of European Directives as non-voluntary borrowing see N. Burrows, 'European Community: the Mega Mix' in Örücü et al., n. 24 above, p. 309.

environmental factors are decisive for the success of legal transplants by using some examples from legal practice.

4. The Success of Legal Transplants as Explained by their Environment

Prestige or quality of the exported legal rules,[39] efficiency,[40] the role of the national elite,[41] chance,[42] practical utility,[43] cultural forces[44] and imposition[45] have been mentioned as factors involved in the taking place of legal transplants.[46] These very diverse factors may be regarded as explaining *why* legal transplants take place and not so much *whether* the transplants have been successful. To judge what factors are really involved in the successful transferring of law, other criteria should be used. It follows from the above that these criteria should first of all be related to the environment into which the foreign legal rule is imported. If the imported rule would have the same effect it has in the 'mother country', that rule would be neutral to considerations of national morality. And – most important – this may be so because *other factors* than national morality had a formative influence on the coming into being of these rules. Here, I will elaborate this idea by looking at both legal transplants in Europe itself and at transplants that have taken place within the mixed jurisdiction of South Africa. In doing so, it is taken as a starting point that where there is uniformity right now, this is caused by successful legal transplants,[47] be it already at the time of the reception of Roman law, and/or, be it at later times.

As to Europe itself, it is striking to see that in some areas of private law, there is already a great deal of uniformity. This is in particular the case in the law of contract. The mere fact that the so-called Lando Commission was able to draft *Principles of European Contract Law*[48] without too much disagreement about what these principles should consist of, is in this respect informative. This can only be explained by the fact that – despite strong national influence on this area of law as well – some other factor has been at work here. It is highly likely that the socio-

---

39 The traditional explanation; cf. Ajani, n. 7 above, and Watson, n. 5 above, p. 345, stressing 'the need for authority'.

40 In particular Mattei, n. 19 above.

41 P.G. Monateri, 'The "Weak" Law: Contaminations and Legal Cultures' in *Italian National Reports to the XVth International Congress of Comparative Law 1998* (Giuffre Editore, Milano, 1998) p. 94.

42 Watson, n. 5 above, p. 339.

43 Watson, n. 5 above, p. 335.

44 R. Evans Jones, 'Receptions of Law, Mixed Legal Systems and the Myth of the Genius of Scots Private Law' (1998) 114 *Law Quarterly Review* 228.

45 As is rightly stressed by E. Örücü, 'Mixed and Mixing Systems: a Conceptual Search' in Örücü et al., n. 24 above, p. 349.

46 Cf. Örücü, n. 7 above, p. 121 et seq.

47 Regardless of whether these can be qualified as transplants in the narrower sense of being initiated by the national courts.

48 See n. 13 above.

economic 'fragment'[49] here was, and still is, a transnational one. Contracts many times are not just made in a national setting, but in an international one: the law of contract is particularly there to facilitate (legal) persons to practice international trade. In doing so, not only goods are transplanted from one country to another, but also national legal rules, for the simple reason that knowledge of the foreign rules is made available to the contracting parties through the contracting process. In the end, this may lead to uniform practices from which uniform legal rules evolve. Evidence shows that this has at least been the case with regard to the *formation* of contract.[50]

In property law on the other hand, uniformity in Europe is to a great extent lacking. If my thesis is correct, this is mainly caused by the absence of successful legal transplants in this area of law.[51] This may indeed have to do with the existence of some national morality in property law, only providing a national environment for the (then unsuccessful) transplants. Gambaro, for example, states the following about the law of real property:[52]

> When one considers the nature of various property rights (obligations between neighbours, riparian rights, condominium law, rights of superficies, servitudes, and the like), it becomes rather clear that much property law is deeply rooted in locally developed legal traditions. And, for this reason it is better left to those local legal traditions which for hundreds of years have addressed these issues in the manner most adapted to the locality

An interesting example with regard to property law is the recent success that the institution of the *trust* seems to have had outside of the Anglo-American legal world. Over the last decade, some civil law countries have accepted trust-like arrangements in their national laws;[53] the Hague Trust Treaty of 1985[54] forces parties to the Treaty to implement foreign trusts in their national legal systems. I believe the success of the trust is caused by the ever-increasing globalization of world trade, leading to the need for a relatively easy way to establish a separate patrimony with effect *erga*

[49] To use Teubner's terminology; see above, para. 3.

[50] Which was the very reason why Schlesinger decided to devote his Cornell-project to formation of contract. See R.B. Schlesinger (ed.), *Formation of Contracts: a Study on the Common Core of Legal Systems* (Oceana, Dobbs Ferry, Vol. I, 1968), p. 18: 'it seemed wise to start with a topic to which the system-builders everywhere almost unanimously have assigned an initiatory, separate, and well-defined place'. See for details Smits (2000), n. 10 above, p. 190.

[51] Although here too, transplants in the Watsonian sense, have taken place. Cf. Watson, n. 2 above, p. 82 et seq.

[52] A. Gambaro, 'Perspectives on the Codification of the Law of Property: an Overview' (1997) 5 *European Review of Private Law* 497.

[53] Cf. U. Mattei, *Comparative Law and Economics* (University of Michigan Press, Ann Arbor, 1997), p. 132 and J.H. Langbein, 'The Secret Life of the Trust: The Trust as an Instrument of Commerce' (1997) 107 *Yale Law Journal* 179.

[54] Convention on the Law Applicable to Trusts and their Recognition, The Hague 1 July 1985.

omnes, but avoiding the continental *numerus clausus* of real rights.[55] It should however be questioned whether this new business environment (again a uniform socio-economic segment) does indeed lead to a uniform trust law for Europe. Here, it is that internal factors, i.e. factors related to the property rules themselves, have to be taken into account. These rules may at first lead to inconsistencies within the property law system, later on to an embedment of the trust *within* that system; the transplant then should be assessed as unsuccessful (cf. paragraph 5).

The great difference between contract law and property law thus seems to be that the former is much more tied to a non-national environment than the latter one, having for a consequence that legal transplants in contract law have been much more successful in the sense that they really led to uniformity. An important point however still needs to be made. If contract law is much more tied to a socio-economic segment than to a national one, it is only as far as *this segment* is concerned that contract law is uniform. In other parts of the law of contract, the transplant that occurred may *not* have led to any uniformity. So, it could very well be that in commercial transactions there is uniformity through legal transplants, as in consumer transactions there is not.[56] Now, let me elaborate this idea of the environment of the transplanted rule as being of great importance by looking at South African law.

South-African law also provides interesting material as to the external factors that determine a successful transplanting of law. In general, the mixed legal systems show which foreign law elements have been regarded to be of use for the development of a national legal system by the national *Rechtshonoratioren*[57] in Scotland, Louisiana, Quebec and South-Africa. In particular, South-African law is of great interest for the venture of creating a European Private Law because of the fact that in this country – unlike the case in for example Scotland, where a civil law system was overlaid by a common law structure[58] – a whole new legal system had to be built up out of elements of both the civil law and the common law. In particular political and cultural forces were at work in doing so. Here too, the socio-economic environment was very much decisive for where the law was transplanted from. In the nineteenth century, it was mainly English law being transplanted because of the strong English orientation of the leading judges and other representatives of the prevailing legal mentality. From 1900 onward, it was however mainly the *Afrikaans* oriented legal elite that successfully managed to drive back the English influence. English doctrines

---

[55] Cf. Mattei, n. 53 above, p. 132: 'Trust has obtained an easy and well-deserved victory in the competition on the market of legal doctrines'.

[56] This thesis should however be mitigated because of the influence of European Directives in the field of consumer protection. Teubner's whole plea against the introducing of good faith in English contract law however, clearly shows that then consistency problems still may occur.

[57] To quote Max Weber. See M. Rheinstein, 'Die Rechtshonoratioren und ihr Einfluss auf Charakter und Funktion der Rechtsordnungen' (1970) 43 *RabelsZeitschrift* 1.

[58] On Scots law as a mixed legal system *e.g.* E. Attwooll, 'Scotland: a Multi-dimensional Jigsaw' in Örücü et al., n. 24 above, p. 17, and Evans-Jones, n. 44 above.

like the consideration doctrine in contract law and the doctrine of nuisance were rejected as being too little Roman-Dutch law oriented.[59]

Problems with the consistency of South-African law however existed as long as there was no prevailing view of the general cultural embedment of the legal system. This is clearly shown by the battle of *causa* and consideration. As long as there was no agreement in the lower courts (reflecting society in general) whether the system was to be influenced by English law or Roman-Dutch law, a 'nightmare of confusion' (to quote Lord De Villiers) existed. The courts of the Cape and of Transvaal had differing points of view in this regard until the Appellate Division of the Supreme Court finally settled the matter in favour of Roman-Dutch law.

Two things may be learnt from South Africa with regard to the successful transplanting of law. The first is that even in the heyday of English and *Afrikaans* nationalism, some areas of South-African law were not influenced by the battle between the so-called Purists and Pollutionists. Again, large parts of the law of contract appeared, to a large extent, to be resistant to considerations of national morality. Secondly, it is apparently so that the more general political and cultural climate in a country very much decides which rules are regarded as a true part of that country's legal system.[60] In the case of legal transplants, only those rules that are regarded by the prevailing legal elite to form part of the national legal culture will be readily accepted as law that is suited for the environment of the importing country. In South Africa, like in the case of the European Union, a whole new society ('state') had to be built up out of differing economic, social, cultural and legal elements. This leads to irreconcilable conflicts as long as there is no predominant view of what that society should look like, and consequently, a coherent system of law cannot arise. In this respect, a consistent political and institutional system is of great importance for the success of legal transplants. This was so in South Africa – where a legal system with an identity of its own – only emerged after the coming into being of a national State in 1910; it will in my view also be the case in Europe.

The point I want to make for the venture of a future European Private Law is that as long as there is a uniform *European* socio-economic or cultural segment (a 'fragment', in Teubner's terminology) present, transplants *may* lead to uniform law in Europe, but that as far as this segment is lacking, uniform law is impossible. In assessing the possible success of legal transplants in Europe, it thus primarily comes down to identifying new European socio-economic or cultural segments. In the law of commercial contracts, this uniformity has already been more or less attained. Other areas that are concerned with the main goal of the European Union, namely the promoting of economic activity within Europe, may also be unified through the use of transplants. Other uniform segments may come into being as well. In case there would be a shared idea in Europe of to what extent consumers should be

59 Resp. *Conradie v Rossouw* 1919 *AD* 279 and *Regal v African Superslate (Pty.) Ltd.*, 1963 1 SA 102.

60 This appears also to be true for Scots law; cf. N.R. Whitty, 'The Civilian Tradition and Debates on Scots Law' [1996] *Tydskrif vir die Suid-Afrikaanse Reg* 227.

protected from unfair trade practices, a segment of consumer protection could come about as well.

To assess what factors are involved in the successful transferring of law, one can however not halt at the external factor of the environment into which the foreign legal rule is imported. The extent to which uniformity is created through transplants is also dependent upon other, *internal*, factors. These factors may also explain why legal transplants have been more vigorous in the field of contract law than in, for example, property law.

5. Internal Factors Involved in the Success of Legal Transplants: Path Dependence and Areas of European Private Law

Apart from the factors related to the environment of which the transplanted rules become parts, there are also *internal* factors that account for the success (or failure) of legal transplants. Some transplanted rules are better able to adjust themselves to their new environment than others. It is this interaction of different types of rules and their environment that is tackled in the concept of *path dependence*. This concept was developed to explain why evolution in general (of species in biology, of economies in evolutionary economics, etc.) might not lead to the best possible result. The central idea is that the path evolution is bound to take in the future, does not only depend on the 'adaptive landscape'. Many times, a true spontaneous order cannot evolve because of internal materials (in organisms these would be genes) that have been shaped by transformations in the past and that are now irreversible. These were responsive once to the environment of previous times, but are now constraints upon adaptive change.[61] The future development is thus affected by the path that was traced out in the past. In biology, especially Gould has pointed out that evolution often depends on 'accidents', leading to an eccentric path.[62] The lesson to be learnt from this for the law is that evolution of legal norms through transplants may not under all circumstances lead to uniform results, *even though a socio-economic or cultural segment may be identified.* So, even though the environmental prerequisite is met, transplants may in these cases not be successful after all.

To decide to what extent uniformity of private law through legal transplants can come about in Europe, it is useful to presume that this is least probable where it is only possible to change the present rules at the expense of high costs. This is so in case of rules that many people rely upon. On the other hand, the amount of uniformity to be attained should theoretically be the greatest in the case of rules that are only of use for the parties that set these rules themselves. If one takes the

61 J. Hirshleifer, 'Evolutionary Models in Economics and Law' reprinted in Ulrich Witt (ed.), *Evolutionary Economics* (Elgar, Aldershot, 1993), 205. For an application to law see M.J. Roe, 'Chaos and Evolution in Law and Economics' (1996) 109 *Harvard Law Review* 641.

62 S.J. Gould, *Wonderful Life* (Norton, New York, 1989).

statement of Gambaro on real property law as being based in local legal traditions,[63] he is certainly right that any uniformity in this field of the law is hard to attain. But the reason why this area of law is looked at as most adapted to the locality has in my view, much more to do with the investments that have already been made in the path of property law, and from which it is too costly to deviate, than with 'the nature' of property rights, as Gambaro states. To change the national law in the areas mentioned by Gambaro would mean that third parties' interests would have to be reconsidered on a very large scale. The reliance of the parties involved on the existence of 'absolute' rights that have effect *erga omnes* would be violated if the applicable rules on, for example, the establishment of limited rights and the registration of these, would be eliminated or even changed. The taking into account of so many different interests has led to delicate static systems of property law with – most of the time – a *numerus clausus* of limited real rights.[64] Moreover, to get to know the ins and outs of property law in a specific system is far more difficult than to get to know a country's law of contract: the information costs of the former are much higher.[65] In this sense, property law is stuck in a 'local equilibrium'. In the bigger part of property law, this does not pose a true problem: any need to have uniform law is virtually absent. It is a problem however, where there *is* a need, namely in the field of security interests: here, the external factor (the coming into being of an international commercial environment) and the internal factor of the specific type of legal rules are the most divergent. Accordingly, it is most difficult to come to uniformity in this area of law.

This is entirely different in case of the law of contract. The parties to a contract would not be truly hampered by a change of the law because of their ability to set the rules for their relationship themselves. The law of contract's dynamic character guarantees the elimination and survival of rules that are respectively the least and the most suited for their new environment. Benson quotes Rubin as he says:[66]

> If conditions change (. . .) and two individuals decide that, for their purposes, behaviour that was attractive in the past has ceased to be useful, they can voluntarily devise a new contract stipulating any behaviour that they wish. That is, old custom can be quickly replaced by a new rule of obligation toward certain other individuals without prior consent of or simultaneous recognition by everyone in the group (or of some legal authority)

This evolutionary thesis is backed up by evidence from both economic analysis of law and comparative law.

63 See paragraph 4.

64 Cf. Smits, n. 10 above, p. 246.

65 Cf. M. Dreher, Wettbewerb oder Vereinheitlichung der Rechtsordnungen in Europa? (1999) 54 *Juristenzeitung* 105, 109: 'Da Wissen und Kosten eng Miteinander Verbunden Sind, Stellt Unwissenheit Zumindest vor Informationskosten und Begrenzt so auch die Faktormobilität Ganz Entscheidend'.

66 B.L. Benson, 'Evolution of Commercial Law' in *The New Palgrave Dictionary of Economics and the Law, vol. i* (MacMillan, London, 1998), p. 90.

Economic analysis of law shows the need for a distinction between default and mandatory rules. Rules should be mandatory when any other rule that the parties adopt would be violating third party interests. Mattei and Cafaggi rightly point out that the amount of mandatory rules should decrease in a system where alternative means of protection of third parties are available. They mention, for example, the lesser amount of mandatory rules in contract law if the tort system protects third parties.[67] It is obvious that property law is much more related to these mandatory rules than contract law. The economic reason for property law being more mandatory thus runs parallel with the evolutionary idea of property law being less able to change when confronted with a changing environment.

Also comparative law provides evidence of some rules being more suited to be transplanted than others. I already pointed out that there is a far greater uniformity in European contract law than there is in European property law. If one turns again to the mixed legal systems, one sees that contract law in South- Africa, for example, is to a great extent a true mix of civil law and common law elements.[68] It has for example rejected the requirement of consideration, but has developed a system of contractual remedies that is to a large extent comparable to English law. Any true influence of English property law on the Roman-Dutch system is however absent: South-African private law has essentially kept its system of a *numerus clausus* of real rights, even though it would not be called that way.[69] In Scots law, a similar tendency can be identified.[70]

Again, I use the trust to illustrate this. Despite the ever-greater use of the trust in civil law countries in recent years, it should be doubted whether its reception will lead to convergence of the civil law and the common law. In both South African[71] and Scots law,[72] the implant of the trust led to an institution that is still called a trust, but is mainly civilian as to its contents. South African law for example does not recognise the English law dichotomy of legal and equitable ownership: the trustee is the full owner of the trust and the beneficiary only has a right *in personam* against the trustee.[73]

---

67 U. Mattei and F. Cafaggi, 'Comparative Law and Economics' in *New Palgrave* I, n. 66 above, p. 348.

68 Cf. on the mixed character of the various areas of South African law: R. Zimmermann and D. Visser (eds.), *Southern Cross; Civil Law and Common Law in South Africa* (Clarendon Press, Oxford, 1996).

69 Cf. Smits, n. 10 above, p. 257.

70 Cf. Smits, n. 10 above, p. 189 et seq.

71 Cf. T. Honoré, 'Trust' in Visser and Zimmermann, n. 68 above, p. 849; and M.J. De Waal, 'The Uniformity of Ownership, *Numerus Clausus* and the Reception of Trust into South African Law' (2000) 8 *European Review of Private Law* 439 et seq.

72 G. Gretton, 'Scotland: The Evolution of the Trust in a Semi-Civilian System' in R. Helmholz and R. Zimmermann (eds.), *Itinera Fiduciae; Trust and Treuhand in Historical Perspective* (Berlin 1998), p. 507.

73 Yet, insolvency of the trustee does not imply that the trust can be liquidated. Cf. Art. 12, Trust Property Control Act 1988. Art. 1 of the Principles of European Trust Law (n. 13 above) also provides a very broad definition of the trust, accommodating both the English trust and the more civilian versions of the mixed legal systems.

Still open for further discussion is what exactly is the relationship between the two types of factors that are decisive for the success of legal transplants. I have shown that the two do not have to run together. In property law, for example, the socio-economic environment may favour legal transplants if international commerce would be in need of a uniform regime of security interests, yet the type of rules involved may prevent a uniform law from coming about (as we saw with law of trusts). On the other hand, the environment of the exporting system may be different from the importing one, while the type of rules (as in the case of contract law) does allow a successful legal transplant to take place. It is most likely that this happens in the case of exporting Western contract law to legal systems in transition to a market economy (as is the case in Eastern Europe). Uniform law will then not come about either, but now because of the external factor preventing this.

6. A European *Ius Commune* through the Use of Legal Transplants?

In the above, the assessment of factors that favour and hamper the successful transplanting of law have been illustrated by using some historical examples. The framework that has been developed in this paper should however not only be suitable to *explain* present uniformity and diversity in Europe, but should also be able to *predict* it. Both the environmental factor of a socio-economic or cultural segment (preferably accompanied by a European political-institutional system) and the internal factor of legal rules of a certain type are decisive for the success of legal transplants.

As to the present environment in Europe, one can on the one hand identify an increasingly global segment of transfrontier trade. Consequently, there will be a good setting for uniformity of commercial law, coming about through transplants. In Europe itself, this segment is politically backed up by the EC Treaty. On the other hand, there are some segments that in a way are auxiliary to the promoting of economic activity, like consumer protection and the avoidance of unfair competition. These segments may also be 'European' ones. As to the type of rules, it is clear from the above that mainly the law of contract (and possibly the law of tort) offers rules with a high potential for transferring these to other legal systems. In property law, this may be different, in particular leading to problems in the field of harmonizing the law of security interests. Any transplant that takes place in this field would probably not lead to uniformity at all, but rather to inconsistencies within the importing legal system.

It is however my profound belief that using legal transplants is still one of the most promising ways to establish a European *ius commune*. Any tension between legal-cultural unity and socio-cultural diversity will be smoothly resolved if it is left to the national courts to decide which rules remain national in character and which rules become part of a European uniform law. Of course, an important consequence of this theory is that diversity of laws in Europe will, to a large extent, remain. This is however not to be regarded as negative, but much more as a strength – as Örücü has recently pointed out as well. In my view, diversity is just as good as uniformity,[74] as long as the *Rechtshonoratioren* have at least taken into account that there are other solutions than the national one, and have seriously investigated whether the foreign legal rule may not have been better suited to solve the case. Any other view on harmonization of law through centralist imposition would strangle the present diversity. In this sense – even though disadvantages of the approach defended here may be identified – the future of legal transplants in Europe will be brilliant.

[74] See Örücü, above n. 7, p. 22, stressing 'harmony' instead of harmonization. Cf. R. Hyland, 'Comparative Law' in D. Patterson (ed.), *A Companion to Philosophy of Law and Legal Theory* (Blackwell, London, 1996), p. 184.

Chapter 9

COMPARATIVE LAW IN A REGIONALLY INTEGRATED EUROPE

*Walter van Gerven**

The following piece also looks at comparative law in a European context. It reminds us that, when looking at the laws of the member states of the EU, the law of the EU and the ECHR must also be considered, and therefore, comparative law in Europe must employ a multi-level approach, as within each state, layers of systems function side by side with a plurality of legal sources. This necessity is also reflected by McDonald in his chapter. A study of the concept of the nation state alone is not appropriate in a regionally integrated Europe. Traditional definitions are artificial.

According to van Gerven, the enactment of uniform rules is not sufficient to achieve uniformity; these must be embedded in the common legal heritage of the European legal order. Common principles must be discovered. In this context, this study discusses 'bottom-up and top-down' harmonization and advocates the bottom-up approach and the use of 'case-books for a common law of Europe', a project which van Gerven himself launched in 1994. He suggests a complementarity between the 'case-book' (bottom-up) approach and the 'European Principles' (top-down) approach. This bottom-up approach should be compared with that of Smits above.

Through harmonization European integration will no doubt lead to some degree of uniformity, but this uniformity will remain limited to areas where member states have transferred jurisdiction to the EU institutions. In this context, the author looks at the impact of the 'Francovich' judgment. He also looks at the impact of the ECHR in areas that have 'escaped Community law so far'. The work claims that the role of comparative law in the context of European integration is no more of persuasive but of strategic importance.

Van Gerven, like Smits, queries European Codifications as the ultimate goal of comparative law research in Europe, and claims that codification at the level of the EU raises important issues, the most serious being the lack of democratic legitimation. For him, existing socio-cultural differences and mentalities are not among these issues, as long as the European Civil Code is limited to certain areas. The national legislator must

---

* Professor at the Katholik University, Leuven, and the University of Maastricht, and visiting Professor at King's College, London.

A. Harding and E. Örücü (eds.),
Comparative Law in the 21st Century, 155–178.

make a choice as to the most desirable programme, and the task of the academic is to facilitate the work of legislators and courts.

The issue of the legitimacy of the emerging ius commune, *and the importance of the involvement of national parliaments in its creation, are highlighted. The aim must be to preserve diversity, but at the same time emphasize commonality; hence the importance of applied comparative law. On this point the views of van Gerven and Smits coincide, and echo the predominant vision of comparatists for the 21st century.*

[A. Harding and E. Örücü]

Comparative law practised in a European context, that is, comparing the laws of EU Member States, is inaccurate if it does not take full account of the law of the European Community (hereafter EC), now the European Union (hereafter EU), and of the European Convention on Human Rights (hereafter ECHR). That is the message that this contribution wants to convey.[1] It concerns both 'theoretical' and 'applied' comparative law, as the distinction is made by Andrew Harding in his stimulating contribution.[2] It implies that understandings of comparative law based on the study of law and legal culture which are seen as the expression of the concept of the 'Nation State',[3] must be left behind in a regionally integrated Europe. For indeed, in such a context, comparative law bears from now on, and in an ever-increasing manner, the unmistakable marks of a 'multi-level approach' based on a continuous interplay between national and supranational legal systems.[4]

1 It is based on experience that the author has had during more than 40 years of professional life, as an academic and a practitioner, devoted half to private and comparative law and the other half to the law of the European Community. In both areas, it is impossible *not* to cross the line between private and public law, nor is it possible to distinguish theory from practice, or to distinguish national laws from supranational laws.

2 See Harding's contribution to this book.

3 As stubbornly advocated by P. Legrand, see n. 50 below; and the criticism in articles by Watson, Van Hoecke and Chamboredon also cited at n. 50 below.

4 See C. Joerges, 'The Impact of European Integration on Private Law: Reductionist Perceptions, True Conflicts and a new Constitutional Perspective' in O. Gerstenberg and C. Joerges (eds.), *Private Governance, Democratic Constitutionalism and Supranationalism* (European Commission, Brussels, 1998), and other writings of the same author. For a recent overview and discussion of the impact of such a non-statal approach, see M. Warrington, *Structures of Europeanization and Comparative Legal Theory*, a doctoral thesis to be presented at the K.U.Brussel (from which I borrowed a number of references to studies in the area of legal theory).

1. Comparative Law to be Re-defined and Its Methodology to be Differentiated

Traditionally, comparative law is about comparing 'the legal systems of different nations' and therefore deals 'necessarily ... with foreign law'.[5] Accordingly, comparing differences between rules of the same legal system is not regarded to be comparative law.[6] That can no longer be true within the Member States of the EU, all of which are moreover Contracting States of the ECHR, where several legal systems function alongside each other, not just as separate legal systems (like international law applicable in all states) but, with regard to both the EU and ECHR legal orders, as systems which are an integral part of the national laws of the Member, i.e. the Contracting States.[7] It is this reality of intimate co-existence, giving expression to an ever-growing plurality of legal sources,[8] which undermines the concept of the 'Nation-State' as a monolitic legislative entity and, by the same token makes the borderlines of comparative law increasingly fluid. To take the example of tort law: is it comparative law to compare EC tort rules on liability of Member States for breaches of Community law, the so-called 'Francovich'-liability,[9] with German or French tort rules on liability of public authorities, having regard to the fact that EC law is an integral part of both German and French law? Is it comparative law to compare such EC rules on liability of Member States for breaches of Community law with the rules on tort liability of States for breaches of the ECHR, as provided for in Article 41 (ex 50) ECHR taking into account that both supranational legal systems are somehow linked to each other as they are each an integral part of the legal systems of 'their' respective Member States? And if those comparisons relating to closely intertwined legal systems are regarded as genuine comparative law, why would it then not be comparative law to compare the rules of German tort law, or English tort law which are modified as a result of the case law of the European Court of Justice's (ECJ) 'Francovich' case law, with the rules of those *same* national laws which, in dealing only with 'purely internal' liability situations, have remained immune from changes brought about by the ECJ's 'Francovich' case law; or to compare the EC tort liability rules for Community institutions set forth in Article 288 (ex 215), paragraph 2 EC, with the EC tort liability rules for Member States as laid down in the Court's 'Francovich' case-law? In other words, why is comparing different sets of rules existing within the same national or supranational legal order

5 K. Zweigert and H. Kötz, *An Introduction to Comparative Law* (3rd edn., T. Weir translated, Clarendon Press, Oxford, 1998), at pp. 4 and 6.

6 Ibid., at p. 2.

7 It may suffice to quote Art. 249 (ex 189), para. 2 EC, which says of a regulation (and the same is true *a fortiori* of directly applicable Treaty provisions) that 'it is binding in its entirety and directly applicable in all Member States'.

8 On the growing plurality of sources, see T. Koopmans, 'Sources of Law: the New Pluralism' in *Festskrift til Ole Due* (Liber Amicorum, GEC Gads Forlag, Copenhagen, 1994), pp. 189–206.

9 So-called after the ECJ's judgment of 19 November 1991 in *Francovich v. Italy*, case C-6/90 and 9/90 [1991] ECR I-5357.

not also comparative law, knowing that the differences between those sets of rules are the result of interferences of a third (supranational or national) legal system?

Regardless of the answers given, those questions show, at the very least, the artificiality of the traditional definition. They also lead us here to take comparative law in its broadest meaning, and therefore also to bring under it the comparison of sets of rules within the same legal order which, although dealing with similar issues, are nonetheless to be differentiated because of interferences of other legal systems or simply because they pursue different objectives.[10]

Someone seeing comparative law in a European context may, in Andrew Harding's terminology,[11] belong to the category of 'regionalists'. However, that does not deny him or her, the right to being called a 'comparatist'. Comparing legal systems that are growing closer to each other, because of their countries' determination to achieve economic and political integration, remains comparative law. The fact that countries are part of an integration process may however have an impact on the methodology, and the outcome of the comparison.[12] To quote the most obvious example: where national systems of EU Member States are compared, as opposed to where a national system of a EU Member State is compared with that of a 'third' State, the terms of comparison will differ to some extent due to the duty of all Member States' courts to construe their national law in conformity with EC law. That difference in methodology may very well lead to a larger degree of convergence between the laws of the Member States concerned than between those of a Member State and of a third State. An even more fundamental difference in legal methodology between Member States and non-Member States may occur because of the use, in connection with Community law, of the method of teleological interpretation, i.e. interpretation of applicable rules in light of the function of the objectives aimed at.[13] It is not unlikely that teleological interpretation, which became common 'technology' for lawyers of all EU Member States, will have a 'spill-over' effect in that lawyers of Member States where that method of interpretation was not used before, may now be inclined to use it also in interpreting national rules outside the scope of Community law.[14]

---

10 So-called 'internal comparative law': J.B.M. Vranken, *Algemeen Deel* of the Dutch *Asser Commentary* (Willink, Zwolle, 1995) at p. 140.

11 See Harding, n. 2 above.

12 That means, to use the terminology of Teubner, the subsystem of law can (at the very least) be influenced by the subsystems of politics and economics: G. Teubner, *Law as an Autopoietic System*, (EUP Press Series, Blackwell, 1993).

13 That this method may lead to a difference in outcome follows from the ECJ's case law according to which the same terms (e.g. in an Association agreement with a third country) may have to be differently interpreted than when they are part of a rule of internal Community law. See ECJ's judgment of 5 February 1982, case 270/80, *Polydor* [1982] ECR 329, pp. 14–20.

14 Teleological interpretation is inconsistent with the old rule of exclusion which binds common law judges to the letter of the statute and prevents them from discovering the intention of the lawgiver: but see R.C. Van Caeneghem, *Judges, Legislatures and Professors* (Cambridge, 1987), at p. 17, where it is

Moreover, those practising comparative law in a context of European integration may tend to be more exposed than others to what is called the 'constitutionalization of private laws'. It means, in the words of an early German Constitutional Court judgment,[15] that:

> the legal content of fundamental rights as objective norms affects private law through the rules which directly apply in this area of the law. Just as new law must conform to the values embodied in the fundamental rights [guaranteed in the *Grundgesetz*], existing law must be aligned [by the courts] with those values ... [through] the interpretation of existing law

'Constitutionalization' enters into higher gear where the laws of States, such as the EU Member States, are influenced by fundamental rights provisions contained in both EC and ECHR law. For EC law, that evolution is most transparent in the field of legal remedies where the ECJ case-law (referring in that connection to the constitutional traditions of the Member States and to Articles 6 and 13 ECHR) requires national courts to offer adequate judicial protection, and therefore to make effective remedies available to plaintiffs who claim their (Community) rights to have been breached.[16] Those remedies must allow national courts to set aside national provisions, of whatever nature and in whatever area of the law, which make the enforcement of Community rights impossible or excessively difficult, and to obtain interim relief, under certain circumstances, as well as to obtain restitution of unduly paid sums and/or compensation for damage sustained.[17]

2. The Bright Side and the Dark Side of Harmonization and the 'Strategic' Importance of Comparative Law in a European Context

At the occasion of the World Exhibition held in Paris in 1900, the great French scholars E. Lambert and R. Salleilles founded the International Congress for Comparative Law. What they had in mind was 'the development of nothing less than a common law of mankind (*droit commun de l'humanité*)'. As Lambert put it:

---

already pointed out that the rule may well be subject to change, which indeed has occurred: see the House of Lords decision in *Pepper v Hart* [1993] 1 All ER 42. And for an even earlier statement, see Lord Denning, *The Discipline of Law* (Butterworths, 1979) at p. 4.

15 Judgment of 15 January 1958, BverfGE 7, 198, at 205–206. See W. van Gerven, J. Lever and P. Larouche, 'Tort Law' in W. van Gerven, J. Lever and P. Larouche, *Ius Commune Casebooks for the Common Law of Europe* (2nd edn., Hart Publishing, Oxford, 2000) in Introductory Note under 2.2.1., at p. 142.

16 Thus emphasizing the concept of the individual ('persona') in Community law upon whom a right of legal action ('actio') is conferred, to use the distinction already present in Gaius' *Institutiones*, as recalled by G. Samuel, *The Foundations of Legal Reasoning* (Maklu, Antwerp, 1994) excerpted in G. Samuel, *Source book on Obligations & Legal Remedies* (2nd edn., Cavendish Publishing, 2000), p. 27 et seq.

17 See, with further references, W. van Gerven, 'Of Rights, Remedies and Procedures' (2000) 37 *Common Market Law Review* 501, at 511 and 525.

> ... comparative law must resolve the accidental and divisive differences in the laws of peoples at similar stages of cultural and economic development, and reduce the number of divergences in law, attributable not to the political, moral, or social qualities of the different nations but to historical accident or to temporary or contingent circumstances[18]

Paradoxically enough, in the same year when such a strong plea for a common law of mankind was made, the German Civil code entered into effect, on the first day of 1900,[19] as a symbol of national unity and pride, and as a new and long lasting divisive difference between the 'Nation State' laws of Western Europe.

Obviously, the dream to unify the laws, particularly the private laws of Western Europe, has not become true, but remains the ultimate objective of some, mainly academic, lawyers. However, that has not prevented the Member States of the EU – which have all now adhered to the ECHR – from sharing a 'common' law in the areas of human rights, economic freedoms and, to a large extent, with regard to consumer, social and environmental rights.[20] As for the latter freedoms and rights, that achievement has been made possible by the introduction in the EC Treaty of an original instrument, known as the directive. In contradistinction to a regulation which is directly applicable in all of the Member States, a directive 'shall be binding, as to the result to be achieved ... but shall leave to the national authorities the choice of form and methods' (Article 249 (ex 189), paragraph 3 EC). The directive thus combines legislative competence of the Community with legislative power of the Member States and, by the same token, combines uniformity of *principles* with diversity of implementing *rules*. It therefore intends to bring about harmonization, rather than unification, and as a result has been extremely successful in putting the internal market into effect.[21]

Regulations and directives are legal instruments of the so-called first (and oldest) pillar, the *EC* pillar, of what is now called the *EU*. The second and the third pillar of the EU, created by the Maastricht Treaty and amended by the Amsterdam Treaty, contain provisions on a common foreign and security policy (Articles 11–28 TEU) respectively, and on police and judicial co-operation in criminal matters (Articles 29–42). Whilst the first pillar aims, from the outset, at integration within the framework of the (then) European *Economic* Community (now the European Community), the second and the third are based on intergovernmental co-operation for which use can be made, however, of the first pillar institutions, such as the Council of Ministers and

---

18 As quoted in Zweigert and Kötz, n. 5 above, at p. 3.

19 Ibid., at p. 142.

20 See on this evolution, N. Reich, *Bürgerrechte in der Europäische Union* (Nomos, Nürnberg, 1999).

21 Notwithstanding the wording of Article 249, a directive may nonetheless have direct effect according to the ECJ case law, if its provisions are sufficiently clear and unconditional, but only 'vertically', that is, against a Member State which has not duly implemented the directive in time.

the European Commission (Articles 3 and 5 TEU).[22] Whilst, under the first pillar, regulations and directives can be issued by qualified majority in accordance with the so-called co-decision procedure of Article 251 (ex 189 b) EC, the institutions may under the third pillar[23] only act by unanimity. In that context they may, amongst other measures, establish conventions, to be adopted by the Member States, or adopt framework decisions which – like directives under the first pillar – are 'binding upon the Member States as to the result to be achieved but (leaving) to the national authorities the choice of form and methods' but which – unlike directives – are not allowed to have any 'vertical' (or 'horizontal') direct effect (Article 34, paragraph 2b TEU).

It will be clear from the foregoing that the European decision-making-process will have a much larger impact on the legal systems of the Member States under the first than under the third pillar. However, once uniform rules have been adopted under the third pillar, they will, as under the first pillar, constitute an integral part of the law prevailing in any one of the Member States, and take precedence over national rules.

So far the bright side of harmonization, which is that European integration will unavoidably lead to a certain degree of uniformity (full uniformity in the case of regulations or conventions, partial uniformity in the case of directives or framework decisions). Now the dark side, which is that the uniformity brought about remains limited, under whatever pillar of EU law, to the areas for which jurisdiction has been transferred by the Member States to the EU institutions. That principle is known as the principle of 'attribution of competences'[24] according to which 'the Community shall act within the limits of the powers conferred upon it by this Treaty and of the objectives assigned to it therein' (Article 5, paragraph 1 EC); a principle which must be combined with the principle of proportionality 'in areas which do not fall within the [Community's] exclusive competence', the Community shall take action 'only if and insofar as the objectives of the proposed action cannot be sufficiently achieved by the Member States' (Article 5, paragraph 2 EC). As a consequence thereof, *outside* the limited areas where powers have been conferred by the Treaties upon the European Community (and the same applies to the European Union as a whole), the European institutions do *not* have legislative powers, *nor* do they have executive and judicial competences. In other words, unification or harmonization takes place only *within* the areas for which the Union has acquired jurisdiction (that is broadly speaking under the first pillar, for *inter-State* commerce and related consumer,

---

22 Which therefore call themselves the EU – and no longer the EC – Council and Commission. Since the European Court of Justice has, unfortunately, very limited jurisdiction under the second and the third pillar, it continues to call itself the ECJ of the European Communities (those are the three initial, first pillar, treaties: the EC Treaty, the Euratom Treaty and the Coal and Steel Community (ECSC) Treaty).

23 I will no longer mention the second EU pillar as it deals with foreign affairs, which is more a concern for politicians and diplomats than for lawyers.

24 See e.g. ECJ, Opinion 2/94 on the accession by the Communities to the ECHR, [1996] ECR I-1759, at para. 24 et seq.

environmental and social matters and, under the third pillar, for *transborder* crime), and for which a legal basis[25] can therefore be found in the European treaties. Accordingly, the unifying viz. harmonizing effect of European measures is limited to those matters and, therefore, does not affect national rules in so far as they regulate purely domestic matters (or relations between individual Member States and third countries).

The overall effect of the above is that Community (and Union) laws cut through existing national laws by dividing areas, governed so far by the same national rules, into two separate branches: *one* for which there are, in each Member State, rules which are identical with, or similar to, the rules existing in the other Member States; and *another* (raising the same issues though) for which the existing national laws continue to prevail in each Member State with the same degree of differentiation between the laws of the Member States as before.

Two examples may help to clarify the foregoing, one regarding legislative measures and the other regarding judicial interpretation. Before the coming into force of (primary and secondary) EC competition law (mainly by virtue of Articles 81–82 (ex 85–86) EC), domestic 'anti-trust' laws (where they existed) governed all anti-competitive practices in the Member-State concerned. Now, as a result of Community law, all Member States have one set of uniform competition rules for anti-competitive practices which affect, broadly speaking, inter-state commerce between the Member States, and another, different set of non-harmonized competition rules for anti-competitive practices which only affect the national market of the Member State concerned. And, as for judicial interpretation, where, before the ECJ's 'Francovich' judgment,[26] the same set of national tort rules applied to all acts or omissions of public authorities in a Member State, there are now, after 'Francovich', in each Member State, two sets of national tort rules for such acts or omissions: one set of 'old' rules which continue to apply to breaches of purely national law, and another set of 'new' ('Francovich') rules for breaches of Community law. Whilst the 'old' rules continue to vary from one Member State to another, the 'new' rules tend to be uniform for all Member States, as a result of the ECJ's case law, in which the conditions for state liability that may arise are spelled out. As a matter of fact, both sets of rules will normally be applied in each Member State by the same national courts.

Community law has therefore a dual effect: it harmonizes the laws of the Member States in a *specific* area but, at the same time, it 'de-harmonizes' the law in each Member State by causing matters which, before harmonisation, were governed by

[25] To ascertain whether there is a legal basis in the Treaties for Community secondary rules (regulations and directives) constitutes one of the ECJ's most important tasks. The Court fulfils this task with great circumspection, because of the fact that the 'legal basis' issue is one of the most sensitive issues, politically and constitutionally, as it relates to the demarcation of competences between the Union and the Member States, and between Community institutions, e.g. Council and Parliament, and the decision-making procedures that they apply.

[26] Cited, n. 9 above.

the same rules, to be now regulated by two different sets of national law rules, one for matters affected by Community law, and one for matters not affected by it.[27] As a consequence thereof,[28] the function of comparative law, when practised in a context of European integration, is no longer of a 'persuasive' nature only – which is to persuade legislatures, judges, teachers to draw lessons from foreign law so as to be better prepared to carry out their own task – but is now also of 'strategic' importance – which is to maintain coherence and consistency within, and between, intertwined, national and supranational (EU and ECHR[29]), legal systems; in other words, to maintain order, and equilibrium, in the face of a growing plurality of legal sources.[30]

In a context of European integration, the strategic importance of comparative law research relates first to the support it can give *European* legislatures and courts in laying down rules, respectively adopting solutions based as much as possible on common principles, or solutions found in the legislation and the case law of the Member States (or, if no common elements exist, in making existing differences accord as much as possible). Such support is especially needed in order to off-set the piece-meal character of EC directives which, although dealing with related subjects, are not always the expression of a consistent underlying philosophy.[31] Secondly, comparative research is also of strategic importance in that it should assist *national* legislatures and courts – called upon to implement, or to apply, Community rules in their national laws – in preserving the convergence between the Member States' law which Community law has brought about in certain areas of national law (the bright side of harmonization), and in safeguarding the internal equilibrium of each Member

27 See further W. van Gerven, 'Comparative Law in a Texture of Communitarization of National Laws and Europeanization of Community Law' in Liber Amicorum in honour of Lord Slynn of Hadley, Vol. I, D. O'Keeffe (ed.), *Judicial Review in European Community Law* (Kluwer Law International, The Hague, 2000), pp. 433–445.

28 See W. van Gerven, 'Bridging the Unbridgeable: Community and National Tort Laws after *Francovich* and *Brasserie*', (1996) 49 *International Comparative Law Quarterly* 507, at 532 et seq.

29 Both supranational legal orders overlap each other in the area of human rights and fundamental freedoms. Within the scope of Community law, those rights and freedoms are safeguarded by the ECJ, not by the European Court of Human Rights, as a result of an implicit understanding between the two supranational courts (which, however, is less certain now than before). See D. Curtin, 'The EU Human Rights Charter and the Union Legal Order: the "Banns" before the Marriage?' in O'Keeffe n. 27 above, p. 303, at p. 307 et seq. The (non-binding) EU Human Rights Charter has in the meantime been adopted at the Nice Summit meeting in December 2000.

30 On the necessity to maintain an equilibrium between institutions which hang so much together, like an 'organic' bond, that to alter one component makes it necessary to reform other components as well, see already H. Battifol, *Aspects philosophique du droit international privé* (Dalloz, Paris, 1956), at p. 50. In modern legal theory the phenomenon is known and analysed as 'organic (or substantive) systematicity': see F. Ost and M. Van De Kerchove, *Legal System between Order and Disorder*, (translation from the French by I. Stewart, Clarendon Press, Oxford, 1995) at p. 62.

31 See W. van Gerven, 'Community and National Legislators, Regulators, Judges, Academics and Practitioners: Living Together Apart?' in B.S. Markesinis (ed.), *Law Making, Law Finding, and Law Shaping* (Oxford University Press, Oxford, 1997) p. 13, at pp. 21–28.

State's national legal system notwithstanding the de-harmonization which harmonization brings about (the dark side of harmonisation as explained above).

The latter point leads to a further remark relating to what is called the 'spill-over' effect of Community law.[32] In the two examples given above, national legislatures viz. national courts may wish to develop their own national laws – even outside the areas where jurisdiction was transferred to the Community institutions – in a way that preserves homogeneity between the 'Community initiated' domestic rules developed for such areas and the 'purely' domestic rules developed for neighbouring areas, and therefore raising similar issues, for which no transfer of jurisdiction has taken place. Thus the Belgian, Dutch and UK legislators have made domestic competition rules for *intra*-state anti-competitive practices to conform as much as possible to the Community competition rules for *inter*-state anti-competitive practices (even to the point that national courts are requested to follow the interpretation which the Community courts, ECJ and CFI have attached to similar wording used in the Community law texts). Likewise, when the House of Lords was led not to apply the defence of immunity of the Crown (as a result of the ECJ's *Factortame I* judgment)[33] in instances of interim relief for alleged breaches of Community law by UK authorities (in that case by an Act of Parliament), it accepted later that neither could the defence against plaintiffs seeking interim relief in 'purely national law' instances[34] be opposed. Obviously, the wish of national legislatures or courts to develop their national rules in accordance with Community law solutions, is not the result of any obligation of Community law – as it relates to matters for which no transfer of jurisdiction has taken place. It is the result rather of those legislators' determination to maintain coherence, and in the case of the courts, to give equal treatment to litigants in instances raising similar issues, regardless of whether the applicable rules find their origin in Community law or in national law. For whatever reason 'spill-over' effect occurs, it is an unmistakable illustration of how the comparison of rules belonging to different (be it intertwined) legal orders, national and supranational, or belonging to the same national legal order but differentiated because of the impact of supranational law, becomes a structural element, so to speak, of legal methodology as applied in a context of integration.

The impact of EC law on the domestic legal systems, and the ensuing need for comparative law, are most obvious in those branches of the law where obstacles to the establishment and functioning of the internal market had to be eliminated; these are commercial and economic laws dealing with free movement of persons, goods, services and capital, including company and banking laws as well as, later on,

[32] See G. Anthony, 'Community Law and the Development of UK Administrative Law: Delimiting the "Spill-Over" Effect' [1998] *European Public Law* 253 et seq.

[33] Case C-213/89, [1990] ECR I-2433.

[34] See the discussion in M. Brealy and M. Hoskins, *Remedies in EC Law*, (2nd edn., Sweet and Mazwell, London, 1998), at p. 192 et seq. where *Factortame I* is analysed; and the 'spill-over' effect is mentioned at p. 153, fn. 14, by reference to the House of Lords *M. v. Home Office* [1994] 1 AC 377; [1993] 3 All ER 537. See also Anthony, n. 32 above, where the judgment is discussed in relation with other case law.

consumer, environmental, social and tax legislation. However, in relation therewith, the ECJ has in its case law increasingly underlined the need for legal remedies, such as restitution, interim relief, and compensation, mainly as against national public authorities, in order to secure the rights that individuals can derive from Community law. To achieve that, it has required domestic courts to do away with any domestic regulation, of whatever rank or nature (many of them in the area of private law), which hinders the full effectiveness of Community law and the full protection of the Community rights of individuals. In this regard, the Court uses a doubt test: one to know whether the enforcement of Community rights is not made virtually impossible or excessively difficult by the regulation concerned, and the other to know whether the national regulation does not treat Community rights claims less favourably than similar domestic claims. The application of the second test has brought the ECJ and national courts in many instances to compare Community rules and national rules in view of determining whether the claims of litigants brought under the former are treated equally well as those brought under the latter.[35]

In contrast with EC law, the impact of the law under the ECHR is primarily felt in areas that escaped Community law so far, namely family law, penal law and procedural law. Many of the judgments of the Strasbourg supervisory organs have caused important reforms in those areas of the law,[36] and have resulted in bringing the legal systems of the Contracting States closer to each other. As a further consequence, comparative law research in the Contracting States will also be carried out there within a framework of growing convergence, which is the expression, in that context, of underlying value judgments, constituting an ethical minimum at the European supranational level, with regard to the organisation of a society in which human dignity is deemed to be of crucial importance. Especially in the EU Member States which are all at the same time Contracting Parties to the ECHR, legal integration will therefore go hand in hand with, and will be the result of political and economic, as well as ethical and cultural convergence leading to commonality which, within the next few years, may very well match that of the United States of America.

3. The Issue of Codification of European Community Law

Should the use of comparative law research, seen as a tool to safeguard coherence and consistency of the law in a context of European integration, go so far as to

[35] See further T. Tridimas, *The General Principles of EC Law* (Oxford University Press, Oxford, 1999), at p. 280 et seq.

[36] Just two examples: *Merckx v Belgium*, 13 June 1979 (Publ. ECHR, Series A, vol. 31) which compelled national legislatures to do away with discrimination against 'illegitimate' children; and *Osman v UK*, 28 October 1998 (excerpted, and commented on, in the Casebook mentioned at n. 15 above, under 9 ECHR 10, at 939 et seq.), which, in fact, condemned the power of English courts to strike out liability claims against public authorities, such as the police, without a more than preliminary investigation of the substance of the claim.

regard European codification as its ultimate goal? According to some,[37] the answer should be in the affirmative, at least for certain areas of private law, like contracts and torts, where disparities between national legislation may constitute an impediment to the orderly functioning of a single market. And indeed, proposals have been made, and important work is in progress, in view of preparing a European Civil Code relating to the law of obligations (contracts and torts), property and proprietary interests.[38] The work does not have to start from scratch. More specifically, in the area of contracts, considerable work has been achieved by a (self-appointed) body of distinguished lawyers from all the Member States of the European Union, under the chairmanship of Professor Ole Lando, who called themselves the Commission on European Contract Law. In the meantime, the Commission has published Parts I and II of Principles of European contract law.[39] Also in the area of European tort law, several doctrinal works have been published[40] as well as a casebook on the law of tort, at the initiative of the undersigned, of which a considerably enlarged second edition was published recently. It contains a large number of cases and other legal materials from different national laws (mainly from England, France and Germany) and from the legal orders of the EC and the ECHR.[41]

Drafting a European Civil Code that is to contain wholly comprehensive and well-structured provisions is a vast enterprise, even when it is limited to the subjects mentioned above. To make it possible, there must, of course, be a legislator who is empowered to adopt uniform legal rules. Within the context of Community law – the only legal framework within which such a legislator can possibly operate – that can only be the case if a solid legal basis is found in the EC Treaty allowing to proceed by way of a regulation which, as we have seen above, is directly applicable in all of the Member States. That means that it should be possible to make use of Article 95 (ex 100a) EC, which authorizes the Council to adopt 'measures' (those are regulations as well as directives), in accordance with the co-decision procedure provided for in Art. 251 (ex 189b) EC – and thus, if need be, by a qualified majority in the Council – 'for the approximation of (national law) provisions ... which [measures] have as their object the establishment and functioning of the internal market' (a concept defined in Article 14 (ex 7a) paragraph 2 EC).

---

37 See, e.g. J. Basedow, 'A Common Contract Law for the Common Market' (1996) 33 *Common Market Law Review* 1169 et seq.

38 The Code is prepared by a Study Group on a European Civil Code, chaired by Professor C. von Bar of the University of Osnabrück in Germany.

39 O. Lando and H. Beale (eds.), *Principles of European Contract Law*, Parts I and II (Kluwer Law International, The Hague, 2000). See also H. Kötz and A. Flessner, *Europäisches Vertragsrecht* (I, J.C.B. Mohr, Tübingen, 1996).

40 C. von Bar, *Gemeineuropäisches Deliktsrecht*, I and II (C.H. Beck, München, 1996 and 1999) in English translation: *The Common European law of Torts*. See also G. Brüggemeier, *Prinzipien des Haftungsrecht* (Nomos, Nürnberg, 1999).

41 W. van Gerven et al., n. 15.

It has long remained controversial whether Article 95 EC is able to supply the legal basis for the enactment of such a uniform Civil Code (albeit limited to contracts, torts and property). The answer to that question turned around the interpretation, in the above quotation, of the words measures 'which have as their object' the establishment and functioning of the internal market. According to some,[42] the expression concerns the approximation of all kinds of national laws which, because of disparities amongst them, have for effect to distort competitive conditions, and therefore to hinder the freedom of movement of goods or services and, in consequence, the realisation of the internal market. According to others,[43] those words must be given a narrower interpretation because of the fact that the expression 'have as their object' must be seen in conjunction with the expression used in the general provision on harmonization, i.e. Article 94 (ex 100) EC Treaty which refers to 'directives [through which it is not possible to achieve *full* uniformity] for the approximation of . . .provisions of the Member States as directly affect the establishment or functioning of the common market'. According to the latter (narrow) view, the juxtaposition of those two provisions shows that the special provision of Article 95 may only be used for the approximation of national provisions which do more than just *affect* the establishment or functioning of the common or internal market,[44] but which, because they specifically regulate the production or marketing of goods or services,[45] pertain to the very *object* of the internal market. If the former (broader) view on Article 95 were to be followed instead, the scope of application of the general provision of Article 94 EC would be virtually reduced to the matters specifically enumerated in Article 95, paragraph 2 EC.

As predicted,[46] in its recent tobacco advertisement judgment of 5 October 2000, the ECJ has now endorsed the narrow interpretation by stating that 'a mere finding of disparities between national rules and of the abstract risk of obstacles to the exercise of fundamental (economic) freedoms or of distortions of competition liable to result therefrom, [is not] sufficient to justify the choice of Article [95] as a legal basis . . . '.[47]

---

42 See J. Basedow, n. 37 above.

43 Cf. I. Schwartz, 'Perspectiven der Angleichung des Privatrechts in der Europäischen Gemeinschaft' [1994] *Zeitschrift für Europäisches Privatrecht* 559 et seq., cited in Basedow, ibid., at p. 1173.

44 In the case law of the Court the expressions 'common market' (old terminology) and 'internal market' (new terminology) are used in conjunction with each other and virtually as synonyms: see Kapteyn, P.J.G. and P.V. van Themaat, *Introduction to the Law of the European Communities* (3rd edn. by L. Gormley, Kluwer Law International, London, 1998), at pp. 779–780, and the ECJ Judgment of 17 May 1994, *France v Commission*, C-41/93, [1994] ECR I-1829, para. 19.

45 As in the ECJ judgment of 11 June 1991, *Commission v Council*, [1991] ECR I-2867, para. 23, and in the judgment of 13 July 1995, *Spain v Council*, C-350/92, [1995] ECR I-1985, para. 32–36.

46 See W. van Gerven, 'Coherence of Community and National Laws. Is There a Legal Basis for a European Civil Code?' (1997) 5 *European Review of Private Law* 465–469, at 467.

47 ECJ Judgment of 5 October 2000, Case C-376/98, *Germany v Parliament and Council* [2000] ECR I-8419, and the Opinion of Advocate-General Fennelly at ECR I-8423.

Where Article 95 (in its narrow interpretation) does not suffice as a legal basis for the establishment of a European Civil Code, such a legal basis can still be found in Article 94. However, that provision allows the adoption of directives only (and not of regulations as pointed out above), which moreover must be adopted by unanimity, instead of qualified majority, in the Council. The only remaining possibility to achieve *full* uniformity needed to promulgate a fully binding Code, is therefore to enact the Code by means of a multilateral Agreement between the Member States, or at least between those which are ready to adopt a Code. Obviously, that should not preclude such a Code from being prepared with the input of expert lawyers from the other Member States, which would make it easier for those States to adhere to the Agreement when they are ready for it. Such Agreement, although not coming within the scope of Article 293 (ex 220) EC, could nonetheless grant jurisdiction to the ECJ to interpret its provisions in a uniform way.[48]

Codification of large areas of civil law at the level of the European Union raises other important issues as well. These involve in the first place, questions as to whether existing socio-cultural differences between the Member States, and differences in legal mentalities prevailing in those Member States, are not such as to make a binding codification of uniform rules virtually impossible. They involve in the second place, questions as to whether the establishment of such a Code can claim sufficient democratic legitimation needed to secure sufficient acceptance of the Code in the Member States' legal orders.

I would be rather confident that existing socio-cultural differences between the Member States are not of a nature to prevent the establishment of a European Civil Code, certainly not when (as envisaged) it is limited to the law of contracts, torts, property and the like. Indeed, the establishment, for many decades now (more than 40 years for the first six Member States), of intense economic, and also later on, extensive professional, social, cultural and educational exchanges between citizens, companies, universities, public authorities, amongst others, *and* the existence in all of the Member States of similar political institutions and (thanks to the ECHR and the case law of the European Court of Human Rights) of common beliefs in human rights, fundamental freedoms and democracy, have forged a sufficiently solid 'acquis communautaire'. That 'acquis' is certainly able to support and to allow the development of common legislation in the areas just mentioned.[49]

---

48 K. Lenaerts and P. Van Nuffel (R. Bray, ed.), *Constitutional Law of the European Union* (Sweet and Maxwell, London, 1999) at p. 599, referring to the 1980 Rome Convention on the law applicable to contractual obligations (but see now Article 65 (ex 73m) EC).

49 It has certainly the effect that 'legal transplants' between the laws of Member States are facilitated. See further on that phenomenon, A. Watson, *Legal Transplants* (Scottish Academic Press, 1974) and more recently, in relation with public law, J. Bell, 'Mechanisms for Cross-Fertilization of Administrative Law in Europe' in J. Beatson and T. Tridimas (eds.), *New Directions in European Public Law* (Hart Publishing, 1998), p. 147 with further references.

What about differences in legal mentalities? Is it correct to say, in the most general of terms,[50] that 'civil lawyers' of the European continental legal tradition (whereby all those legal systems, and all branches of their laws, are lumped together) follow a principled approach, whilst common lawyers would apply, and only understand, an incremental approach; and that convergence is therefore 'epistemologically' excluded from the very outset;[51] as if the French law of strict liability has not been forged by case law, and as if under English law, the principled approach has not given rise, with ups and downs, to the establishment of the more general tort of negligence?[52] In that regard, one may have some misgivings about the term 'mixed legal systems', which has the connotation that there are legal systems which are not mixed at all. Obviously, it is interesting to see how the Quebec Civil Code, regarded as a genuine mixed codification, deals with the law of trust (through the European institution of *fiducie* derived from the Roman *fiducia cum amico*). But, where is the borderline? Are not all modern legal systems to some extent mixed legal systems? Can any European lawyer tell whether his legal background is more influenced by Rousseau or Montesquieu than by Locke, Machiavelli or Grotius? Is Belgian private law, belonging to the French legal family but during the last decades much influenced by Dutch law, still a non-mixed legal system? And what about the Dutch Civil Code which was first based on a draft prepared between 1822 and 1830 (when Belgium and the Netherlands were united) by a commission of Belgian and Dutch lawyers, following the example of the French Code,[53] to be replaced in 1992 by a new Code which is now also influenced by German and Swiss law? And how would it have been possible for students of the common law, in the US and the UK, not to have

50 Thus P. Legrand, *Fragments on Law-as-Culture* (Tjeenk Willink, Deventer, 1999), a collection of earlier publications, in which according to well-informed readers (see M. Adams, review in *Rechtsk. Weekbl.* 2000, 326) the same arguments are exposed over and over again. For a severe rebuttal, see A. Watson, 'Legal Transplants and European Private Law' *Ius Commune Lectures on European Private Law* (2000) who writes: 'I confess that in large measure I do not comprehend what he is about. I see no substance, just big words... ' at p. 1. For a more subtle rebuttal, see M. van Hoecke, 'The Harmonization of Private Law in Europe: Some Misunderstandings', in M. van Hoecke and F. Ost (eds.), *The Harmonization of European Private Law*, Hart Publishing, Oxford, 2000), at pp. 1–20; see also A. Chamboredon, 'The Debate on a European Civil Code: For an "Open Texture"' at pp. 63–99 in the same book, for a detailed and precise rebuttal.

51 That does not mean that codification should ignore relevant national and regional diversity. Quite to the contrary, as it is stated in Article 151 (ex 128) EC with regard to the EC institutions, it is for them, as it is for all those involved in building the Union, to respect national and regional diversity, but at the same time to bring the common cultural heritage to the fore. This duty to respect diversity is an element that may eventually point in the direction of harmonization, rather than of unification, of national laws.

52 See van Gerven et al., above n. 15, Introductory Note under 1.4.1.B at p. 50–54, and Introductory Note under 2.4.1, at p. 209–211, with special reference in litt.d, at p. 211, to *Henderson v Merrett Syndicates Limited* [1995] 2 AC 145, in which the House of Lords recently reformulated the *Hedley Byrne* principle into a more general liability principle for the provision of services.

53 See C.J.H. Brunner, 'De invoering van een nieuw B.W. in Nederland' [1991] *Tidschrift voor Privaatrecht* 735 at 736.

undergone, in some way or another, the teachings of the great German and Austrian comparatists who, before World War II, immigrated to those countries? And, to come back to the 1960s, how 'unmixed' was the legal education of the many young students who have spent a year or more at one of the great American law schools; not to speak of the numerous students, teachers, judges and advocates, including those from the new candidate Member States, who from the 1980s have been exposed, in ever growing numbers, to contacts with colleagues from other Member States?[54]

In my view, the problems with codification lie elsewhere, that is with the lack of legitimacy of the legislature, and therefore with regard to the principle of democracy.[55]

Recently in a 'plea against minimum standards' and 'a praise of diversity', strong objections have been voiced against the efforts undertaken to codify European civil laws and, therefore, to lay down common rules (explicitly or implicitly seen as a precursor to a European Civil Code).[56] By necessity, such common rules are minimum standards, or principles, and as such abstracted, i.e. 'scraped off', from the innate moral character which is characteristic for value judgments (based on different national moralities) underlying the more specific legal rules. Such principles can therefore 'never be a *restatement* of the existing law'.[57] In addressing a given legal system, one should rather try 'to uncover the hidden policy issues and the contrasting values covering underneath the national rules'.[58] In consequence, jurists who believe 'in the need for a common law for Europe...have to look *forward* to what we wish the legal system to be, and not backward to the mass of national legal materials ... [and must] do something with that material, eliminating some parts of it, extending other parts, rethinking it all'.[59] In other words, European private law

---

[54] Cf. Article 149 (ex 126) EC of which para. 1 reads: 'The Community shall contribute to the development of quality education by encouraging cooperation between Member States and, if necessary, by supporting and supplementing their action, while fully respecting the responsibility of the Member States for the content of teaching and the organisation of education systems and their cultural and linguistic diversity'.

[55] Which Article 6 (ex F) TEU names as one of the principles on which the Union is founded.

[56] Jan M. Smits, *The Good Samaritan in European Private Law: on the Perils of Principles without a Programme and a Programme for the Future* (Kluwer Law International, The Hague, 2000) at pp. 40,43.

[57] Ibid., p. 19: that applies, according to the author, also to European contract law; see Lando and Beale, n. 39 above.

[58] Smits, n. 56 above, at p. 47. I fully agree with that position: see W. van Gerven, *Het Beleid van de Rechter (The Policy of the Judge)* (3rd edn., Standaard Wetenschappelijke Uitgeverij, Antwerpen, 1973), in which I tried to stress the need for 'value-oriented jurisprudence' (the term comes from H.D. Lasswell and M.S. McDougal, *Jurisprudence for a Free Society: Studies in Law, Science and Policy* (Nijhoff, Dordrecht, 1992), at p. 66). As for the 'good Samaritan' (which is the subject of Smits' inaugural speech), I would not draw the difference between the common law and continental laws as deep as in Smits' approach, since also in the latter laws, there exist different shades in civil or penal law enforcement, but, that is a different story.

[59] Ibid., at p. 48.

should have a 'programmatic' character, in that it should single out the parts of private law where differences are not going to disappear in any meaningful sense, and the parts, particularly in the more 'commercial' area of the law of obligations and property law, which 'can be newly founded on the basis of a universal programme'.[60]

These objections must be taken seriously, but should be considered in connection with the role of legislatures and of judges, and not so much (at least not in the first place) with the role of academics.[61] That has to do with what I have called above as the legitimacy of the law and the principle of democracy. According to that principle,[62] it is for a generally elected legislator to make the choices as to what a 'programme' for a European private law necessarily entails, as it is for the courts, in last instance for the supreme courts, to find solutions to concrete situations, thereby contributing, on a case-to-case basis, to the emergence of judicial rules. The task of academics lies elsewhere: it is to facilitate the work of legislators and courts, by helping them in the preparation of their work, and commenting on it when it is done. It is within that institutional framework of decision making that the issue of legitimacy of European supranational law must be situated.

Before elaborating that point, I would like to refer the reader to the distinction between 'law' and 'legislation', which F.A. Hayek has exposed so well.[63] *Law*, according to him, belongs to the category of 'endogenous' orders, growing or originating from within, which means that it originates in, and grows almost spontaneously through, rules which people in a given society live in accordance with.[64] Such rules are articulated in customary law and judge made law. *Legislation* belongs to the category of 'exogenous' orders which are conceived and imposed from the outside, that is in the legal area by a legislature, and tends to influence the endogenous rules when they are evolving in a direction regarded to be wrong or one-sided. Obviously, much is to be said for and against that distinction. However, the point I wish to make here, in conformity I would think with modern theories of deliberative democracy, is that the legitimacy of the law does not only, and not

60 Ibid. Compare with Lambert's statement made one century earlier referred to above in the text accompanying n. 18 above.

61 The distinction between these three categories of jurists is at the basis of van Caenegem's book, n. 14 above.

62 'Democracy is in itself an idea of great abstraction if not ambiguity', thus R. Dworkin, *Sovereign Virtue* (Harvard University Press, Cambridge, 2000) at p. 185, who adds however, that it 'requires that officials be elected by the people rather than chosen through inheritance or by a small group of prominent families or electors'. Obviously, democracy has also other aspects, less 'procedural' and more 'substantive', such as equality and universality values flowing from the fundamental concept of human dignity.

63 *Law, Legislation and Liberty*, I: *Rules and Order* (Routledge, London, 1973).

64 To be compared with F.C. von Savigny's view of the law as a living entity moving and changing with the broad stream of a nation's ideas ('Volksgeist'). However, this view leads von Savigny to oppose codification because, codes fix the law at a given moment in history, and to turn instead to learned jurists, academics, who are to ascertain this 'folk-law': see R.C. van Caenegem, n. 14, at pp. 51–52.

ultimately, come from above (top-down); but also, perhaps mainly, from below (bottom-up). Which implies that, in addition to legitimacy emanating from above, judge-made law is crucial in the promotion of pluralist discourse and, therefore, to enhance democratic legitimacy. Moreover, in the absence at the European level of a full fledged legislator, judge-made law may well present in some areas of the law an indispensable and readily available form of deliberative democracy.[65]

4. The Issue of Legitimacy of an Emerging *Ius Commune Europaeum*

European codification of private law (limited to the law of obligations and property) needs to be considered in light of the foregoing. It may be argued that, apart from the necessity to find a legal basis for codification in Community law (which cannot be found in Article 95 EC), there is a need for codification to obtain the highest degree of democratic legitimacy and credibility that can be achieved[66] in order to be acceptable in all Member States. Credibility requires that the academic endeavour to prepare a civil code be embedded in a legal environment which has solid roots in the legal systems of the Member States. Democratic legitimacy requires that the codification must somehow have the approval of the people, that is through its legally elected representatives.[67] The former can be secured by a group of experts coming from the various Member States involved. The latter can only be achieved by such a group of experts if each of them has a clear official mandate from the *national* authorities of his or her Member State and, moreover, if the group does have unambiguous political backing at the *European* level – which must be broader than support from certain fractions of the European Parliament.[68] Even where the Code would be adopted by a qualified majority in the Council, as is made possible by the procedure of Article 251 EC to which Article 95 refers (assuming again that such provision were to offer a sufficient legal basis, *quod non*), democratic legitimacy would still be fragile. That is so because of the complicated procedure of article 251 EC, which requires that once the Commission is prepared to submit a proposal to the

65 On deliberative democracy, see E.O. Erikson and J.E. Fossum (eds.), *Democracy in the European Union. Integration through Deliberation* (Routledge, London, 2000): 'The specific characteristic of this approach is that it conceives of "supranational" law not as given rules, which pre-empt and have supremacy over national legal systems, but as law that derives its validity from the "deliberative" quality of its production', thus C. Joerges and M. Everson in their contribution to that book, at p. 181.

66 See, for a more extensive assessment of the need for codification at the European level, W. van Gerven, 'A Common Law for Europe: the Future Meeting the Past' (2000) 8 *European Review of Private Law*, forthcoming.

67 Cf. Dworkin's definition of democracy in Dworkin, n. 62 above.

68 To my knowledge, the other components of the legislature – the Commission which has the right of initiative, and the Council – have not expressed any unequivocal support: the statement of the Tampere European Council of 15–16 October 1999 (which is not the Council of Ministers in the EC context) to achieve greater coherence in civil law, was made in the limited context of eliminating obstacles to the good functioning of civil proceedings (para. 39 of the conclusions of the Presidency) and, moreover, has not been followed up at the Intergovernmental Conference of December 2000 in Nice.

Parliament and to the Council, both those institutions must reach an agreement on the final version. In other words, under that procedure there remains a decisive part of decision-making power with the Commission (which has the right of proposal) and with the Council (which has an equal say as Parliament), two institutions which, unlike the European Parliament, are non elected components of the European legislature and, more importantly, are not directly (and, as a college, not even indirectly) accountable to the Parliaments of the Member States. That may be seen as a serious impediment, especially in those Member States where codification is an instrument that does not belong to the legislative tradition.[69]

If the involvement of national Parliaments in carrying out such an important undertaking as the enactment of a Code is seen as an essential element to lend additional credibility and legitimacy to the undertaking, the only way to involve national Parliaments[70] is by adopting the Code by means of an Agreement between Member States – which necessitates parliamentary ratification in the Member States that have chosen to adopt the Agreement. That may seem a long way to go, but also, the enactment on the (highly controversial) legal basis of Article 95,[71] or on the (non controversial but not fully satisfactory) legal basis of Article 94, is less likely to occur, taking into account the complicated procedure and the lack of genuine interest, at least for the time being, on the part of the Council (and, it would seem, also of the Commission).

There is another reason why the proposed codification should preferably *not* occur within the legal and institutional framework of Article 95 or, for that matter, Article 94 EC but rather, by way of an Agreement between Member States. That is because, only the latter instrument allows the enactment of uniform rules to be extended to areas for which the European Community does not possess jurisdiction under the principles of attribution of competences and of subsidiarity; or, for which it has received jurisdiction but only in so far as necessary to achieve the objectives of the EC Treaty (Article 5, paragraph 3 EC), that is, in the terminology of Article 94 EC, in so far as divergent national rules may 'directly affect the establishment or functioning of the common [internal] market'. Those restrictions on the EC legislature's competence may indeed encourage the draftsmen of a Code – in order to avoid criticism as to the legality of their proposals – to view the provisions of the

[69] It might help those countries to call the enactment of uniform rules in the areas of contracts, torts and property not a *Code*, but rather to let the enactment take the form of three separate *Acts*.

[70] Article 95 may constitute a legal basis but only for harmonization through directives and with unanimity in the Council of Ministers, and of course does not involve national parliaments (unless the original but *praeter legem* technique would be used that was put into effect in the preparation of the European Charter of fundamental rights, adopted at the Intergovernmental Conference in Nice, that is, by convening a so-called 'Convention' in which not only the European institutions but also the national Parliaments were represented).

[71] The worst thing that could happen to the codification effort is that enactment on the basis of Article 95 would be successfully attacked for nullity by one or more Member State before the ECJ, on the basis of Article 230 EC.

Code mainly in a context of the objectives of the internal market. Those objectives are to eliminate or approximate national laws, regarded as obstacles to the free movement of goods, services and capital, to establish a system of undistorted competition and, in the process, to safeguard the interests of consumers and of the environment. Drafting a Code in light of those objectives may lead the draftsmen to give preference to specific interests or objectives, instead of taking a neutral view of all interests involved, general and specific, as is required in the case of a document of general legislation.[72] In the law of torts, that attitude might lead for example, to giving preference, as a matter of principle, to a form of strict liability, in order to better protect consumers and the environment and (through compulsory insurance directives) victims of road accidents, instead of examining the issue of strict liability as opposed to fault liability in a neutral way, that is without 'prejugé favourable' for either of them.

To use the instrument of an Agreement to enact a Code (and therefore to involve the national Parliaments in the enactment) must obviously go hand in hand with the creation of a preliminary ruling procedure enabling a Community court to interpret the Code provisions in a uniform way at the request of a national court before which litigation is pending. There is no reason why an existing Community court (ECJ or CFI) might not be given jurisdiction to that effect in the Agreement concerned.[73] However, given the probably substantial amount of litigation concerning the interpretation of the new rules, it may be unavoidable to set up a new Community court which, obviously, would require a substantial amount of budgetary means. It is not at all certain that the Member States would be ready to give such high priority to the project of European codification.

The enactment of uniform rules at the European level preferably, as indicated, through an Agreement between Member States is not sufficient in itself. In order to make European codification consistent with the historical development of the underlying national legal systems, i.e. in order to make, in Hayek's terms, European *legislation* accord with the *law* of the Member States as it has grown, through national statutory and judge-made law, in those Member States' legal systems, it is absolutely necessary to embed such codification in principles and solutions which are firmly rooted in the common legal heritage of the European legal orders.[74] Only then will it be possible to create and to maintain uniform rules, which are not 'scraped off' from underlying and changing value judgments, and which are able, notwithstanding

[72] Unless, of course, one chooses from the outset two different sets of civil codes, more particularly contract law: one for merchant transactions and one for transactions with consumers: thus Smits, n. 56 above, at pp. 45–46.

[73] See Lenaerts and Van Nuffel, n. 48 above, at p. 599.

[74] See R. Zimmerman, 'Roman Law and European Legal Unity' in A. Hartkamp (ed.), *Towards a European Civil Code* (2nd edn., Kluwer Law International, 1998), at pp. 33–34: 'The idea that a codification should be able entirely to cut off the continuity of historical development, has proved to be a rather simplistic illusion . . . [T]he re-appearance of ideas and solutions from the treasure-house of the *ius commune* is by no means a rare . . . phenomenon.'

uniformity, to allow differences in innate moralities and mentalities to subsist and to evolve, and with time to converge.

This reality underlines the need for Community or national legislators, draftsmen or courts creating or interpreting uniform law, to look for common principles that are already present in the Member States' laws *and* judge-made rules.[75] That is what Article 285 (ex 215), paragraph 2 EC requires the ECJ to do with regard to the extra-contractual liability of Community institutions, and what the Court has done in developing a catalogue of basic rights and fundamental freedoms (now explicitly stated in Article 6, paragraph 2 TEU) as well as in other areas of Community law. There is no reason why other *Community institutions*, i.e. the Council, Parliament and the Commission – where they act within the competences conferred upon them by Community (or Union) law – or for *Member States* – where they conclude Agreements in areas within or outside the realm of the EU – should not act accordingly. Only by founding uniform supranational rules on such a common substratum of national 'law' and 'legislation' will it be possible to prevent such rules to be regarded in the Member States as a foreign legal artifact (*Fremdkörper)* to which those Member States and their citizens are submitted from above, that is by a distant, and too often perceived as a bureaucratic, supranational authority.[76]

To draw on principles which the Member States' legal orders have in common is of even greater importance in the large areas of the law (such as family or penal law), which fall outside the scope of Community law and for which there is no European legislator whatsoever. That does not prevent a European *ius commune* from emerging, also in those areas of the law, partly as a result of the case law of the European Court of Human Rights, and partly as a result of increasingly growing contacts between citizens of the EU as well as of immigration of non-citizens into the EU. In those areas, it is even more imperative to uncover elements of 'commonality' in the legal orders of the European States.

5. 'Bottom-up' and 'Top-down' Harmonization

It is precisely to fulfill that task, i.e. to help commonality – where it exists, or is bound to exist – to come to the fore, that a project of 'Casebooks for a common law of Europe' was launched in 1994 by the author of this contribution, with the support of a Steering Committee of leading judges and scholars from many Member States.[77] The project and the comparative method applied, presented as a 'bottom-up' approach (in contrast with a 'top-down' approach), was described in a short article

[75] Such principles are, by nature, 'open texture' rules: see, further, Chamboredon, n. 50 above.

[76] See further W. van Gerven, 'Taking Article 215 (2) EC Seriously' in J. Beatson and T. Tridimas (eds.), *New Directions in European Public Law* (Hart Publishing, Oxford, 1998), at pp. 45–47 (Article 215 (2) EC is *not* Article 288 (2) EC).

[77] On the emergence of 'A new Common Law for Europe', see Lord Bingham of Cornhill, in B.S. Markesinis (ed.), *The Clifford Chance Millennium Lectures: The Coming Together of the Common Law and the Civil Law* (Hart Publishing, Oxford, 2000) at p. 27, where the case book project is welcomed at

published in 1996.[78] Each of the books tends to reproduce legal materials – judgments mainly but also legislative acts and, where relevant, excerpts from doctrinal writings – which are drawn primarily from the three major European legal systems (English, French, German) and, in combination therewith, from the two European supranational legal orders (the EU and the ECHR). The project's objectives are twofold. *Educational*, first, which is to supply teachers and students from all over Europe with comparative teaching material, in order to make them acquainted with the style, substance, reasoning – in one word, with the mentality of the main national and supranational legal orders,[79] in view of bringing mentalities closer to each other. The objective of the casebooks is also *political*, in the sense that, as explained above, the project wants to help create credibility and legitimacy to the emerging common law. By uncovering similarities and differences in legal concepts and principles, as well as in value judgments and policy decisions which are applied in the national legal orders,[80] it is hoped that commonality between European legal systems will come to the fore and that the legitimacy of a common law for Europe will be strengthened.

The 'bottom-up' approach, based on the examination of statutory and judge made law in the Member States' legal orders – regarded, in the absence of a full fledged Community legislature, as a prime source of democratic legitimacy of a European *ius commune* – does not make the 'top down' approach superfluous, that is to stimulate convergence through the elaboration of principles. Both approaches are indeed complementary to each other. An excellent example of such a 'top-down' approach is found in the 'Principles on Contract' prepared by the Lando group referred to above,[81] and in similar projects. Together, the 'top-down' approach (principles) and the 'bottom-up' approach (case books) supply judges, teachers and

pp. 33–34. See also, in addition to many of the other contributions, the concluding contribution of Lord Goff of Chieveley, 'Coming Together, the Future' at p. 239 (also discussing the feasibility of a Code, at pp. 241–244).

[78] W. van Gerven, 'Casebooks for a Common Law of Europe' (1996) 4 *European Review of Private Law* 67–70.

[79] The second, revised and substantially enlarged edition of the casebook on tort law (van Gerven et al., n. 15 above) was published by Hart Publishing in December 2000. The table of contents and part of the materials can be consulted at the Internet site <http://www.rechten.unimaas.nl/casebook>. The casebook on contract law will appear in 2002 and the casebook on judicial review will hopefully be published in 2003.

[80] For a telling example, see the case law existing in various countries relating to medical liability in unsuccessful abortion or vasectomy cases. See in particular, the recent House of Lords judgment in *Macfarlane v Tayside Health Board* [1999] 3 WLR 1301, as compared with the judgment of the Dutch Hoge Raad of 21 February 1997: although both courts come to a different conclusion on whether compensation can be claimed for educational expenses to be made in the future for the healthy born child, the same value and policy arguments were used, and weighed against each other. Moreover, in the Dutch case, the Advocate General, J.B.M. Vranken, came to the same conclusion as the House of Lords. Excerpts from the cases with comments can be found in van Gerven et al., above n. 15, under 2.E.6, at pp. 92–98 and 2.NL.25, p. 133–136.

[81] Lando and Beale, n. 39 above.

other lawyers with an excellent overview of the 'law' as it stands. Together, they account for the diversity and commonality of Europe's legal cultures and how they are gradually turned into a common European legal culture.[82]

In developing a European *ius commune*, it is obviously not the aim to duplicate the past (if that were possible), nor should it be the aim to establish unity, or even convergence, just for the sake of it. And indeed, convergence must be pursued only if it is in line with desirable tendencies in society (including the tendency towards European integration), and if it is not inconsistent with the need to preserve diversity in areas (primarily outside the scope of Community law and of the ECHR) where such diversity is required because of pluralism and multi-culturalism in present society.[83] To preserve diversity, but at the same time to emphasize commonality is the delicate balance which Article 151 (ex 128) EC requires all Community institutions to strive for, i.e. 'to contribute to the flowering of the cultures of the Member States, while respecting their national and regional diversity and at the same time bringing the common cultural heritage to the fore'.

6. Subjects of Applied Comparative Law

There are many areas within and outside the scope of EC law where comparative law is 'of strategic importance' as mentioned above, or as Harding puts it,[84] where comparative law constitutes 'a practical method by which we can decide inter-jurisdictional questions to do with legislation, legal transplantation and legal development or reform, with the possible higher aim of unification or standardization of principles of justice in pursuit of humanistic, economic or environmental goals'. That is particularly the case in the context of an integrated Europe.

82 See van Gerven, n. 66 above. To show that this is not just an illusion, it may suffice here to quote the following passage from R. Zimmerman, *Opus Magnum. The Law of Obligations, Roman Foundations of the Civilian Tradition* (Clarendon Press, Oxford, 1996), at X and XI of the Preface: 'In the Middle Ages, the whole of educated Europe formed a single and undifferentiated central unit, and the Roman-canon "common law" was part and parcel of this European culture. Law professors moved freely from a chair in one country to one in another; the same textbooks were used at Pavia or Bologna as much as at Halle, Alcalà or Oxford . . . ' and '. . . the "European" ius commune and the "English" common law were (and are) not really so radically distinct as is often suggested. This applies to the methodological approach and framework . . . as much as to the substantive legal rules. Thus, firstly, the continental ius commune of the 16th, 17th and 18th centuries displayed many features what we like to regard today as typically English. For it was not a professorial law characterised by impractical abstractions, deductive reasoning and conceptual jurisprudence . . . And secondly: England in reality was never completely cut off from continental legal culture'.

83 Thus also J.M. Smits, 'Multiculturalisme in Europees privaatrecht: een pleidooi' in *Nederlands Tijdschrift voor Burgerlijk Recht* (2000) p. 289, who, at p. 291, refers in that context to the openness of the case law of the Privy Council which allows itself to take account of differences between common law countries, as in *Invercargill City Council v Hamlin* [1996] 2 WLR 367, [1996] AC 264 (also briefly discussed in van Gerven et al., n. 15 above, at 53 of the second edition).

84 Harding, above n. 2.

Let me therefore, to conclude, just mention some subjects to which the method of comparative law, as described in this article, can be applied. All subjects relate to public law, that is an area of the law which – because of its close association with the concept of the 'Nation State' and before the emergence of the 'new pluralism'[85] – has too long been neglected.[86]

Those subjects are: (i) the shaping of legal remedies (mainly compensation, injunctive relief, restitution) primarily on the part of private persons *vis-à-vis* the State;[87] (ii) the establishment of a 'constitution' for Europe, to be based on principles which the Member States have in common, and turning around three subject-matters: a catalogue of basic rights and freedoms of citizens adopted at the summit meeting of the European Council held in Nice in December 2000; the European Union's institutional balance, encompassing both the division of powers between the national and the supranational level and the division of powers between the three pillars, and the institutions, of the Union; and the governmental form which the Union is to take (bi-cameral parliament, presidential or purely parliamentary system) including the delicate question – which led to the collective resignation of the previous European Commission – of accountability and political responsibility of the Commission towards the Parliament and the Council;[88] and (iii) the structuring of the European Union's legal framework to counter fraud affecting the financial interests of the Community,[89] and even more so, to combat serious transborder crime,[90] which concerns, the issue of establishing a European Public Prosecutor's Office.[91]

All of these subjects need significant comparative research in the laws of the ever-increasing number of Member States, with the higher aim of 'standardization of principles of justice in pursuit of humanistic ... goals'.[92] In the absence of comparative research, solutions would be more difficult to find or would be too artificial, or lack credibility and legitimacy, for not being rooted in the hard core of principles that Member States have in common.

---

85 See Koopman, above n. 8.

86 Is it not indicative that Zweigert-Kötz, n. 5 above, which has an excellent introduction to comparative law, that all subjects discussed in the special part relate to private law?

87 See van Gerven, above n. 17.

88 See on those subjects, van Gerven, 'Managing the European Union: For Better or for Worse?' in Markesinis, n. 77 above, at p. 91 et seq.; and 'Het voor en tegen van een Europese Grondwet' in A.K. Koekkoek (ed.), *Bijdragen aan een Europese Grondwet* (Staatsrechtconferentie, Tilburg, 8 December 2000) at pp. 27–44.

89 See Article 280 (ex 209a) EC.

90 See Article 29 (ex K1) TEU.

91 See W. van Gerven, 'Constitutional Conditions for a Public Prosecutor's Office at the European Level' in G. De Kerchove and A. Weyembergh (eds.), *Vers un Espace Judiciaire Pénal Européen/Towards a European Judicial Criminal Area*, (*Institut d'Etudes Européennes, Université Libre de Bruxelles*, Brussels, 2000), at pp. 301–325.

92 Harding, above n. 2.

Chapter 10

THE CONTRIBUTION OF COMPARATIVE LAW TO THE HARMONIZATION OF EUROPEAN PRIVATE LAW

*Efstathios Banakas**

Banakas' contribution, like those of Smits, van Gerven and McDonald, explores an area of comparative legal study which will be of enormous importance both in itself and for the light it will shed, by its example, on the future of law more generally: that is European integration. He indicates the practical role that comparatists can play in debates concerning this issue that currently appear to be somewhat disconnected from the experience of legal sociology, comparative law, and even legal history. Although comparatists could well be seen as advocates of narrow legal nationalism, attempting to prevent destruction of the 'Alhambras of national legal art', and emphasizing differences as against similarities, they can also, he points out, be of practical help in trying to overcome the formidable obstacles which integration encounters at both the macro and micro levels. Interestingly enough, he sees comparatists as potential advocates for either side *in these debates.*

In elaborating on this theme, Banakas brings into play the diverse forms of European legal culture and tradition, echoing here the concerns of Rafenne and Foster, for example. He also adverts to the perennial debates about legal transplantation; and to some interesting examples such as good faith in consumer transactions, assessment of damages, tort liability for defective products and of public bodies.

Are there any compelling reasons for harmonizing private law in Europe, he asks? He does not provide a dogmatic answer to this question, but presumably comparatists should play a part in these large political decisions as well as trying to bridge the gaps between legal traditions. Banakas would prefer the process of legal integration to be left outside politics and sees political will as ultimately an obstacle rather than a necessity; yet the new Dutch Civil Code was achieved only by co-operation between politicians and lawyers, and also involved looking at different solutions in comparative vein. To facilitate the process of legal integration and the drafting of an effective and legitimate

* Senior Lecturer, University of East Anglia, Norwich.

A. Harding and E. Örücü (eds.),
Comparative Law in the 21st Century, 179–192.

European Civil Code, he advocates the setting up of an European Law Institute, and draws inspiration from the American Restatements.

[A. Harding and E. Örücü]

1. Looking for a Role for Comparative Law in European Legal Harmonization

The harmonization of European private law is an unstoppable process, its momentum increasing, it seems, in reverse proportion to the objections and criticisms it provokes. Politicians, academics, pressure groups and the media are all, for different reasons, attracted by it, and involved in increasing its momentum. Academic objections, in particular, from those among us that are concerned about the degrading effect of piecemeal harmonization on national private law theory built on centuries of painstaking labour of scholars and practitioners, seem more and more futile. The Alhambras of national legal art are falling as Europe is hurrying on to greater integration. The question now is what will emerge in their place, and it is in this connection that comparative law may be of some help.

First, however, comparative law needs to be tuned into shape. Whether it is a science or not,[1] it is certainly a discipline today submerged in a self-analysis of its own aims and methods. A reason for this is, perhaps, not so much the state of the health of its methodology, but, rather, the 'boundless freedom that it offers', described by Kokkini-Iatridou as 'the great attraction of comparative law.[2] This freedom is, indeed, dangerous, and one should heed to the warning of Ludwig Wittgenstein, the most cautious among modern thinkers, when defining the premises of communicating knowledge through the unique instrument of language. Talking about comparison in general, he pointed out the great risk of confusing the prototype with the object of comparison, which we are viewing in its light.[3] I do not propose to enter here into the controversy about whether comparative law is a science or, less pretentiously, only a method or, finally, only a humble craft, acquired through experience and intuition. If it is a method, it is better based on empirical premises. As Maurice Merleau-Ponty, the French philosopher, put it, '[T]he perceived world is the always presupposed foundation of all rationality, all value, all existence.[4] Law is understood as perceived; and its origin is perceived as

1 A passionate argument in favour of a 'science' of comparative law is presented in L.-J. Constantinesco, *Traite de Droit Compare, vol. iii* (Economica, Paris, 1983), published posthumously.

2 D. Kokkini-Iatridou, 'Some Methodological Aspects of Comparative Law – the Third Part of a (pre-)Paradigm'.

3 L. Wittgenstein, *Culture and Value* (trans. by P. Winch, Oxford University Press, Oxford 1980), p. 14e.

4 M. Merleau-Ponty, '*Le Primat de la Perception et ses Consequences Philosophiques*' (1947) XLI *Bulletin de la Société Française de Philosophie* 120.

rooted in, chiefly political power relations.[5] But the phenomenon of law is, also, a *cultural* phenomenon; it is, therefore, important to explore this, and the phenomenon of *legal culture* itself, as a methodological basis, a *prototype* in Wittgenstein's words, of comparative law. Understanding the political process and the dynamics of legal culture are important skills in dealing with comparative law. They are equally important for easing the pain of European harmonization.

The political process of European legal harmonization involves three major Community players: the Commission; the European Parliament; and the Economic and Social Committee.[6] Of course, the major instruments of harmonization, i.e. directives, are agreed by the Council of Ministers, but the importance of regulations issued by the Commission, under powers delegated by the Council, for the harmonization of private law, should not be underestimated. Such Regulations are issued in great number every year, as a quick search of any legal database will show. A new area of harmonization can be proposed by any of the above Community bodies to the Commission, or decided directly by the Council. The Commission will draft the directive (or regulation) with the help of legal experts. At this point, comparative lawyers can offer important knowledge and skill. Knowledge of the actual state of theory and practice in national legal systems of member states is obviously important; but beyond that, skill in understanding the national legal cultures is even more so. It is legal culture that will in fact determine the degree to which harmonization will be effective.

Knowledge of theory and practice of other systems can prevent embarrassing initiatives from coming into existence. It is still the case that among European lawyers, even legal scholars, there is ignorant hostility of institutions and practices in other countries. The Regulations on Unfair Terms in Contracts provoked great concern among scholars in this country, unfamiliar with the German theory of 'good faith'; and a new initiative of the European Parliament to propose a draft directive on harmonizing the mode of assessment of personal injury damages has surprised French lawyers, who saw in it the adoption of their own system of invalidity scales (IPP), which they despise and want to reform, probably because alternative methods, such as the English tariff system, are widely unknown or misunderstood among lawyers in other European countries. For the same reasons, after the harmonizing instrument is put into force, comparative lawyers have a further important role to play. They can be advocates for either side: for the Commission, when it monitors the implementation of the harmonizing instrument as it is its duty; or, for a member state, resisting such implementation on the ground that the national legal system provides already answers of sufficient proximity to the Community model. Successful defence of the national system's existing provision should be no small matter for those concerned with preserving national systematic purity. A good

---

5 See W.S. Hamrick, *An Existential Phenomenology of Law: Maurice Merleau-Ponty* (Dordrecht/Boston/Lancaster 1987), p. 116; translations of Merleau-Ponty's French writings are borrowed from this book.

6 Article 94 (new) EC Treaty.

example is France's lost battle to resist enacting a new legal instrument to implement the Product Liability Directive of 1985.[7] French lawyers failed to win the argument that such implementation was unnecessary, in the light of the jurisprudential development, in celebrated decisions of the Cour de Cassation, of Article 1384 of the Code Civil (*responsabilité du fait des choses*). As a result, the once elegant tort law section of the Code Civil has now been marred by a long list of new articles reproducing verbatim the articles of the directive, in a style and language alien to the honoured Napoleonic original.

While all of this is obvious for anyone to see, more needs to be said about the importance of legal culture for the harmonization process; even more so, in view of the fact that the nature and function of legal culture is often overlooked by comparative lawyers themselves. Merleau-Ponty made the important point that culture in general, and, one should also add, legal culture, in particular, cannot be wholly deduced from the perceived world – this only contains the *foundation* of that which is cultural.[8] Legal culture is not only an empirical reality, but, also, a basis of meaning, i.e. of talking about the law. As pointed out by the American pragmatist philosopher Dewey, all description of social and cultural phenomena by language is itself, purposeful: for, as he put it, social and cultural phenomena are never 'over and done with', but remain always open, are 'goings-on.[9] Law, itself a social and cultural phenomenon, is also a 'going-on' phenomenon, that can only be perceived to *be* what it functions *as* in the social and cultural context. The great German anthropologist Richard Thurnwald, argued for the law to be perceived and understood 'functionally out of the cultural system.[10]

2. What is Legal Culture?

The great legal anthropologist, Bronislaw Malinowski, has described all culture as 'normative'.[11] This important aspect of all culture, especially, of *legal* culture, implies that a group's or a community's conformity to aspired aims and goals, serves the function of providing answers to *normative* problems. A basic distinction is the one between 'lay' and 'internal' legal culture. *Lay* legal culture, far from being uniform, can exist on several different levels: one can speak, for example, about the lay legal culture of a whole country or nation, or that of a social class, or of a regional or local, or other (for example, religious) group of people. It is pointed out that in most of the world's contemporary states there are more than one social class or culture group in one or more of these senses, and, therefore, also several legal cultures

7 EC Directive 85/374.

8 Hamrick, above n. 5, p. 3 et seq.

9 Quoted in A. Ryan, 'Pragmatism and Property', unpublished paper, IALS, 1993.

10 R. Thurnwald, *Werden, Wandel und Gesteltung des Rechts im Lichte der Voelkerforshung* (Berlin, Leipzig, 1934), vol. ii, 6.

11 B. Malinowski, *The Dynamics of Cultural Change: An Inquiry into Race Relations in Africa* (Yale University Press, New Haven, 1945), 44–5.

(*cultural pluralism*). *Internal* legal culture is the process of law-making and law-finding, the methods of legal reasoning of judges, the structure of the legal system and the administration of justice in a given jurisdiction, and the training and organisation of the legal profession.[12] Comparative legal historians and mainstream legal comparatists, primarily with legal training, use concepts such as 'legal tradition', or 'style of legal systems', in much the same way as sociologists use the concept of legal culture. Merryman's definition of 'legal tradition' includes 'historically conditioned attitudes about the nature of the law, about the role of law in the society and the polity, about the proper organisation and operation of a legal system, and about the way law is or should be made, applied, studied, perfected and taught.

A comparatist who likes to use the concept of legal culture more than anything else to understand differences in legal systems is Alan Watson. Watson argues that legal culture is a powerful and autonomous factor of legal change, or, for that matter, of legal inertia in the face of changing social and political conditions. For him, legal culture must be distinguished into that of lay people, lawyers and lawmakers.[13] Watson argues that social or economic pressure for legal change starting with lawmakers, operates only within their own culture, whereas if such pressure 'starts with the lawyers, their own culture is involved and the pressure must be directed against the culture of the lawmakers. For Watson, the existence of a distinct culture of lawmakers explains, firstly, the historical phenomenon of legal orders borrowing socially and economically 'dysfunctional' legal transplants (for he believes that '[T]o a considerable degree, the lawmakers of one society share the same legal culture with lawmakers of other societies')? Secondly, the separate legal culture of lawmakers is, for Watson, responsible for what he considers to be the 'positive disinclination' of lawmakers to change formally the rules, institutions, and, especially, the *sources* of law, when the law is out of date. The question is whether culture in general, and legal culture in particular, are *significantly autonomous*, from the aims and goals of the socio-political and economic model, in which the law also operates.

This question is particularly important in relation to the role that legal culture can play in the process of harmonization of European private law. Furthermore, it has rightly been pointed out that: '[A]lthough the careful study of a single legal culture can yield valuable insights, only the analysis of a variety of legal cultures will recognise what is accidental rather than necessary, what is permanent rather than changeable in legal norms and legal agencies, and what characterises the beliefs underlying both As everything else is perceived and understood, law and legal culture is perceived and understood comparatively. But comparison presupposes a separate identity: a thing cannot be compared to itself. How culturally specific is law? A leading legal sociologist of our time has observed that '[T]he modern world makes

[12] L.M. Friedman, *Law and Society: an Introduction* (Englewood Cliffs, NJ, Prentice Hall, 1977).

[13] A. Watson, 'Legal Change: Sources of Law and Legal Culture' (1983) 131 *University of Pennsylvania Law Review* 1121, 1152 et seq.

a strong case against cultural specificity.[14] A quick look at the World's modern societies shows that diverse, or similar social structures and economies, rather than 'cultures' in the sense of values and attitudes of lawyers and laypersons, account for diversity, or convergence, in their laws. But, as with many other things in life, the truth about what gives to law, and to a legal system its specific characteristics, probably lies *via media* between Montesquieu's view of law as a product of national and cultural forces, and the views of more modern comparatists,[15] underlining the importance of the social and political environment.

Indeed, it appears that the more societies advance in their political, economic and social structures, the more powerful these structures themselves become over cultural specificity in shaping the law's real identity, behind its symbolic or ritual image. Elsewhere I have argued that because cultural roots and historical choices are an integral part of any description, or explanation of law at a particular place and time over a particular community, comparative law must be alert to the need of a *tertium comparationis* that, in taking into account cultural specificity, this does not have a Procrustean effect on the proper understanding of foreign legal systems.[16]

3. Legal Culture and the Harmonization Process

The pace of Europeanization of legal life in the last few years in the European Community must weigh heavily in answering the question of how culture-specific national legal systems still are. From universities to law firms, the European mix increases, and the European Courts in Luxembourg grow every day in confidence in laying foundations for common principles of European private law.[17] Law students already have a European casebook on tort Law,[18] and judges and practitioners a European textbook on contract Law.[19] Several groups of European academics are at work developing common principles and rules or contract law (Lando group), tort (Vienna group), or, casting a wider net, a European Civil Code and the Common Core of European Civil Law (the Trento project). The European Academy in Trier is only one of many academic institutions offering a relentless programme of seminars

14 L. Friedman, *The Legal System: A Social Science Perspective* (Russell Sage Foundation, New York, 1975), 195.

15 E.g., O. Kahn-Freund, 'On Uses and Misuses of Comparative Law' (1974) 37 *Modern Law Review* 1; R. Seidman, 'Administrative Law and Legitimacy in Anglophonic Africa: A Problem in the Reception of Foreign Law' (1970) 5 *Law and Society Review* 161.

16 E.K. Banakas, 'Some Thoughts on the Method of Comparative Law: The Concept of Law Revisited' (1981) LXVII *Archiv fur Rechts- und Sozialphilosophie* 289, 292 et seq.

17 A good example is the effect of the case of *Brasserie du Pecheur* [1996] Common Market Law Reports 889 (joined cases C-46/93 & C-48/93). On English law cf. *R. v Secretary of State for Transport, ex p. Factortame & ors.* [2000] 1 AC 524, HL.

18 See W. van Gerven, J. Lever and P. Larouche, 'Tort Law' in W. van Gerven, J. Lever and P. Larouche, *Ius Commune Casebooks for the Common Law of Europe* (2nd edn., Hart Publishing, Oxford, 2000).

19 H. Kötz, *Europäisches Vertragsrecht* (J.C.B. Mohr, Tübingen, 1996).

in European private law, attended by practitioners of member states as part of their continuous education programme. What is the effect of all this on national legal cultures? This is an enormous question, of an enormous significance, which comparative lawyers in Europe must see as a big challenge.

The answer to that question will enlighten the debate of whether legal harmonization is a good or a bad thing for Europe, and whether it proceeds on the right path. For, whatever the political power of the market may be (and effecting the common market is the unique basis of harmonization of private law in the European Union at the present moment), the market, as the American experience shows, is only concerned with economic efficiency, and will not provide answers to wider questions of validity and value of legal rules and practices. It is difficult to foresee how far national legal cultures will be defended by national communities, against the onslaught of continuing European integration. There may be objectively little to regret, in terms of moral, artistic or other value, in the disappearance of national legal cultures in Europe. But there is evidence that in some member states other parallel to the legal national cultures, such as religion or literature are emerging as political flagships of resistance in support of national identity. And there is also evidence that certain benchmark principles of national private law are now being defended as part of the constitutional fabric of member states, in anticipation of a further advance in harmonization, such as the French principle of *faute* or the English doctrine of public authority immunity in exercising discretion. More importantly perhaps, judges and practising lawyers in member states are increasingly unhappy with the scholarly rush to create a uniform theoretical basis of European private law. Private law is more than competition in the market or corporate and commercial transactions. It is also about intimate, very important aspects of personal life, that judges are convinced are better dealt with in the environment of the local culture and tradition. There is evidence that in some member states, judges and practising lawyers are already looking to their national governments for support in their defence of national legal culture against new Brussels initiatives. Could this be the beginning of the unfolding of the great process of harmonization of European private law?

4. Taking Harmonization Seriously: A Review of Some Basic Issues

4.1. Obstacles

Whatever might have been the reality of the *ius commune* of Europe in the middle ages, supported at that time by common feudal structures in the national legal cultures of modern Europe, emerging one by one after the watershed of the French Revolution, private law has been seen as a matter of national pride and prestige. Only as recently as eight years ago, and in the midst of hectic negotiations to move European integration forward afield in areas hitherto not envisaged by the original treaties, the Dutch, who spearheaded these negotiations, brought into force their new Civil Code. In the two centuries since the first European Civil Code (the Code

Napoleon), marked the new era of national legal pride in Europe, the other countries that presently form the European Union, with the exception of United Kingdom, Ireland, Belgium, Luxembourg and the Scandinavian countries, created, one by one, their own, proud codifications. Belgium and Luxembourg are still using the Code Napoleon. The United Kingdom resisted the introduction of civil law-style codifications as alien to the culture of law-makers in this country, and so did Ireland, where, however, there is now, at this advanced stage of European integration, talk of an Irish Civil Code. As for the Scandinavian countries, they have consolidated centuries of judge-made rules of civil liability in fairly recent legislation, preserving the individuality of their solutions, even as they were entering the European Union.

Civil Codes in Europe have always been seen as important declarations of national legal identity, and the law of civil liability, the most dynamic part of civil law, has been the focus of efforts for distinctive national styles. Thus, in the two common law countries, United Kingdom and Ireland, the law of torts is jealously guarded as an idiosyncratic, judge-made branch of civil law with a practical and systematic importance unknown to Continental legal systems. The German Civil Code openly chose to differ from the Code Napoleon in its design of Liability for Unlawful Acts, after rejecting the idea of general clauses of liability similar to those of Articles 1382 *et seq.* CC, originally put forward in the first draft of the German Code produced by the first Commission. Germanic ideas of unlawfulness as an additional condition of delictual liability influenced, in different ways, the Spanish and Italian law of civil liability, both originally closer to the French, leading to separate development of the law by the courts in these two countries. The Greek and the Portuguese Civil Codes chose also their own ways of styling civil liability as important expressions of national legal culture, and the newest Dutch Civil Code ambitiously combined elements of all traditions. Extra-contractual liability, and its relation to other sources of civil liability such as breach of contract, has, in short, always been seen in the European legal systems as an issue of great intellectual, social and cultural importance, close to the definition of citizens' basic rights, reflecting the individual sensitivities of law and policy makers in different legal systems.

Despite the cultural resistance, it is true that a limited, piecemeal harmonization, of specific private law regimes, in areas that directly affect the operation of the common market or the free movement of persons and goods, has been agreed by Governments and attempted through Directives and Regulations. There have been a number of Directives and Draft Directives in diverse areas, such as: Product Liability for Defective Products,[20] Consumer Protection,[21] Consumer Credit,[22] Package

[20] Council Directive 85/374/EEC of 25 July 1985, now fully implemented by all EU member states.

[21] Council Directive 85/557/EEC of 20 December 1985 on Consumer Protection in Contracts negotiated away from business premises.

[22] Council Directive 87/102/EEC.

Travel, Package Holidays and Package Tours,[23] Unfair terms in Contracts,[24] Proposal for a Directive on the Liability of Suppliers of Services,[25] Proposal for a Directive on Liability for Injury caused by Waste.[26]

But such areas apart, it is not immediately obvious whether there is the will, or, indeed, the need, for a systematic harmonization of private law in Europe, and the creation of a common European law. The question applies also to the broader issue of creating a European Civil Code, very much discussed among European politicians and academics recently. If there is a need, the will must be found. But present discussions and concerted efforts by various academic groups to formulate proposals for a European civil liability law or Civil Code, seem to put the cart before the horse in so much as they concentrate their efforts on how best to achieve harmonization, and much less on why such harmonization is needed. Are there any compelling reasons for harmonizing private law in Europe?

Such reasons, if they exist, must be weighed against the following considerations addressed below.

First, whether or not there is a legal basis, there is definitely no legal obligation, arising out of the European Treaty, of member states to proceed to wholesale harmonisation of private law by Community legislation. This has been confirmed recently by the European Court of Justice in the tobacco advertising ban case,[27] where the Court pointed out that the European Treaty does not confer in the (new) Art. 95 (1) a general power on Community legislature to regulate the internal market.[28]

Secondly, civil Liability for damage caused by competition distortions, business practices in banking, corporate or insurance matters or failures to implement Community rules has already been harmonized by the Treaties themselves, and by several directives and regulations.

Thirdly, specific areas in which there is a need for uniform protection of European citizens in their exercise of their right of free movement can, and should be singled out for individual harmonization, such as liability for traffic accidents, currently under consideration by the European Parliament working group led by Professor Busnelli of the University of Pisa.

4.2. The Arguments for a Common European Private Law

A political ground for the harmonization of European private law can be found in the quest for a common European citizen's identity, a task that seems to be on its way to be confirmed as a political goal of the Union in the Charter of Human Rights,

[23] Council Directive 90/314/EEC.
[24] Council Directive 93/13/EEC.
[25] 91/C12/11 revised in 1992.
[26] 89/C251/04.
[27] ECJ, 5 Nov. 2000, C-376/98.
[28] See also (new) Art. 5 EC.

agreed in the European summit in Nice in December 2000. Uniform Human Rights can be seen as inevitably leading to uniform civil rights. If this is accepted, it will be a powerful argument for the harmonization of the law of civil liability in Europe. However, a number of Governments take a narrower view of the Charter, as addressing only the question of the protection of human rights internally in the Union, before Union organs and institutions, whereas others look at it as the first step of a constitutional restructuring of Europe, and an element of a common European identity to be projected also externally to the rest of the world.

To the extent that private law rules are more generous in their remedies in some countries than others, the equal treatment of all European nationals in the geographical area of the Union necessitates harmonization of national systems. Privacy is better protected at the present moment in Germany than in the United Kingdom;[29] defamation is a more lucrative tort for a claimant in the United Kingdom than almost anywhere else. And citizens are compensated for disproportionate financial burdens imposed by *lawful* administrative action only in France.

Not to be underestimated is the excitement of academicians and some other lawyers caused by the unique opportunity, and challenge, of redrafting civil law on a global European basis. Ideas have a power of their own.

It is a well-known mantra that European unity must constantly evolve or perish. Some nations, and politicians, are driving hard towards a common public and private law structure.[30] The European Parliament has long ago (1989) asked for a European Civil Code to be put on the agenda of the Commission and the Council,[31] and will routinely support all initiatives for harmonization, undeterred by Governments or decision of the European court. This is significant, as the Parliament, for all its defects and shortcomings, may be seen as representing the people of Europe better than any other European institution. Academics are drafted to the political task, and some will pull all the stops to sell projects such as the European Civil Code or a Uniform Law of Civil Liability to the weary local legal communities of member States. In a recent Conference on the European Civil Code organised by the European Law Academy at Trier, we were presented by Professor Christian von Bar from Osnabrück with a draft of Uniform European Law entitled 'Part X: Tort Law', without been told what this tort law was part of! Presumably, it was part of a draft of European Civil Code. We were also told by Professor von Bar that there is no reason why the new European Civil Code could not be used in member States *together* with national Civil Codes, which would not necessarily have to be abolished. A proposal that could be seen as a Trojan horse in some countries or

[29] Although there is change in the air, following the introduction of the Human Rights act 1998: see *Douglas and Ors v Hello! Ltd* [2001] 2 WLR 992, CA.

[30] Joshka Fischer, the German Foreign Minister, in a controversial lecture in May 2000 at Humboldt University in Berlin spoke of a 'constitutional re-establishment of Europe' that should include the 'firm establishment' of not only 'human' but, also, 'civil' common European rights.

[31] Official Journal of EC 1989, No. C 158/400.

as discriminatory in others, such as the United Kingdom, with no national Civil Code to hold on to.

Admittedly, complete political Union in Europe cannot be achieved without a uniform private law. Looking to the United States, the success of the Union there is due to four important common elements: common market, common currency, common language and common law. The common language is almost impossible, perhaps, to achieve in Europe, but is it possible to achieve the common law?

Those pulling political weight behind the unification of civil law in Europe may, however, be rendering the cause a very bad service. Left outside politics, such unification might have been more palatable, indeed almost natural. Private law, unlike criminal or public law, does not need to be political or bound with particular state interests. The citizens of Europe will probably be happy with a change in their private law for the better, and their lawmakers should aspire to give them such change, which could take the form of a uniform system encompassing what is best in the rich European national legal systems. Unfortunately, such projects as we are offered so far by the various working groups are plans to iron out through conceptual compromises, existing differences of black letter law between member states, seeking, so to speak, the lowest conceptual common denominator, with no creative aspiration to move the Droit Civil of Europe to a new era. Thus, they expose themselves not only to political but, also (and quite rightly so) to scientific attacks, mainly for their uninspiring and degrading vision of European private law. These are products that the consumer can, and must, easily resist. A new European private law, with forward looking principles based on some of the best ideas of national legal systems, might have been a much harder job to do, but, perhaps, also harder to resist, and a true service to European unity.

4.3. Method of Production

Common principles of European private law will be a sizeable transplant for all EU member states. As with all legal transplants, their introduction, survival and success depends on their reception in each country, first, by lawmakers (including judges) and other lawyers, practitioners and academics, and, second, by business interests, the insurance industry and the wider community. The experience from working with a group preparing a draft directive on the important issue of assessment of personal injury losses from car accidents has taught me that it is the reaction of the former group rather than the latter that is crucial.[32]

In the light of the thesis advanced in this paper, that a common European private law must be forward looking, based on new principles, and not a conceptual legal syncretism of existing, and often outdated, national styles, it is important to educate and persuade national lawmakers and lawyers. The American experience of the

[32] See on this, E.K. Banakas, 'The Method of Comparative Law and the Question of Legal Culture Today' (1994) 3 *Tilburg Foreign Law Review* 113–153, esp. at 123 et seq.

democratic adoption of the Restatements is very useful in this connection. We need in Europe, an institution, independent from Community and State authorities, such as the American Law Institute. The American Law Institute was organised in 1923, following a study conducted by a group of prominent American judges, lawyers, and teachers known as 'The Committee on the Establishment of a Permanent Organisation for the Improvement of the Law'. The Committee had reported that the two chief defects in American law, its uncertainty and its complexity, had produced a 'general dissatisfaction with the administration of justice'. According to the Committee, part of the uncertainty of the law, as it then existed, was due to the lack of agreement among members of the profession on the fundamental principles of the common law. Other causes of uncertainty were reported as 'lack of precision in the use of legal terms', 'conflicting and badly drawn statutory provisions', 'the great volume of recorded decisions', and 'the number and nature of novel legal questions'.[33] The law's complexity, on the other hand, was attributed in significant part to its 'lack of systematic development' and to its numerous variations within the different jurisdictions of the United States. Clearly, Europe would benefit from an institution like this, not only in making harmonization of private law possible, but, also, in preserving the uniformity of the development of the common European law after its harmonization. The new law will have to be applied uniformly in all member states, and, in the light of the variety of judicial style and culture in the member states, will only survive with the discipline of a moderate rule of *stare decisis*.

The European Law Institute should be a private law organisation encompassing all sections of the legal profession and others closely related with the law-making process. Following the example of the American Law Institute, its membership should be elected and consist of judges, lawyers, and law teachers from all member States as well as some other countries, selected on the basis of professional achievement and demonstrated interest in the improvement of the law. Ex officio members should include the Judges of the European Court of Justice and those of the highest court of each member state, law school Deans, and the Presidents of the Bar Associations, and other prominent legal organisations from each state.

The American experience of Restatements provides a successful model of how to democratically achieve the consensus of the legal world in Europe, vital for the success of any large-scale harmonization project. In the American law Institute, a project is undertaken by the consideration and prior approval of its officers and Council. When a project has been authorized, an expert in the field of law to be considered, usually a legal scholar, is designated as 'Reporter'. With the help of assistants, the Reporter does the basic research and prepares the initial draft of the material. This initial draft is submitted for suggestions and revisions to a small group of Advisers – judges, lawyers, and law teachers – with special knowledge of the subject. In most projects the draft is also reviewed by a Members Consultative Group consisting of members of the Institute with particular interest in the subject.

---

[33] See <http://www.ali-aba.org/ali/thisali.htm>.

The revised draft is next submitted for further analysis and consideration to the Council of the Institute, a group consisting of some sixty prominent judges, practising lawyers, and law teachers. The draft can then be referred either to the Reporter and the Advisers for further consideration or to the Annual Meeting for review by the membership. When approved by the Council, the draft as further revised is presented as a Tentative Draft to an Annual Meeting of the entire membership for debate and discussion, and is then made available for public distribution. In any Restatement or codification project, a series of Tentative Drafts is produced in this manner over a period of years. When the treatment of a subject has thus been completed, a Proposed Final Draft, consisting of all prior Tentative Drafts and reflecting membership action, may be submitted to the Council and the membership. When the project has been approved by both, the official text of The American Law Institute is prepared for publication. The final product, the work of highly competent group scholarship, thus reflects the searching review and criticism of learned and experienced members of the Bench and Bar.

There is no reason why a similar process cannot be instituted in Europe, provided, of course, there is the political will for it. But then, introducing in Europe a common private law requires the greatest and strongest political will for political and legal unity. Is there such a will in Europe today? This remains to be seen. The last successful major codification in Europe, the Dutch Civil Code, was only made possible because the political will created a harmonious collaboration of politicians, lawyers and the community at large, in the process of which the enormity of technical detail that needed to be agreed upon was trustingly left to the experts, who were allowed to proceed on basis of agreed principles. This is the climate that needs to be created, before a new European private law can become a reality.

Chapter 11

HUNDRED HEADLESS EUROPE: COMPARISON, CONSTITUTION AND CULTURE

*Angus McDonald**

The concerns of McDonald in the following piece highlight in several respects the inevitability of a new type of comparative law. It is not just the challenge of emergent legal systems that breaks the mould of European comparative law: Europe itself demands new approaches to comparative law in a way that would have amazed scholars and legislators in the 'great tradition'. McDonald places the notion of a European constitution at the centre of attention, embedded in cultural (or multi-cultural) contexts where 'law meets government meets democratic demands meets economics meets social responses'. The significance of this piece is, however, not just European. By raising the possibility of a 'new geometry' or a 'pyramidal' approach to comparative law, McDonald shows us that regional and international questions create a new dimension to the subject which is very much post-modern: ideas, norms, precedents and comparisons flow not just horizontally across borders but vertically between international and national contexts (compare Bell). One might add that a similar thing occurs in the little-studied area where constitutional norms percolate into areas of local and even private governance. In a world in which a Constitution, like that of South Africa (see Carey-Miller), can permit the courts to consider precedents from other jurisdictions and require them to consider international norms, the possibilities and the demands for comparison become more than merely interesting: they set the parameters of legal change itself. In this environment we need to 'interrogate contexts' much more closely than comparative law has normally done. The way in which Europe responds to the challenge of constructing a constitution out of the disparate available material, the part which comparison plays in that response, and the way it is all regarded by comparatists will be an interesting and creative aspect of comparative law in this century.

[A. Harding and E. Örücü]

* Law School, Staffordshire University.

A. Harding and E. Örücü (eds.),
Comparative Law in the 21st Century, 193–210.

1. INTRODUCTION

As comparative law is not a field of law amongst others, but rather a method, the most demanding challenges for comparative law in the twenty-first century will not be merely those which apply the method to new fields, but will be those which put into question the methodological assumptions of the discipline. This method has not been a value free scientific instrument. The method of comparative law has been comparison *with the purpose of harmonization*. This method cannot remain unaffected by the challenge of Europe.

In some respects, the European dimension can be accommodated by traditional comparative method: where it is a question of comparing specific private law techniques across two or more European jurisdictions, comparative method will be quite comfortable. It is in the field of public law that the challenge arises, and it is in the question of European constitutional arrangements that the challenge becomes most demanding. The question whether Europe needs a constitution is posed, yet between English common law and European codification there is no consensus concerning what a constitution is. It is this dissensus that poses the most interesting challenge to comparison.

Further, we must not assume that we know what Europe *is*, if we wish to understand what Europe can be, and the nature of the challenge that Europe poses to comparison. Certainly since Europe stopped being a synonym for Christendom, European identity has been more opaque than is often presumed, both by those who would defend it and by its opponents. The criticism of eurocentrism still makes too quick an assumption that we know what euroculture is. The advocates of multiculturalism also assume that the identity of cultures is established and a multi-culture is achieved by an additive, arithmetic method, and the sum total of cultures present reduced to one. If European cultural identity is not fixed we cannot expect to locate its essence.

So, the challenge posed to comparison by Europe gives rise to differences in the purposes of comparison, differences in the notions of constitutionality and differences in the claims for European identity.

2. COMPARISON

Does Europe need a constitution? Does Europe have a constitution already? Does Europe have an adequate and appropriate constitution? What does the notion of a constitution mean in relation to Europe? What could it mean to ask whether Europe needs a constitution? How does comparative method respond to such questions?

The conceptual territory occupied by these questions is of a different order to the traditional concerns of comparative studies. These can be understood in plain terms as, 'What can we learn from our neighbours, and could we with advantage adopt some of their different solutions to common problems?' But, Europe is not a neighbour to France, Germany or Italy, and this approach will not work. A comparative approach, if it is to be useful to an investigation of the first question, must therefore question some of its traditional methods and assumptions.

Comparative approaches rest on the claim of the existence of different systems – without a plurality of different systems, there would be nothing to compare. However, this obvious diversity must also contain some similarity, even some unity, otherwise comparison would be pointless. The unity that informs public law specifically is the liberal model, which assumes a separation of powers: rather than the well-known approach of Montesquieu, let us consider the definition offered by Kant. In Kant's statement of this principle,[1] the doctrine of separation of powers is aligned with the very operation of practical reason itself. Kant defines three propositions of practical reason: the major premise, which contains the *law* of the sovereign will, the minor premise, which contains the *command* to act in accordance with the law (subsumption) and the conclusion, which contains the *legal decision* (the sentence). These are also the three powers: ruling (legislator), executing (governing in accordance with the law) and judging (allotting to everyone what is his by law). These three are, institutionally, a legislature, an executive and a judiciary. The extent to which these three institutions exist and operate within Europe, or *should*, is the issue on which the common ground of comparison begins to look like an untenable assumption. It is not self-evident that, for example, given the existence of two of these institutions, an executive and a judiciary, that the necessary next step is the creation of a Parliament which would be a legislator.

The question of the point of comparison arises at a more specific level – what can one system learn from another? Specifically, can one system adopt concepts and practices from another? These matters all bear upon the nature of the work a comparatist can do in relation to the issue of a constitution for Europe.

There exist European constitutions – those of the European nation-states (and this family grouping extends beyond the current, possibly even beyond the future, membership of the European Union). Over the last few years, to ask what constitutional features a newly emergent European nation-state, such as Slovenia or an independent Scotland, or potentially a Basque nation-state, might wish to adopt from its neighbours would be a fairly obvious question for a comparatist to ask.

To ask what sort of constitution Europe as a whole might adopt is a question of a different order. There may or may not exist a European constitution, in the sense of a constitutional framework structuring the functioning of the institutions of the European Union. The answer will depend on how we define 'constitution' – or more precisely, on whether we adopt a definition of 'constitution' from one or another national understanding of the meaning of the concept.

How the methodological issue meets the definitional debate is best illustrated by revisiting a longstanding question: is law best understood in isolation from other factors, or situated in appropriate contexts? As a constitutionalist and a comparatist, I believe I have two good reasons for being a contextualist. Even if other legal fields

---

1 I. Kant, *Political Writings* (2nd edn., Cambridge University Press, Cambridge, 1991), p. 138.

might make a convincing argument for a 'black letter' conceptual purity, constitutional questions at their very heart address the point where law meets government meets democratic demands meets economics meets social responses. Also, comparative approaches have long learned the lesson that attempts to compare specific legal instruments and contemplate their chances of success or failure as grafts from one system to another cannot be a purely legal issue but is necessarily also a historical, sociological, political and cultural inquiry.

Putting law in context, and selecting which contexts, has as its purpose producing an understanding of the constitution which balances a recognition of the degree of autonomy which the constitution has in relation to its contexts with an equal recognition of the degree of integration. The relations of the constitution, whether autonomous or integrated, with its key contexts must be examined in turn. It is not the aim of a contextualist understanding to reduce the constitution to an effect caused by its contexts, nor can it accept the view that the constitution has no relations at all with its environment. Further, a critical theory of law must interrogate the contexts as much as the law, to avoid accepting the perspectives on the law produced from the points of view of the contexts. The aim is an understanding of the constitution informed by political and social, economic understandings. This is best achieved by locating the question of the constitution between social and political perspectives. More specifically, the social question subdivides into two aspects. There is the question of the economy, and there is the question of society more strictly defined, as the question of civil society, or polity. Political perspectives likewise can be subdivided into two aspects. The question of the state is one aspect; the other is the question of politics in the broader sense of questions concerning democracy, best understood as the activity of a public sphere.

If this framework is transposed to the European dimension, it has the advantage of distinguishing tangled issues, and also laying an agenda for inquiry. For example, in contemporary British politics, the single currency debate, an example of the economic aspect, and the associated debate concerning the closer integration of the European economies, has received considerable attention, sometimes in relation to debates about globalization.

The Euro-sceptic position has emphasized the claim that a European superstate is furtively under construction – an example of the state aspect. However harmonization of European laws has remained something of a specialized topic, whilst the issues of the existence or otherwise of pan-European democratic politics or social identities are scarcely addressed at all.

'Is Europe in need of a Constitution?' asks different things within different national traditions. Understanding this is a prerequisite to understanding the question. Understandings of the European project are unavoidably plural, and that the imposition of one understanding over others would do violence to this debate. A consensus is not to be expected.

We could expect the growing pan-European negotiation and co-operation to make the following demand upon comparative law as a discipline: show us how to find our common legal core, and how to integrate our divergent legal practices. Yet comparative law cannot simply deploy its battery of established techniques upon the European terrain. The unique manner in which pan-European co-operation is evolving poses a challenge to the methodology of comparative law. For it is no longer a matter of putting two or more legal systems alongside each other and performing a comparative analysis. The European dimension is just this: a new *dimension*, which requires comparison to operate within a new geometry.

Hitherto, comparison has proceeded by horizontal studies, in two dimensions: comparable systems on the same plane have been analysed for component parts – mostly in private law fields. The European dimension opens up a third dimension, a cubic volume in contrast to the flat surface upon which comparison has hitherto operated. To assert this is not to suggest that comparatists have lacked ambition. It is to say that, until the coming to maturity of the development of the European Union, there was at first only one level, allowing only comparisons on the flat surface occupied by nation states. In a transitional period – say, the fifty years since the Treaty of Rome – comparisons remained two dimensional, but supplemented the horizontal relationship with the vertical one. Thus comparisons between, for example, France and Germany, could be supplemented by comparisons between France and the European Community. This is to imply that there is now the possibility of thinking in terms of a third dimension: the European dimension opens up a third dimension, a cubic volume in contrast to the flat surface upon which comparison has hitherto operated. This is to assert more than a shift from horizontal to vertical comparisons, both of which remain two dimensional, linear connections on different planes. It is to assert the necessity of awareness that the possibilities for comparison are now in a space that occupies a cubic volume. Comparison need not only be imagined as a line that connects points on the same plane. It can also be a matter of connecting multiple points on various planes into three-dimensional models, and comparing the lines of intersection thereby generated.

The comparative method has its strengths and its weaknesses. One strength is the sense of relativism and contingency that arises from acquaintance with the variety of different legal approaches to similar problems. The method necessarily sustains the critical insight that the arrangements of power under which we live could be otherwise, and so embodies the critical maxim that one should never theorize in such a way as to eternalize or naturalize the arrangements of power under which we live. An associated weakness is an assumption of a mechanical functionalism. That is, to claim that what laws do can be reduced to function, defined in a utilitarian way, and that these functions are identical or similar in all societies, neglectful of the more subtle symbolism which law can possess in terms of, for example, national cultural identity.

A second strength of comparison is an ability to propose relationships between law and other elements of a totality that would not be available to the purely legal analysis. The associated weakness is a tendency towards organicism, defining the role of a legal institution in relation to a larger totality viewed as evolutionary and quasi-biological, thereby underestimating the fragmentation, friction and dissent that can operate within a system by presuming harmony amongst the parts.

The challenge for comparative legal research is to develop appropriate methods in response to this. This can only be done if we do *not* start from the presumption that the European dimension is about harmonization: harmonization flattens the third dimension and reduces the scope of comparison to just another exercise in relating two or more systems. This is not appropriate to the reality or the opportunity represented by the European dimension. Observing the development of the European project, two contrasting directions can be identified: the project of harmonizing and ultimately unifying the elements of a common European identity, or the project of diversifying the development of various aspects of European difference. What I am proposing is a shift from comparison in the service of harmonization to comparison in the service of what Lyotard calls 'paralogy':[2] the emphasizing of incompatibilities.

3. Constitution/Sovereignty

The risks of unreflective transpositions of terms such as constitution, sovereignty, democracy from nation-state contexts to a European context can be illustrated by asking, 'does the notion of a European dimension work in relation to each term, and what are the national inflections on the key terms?'

In English legal thought the constitution is about sovereignty. To English minds, a development of the European dimension can only mean a European sovereignty, and sovereignty means a state. A sovereign state is one not subject to superior orders, and so a European state would mean the death of UK sovereignty. This manner of analysis is the legacy of positivism, traceable all the way back to Hobbes.[3] Sovereignty is indivisible and must be unlimited. It is political and legal. Dicey's contribution[4] to this tradition focuses on the legislature as sovereign. So, the aspect of the state that matters is its function as legislator. Such power cannot be shared, although certain delegations of law-making power are conceivable. It is in this way that English jurisprudence might reconcile itself to European laws, but it is a position stretched to breaking point by the dominant sovereignty perspective.

The English tradition in philosophy of law which dominates in the United Kingdom is best summarised in the doctrine of Parliamentary sovereignty, as clarified at the beginning of the 20th century by Albert Venn Dicey. Originated ultimately in the midst of the English civil war of the seventeenth century by the Thomas Hobbes, Hobbes' legacy in England is the notion that sovereignty is indivisible, and must be in the sole possession of one institution or another.

---

[2] J.-F. Lyotard, *The Postmodern Condition* (Manchester University Press, Manchester, 1984), p. 60.

[3] T. Hobbes, *Leviathan* (Penguin, Harmondsworth, 1968), p. 228.

[4] A.V. Dicey, *An Introduction To The Study Of The Constitution* (10th edn., Macmillan, London, 1967), p. 39.

Legally, either Parliament is sovereign, that is, has the last word, or the constitution is, that is, has the last word. In the latter case the last word will be spoken by the judiciary, adjudicating on the constitutionality of parliamentary law making. The notion of Parliamentary sovereignty is also expressed as Parliamentary omnipotence, Parliamentary omni-competence. The root is clearly theological: sovereignty as an attribute of God. So, sovereignty was wrested from god, by means of the execution of his representative on earth, the monarch, and vested in Parliament.

Much later, a legitimation from below replaced the legitimation from above. Parliamentary sovereignty could also be justified on democratic grounds. The will of the people sends representatives to Parliament, which must have sovereign power in the state as the arena in which democracy, the government of the people, channels its will into policy.

This discourse of sovereignty still dominates the English imagination. The 'European debate' in England is still one of a struggle between claims on sovereignty: has Westminster ceded British sovereignty to Brussels, and so on. Some in Europe wish to debate European sovereignty, how to achieve a European sovereignty, and how to make that sovereignty democratic. For the reasons stated, in England this debate cannot find a voice.

Defining the European constitutional debate in terms of how to make sovereignty democratic leads to demands for amore powerful European legislature, but this direction only really coheres if we assume the English view that constructing sovereignty is what a constitution is for. If this assumption is challenged then the democratization of that sovereignty becomes irrelevant. To argue that sovereignty is created deficient only in democracy ignores the possibility of thinking about Europe in a way other than the template laid down by the historical evolution of eighteenth and nineteenth century nation-states.

4. Constitution/Democracy

A European democratic politics is the question of the existence of a European public sphere. In this notion, the ideal of public opinion performs the democratic role of pressurizing the government into responsiveness to the wishes of the people. Here, the role of Parliament that matters is not so much its role as legislature, but its role as check upon the executive. The matter has been most usefully analysed by Habermas.[5] It relies upon a claim of the close link between Parliament and people produced by elections. There are many problems with this notion transposed to the European level. This shows that the so-called 'democratic deficit' debate is far deeper than an institutional issue of the balance of powers between the branches of the European institutions. The key problem is the non-existence by all measurable

[5] J. Habermas, *The Structural Transformation Of The Public Sphere* (Polity Press, Cambridge, 1989), p. 57.

criteria of a meaningful European public sphere. This is indicated, for example by low turnout rates for European elections, but also by intractable problems like the lack of a Europe wide news medium. The relative failure of attempts to launch European newspapers is one index. The lack of a common language or of widespread ability in foreign languages (particularly in the UK) is also a problem. What the European Commission has called a 'lack of seriousness' in news reporting of European issues – the repeated resort to 'Brussels bureaucrat' stories and lack of interest in other issues is indicative. At a conceptual level, the question is whether the function of the public sphere is to reach consensus, as Habermas would have it, or to voice difference, as Lyotard would have it. This level is superfluous however in the context of the inapplicability of the notion of a public sphere in relation to Europe. A European Parliament without a European public sphere declines into simply an institutional feedback loop, and fails to even engage with the question of democracy. Democracy in the context of the public sphere is not about electoral processes, but about a dialogue between state and civil society. The public sphere is civil society collectively asserting control over the state.

One of the still useful conclusions to be drawn from Bagehot's work on the constitution[6] is that political and legal institutions must not only be efficient, but must also offer the public reasons for enthusiasm, loyalty and attachment to them, if they are to prosper. This symbolic level asks the question, what would make us *want* to think of ourselves as Europeans? An answer not based on the assumption of any unified substantive European identity is proposed here.

The question considered here concerns in the broadest sense the past, present and future of Democracy in Europe, or, European Democracy. This fine distinction hides a fundamental question: what is the relation between democracy and Europe? Either we know what democracy is, an ideal, and we desire to see it achieved in Europe, overcoming the deficit in democracy of which Europe is often accused; or, we are reflecting on a tradition, perhaps even an invention, 'European democracy', imperfect and incomplete, in order to assess our present prospects.

If our question is distinguished with a little more precision as the question of democracy in relation to the European Union, are we any clearer? In this I follow the argument of Castoriadis,[7] that democracy is an attribute of a polity, a self-instituting practice expressed in but not reducible to a set of institutions. He is speaking of direct democracy, and so will I. If this is what democracy, European democracy, means, then clearly there is not merely a deficit but rather a complete absence of democracy in relation to the European Union. The reason is clear enough: there is no European polity, no European public sphere.

Further there is no sense that a pan-European civil society is emerging. In most cases, commentators still claim that 'organic' nations defined by common cultural memory, experience, traditions and language are the units within which most people

[6] W. Bagehot, *The English Constitution* (Collins, London, 1963), p. 239.

[7] C. Castoriadis, *Philosophy, Politics, Autonomy* (Oxford University Press, Oxford, 1991), p. 81.

define their identity. A Europe wide civil society – one of associations, not just economic links – is seen as dead since either the decline of Christendom as another name for Europe, or the decline of international socialism on the eve of the First World War. The civil society theme is one of the most contested, as it relies on identity claims not grounded in institutions or susceptible to rationality. The German tradition gives us the notion of a civil society animated by the *Volksgeist*. This concept, of the spirit of the people, is subject to different emphases in Herder, Savigny and Hegel. In this tradition, the constitution does not embody an abstract reason, but a spirit of the people. A civil society cannot be an external construction but must evolve with the organic life of the community. In Kristeva's analysis,[8] for Herder, the *Volksgeist* is a mystical concept of the nation 'rooted in soil, blood and language'. Kristeva judges the *Volksgeist* of Herder, and its romantic interpretation and Nazi implementation as a notion to be dreaded and rejected. She wishes to endorse instead Montesquieu's *Esprit Generale*, which she views as a more cosmopolitan and liberal variant of the notion. Savigny's development of the notion emphasises the historical and customary nature of the *Volksgeist*, and ends up with a position akin to the English view of the common law, that law is an organic evolving institution to be judicially discovered rather than a technical instrument utilised by the legislator. Hegel also endorses an organic notion, observing against the Prussians of his day who wished to form a union of German states, in a way resonant for European nation states and their relationship with Europe, that:

> Those who talk of the 'wishes' of a collection of people constituting a more or less autonomous state with its own centre, of its 'wishes' to renounce this centre and its autonomy in order to unite with others to form a new whole, have very little knowledge of the nature of a collection or of the feeling of selfhood which a nation possesses in its independence[9]

Kristeva is, I think, overly dismissive of this German romantic tradition. Whilst her fears of its ramifications as a state politics are certainly valid, she fails to distinguish the cultural specificity in which Herder in particular seems to be interested. The cultural level need not be collapsed into a narrower political claim quite so abruptly.

5. Constitution

In the absence of European sovereignty, European public sphere and European civil society, is there European constitutional law, and what would it mean to (re)constitutionalize the activities of the European institutions? To the English

[8] J. Kristeva, *Nations Without Nationalism* (Columbia University Press, New York, 1993), pp. 7, 32. This is a summary of the argument developed at greater length in J. Kristeva, *Strangers To Ourselves* (Columbia University Press, New York, 1991).

[9] G.W.F. Hegel, *Philosophy Of Right* (Oxford University Press, Oxford, 1967), p. 208.

Hobbesian/Diceyan tradition, the function of a constitution is to establish a sovereign. This is true also of the Lockean tradition where the constitution limits the sovereign – sovereignty is still the point. To such perspectives this question merges immediately with the question of a European state.

From a continental perspective premised on the French revolutionary example, a constitution is a document produced by contracting parties in a special assembly gathered for that purpose which codifies the powers to be distributed to various bodies thereafter. This is most clearly expressed in discussions of the French revolution.[10] A constitution can be a clarification of the location of powers, either in a federal structure or by a principle of subsidiarity. As part of this, a Charter of Fundamental Rights can declare the position of the citizen. The absence of these formal measures is more troubling to the continental approach than it is to the pragmatic English approach. The English quite literally do not understand what the point is. Hence Blair's wish to describe such initiatives as 'only restatements of the current law', a position which ignores what happens when you change the form in which a certain content is expressed.

When a comparative public lawyer interested in constitutional questions (at least, one starting from a British perspective) turns to a consideration of the European dimension, the unavoidable starting point is the contrast between the two legal traditions of Europe, the common law and the Roman law. It is not only a question of the existence of these two traditions, but that theorists within both traditions have argued about the strengths and weaknesses of their traditions by contrast with the other. These mutual interpretations – misinformed or otherwise – have structured the terms in which the contrasts between the two traditions have been understood. We think here of Montesquieu lauding the benefits for freedom to be derived from the English structure of separation of powers, or Dicey likewise praising the English tradition above all for its avoidance of the pernicious effects of the French *droit administratif*.[11]

Certain aspects of the current situation give extra interest to a re-examination of the relevance of the two traditions and their different approaches to the question of the constitution. The key aspect is this: the evolution of European states, laws, politics, societies and economies is at a stage where the question is being asked, does Europe need a constitution? This question presupposes that Europe currently lacks a constitution. This situation, of the absent constitution, has of course a different meaning for the common law tradition than it does for the Roman tradition. To the continental approach, it is clear that Europe lacks a constitution simply because it lacks a foundational statement of fundamental rights secured in a single public document. To the English approach, this question is more ambiguous. Constitutional law in England starts from the premise that a constitution must exist if organs of government and law are actually operating, and the form of the constitution,

[10] E. Burke, *Reflections On The Revolution In France* (Penguin Books, Harmondsworth, 1968).
[11] Dicey, n. 4 above, p. 328.

whether it is a distinct document, and has special constitutional status, is only that, a formal question. Therefore to English legal minds, the question, does Europe need a constitution, is liable to receive a quizzical response. If Europe has, as it appears to have, functioning organs of government and law, then by definition it must also have all the constitution it requires. This at least would be the traditional English response. However, the contrast is now less clear-cut than hitherto, as English theorists and politicians have moved away from the Diceyan orthodoxy and adopted something akin to a continental approach. It is indeed in England that politicians and legal theorists alike are showing the greatest enthusiasm for 'correcting' the absence of a constitution, under the catchphrase of modernization. This has given rise to the Human Rights Act 1998 and is a persistent pressure in the direction of a constitutional document in the continental style for the UK.

Hegel adopts the view that a people only achieves actuality worthy of conceptual recognition, if it is indeed a people, and a people, as part of that definition, must already have a collective institution:

> Another question readily presents itself here: 'who is to frame the constitution?' This question seems clear, but closer inspection shows at once that it is meaningless, for it presupposes that there is no constitution there, but only an agglomeration of atomic individuals. How an agglomeration of individuals could acquire a constitution, whether automatically or by someone's aid, whether as a present or by force or by thought, it would have to be allowed to settle for itself, since with an agglomeration the concept has nothing to do. But if the question presupposes an already existent constitution, then it is not about framing, but only about altering the constitution, and the very presupposition of a constitution directly implies that its alteration may come about only by constitutional means. In any case however, it is absolutely essential that the constitution should not be regarded as something made, even though it has come into being in time. It must be treated rather as something simply existent in and by itself, as divine therefore, and constant, and so as exalted above the sphere of things that are made[12]

A constitution should not be regarded as something made, and, furthermore, those who would make constitutions must either presuppose an already existent constitution, or be lacking in real historical existence. This is the real challenge to constitution-makers.

A constitution unconnected to a public sphere, a civil society or a state: is this desirable? One camp views the autonomy of law, including its independence from the pressure of public opinion, as a good thing. This camp includes Weber in Germany, and Dicey in England. Max Weber described English law as lacking in formal rationality, and to that extent pre-modern. His observation on the reasons for the divergence between the English and the continental system bears repetition:

---

[12] Hegel, n. 9 above, p. 178.

> It was not indeed the greater appropriateness of the *content* of Roman Law to the needs of emerging capitalism which was responsible for their victory on the Continent: all the specific legal institutions of modern capitalism are in fact alien to Roman Law and are of medieval origin. What was decisive was its rational *form* and above all the technical necessity of placing the conduct of trials in the hands of rationally trained experts (that is, university-trained experts in Roman Law) ...[13]

Only this *form* of law described by Weber would give constitutionalising the real existence Hegel requires. A European constitution would have to be a constitution in the European manner. But Hegel shows the self-contradiction inherent in that approach. A European constitution in the English manner would pass Hegel's test, as something 'not made' but found in history, but would not satisfy European constitutionalists. There seems to be an aporia. It is necessary to step back from this dissensus and try to find common ground, if not at the constitutional level, then at another level 'not made' but found in history – which is to say, culture.

6. Europe

Is European culture cosmopolitan or nationalist? One possibility for the European project is the development of a European cosmopolitanism: composed of people or elements from all parts of the world or from many different spheres.

An opposite tendency is the development of a European nationalism: an aggregation of people or peoples of one or more cultures, races, etc, organised into a single state. Nationalism can be a sentiment based on common cultural characteristics that binds a population, but where a plurality of cultural characteristics is present, nationalism is predicated on the unifying factor of a common state that guarantees the common identity of citizenship in that state. The principle that establishes state power is sovereignty: the outcome of this position is a focus on national sovereignty.

By method, strategy and intent the comparatist project is wedded to a cosmopolitan perspective. Adopting the term cosmopolitan avoids the dilemmas associated with deciding how comparison deals with nations: is it international, multinational, supranational? The shades of meaning in the notion of cosmopolitan serve to highlight the point of this opening assertion: it means 'having interest in or familiar with many parts of the world', and also carries the sense of 'one who is free of national prejudices'. *Cosmo*: the world considered as an ordered system. *Polites*: citizen. A cosmopolitan is a citizen of an ordered world.

Although I suggest we cannot usefully talk about European state (the language of sovereignty), public sphere (the language of democracy), or society (the language of community), we can nonetheless talk about European culture. At the cultural level it

[13] M. Weber, *Selections In Translation* (Cambridge University Press, Cambridge, 1978), p. 353.

is possible to enter into a European argument – not least because it is an argument. European culture is a collage of diverse elements.

'Perturbation, my sister, the Hundred Headless Europe' is a detournement of the title of a collage-novel produced by the surrealist artist Max Ernst in 1927–1929, called in French 'La Femme Cent Têtes',[14] the hundred-headed woman, a phrase that can also be heard as 'La Femme Sans Tête', the headless woman. When Ernst's wife Dorothea Tanning translated the book into English she attempted to combine the two meanings as 'The Hundred Headless Woman'. I wish to suggest an analogy with Europe – both hundred-headed and headless.

I also wish to invoke the technique that Ernst employed in 'La Femme 100 Têtes': the technique of collage. Collage is a mechanism that, in the words of Ernst (adapting Lautreamont) exploits 'The chance meeting of two distant realities on an unfamiliar plane'.[15] Quoting Andre Breton, Ernst refers to:

> The marvellous faculty of reaching two distant realities, without leaving the field of our experience, and, at their conjunction, of drawing forth a spark ... and, in depriving ourselves of a system of reference, of displacing ourselves within our own memory.... Who knows if, thus, we are not preparing ourselves to escape someday from the principle of identity?[16]

This description is also an apt statement of the claim I wish to pursue in relation to one of the neglected possibilities of Europe. The idea that Europe can be the terrain upon which the aesthetic process Breton describes takes place as a political and social process; what Breton calls the marvellous faculty, this displacement, this escape from identity, is this not an attractive vision of one adventure that can be played out in the arena of European culture? At least, this is a more attractive vision than the dull pursuit of some conformist and consensual common European identity – European Perturbation (agitation, confusion, disorder), rather than European Community and European Union. Not forgetting that democracy is also a perturbation.

This is my response to the question initiated at the outset of my paper. How should we fully utilize the European dimension that is now potentially three dimensional, a cubic volume? The answer I propose is that a cubic volume requires a cubist strategy, in the modernist sense. The cubist and surrealist technique of collage is one key to this understanding.

One of the captions to the collages in Ernst's book is 'Perturbation, my sister, the hundred headless woman'.[17] In substituting the idea of Europe in this phrase, I am attempting to think of another Europe than that of a common set of state-like institutions, a common law, a common economy, a common currency.

---

[14] M. Ernst, *The Hundred Headless Woman* (George Brazilier, New York, 1981).

[15] M. Ernst, quoted in E. Quinn, *Max Ernst* (Ediciones Poligrafa, Barcelona, 1984), p. 166.

[16] A. Breton, quoted in Quinn, ibid.

[17] Ernst, above n. 15, at p. 83.

I am also responding to work in which Jacques Derrida reflects on European identity. He analyses the cosmopolitan/nationalist opposition we have already encountered, while pointing out that the two are by no means incompatible. Where Kristeva uses Herder and Montesquieu to discuss this theme, Derrida uses Valery and Heidegger. In 'The Other Heading',[18] Derrida discusses the notion of a European public sphere, and implicitly opposes the Habermasian model. One of his key points, in parallel to the notion of social and political collage that I have derived from the practice of Ernst and the theory of Breton, concerning European cultural identity, is that:

> . . . What is proper to a culture is not to be identical to itself. Not to not have an identity, but not to be able to identify itself, to be able to say 'me' or 'we'; to be able to take the form of a subject only in the non-identity to itself or, only in the difference with itself. There is no culture or cultural identity without this difference with itself[19]

Any political or legal project that seeks to efface this instability ought to be opposed. Derrida writes of another heading, another head. I push this perhaps too neat dualism of identity and other further, towards the hundred-headed Europe, and the headless Europe.

I shall develop these two images in turn. First, a tale of a hundred heads and of Europa. In thinking about Europe, we have to consider stories of origins and ends. Before the social contract story that marks the birth of a notion of modern Europe, there is a mythical tale, which has a curious resonance for our present debate.

The hundred heads do not belong to Europe but to Typhon. I shall tell the story using Roberto Calasso's rendering of it in 'The Marriage of Cadmus and Harmony'.[20]

What is Europe? The figure of Europa in Greek myth provides one perspective. Europa is a girl abducted by Zeus in the form of a bull. Europa's brother Cadmus is dispatched to find his sister. In the search for his sister Europa, he chances across the following scene: the hundred-headed monster Typhon, a primordial and evil creature, has defeated Zeus, the sovereign god, by cutting through the sinews of his hands and feet, and drawing them out from his body. In homage to absent gods, Cadmus begins to play the just music upon his pipes, and Typhon challenges Cadmus to a contest, pipes versus thunder. Cadmus says that he cannot compete with his pipes, but perhaps with a lyre. He contrives to have Typhon let him gather up the sinews of Zeus as strings for a lyre, and Cadmus leaves the sinews available for Zeus to retrieve and plays harmony on his pipes. His harmony distracts and subdues Typhon. Zeus recovers his sinews, defeats Typhon and rewards Cadmus by

[18] J. Derrida, *The Other Heading* (Indiana University Press, Bloomington, 1992). See also, J. Derrida, *Of Spirit* (University Of Chicago Press, London, 1989).

[19] Derrida, above n. 18, at p. 9.

[20] R. Calasso, *The Marriage Of Cadmus And Harmony* (Vintage, London, 1994), p. 4.

promising him the woman Harmony. Later, Cadmus arrives at a banquet where he is asked to tell his story. He tells of his search for his sister Europa, but left out the most important thing, '[T]hat while looking for his abducted sister, he had in fact come to Samothrace to win another girl, Harmony'. He never finds Europa. With the intervention of Zeus, he marries Harmony.

For our present purpose: the message is, let us beware the error of Cadmus. Many set out searching for Europe but are sidetracked into dilemmas where fear of the monstrous and the uncontrolled lead into an alliance with power where the ultimate value of order (Harmony) is embraced, and Europe is betrayed. Let us search for other Europes. The error of Cadmus is to forget his duty to Europa, to make an alliance with the power that abducted Europa in the first place, and, in horror of uncontrolled nature (symbolized by Typhon), to offer his power, which is the power of harmonising, in the service of sovereignty (symbolized by Zeus).

A practical application of this leads to a challenge to those who abandon Europe for Harmony, or confuse Europe with Harmony. Harmonization is not the only way of retrieving Europe from the clutches of Sovereign Power. Zeus is the symbol of sovereignty, and it is this discourse of sovereignty that I think should be especially resisted.

The 'sovereignty perspective' amounts to the attempt to build a 'head' for Europe. It may be the attempt to build a unified state to control a unified economy, but this socialist response has already been left behind by the development analysed by Jacques Camatte:[21] whereas the revolutionary project consisted of society emancipating itself from the economy what has happened is the reverse. Europe illustrates this very well. The economy, capital, has emancipated itself from society. It is unlikely that state regulation can reverse this tendency. Against the European head, I oppose the hundred-headed Europe, which is a many powered Europe, nation-states, but also the various claims to power within states and societies, within regions – for the European possibility includes quite explicitly the gain of undermining national sovereignty, an idea which has outlived its usefulness. I also propose the idea of a headless Europe, to which I now turn.

Headless Europe evokes first of all Georges Bataille's idea of acephality,[22] then Claude Lefort's notion that democracy is the order in which the place of power remains empty;[23] finally, via Jean Baudrillard,[24] an implosion well evoked by the notion of the black hole.

There is an image of the end of all ends – the 'image' (but this is inappropriate) is the black hole. The black hole is the ultimate end of astronomical development. A star develops through phases, initially producing energy from its core, then activity moves outwards, energy increases, the star expands and swells, becomes a red giant,

[21] J. Camatte, *Echoes Of The Past* (Bojyjob Press, Newton, 1983).
[22] G. Bataille, *Encyclopaedia Acephalica* (Atlas Press, London, 1995).
[23] C. Lefort, *The Political Forms Of Modern Society* (Polity Press, Cambridge, 1986).
[24] J. Baudrillard, *Simulacra And Simulation* (University Of Michigan Press, Ann Arbor, 1994).

then a brief contraction is followed by a huge expansion, with outward layers eventually breaking off and a tiny inner core shrinking under the force of its own gravity, into the terminal stage, the black dwarf, when little energy is emitted, followed finally by the black hole, implosion into an anomalous singularity which cannot be seen but only detected by its effects which consist of sucking in any matter within its gravitational pull. Within a black hole all the laws of physics are suspended.

From myth to science; does this work as a metaphor for Europe? It is tempting to apply the language of assessing whether Europe is producing or consuming energy, whether it is expanding and whether this expansion will lead to a catastrophic collapse, a black hole from which the fragments of Europe will struggle in vain to escape. This language is, precisely, too catastrophic, apocalyptic, millennial. The notion of a black hole is however available as part of our repertoire of ways of thinking. Here the black hole stands for headless Europe, a Europe that absorbs and defeats any attempt to stabilize a representation upon the face of its substance. This is not entirely a negative point. The black hole, the empty space is democratic, and its absorption of any attempt to stabilise a representation upon its face is not undesirable.

The language of 'democratic deficit' sounds too much like a provisional bank balance. There is an account, there is a project, the framework is there, the institutions are operating, but we need to make a few more payments in the democracy account. This financial language does not capture the nature of the legitimation crisis facing Europe – it suggests that if we just add extra elements of democracy – more power to the Parliament, better proportional representation based electoral systems, referenda, then we can correct the imbalance. Some scepticism regarding this seems appropriate.

What are the alternatives to sovereignty? Consider the possibility of arguments concerning a constitutional Europe, but a non-sovereign constitutional Europe. A constitutional but non-sovereign Europe: then, the project is to develop a democratic constitutionality. If this is not about the representation of peoples, an aspect of sovereignty – and an aspect which Lefort warns us can quickly become totalitarian in the attempt to represent unity – then it must be about making the adjudication of constitutionality a democratic process. Focus shifts to the European judiciary. How does the process of adjudication measure up to the accusation of a democratic deficit? What might it mean to demand democratic adjudication? As we know from the example of the USA, if we proceed towards a federalisation, what we will do is create an empowered judiciary. If we are not applying the nation-state blueprint to this situation, and offsetting judicial power with legislative power, then the key challenge will be how to control (democratically?) the judges.

This is double edged. As democrats, the judges are our best hope for control over the actions of the executive. Yet, they are not as such a democratic institution. They defend not so much democracy as rights. These are not co-terminous concepts. The example of the English judiciary should be borne in mind: a tradition which identifies the judiciary as the guardians of liberty as well as as the developers of the common law, a law which is only effective when adjudicated upon. Perhaps it is time in Europe for a project analogous to that of the American legal realists: a project to understand what the European judiciary is actually doing, a judiciary moreover not trained in the common law tradition where such an understanding of their role against the state is commonplace.

Neither democratic deficit nor legitimation crisis is the appropriate framework for thinking about a democratic Europe. Let us be clear whether we mean a democratic sovereignty, a democratic constitutionality, a democratic polity, a democratic public sphere. These last two notions are the most difficult to discuss. Considering the development of a European public sphere, the experience of national public spheres is to the point. National public spheres have already collapsed under colonisation by the forces of the media, as analysed more than 30 years ago by Habermas, and amplified by Negt and Kluge.[25] Realistic prospects for a European public sphere that could escape this fate are not in evidence. Baudrillard's hypothesis concerning the implosion of the masses is also relevant here: if valid, then Europe is poised between two equal but opposite black holes, the one being the resistance of the masses to representation, the other being the absence of representative institutions. A precarious equilibrium may actually emerge from this position.

Black hole headless Europe at least alerts us to the situation in one specific way. For the value of Lefort's empty space of democracy to work, is it essential that there is a site that is visibly empty, an institution unoccupied by power? Or can the black hole that enforces a collapse upon any would-be head also be an engine for democracy in Europe? At least it reminds us that the social contract story, by means of which the European powers ceded their powers to a new institution, was never carried through. Headless Europe remains also hundred-headed Europe. The social contract story is supposed to abolish the originary powers in nature, but these powers, the sovereign states, still haunt the European stage. My suspicion of the would-be constitutionalisers of Europe is that the desire is to use the constitution to institute a *gap* between politics and law. This is what constitutions do: powers convene and impose a blueprint, but this political act becomes in hindsight a purely legal act. Do we really want to convene them once again, in inter-governmental conference, to constitutionalise Europe? Surely they will not accept the role attributed to the English electorate, using their sovereignty only to transfer it to the institutions. Or, like the furies, accept law in the community. We might do better to accept and remember that Europe is a politics of powers, not a law of constitutions. In which case, Europe, the abandoned sister of Cadmus, will remain a perturbation. Unlike Cadmus, it is open to us to acknowledge this perturbation, instead of marrying Harmony in a marriage engineered by Zeus/Sovereignty. This perturbation would be truer to the possibility of a European identity in non-identity such as that described[26] by Derrida.

[25] Negt, Oskar and Kluge, *Public Sphere And Experience* (University Of Minnesota Press, London, 1993).

Chapter 12

OPPOSITIONS AND FRAGMENTATIONS: IN SEARCH OF A FORMULA FOR COMPARATIVE ANALYSIS?

*Peter Leyland**

Leyland and an Italian colleague, embarking on a research project comparing contemporary developments in public administration in the United Kingdom and Italy, encountered a problem familiar to comparative lawyers and indeed discussed by several contributions to this book (see especially, in a public law context, Bell and Harding). Given a number of the common elements such as the introduction of market-based disciplines leading to new management strategies, reallocations of power, and redefinitions of the public and private sectors and methods of accountability; but given also the differences in legal tradition, administrative style, state structures determined by history and politics, and substantive differences in public law, how could the two countries be compared? In particular the organization of public administration in Italy is the subject of extensive and detailed legislation whereas under the United Kingdom's unwritten constitution it is purely an executive matter, and ministerial responsibility, that most peculiar invention, looms large in importance. The authors also accepted that comparison in public law is different from comparison in private law in that there are more variables.

Their solution was both interesting and potentially adaptable to other public law questions, and brings to mind the comparatist's search for the holy grail of a metalanguage to use as a tool of comparison. The solution, which we could call 'comparison by oppositions', was to use a variant of Weber's notion of ideal types of state model in conjunction with Foucault's ideas relating to power and knowledge.

*The basic idea is expressed by Weber in this way: 'An ideal type is formed by the one-sided accentuation of one or more points of view and by the synthesis of a great many diffuse, discrete, more or less present and occasionally absent concrete individual phenomena, which are arranged according to those one-sidedly emphasized viewpoints into a unified analytical construct (*Gedankenbild*).'*

* Senior Lecturer in Law, University of North London. I would like to thank Professor John Bell, Professor Sabino Cassese, Professor Bill Bowring and Professor Andrew Harding for their helpful comments on an earlier draft of this chapter.

A. Harding and E. Örücü (eds.),
Comparative Law in the 21st Century, 211–234.

Leyland concedes that ideal types 'will need to be expanded and refined in terms of the particular areas that are made subject to detailed analysis'. The chapter continues to do precisely that, outlining the characteristics of two ideal types: the 'Mixed Economy Welfare State' model and the 'Mixed Economy Public Choice' model. Leyland then adds to the model another ingredient (and here is where Foucault comes in) – that of 'multi-directional and multi-layered exercise of power'.

The reader will have to judge for herself whether the attempt to use these ideal types as a tool of comparison, in this instance and more generally, succeeds, or whether they prefer Bell's scepticism regarding this type of analysis. The point is securely made that public law is a legitimate subject for comparative study, and the chapter itself is a fine example of the genre.

[A. Harding and E. Örücü]

1. Introduction

This chapter arises from a practical problem in the form of a comparative analysis of the relationship between government and public administration in the United Kingdom and Italy undertaken with an Italian colleague.[1] An appropriate method was required in order to embark on this project and the present chapter seeks to explore some possible ways forward. Although these ideas are discussed mainly in relation to ministerial powers and the accountability of government, the intention is to attempt to develop a transferable method of comparison that could be employed to consider other areas of public law. For example, the proposed method would appear suitable as a way of considering respective trends towards devolution.

The projected work[2] analyses government and public administration in these two nations in order to examine the relative impact of reforms in administrative structure to the central question of the political accountability of the executive.[3] At an empirical level, the discussion[4] is organised around certain important issues common to both nations which include: the allocation of responsibilities at the level of ministers and senior civil servants; the structural re-organisation of central government by way of legislation; methods of appointment and dismissal of ministers and civil servants; the varying degrees of political involvement in the policy making process; and the relationship between central government powers and those

1 Daniele Donati at SPISA, University of Bologna.

2 See P. Leyland and D. Donati 'Executive Accountability and the Changing Face of Government: UK and Italy Compared' (2001) 7 *European Public Law* 217–257.

3 See L.I. Ortega, 'Rapporti fra Direzione Politica e Direzione Amministrativa in Propettiva Comparata' (1998) No. 5 Le Istituzione del Federalismo 769–782: this is an Italian study that features a comparative discussion of the relationship between ministers and civil servants.

4 In the projected work for which the comparative method considered here is intended.

of local government and other bodies. Further, it involves an investigation into how the re-distribution of powers between different bodies has led to new criteria of demarcation between the public sector and private, with a redrawing of boundaries and roles. A number of other important issues are encountered as part of the discussion. For example, the use of contract in and by government, new public management strategies, the incorporation of codes of practice, the development of accounting techniques, competitive tendering and citizen involvement in the administrative process. At the outset it should be noted that consideration of the reforms in this area is made more problematic by a continuous process of transformation that has led to the fragmentation of what was previously considered to be a public sector. A central concern is to assess the relative accountability of the executive branch of government to Parliament in the light of transformations brought about by the introduction of these reforms, and in particular by market-based disciplines.[5]

However, it is recognised that far reaching historical, cultural and institutional differences lie not only between the ideas behind these reforms but also behind the institutional architecture that has given origin and shape to these two systems. This has to be taken into account when considering such issues. To put it simply, we would expect to find that different implications would follow from similar kinds of initiative, as each is pursued in distinct ways. To take one instance, although

---

[5] Some of the texts which will form the basis for the UK: P. Barberis, 'The New Public Management and a New Accountability' (1998) 76 *Public Administration* 451; M. Freedland, 'Government by Contract and Public Law' [1994] *Public Law* 86–105; C. Painter, 'Public Service Reform From Thatcher to Blair: A Third Way' [1999] *Parliamentary Affairs* 94; A. Gray and W. Jenkins 'Government and Administration 1998–99: Overcoming "Conservatism" – A Job Half Done?' [2000] 53 *Parliamentary Affairs* 219–241; C. Graham and T. Prosser, *Privatizing Public Enterprises: The Constitution, the State and Regulation in Comparative Perspective* (Clarendon Press, Oxford, 1991); N.D. Lewis, 'A Civil Service Act for the United Kingdom' [2000] *Public Law* 463; N. Lewis and D. Longley, 'Ministerial Responsibility: The Next Steps' [1996] *Public Law* 490; G. Majone, 'From the Positive to the Regulatory State: Causes and Consequences of Changes in the Mode of Governance' [1997] *Journal of Public Policy* 139–167; R. Scott, Sir, 'Ministerial Accountability' [1996] *Public Law* 410; M.J. Smith, 'Reconceptualizing the British State: Theoretical and Empirical Challenges to Central Government' (1998) 76 *Public Administration*; A. Tomkins, *The Constitution after Scott*, (Oxford University Press, Oxford, 1998); J. Tonge, *The New Civil Service* (Baseline Books, Tisbury, 1999); P. Hennessey, *Whitehall* (Fontana, London, 1990); C. Turpin, 'Ministerial Responsibility: Myth or Reality', in J. Jowell and D. Oliver, *The Changing Constitution* (3rd edn., Clarendon Press, Oxford, 1994); D. Woodhouse, 'Ministerial Responsibility: Something Old, Something New' [1997] *Public Law* 262; D. Woodhouse, *In Pursuit of Good Administration* (Clarendon Press, Oxford, 1997). Some of the texts for Italy are: A. Brancasi, '*Il Nuovo Ruolo della Dirigenza tra Conti Pubbilici e Regole Contabili*' *Le Istizioni del Federalimo* 5/98; D. Hine, *Governing Italy: The Politics of Bargained Pluralism* (Clarendon Press, Oxford, 1993); C. Musillo, 'Italian Administrative Reform: Its Completion and Implementation' [2000] *European Public Law* 363–372; R. Perez, '*L'Efficienza per Decreto*' 28 *Giornale di Diritto Amministrativo*, N.1/2000; C. Pinelli '*Ministri, Diriginti e Amministrazioni: Uno Sguardo Costituzione sulla Nuova Disciplina*' No. 5/1998 *Le Istizioni del Federalimo*; G. Rebora, '*Teoria e Prassi della Valutazione dei Risultati: Una Ricerca sulle Esperienze delle Amministrazioni Pubbliche Italiene*' [1999] *Studi Organizzativi* n. 3, 145–178.

privatisation and aspects of new public management are a common concern, we can anticipate that their impact in each nation will be significantly different. Most conspicuously, the basic constitutional distinction compels each proposed study to have a distinct point of departure. For example, the lack of a written constitution of the United Kingdom setting out a framework of government means that such matters as the crucial relationship between ministers and civil servants is considered as part of the imprecise and much debated convention of ministerial responsibility.[6] On the other hand, the role of ministers and civil servants in Italy is found in a number of specific laws that set out and modify the role of ministers and civil servants, and these provisions delineate in considerable detail the precise functions of administration. In both nations a trend towards streamlining bureaucratic practices will be identified. In Italy this is approached through re-writing of the laws (in the guise of reforms to either the legal or the administrative structure), whilst in the United Kingdom, the 'Next Steps' initiative was introduced without the need for direct legislation and, as a consequence, there has been much less uniformity in the way this reform has been introduced.

The first part of this chapter touches upon some of the more general problems a comparatist might face when approaching a task of this kind. The next section entitled 'Comparison by Oppositions' proposes a method operating at a macro level that employs a variant of Weberian ideal types to identify more general national trends in state organisation that is set against contrasting models of the state. However, in common with other recent studies, the intention is to avoid a 'linear and partial view' of the subject that merely considers the nature of what is now sometimes termed the 'contract state'.[7] The final section of our discussion attempts to look for a comparative approach that addresses issues beyond the state. Michel Foucault argued that 'the state is no more than a composite reality and a mythicized abstraction' which has been afforded exaggerated importance. He recognised that the discipline of managing a population 'not only concerns the collective mass of phenomena, the level of its aggregate effects, it also implies the management of population in its depths and details'.[8] For Foucault historicizing the mechanisms of power reveals that 'governmentalization' is at once internal and external to the state. Thus it can be proposed that 'transformations of public administration have made more transparent the dense networks of accountability within which power is exercised'.[9] For us, an important theme is that the modern state '... is involved in a series of complex relationships with policy communities and policy networks and, as with other aspects of the process of hollowing out the state, this has ... national,

---

6 See e.g., Tomkins, above n. 5, at pp. 25–63; Turpin, above, n. 5; D. Woodhouse 'Ministerial Responsibility: Something Old, Something New' [1997] *Public Law* 262.

7 See e.g., I. Harden, *The Contract State* (Open University Press, Buckingham, 1992).

8 M. Foucault, 'Governmentality' in G. Burchell, C. Gordon and P. Miller, *The Foucault Effect: Studies in Governmentality* (University of Chicago Press, Chicago, 1991) at p. 102 et seq.

9 See C. Scott, 'Accountability in the Regulatory State' [2000] Journal of Law and Society 38, at p. 40.

regional and international dimensions'.[10] Any comparative approach will seek to take account of an emerging trend that considers constitutionalism to be a 'discursive practice' that can be investigated to reveal the strategies of power that it contains.[11]

2. The Route to a Comparative Method?

In order to undertake any comparison a viable approach has to be developed but there are many pitfalls to overcome in formulating a suitable method. Even at a practical level the translation of terminology can present a formidable obstacle. For example, learning when not to translate is one of the skills that needs to be developed and to some extent mastered.[12] However, the difficulty goes beyond the mere translation of terms. The accepted definition of what an intellectual discipline itself involves is quite distinct. It has been claimed that there are two separate paths that shape national administrative law traditions.[13] The first regards administrative law as being about the control of the administration, and the second involves examining the methods for reaching social goals through collective action. This is reflected in the divergence in form of administrative and constitutional law syllabuses and the academic concerns of university departments. For example, where administrative law of the United Kingdom concentrates on the control function of the courts, Italian administrative law concentrates more generally on the structure and function of public administration, which means that the issues tend to be conceived in wider terms.[14]

Next, it is crucial for comparatists to consider whether they are actually looking at the same thing. Indeed, the test of 'functionality' has been regarded as *the* basic methodological principle of comparative law and the starting point for this approach is the proposition that it is only possible to adequately compare things that fulfil the same function. To discover whether this is the case, the problem of discovering function is posed in abstract terms without reference to the system under discussion. This works on the assumption that every legal system is faced with the same

---

10 J. Morrison, 'The Government-Voluntary Sector Compacts: Governance, Governmentality, and Civil Society' (2000) 27 *Journal of Law and Society* 98–132, at p. 108.

11 J. Harvey, J. Morison and J. Shaw, 'Voices, Spaces and Processes in Constitutionalism' (2000) 27 Journal of Law and Society 3.

12 P. Legrand, 'How to Compare Now' [1996] *Legal Studies* 234. In this case co-authorship with an Italian colleague helps tackle this problem.

13 J. Bell, 'Mechanisms for Cross Fertilization of Administrative Law in Europe' in J. Beatson and T. Tridimas (eds.) *New Directions in European Public Law* (Hart Publishing, Oxford, 1998), p. 148, refers to two distinct emphases in public law identified in S. Cassese, *Le Basi del Diritto Amministrativo* (2nd edn., Bologna, 1995).

14 See H.W.R. Wade and C. Forsyth, *Administrative Law* (8th edn., Oxford University Press, Oxford, 2000) as an example of the UK court centred approach, e.g., p. 5 'The primary purpose of administrative law ... is to keep the powers of the government within their legal bounds'.

problems and has to solve them in their own particular way.[15] For the study in hand, it will be suggested at a broad level of generality that a common concern can be identified, namely, the attempt to approach the distribution, exercise and containment of state power, an objective that has been considered only to be attainable by the modification of state institutions and the introduction of regulatory mechanisms. This is recognised as a central issue of modern governance that, as we have already noted, is approached in different ways. Nevertheless, it should be emphasized that despite any divergence in domestic constitutional and legal arrangements, we find that at a supra national level, the administrative machinery of the European Union (EU) and other international trading organisations are faced with having to grapple with identical issues.[16]

A further list of potential obstacles for comparatists to negotiate has long been recognised.[17] For example, Montesquieu believed that environmental difficulties stood in the way of transplantation from one system of law to another. Kahn-Freund in a famous article further developed the idea by proposing that the degrees of transferability varied with the type of law under consideration. With regard to our current concern, he maintained that the problem was more difficult at the public law end of a continuum because of the proximity to the organic power structures which organise constitutional, legislative, administrative or judicial institutions and procedures[18] which, taken together, formed an effective barrier. This all means that the comparatist seeking to transplant ideas needs to be conscious of crucial variables in the form of similarities and differences, in both the arrangements for the separation of powers between state institutions, and the distribution of power between organised groups at many different levels, including economic interests, consumers, trade unions and so on.[19] The proposal in this chapter is to formulate distinct, abstract, ideal typical models of the state that will allow the analyst to identify the interplay of such factors.[20]

The approach of Kahn-Freund prompted a well known debate in which Watson not only argues that Montesquieu seriously underestimated the amount of successful borrowing, for example, the transfusion of Roman law throughout Western Europe, but also contests the view that the degree to which any rule can be borrowed depends

[15] K. Zweigert and H. Kötz, *An Introduction to Comparative Law* (3rd edn., trans. A. Weir, Oxford University Press, Oxford, 1998), p. 34. See also A. Harding, 'Comparative Public Law: A Neglected Discipline' in I.D. Edge (ed.), *Comparative Law in Global Perspective* (Transnational, New York, 2000), at p. 115.

[16] 'The EC has made its own substantial contribution to juridification'. See C. Harlow, 'European Administrative Law and the Global Challenge', *European University Institute*, Working Paper RSC No. 98/23; see section III thereof, 'Law's Expanding Empire', p. 11.

[17] See e.g., J.W.F. Allison, *A Continental Distinction in the Common Law* (Oxford University Press, Oxford, 1996), p. 12 et seq.

[18] O. Kahn-Freund, 'On Uses and Misuses of Comparative Law' (1974) 37 *Modern Law Review* 6.

[19] Ibid., pp. 11–12.

[20] See later section 'Comparison by Oppositions'.

on how closely it is linked to the foreign power structure.[21] It is not necessary for us to pursue this much-discussed disagreement further, but perhaps it is significant to note that the original article was based on a lecture delivered shortly after the United Kingdom entered the European Economic Community (EEC), as it then was, and it almost coincides with Lord Denning's famous statement about 'the incoming tide' of European law in *Bulmer v Bollinger* [1974] Ch. 401. Today, in the light of so much evidence of continental influence, it seems that the question of transplantation has to be revised and updated. For one thing, the Kahn-Freund view partly appeared to rest on the assumption that entire tracts of law move from one system to another. But certainly in the field of public law, a more useful approach to considering the formulation and development of law would be to identify an absorption of influences and a recognition that a 'process of cross-fertilization' is already taking place.[22] This '... implies that an external stimulus promotes an evolution within the receiving legal system' prompting an adaptation by the receiving system. In the United Kingdom there have been many instances of judicial reasoning and drafting of statutes that have been wholly or partially derived from other national or European models.[23] Lord Woolf has stated quite recently that 'What the judges do not learn for themselves in the course of judicial exchanges, has been taught by advocates, ... , who have persevered, sometimes in the face of vigorous judicial opposition, in educating the judiciary as to the developments overseas'.[24] This confirms what we already know – namely, the existence of 'continental influence' obviously in the form of EU law, but also overseas and Commonwealth influence generally in public law,[25] and additional continental influence would appear to be inevitable as a result of the Human Rights Act 1998. In fact, it can be argued that despite the continued predominance of the common law in the United Kingdom and of a continental system in Italy, both nations are progressively accumulating through a process of 'cross-fertilization' a kind of composite system of law and of governance.[26]

Moreover, it has been widely acknowledged that comparative work is of particular importance in public law. This is because of shared problems that are

---

[21] A. Watson, 'Legal Transplants and Law Reform' [1976] *Law Quarterly Review* 79–84. This is referred to by Allison, above n. 17.

[22] Bell, above n. 13, at p. 147; D. Oliver, *Common Values and the Public-Private Divide* (Butterworths, London, 1999), p. 117 et seq. See also R.C. Van Caenegem, *An Historical Introduction to Western Constitutional Law* (Cambridge University Press, Cambridge, 1995).

[23] E.g., the concept of proportionality in administrative law; and the interpretative obligation in s. 3 Human Rights Act 1998 is closely modelled on EU law. See *Marleasing SA v La Comercial Internacional de Alimentacion SA* (case C-106/89) [1990] ECR I-4135. See further, Thomas' chapter in this volume.

[24] See Woolf Lord, 'Droit Public-English Style' [1995] *Public Law* 57–72, at p. 59.

[25] Allison, above n. 17, at p. 23, n. 135 and 136. See also Thomas' chapter in this volume.

[26] See L. Torchia, 'Developments in Italian Administrative Law through Cross-fertilization' in Beatson and Tridimas, above n. 13; and M.P. Chiti, 'Tendencies towards European Standards in National Administrative Law, Italian Report' in J. Schwarze (ed.), *Administrative Law under European Influence* (Sweet and Maxwell, London, 1996).

common to all developed and developing countries in respect of the question of how government can be controlled in the interests of both state and citizen.[27] Public law has been defined by Loughlin as 'a sophisticated form of political discourse'. In one sense this approach confirms that 'controversies within the subject are simply extended political disputes' but this also suggests that the analyst must ensure that any inquiry is 'embedded in the realities of the times'.[28] In other words, it is crucial to take account of the social, political, economic and historical context. However, the task of analysis is far from straightforward because of fundamental distinctions that have to be recognised, not only in respect of the tradition of law, but also concerning the nature of the state itself. Perhaps the most obvious problem for any discussion of the United Kingdom from a comparative angle is that there is no fixed point of reference in the form a written constitution that might encapsulate a normative theory of the separation of powers and of the state. Thus a cartographer of the constitution is compelled to proceed on the basis of a few central constitutional principles, for example, the sovereignty of Parliament and the rule of law; statutes that define key aspects of the operation of the constitution; and some important but in a number of cases alarmingly imprecise constitutional conventions.[29] It has been pointed out that a clear conception of the state would enable the special powers of government to be more adequately acknowledged.[30] For instance, on one view a single theory of the state, defined mainly in terms of degrees of centralization following privatisation, is the prime requirement to evaluate trends in public and private law.[31] An alternative approach seeks to address the increasingly evident blurring of boundaries between notions of public and private by developing general principles available for any significant exercise of power.[32] While it can be acknowledged that law clearly has an important mediating role in regard to the exercise of monopoly power, no theoretical way forward for undertaking this challenging task is actually proposed.[33] It should be noted that aspects of this theme will be taken up later, as there will be an attempt to outline a particular view of the

---

27 N. Brown and J. Bell, *French Administrative Law* (3rd edn., Oxford University Press, Oxford, 1998), p. 1.

28 M. Loughlin, *Public Law and Political Theory* (Oxford University Press, Oxford, 1992), p. 4.

29 Ministerial responsibility, which is an important subject for this analysis is a good example of an imprecise convention. See e.g., Tomkins and Woodhouse, above n. 5.

30 M. Loughlin, 'The State, the Crown and the Law' in M. Sunkin and S. Payne (eds.), *The Nature of the Crown*, (Oxford University Press, Oxford, 1999), p. 76. In calling for a more appropriate conception of the state Loughlin points out that such a concept is relatively unknown in UK law and that the idea of the Crown has been substituted.

31 Allison, above n. 17, at p. 239.

32 See D. Oliver, *Common Values and Public Private Divide* (Butterworths, London, 1999), e.g., at p. 31 et seq. She examines the nature of power and stresses the concern of law to protect vital interests against abuse of power, whether it be public or private.

33 In regard to an earlier article on this subject, Allison points out that no new conception of power is elaborated by Oliver (Allison, above n. 17, at p. 244). See D. Oliver, 'Is the Ultra Vires Rule the Basis of Judicial Review' [1987] *Public Law* 543–569.

multi-faceted exercise of power in regard to the comparative models of state organisation.[34]

Turning to Italy, the Italian constitution of 1948 provides an entirely different starting point. Not only does it address the rights of the citizen and make provision for certain economic relations,[35] but it sets out the characteristics of government based upon a limited separation of powers and a system of checks and balances.[36] There are other significant differences, for example, in the way a government is formed after a general election. This is from a combination of parties in Parliament with the agenda for national policy reached after the government has received a vote of confidence before it assumes power. It is then that an agreed programme is approved separately by each chamber. Following such an agreement the survival of coalition governments depends on sustaining parliamentary support. However, it will be apparent that the structure of government and administration has been transformed in recent years so that the accepted concept of the Italian state as a single 'legal entity with its own personality, all encompassing law, statutes, rights, public bodies, private citizens' has been largely abandoned only to be replaced by an array of different concepts. In effect, it has become *a* subject and not any longer *the* subject of the internal legal order. Although the state remains sovereign, there are other public bodies with a high degree of autonomy, perhaps most important of which are regions and municipalities.[37] In one important respect, the new laws in Italy,[38] which have been termed 'administrative federalism', tend strongly to accentuate this trend towards regionalism. For example, Law 59/97 puts the mechanism in place for the transfer of administrative functions from central government to the regions, provinces and town councils (this is with the exception of certain reserved functions for central government).[39] At a political level, it includes provision for the direct election of Regional Presidents and City Mayors,[40] and there are new localized accountability mechanisms located in Parliaments and Assemblies.[41] Despite these important reforms, the system still lacks uniformity, as the enabling legislation allows scope for changes to be introduced at different rates and

[34] See section entitled 'Michel Foucault: Two Histories of the Present'.

[35] T. Glyn Watkin, *The Italian Legal Tradition*, (Dartmouth, Ashgate, 1997), p. 87.

[36] E.g., Article 70 allocates the legislative function to both houses but Article 76 allows for the delegation of that function. Article 94 provides that the government must enjoy the confidence of both houses. Article 100 provides that the Court of Accounts exercises preventive control on the legitimacy of government measures. Article 104 provides that the judiciary is an autonomous institution independent of any other power.

[37] See Articles 114 to 133 of the Italian Constitution.

[38] Law no. 241/1990, Decreto legislativo no. 29/1993, Law 59/97 (So called Basanini Acts etc.) See e.g., Torchia, above n. 26, at p. 139.

[39] Some functions are specifically identified to be excluded from this process e.g., justice, national security defence, international relations and trade, macroeconomic policy, energy policy, telecommunication, transport, education and research.

[40] Law 81/93.

[41] Const. law 1/99.

in different ways. In preference to any side-by-side description of institutional developments in Italy and the United Kingdom, the proposed method for considering these diverse systems will be by way of two contrasting Weberian ideal typical models of the state, with each displaying distinct political, administrative and economic characteristics.

Another criticism is that comparative legal studies has frequently failed to meet the call for 'an expanded intellectual range' and that, at times, it has even failed to reach beyond the mere description and comparison of systems of rules.[42] Critics have argued that the comparatist needs to be equipped with a theory about law which recognises that it is part of a social sub-system[43] and that it needs to take on board the notion that that which takes place at other levels of discourse is not necessarily peripheral or irrelevant. Such a view recognises law as a social phenomenon related to the historical, social, economic, political, cultural and psychological context that will be able to reveal deeper understanding. The comparatist is required not to stop at the surface, since there is a great deal more to comparison than that which comes from a descriptive examination of legal texts. The dangers of superficial comparison that overlooks the socio-cultural or the socio-historical context have been demonstrated by reference to examples that might suggest that deeper comparative inquiry is essential to avoid serious misconceptions.[44]

In this chapter, there is an attempt to develop a limited theoretical framework by adopting the notion of 'ideal types' and by employing Foucault's ideas relating to power/knowledge and history. This is in order to extend the scope of analysis beyond a mere description of institutions and rules. But how far should and can any theoretical approach extend? It has been suggested that to achieve satisfactory results the comparatist should possess a 'mentalité' which is inevitably socially, historically, culturally, and epistemologically situated.[45] The scholar from abroad is faced with the formidable obstacle of having to understand the common law mind before studying the cognitive framework of our law and vice-versa. Integration of foreign ideas and principles is made virtually impossible because only those who have the perception and understanding of the culture will approach or interpret a concept as a native would.[46] These are deep-seated problems to be discovered beneath the surface. Can all these requirements be realistically set as a precondition? If so, to embark upon an intellectual mission of this kind demands an open commitment to interdisciplinarity and a vast intellectual range. Yet another problem that such an all-embracing approach raises is where to limit the field of inquiry, since this poses

---

42 P. Legrand, above n. 12, at pp. 233–234.

43 E.g. N. Luhmann, *A Sociological Theory of Law* (Routledge, London, 1985).

44 See Legrand, above n. 12, p. 235 et seq; he explains how cultural phenomena such as a painting by Jacques-Louis David of Napoleon, can provide insights into the French legal mind. The task is to search beyond legal rules and propositions and find that these have been partly shaped by cultural representations.

45 Ibid., p. 236 et seq.

46 Bell, above n. 13, at p. 155.

the familiar problem of deciding where law begins and where it ends and to what extent the contextual elements ought to be pursued.[47]

According to Zweigert and Kötz '... comparatists all over the world are perfectly unembarrassed by their methodology, and see themselves at the experimental stage'.[48] It will always be crucial to consider first what we are trying to achieve by undertaking any comparative work. 'Before we talk about method, we need to know what is the point of the whole enterprise'.[49] Then, the work has to be based upon sound historical and empirical investigations of law and social change, and this should demonstrate an understanding of the subject matter in context and evaluation of its significance. But although a basic methodology is essential, at one and the same time, a certain pragmatism is called for. Thus 'Even today the right method must largely be discovered by trial and error' and 'comparative inquiry is a field whcrc allied to any method one needs 'sound judgment', 'common sense' and 'intuition'.[50] The analyst tests the usefulness and practicality of a hypothesis by demonstrating its explanatory potential.

In sum, I suspect that the challenging call for a theoretical basis to any inquiry may deter many public lawyers wishing to undertake important comparative work. Indeed, it is interesting that the distinguished American comparatist Merryman responded to Legrand's suggestion that an all embracing cultural analysis geared towards finding out how lawyers think was a pre-condition to reaching a deep understanding by disposing ' ... of the fallacy of omnicompetence. No human being can do all what you have just suggested. Next, let us agree to reject the all-or-nothing premise. It is perfectly acceptable for a scholar to attempt to deal with a manageable piece of reality rather than take on everything'.[51] The approach discussed below is presented as a flexible method for analysis based on a particular view of the subject matter rather than a general theory of comparison.

3. Comparison by Oppositions

This section outlines a possible method for comparison that has been developed to deal with the particular subject matter under consideration.[52] In situations where an

---

47 Legrand, above n. 12, at p. 234.

48 K. Zweigert and H. Kotz, above n. 15, at p. 33.

49 P. Legrand, 'John Henry Merryman and Comparative Legal Studies: A Dialogue' (1999) 27 *American Journal of Comparative Law* 3, at p. 50.

50 Zweigert and Kötz, above n. 15, at p. 33.

51 Legrand, above n. 49, at p. 40.

52 Other off-the-shelf methods could have been tried e.g., M. Van Hoecke and M. Warrington 'Legal Cultures, Legal Paradigms and Legal Doctrine: Towards A New Model for Comparative Law' [1998] *International Comparative Law Quarterly* 495, at p. 514. This proposes a paradigm of legal orders that could be used at a micro or macro level and consists of: (1) A concept of law. What is law? What is its relationship to other social norms? (2) A theory of valid legal sources; (3) A methodology of law, both for the making and for the adjudication of law; (4) A theory of argumentation; (5) A theory of legitimation of law; (6) A common basic ideology.

analyst is faced with having to select from an endless stream of individual cases, Weber's conception of the 'ideal typical' offers a widely tested method of analysis.[53] The first stage is the construction of certain elements of reality into logically precise, controlled and unambiguous conceptions that are removed from historical reality. This provides extreme and pure cases and allows the analyst to consider that the real meat of history falls somewhere between these extreme types.[54] Its purpose has been summarised thus:

> ... the ideal type is a category of historical interpretation; it is a structure of understanding for the historian who seeks to integrate, after the fact, a certain set of data: it allows him to recapture an 'essence' working from general principles which are not at all present in the thought of individuals whose concrete behaviour is nevertheless to be understood on their basis[55]

Weber explains how the analyst proceeds:

> An ideal type is formed by the one-sided accentuation of one or more points of view and by the synthesis of a great many diffuse, discrete, more or less present and occasionally absent concrete individual phenomena, which are arranged according to those one-sidedly emphasized viewpoints into a unified analytical construct (Gedankenbild). In its conceptual purity, this mental construct cannot be found empirically anywhere in reality. It is a utopia. Historical research faces the task of determining in each individual case, the extent to which the ideal-construct approximates or diverges from reality[56]

Before we proceed further, it is important to recognise, first, that these proposed ideal types are contrasting and opposing models of the state and its institutions. They will provide a general description and will need to be expanded and refined in terms of particular areas that are made subject to detailed analysis.[57] A recognised problem with this method is achieving an appropriate level of generality when constructing ideal types.[58] Secondly, the choice of the type of state model itself might differ. For example, if one were comparing changes between Russia or Eastern

---

53 See e.g., M. Loughlin, above n. 28, at p. 59, who uses this approach to describe the main styles dominating public law, which for him, are normativism and functionalism.

54 H.H. Gerth and C. Wright Mills, *From Max Weber* (6th edn., Routledge, London, 1967), p. 59; R. Cotterrell, *The Sociology of Law: An Introduction* (Butterworths, London, 1984), pp. 159, 166.

55 M. Foucault, above n. 8, at p. 90.

56 M. Weber, *The Methodology of the Social Sciences* (Glencoe, Illinois, 1949) quoted by Allison who also utilises Weber's ideal type but rather differently (Allison, above n. 17, at p. 31). E.g., his model does not deal with the locus of political and economic power and he does not deal with two contrasting types as is proposed here (see chapter 3).

57 Weber was sceptical of Marx's claims to scientific value and laws of historical change. His methodology was rather 'to understand contingent tendencies, developmental possibilities and historical phases'. See B. Turner, *Max Weber: From History to Modernity* (Routledge, London, 1992), p. 214.

58 Allison, above n. 17, at p. 32 n. 186.

European States and the United Kingdom – in view of the recent history of the nations concerned, it would be more relevant to construct a variant of a centrally controlled state to contrast with a liberal model.[59]

3.1. Model A: Mixed Economy Welfare State

In brief, although it will be described in 'abstract' terms, this is a model similar to the 'post-war settlement' in the United Kingdom.[60] The main characteristics can be summarised as a centralised state with a democratic system of government 'characterised by universalism and the usurpation of markets'[61] in which the balance of economic and political power rests in an interventionist state which is not in the hands of business or capital. This means that crucial sources and levers of economic power have been transferred from private business to government and governmental organisations. The government operates principles of 'Keynesian' demand management. The power of private employers is limited by government and the outcome of clashes of group or class economic interests is frequently settled in favour of employees. Limited priority is given to achieving profit. The effect of such a distribution of power means that economic decisions in many sectors have passed out of the hands of private industry to a new class of public managers, and indirectly to the government.

The state accepts responsibility for full employment, the rate of growth, the balance of payments and the distribution of incomes through direct taxation. Crucially, the state has a central role, as in the blueprint produced by Beveridge, by having to fulfil a general commitment to universal benefits. It acts as provider, offering in Churchill's phrase, 'national compulsory insurance for all classes for all purposes from the cradle to the grave'.[62] In other words, this resembles the kind of state Crosland observed when writing in the fifties and sixties during a period of the supposed post-war consensus politics.[63]

However, the feature of our model, which is central to the work in hand, is that a substantial government and local government bureaucracy is charged with the task of implementation of the welfare policies of government. The policy areas for

---

59 For a critical discussion of the problems with comparing socialist legal cultures, see B. Puchalska-Tych and M. Salter, 'Comparing Legal Cultures of Europe: the Need for a Dialectical Analysis' (1996) 16 *Legal Studies* 157. See also F.J.M. Feldbrugge (ed.), *The Constitutions of the USSR and the Union Republics: Analysis, Texts, Reports* (Sijthoff & Noordhoff, Netherlands Germantown, Md: Alphen an den Rijn, 1979); *Russian Laws: the End of the Soviet System and the Role of Law* (Dordrecht, Boston, 1993); G. Golosov, 'Modes of Communist Rule, Democratic Transition, and Party System Formation in Four East European Countries' (Henry M. Jackson School of International Studies, University of Washington, Seattle 1996).

60 D. Fraser, 'The Postwar Consensus: A Debate Not Long Enough' [2000] 53 *Parliamentary Affairs* 347.

61 D. Jahn and M. Henn, 'The "New" Rhetoric of New Labour in Comparative Perspective: A Three Country Discourse Analysis' (2000) 23 *Western European Politics* 26, at p. 28.

62 See e.g., A. Crosland, *The Future of Socialism*, (2nd edn., Greenwood Press, New York, 1963)

63 Fraser, above n. 60.

universal state provision include: health, education, housing and social security. The bureaucracy is deliberately part of government and the political responsibility for its operation lies directly to Parliament. For this model there are a number of hybrid institutions, and this presents us with something of a definitional problem[64] since they exist between the public and private sphere and are common to both models.

3.2. Model B: Mixed Economy 'Public Choice' Model

In summary, this is also a democratic system of government and it shares certain constitutional characteristics with the welfare model by operating on the basis of the rule of law and a bill of rights. It includes a general reliance on liberal constitutionalism, but crucially there is a quite different view of the nature of state. In general, state power is managed so as not to encroach on individual liberty and there is resistance to interference with individual freedom. The system is based on what Hayek called the 'the discovery of a self-generating or spontaneous order in social affairs'.[65] This is a system based upon a spontaneous organisation resembling a free market, which generates a plurality of values. Social and interpersonal transactions are modelled on market exchanges and the role of government is limited to keeping order.[66]

Focusing on the area under discussion, this involves a significant change in the role of the state and a narrowing of its functions (from Model A), with the objective of maximising the areas open to private interests. The economic system operates on the basis that direct taxation is not a legitimate source of state revenue. This is a model where 'the state steers and does not row' and one in which we find a more limited conception of government.[67] For example, government has only marginal responsibility for education, health and social welfare. The norm is that education is paid for out of fees and that private insurance schemes fund health and pensions. Social benefits are restricted to covering only a bare minimum of social needs, and in such a system it follows that government has a much more limited function. In most areas, including social policy and education, it is not directly responsible for the implementation of policy. This role is performed by private organisations and the device of contracting with the central core civil service is deployed to specify the basic parameters of service provision. The residual civil service and local government organisation is subject to the strategies of private management that set a premium on economic efficiency. Further, there are no significant publicly owned industries. In a system where services are delivered privately, the mechanism for accountability of

64 See Allison, above n. 17 above, at p. 84.

65 M. Loughlin, above n. 8, at p. 84 et seq. provides a useful discussion of Hayek's political thought.

66 B. Goodwin, *Using Political Ideas* (John Wiley, Chichester, 1982), p. 53.

67 C. Harlow and R. Rawlings, *Law and Administration*, (2nd edn., Butterworths, London, 1997), p. 131 et seq.

these services is not directly to Parliament. Finally, the citizen has become empowered as a consumer of services as well as goods.

Two distinct abstract models that represent contrasting versions of the state have been briefly set out. It has been argued that:

> Comparative study and historical study are very deeply involved with each other. You cannot understand the under-developed, the communist, the capitalist political economies as they exist in the world today by flat timeless comparisons. You must expand the temporal reach of your analysis ... Knowing that what we are studying is subject to change, on the simplest of descriptive levels we must ask: What are the salient trends? To answer this question we must make a statement of at least 'from what' and 'to what'[68]

It should be emphasized that the main objective is to set a standard against which to assess the degrees of change in a way that allows a multi-dimensional (rather than accurate) map to be drawn.[69] At this juncture, we need to remember that a central concern for our comparison is the accountability of central government following its re-structuring. From the empirical data it is immediately apparent that both our systems, Italian and British have been subjected to doses of modernization and reform, privatisation, contracting out and so on. In fact, it is widely recognised that there has been a certain amount of convergence on policies such as privatisation leading to the dismantling of state monopolies, reduction in public sector employment, and the blurring of the divide between the public and private roles of the state[70] and it would seem to follow that, in some respects at least, national state institutions will have become through this process similar. Why then go to the trouble of constructing these abstract models? The purpose of such analysis is to map movements that are taking place at a macro level, and by doing so, identify the changing patterns of state organisation. This is a formidable challenge as our models are likely to reveal that any such movements ebb and flow in different directions. For example, Paul Craig, commenting on the agenda of the Blair government, has recently noted that:

> It is clear that efficiency and competition will still be important considerations in the new order, but it is equally clear they will not be the sole considerations in the new order, nor will they be adhered to with the degree of doctrinal fervour which characterised the policy of the previous administration[71]

To refine this comparison further, it is suggested that these ideal typical models can be developed by recognising oppositions selected to draw out contrasting trends.

---

68 C. Wright-Mills, *The Sociological Imagination* (Penguin, London, 1970), pp. 168–169.

69 See Loughlin, above n. 28, at p. 37, who bases his approach on C. Taylor, 'Social Theory as Practice' in *Philosophical Papers 2, Philosophy and the Human Sciences* (Cambridge University Press, Cambridge, 1985).

70 Bell, above n. 13, at p. 152.

71 P. Craig, *Administrative Law*, (4th edn., Sweet and Maxwell, London, 1999), p. 43.

For example, at the surface level there is evidently an obvious opposition between the public welfare characteristics of Model A and private choice characteristics of Model B. At first glance, recent changes in government in both nations in the forms of privatisation and the new public management[72] would veer towards the predominance of the public choice model. But if we were to see this in terms of an opposition between regulation associated with Model A, versus deregulation associated with Model B, the results might be more difficult to interpret. We will have seen that each nation has experienced privatisation, which we noted as a central feature of Model B, but, at the same time, 'public control' remains extremely important. In the United Kingdom the positive state of macroeconomic stabilization has been superseded by the regulatory state, whose main function may have been intended to perform the task of the correction of market failures.[73] This originated with a framework of enabling legislation in each area, with regulators having an active role, and there has been increasingly significant legal involvement in the process with the drawing up of carefully drafted licences and contracts[74] and subsequent attempts to strengthen the powers of regulators.

Turning to Italy, we also find that new regimes of regulation have been introduced to accompany the constitutional and legal changes of recent years.[75] It has been suggested that:

> The changing nature of public control has led to a trilateral relationship, between independent regulatory commission responsible for control, the private subject responsible for complying and other private subjects whose interests are protected through public control[76]

The new regime of regulation applies across an impressive range of government bodies and decentralised agencies. Legislative Decree 30 July 1999 no. 286 provides for the introduction of internal control structures for the public administration at central government level and establishes in principle similar guidelines for regions and cities.[77] The point is that the trends to privatisation are consistent with a shift to

---

72 The term governance has been deployed to refer to a wider conception of government that includes its exposure to privatisation and marketization. See e.g., N. Lewis, *Choice and the Legal Order: Rising Above Politics*, (Butterworths, London, 1996).

73 G. Majone, 'From the Positive to the Regulatory State: Causes and Consequences of Changes in the Mode of Governance' [1997] *Journal of Public Policy* 139, at p. 140. See also J. Black, 'Constitutionalizing Self-Regulation' [1996] *Modern Law Review* 24.

74 Harlow & Rawlings, above n. 67, at p. 320.

75 See e.g., Brancasi, above n. 5, at p. 821.

76 Torchia, above n. 26, at p. 144.

77 V. Irelli, 'Simplification of the Sources of Administrative Action: Simplification as De-legislation' in L. Vandelli (ed.), *The Administrative Reforms in Italy: Experience and Perspectives* (Clueb, Bologna, 2000) 91, at p. 130; but these reforms are not imposed on regional bodies enjoying legislative autonomy. Thus, there is no uniformity of application at a regional level.

Model B while the regimes of regulation, and especially regulation of markets, are very much a characteristic of Model A.[78]

In order to approach other areas of analysis it might be possible to suggest further oppositions, justified on pragmatic grounds which would be suitable to the task in hand. This might concentrate upon the tensions underlying the 'institutional setting':[79] decentralization of state power set against centralization of state power; the provider state opposed to the minimal state; trends towards competition set against moves towards monopoly power. Perhaps the important issue from a public law perspective surrounds the changing patterns of executive accountability.[80] Such trends might be assessed by setting accountability (in the sense of responsibility for executive actions of government to parliament and ultimately to the electorate) characteristics of Model A against autonomy (in the sense of freedom to determine actions without institutional control) characteristics of Model B. What this might involve is very difficult to assess given the divergent constitutional framework and institutions. For example, the United Kingdom has a non-statutory civil service that has been transformed by the 'Next Steps' initiative. As we noted earlier, such changes were brought about unevenly without recourse to legislation. The character and duty of the Italian civil service is partly based on the requirements of the constitution and on related legislation. Subsequent reform by means of the Bassanini Acts[81] and related enabling legislation or legislative decrees has been by the same method. However, by assessing the impact of respective reforms in Italy and the United Kingdom in terms of *accountability* on the one hand, and *autonomy* on the other, certain intersecting patterns will emerge, which are likely to be centred on a discussion of the respective mechanisms for separating policy and administration and distinguishing policy from operations.[82] The intention is not simply to recognise that there are movements in different directions, but to chart these trends at a macro level. This enables the analyst to identify the changing patterns of state organisation measured against the ideal types and relevant sets of oppositions. Due account has to be taken of the context, legal order and time.

4. Michel Foucault: Two 'Histories of the Present'

So far, we have discussed two contrasting ideal typical models both of which have been sketched out as diverging variants of capitalism, but it is interesting that Weber identified the inevitable growth of rule-making as a feature of the bureaucratized

[78] For a study that considers the place of regulation set against deregulation in the area of governance see G. Majone, 'The Regulatory State and its Legitimacy Problems' (1999) 22 *West European Politics* 1.

[79] See Bell's chapter in this volume.

[80] E.g., in Italy, Article 95, clause 2 of the 1948 Constitution and Legislative Decree No. 29 of 1993; and in the UK, the evolution of the convention of Ministerial Responsibility. See Tomkins, above n. 5.

[81] See e.g., L. No. 59/97 and L. No. 127/97, i.e., so called Bassanini Laws.

[82] C. Musillo, 'Italian Administrative Reform: Its Completion and Implementation' (1999) 5 *European Public Law* 363, at p. 370.

world of 'organised monopoly capitalism'. He recognised that such systems contribute through the growth of neutral rules, practices and procedures to a formidable and irreversible system of legal regulation, which according to Weber, comes to be accepted without question;[83] and it is possible to observe that an intricate web of bureaucracies and the related domination of rules remain a central feature of the modern European state. Further, notwithstanding any changes to the shape of state organisation that emerges from any foregoing analysis, it will also be apparent that a crucial characteristic of contemporary governance is that it is a process that operates at many different levels. What Morrison has recently referred to as 'the essential Foucauldian insight that power as well as being concentrated in the state is dispersed throughout society'.[84] Thus, it needs to be recognised that such 'power is not homogeneous but can be defined only by the particular points through which it passes' and this includes private as well as public bodies and institutions. It would appear to follow from this view that any form of comparative analysis needs to address the way power has come to be exercised, not only in the contemporary state, but beyond it. In effect, it is suggested that any attempt at mapping will need to be multi-dimensional.

Certain aspects of the work of Foucault provide a means of approaching the subject in order to chart 'long term practices and the field in which those practices operate'. As we noted earlier, an attempt to identify multi-directional shifts in power forms an important concern for this type of analysis. Further, it becomes evident that: 'We have entered a type of society where the power of law is not regressing but rather merging into a much more general power ... ' and where 'legality combines with other discourses to form the individual as the locus of ever greater networks of administrative control'.[85] This proposes that against the positivist model representing legal autonomy from power politics, law has to be analysed from within as an internally generated set of institutionalized mechanisms of power/knowledge. Such an approach might ' ... focus[es] on the connections between the ways in which individuals are politically objectified and political techniques for integrating concrete aspects of their lives and activities into the pursuit of states objectives'.[86]

In a significantly different context, the study of legal history has been seen as a vital precondition to the critical evaluation of law (for example, Maitland) and to achieving an understanding of the operation of legal concepts from a comparative perspective. For example, historical analysis has long been regarded as fundamental to comparative study,[87] providing what might be regarded as a vertical dimension, as

---

83 Cotterrell, above n. 54, at p. 166.

84 Morrison, above n. 10, at p. 124.

85 P. Leyland and T. Woods, 'Public Law History and Theory: Some Notes Towards a New Foundationalism: Part 2', in P. Leyland and T. Woods (eds.), *Administrative Law Facing the Future: Old Constraints and New Horizons* (Blackstone, London, 1997), p. 444.

86 G. Burchell, 'Civil Society and "the System of Natural Liberty"' in Burchell et al., above n. 8, pp. 122–123.

87 Zweigert and Kötz, above n. 15, at p. 8.

opposed to the horizontal study of legal systems. However, in several of his works Foucault attempted something altogether different. He was writing what has been termed a 'history of the present'[88] which recognises that '... if history is to show how we have become what we are then it is about the 'small' happenings, not themselves part of any master plan or subject to any grand design'.[89] For Foucault this is a complex enterprise of research that Deleuze explains in the following terms:

> He does not write a history of mentalities but of the conditions governing everything that has a mental existence, namely statements and systems of language. He does not write a history of behaviour but of the conditions governing everything that has a visible existence, namely a system of light. He does not write a history of institutions but of the conditions governing their integration of different relations between forces, at the limits of a social field. He does not write a history of private life but of the conditions governing the way in which the relation to oneself constitutes a private life. He does not write a history of subjects but of the process of subjectification, governed by the foldings operating in the ontological as much as the social field[90]

For the historian of the present, the starting point is to approach a particular 'ritual of power' and suggest that the formation of a political technology of power can be traced back in time. The analyst concentrates on cultural practices in which power and knowledge intersect in order to obtain a grid of intelligibility.

It should also be emphasized that the state for Foucault is an effect of power. It is the effect of the assembled forces of governmentality placed at another level.[91] 'The state like all other organisations simply organises the supposed relationships of governmental power and these forces are microphysical'.[92] From the standpoint of an analyst, this encourages a recognition of the multi-directional and multi-layered exercise of power. We discover that 'The formal limits between civil society and the state are in reality traversed by networks which operate across constitutional boundaries'. Further, it is important to remember that for Foucault writing a 'history of the present' was not merely reading present interests, institutions and politics back in history to claim that they have current significance. For he explicitly rejected the supposition of historical progression or the idea of a march of progress towards some fixed point – or any kind of causal historical approach.[93] The forces operating in history are not controlled by destiny or regulative mechanisms, but

[88] E.g., M. Foucault, *Discipline and Punish* (Penguin, London, 1977), p. 308; and M. Foucault, *The History of Sexuality* (Pelican, London, 1981), Pts. 1–3.

[89] A. Hunt and G. Wickham, *Foucault and the Law: Towards a Sociology of Law and Governance* (Pluto Press, London, 1994), p. 33.

[90] G. Deleuze, *Foucault* (University of Minnesota Press, 1986), p. 116.

[91] Ibid., p. 25.

[92] Bové's introduction to Deleuze, above n. 90, p. xxx.

[93] H. Dreyfus and P. Rabinow, *Michel Foucault: Beyond Structuralism and Hermeneutics* (Harvester Press, Brighton, 1982), pp. 118 et seq.

rather they respond to haphazard conflicts.[94] His work represents a number of attempts to identify how the current situation has been reached by examining the combination of circumstances to be found in a range of types of social activity.

At this point we need to forge a link between these ideas and the task before us. In dealing with the fragmentation of responsibility and accountability associated with the modern regulatory state, some recent work represents a move away from a relatively narrow definition of the concept of accountability and has discussed this question in multi-directional terms: for example, there is regulation upwards to a higher authority, horizontally to a broadly parallel institution and downwards to the lower level institutions and consumers.[95] So that 'the identification and mapping out of relationships of interdependence within policy domains has been one of the key contributions of the recent pluralist literature in public policy'.[96] We find that such models provide results which reveal that 'the various accountability networks which operate uniquely within each policy domain have the character of a complex system of checks and balances in which particular forms of behaviour are inhibited or encouraged by the overall balance in the system at any particular time'.[97]

In terms of the proposed comparative analysis, I am suggesting that we are seeking to observe two parallel and intersecting histories of the present, one for the United Kingdom and one for Italy that must be tackled at the same time. In each instance the analyst attempts to identify the rituals of power that are involved and the results of the respective analysis can be compared. This is a recognition that we will find that the institutional structures under consideration are organised around a complex series of rationalities rooted in very different objectives which are not co-ordinated as part of a plan. The focus will tend to shift towards examining downwards accountability mechanisms that have been the subject of much recent discussion. For example, to take the United Kingdom, this might involve the interaction of: the new public management and strategies of employment in the public sector;[98] strategies for deregulation of government procedures;[99] the use of internal review procedures;[100] the role of contracts in public administration to modify the managerial functions of government;[101] the use of contracts to determine

94 M. Foucault, 'Nietzche, Genealogy, History', in P. Rabinow (ed.) *The Foucault Reader: An Introduction to Foucault's Thought* (Penguin, London, 1984), at p. 88.

95 Scott, above n. 9, at p. 42.

96 Ibid., p. 50.

97 Ibid., p. 55.

98 G. Morris, 'Fragmenting the State: Implications for Accountability for Employment Practices in Public Services' [1999] *Public Law* 64.

99 D. Miers, 'The Deregulation Procedure: An Expanding Role' [1999] *Public Law* 477.

100 J. Baldwin, N. Wikely and R. Young, 'Adjudicating in Local Offices' in J. Baldwin, N. Wikely and R. Young (eds.) *Judging Social Security* (Clarendon Press, Oxford, 1992).

101 M. Freedland, 'Government by Contract in Public Law' [1994] *Public Law* 86.

relationships between service providers and purchasers;[102] the empowerment of the citizen as consumer for example, by means of Citizen's Charter.[103]

It has been suggested that 'power exists beyond the state: power is less about imposing sovereign will and more about engaging with the many networks and alliances that make up a chain or network which translates power from one locale to another'.[104] This recognition that the exercise of power exists beyond the state has far reaching implications. In one sense it exposes and challenges any narrow distinction between the public and private sphere. We are charting the demise of the monolithic state.[105] The issue at the micro level becomes one of the exercises of the bio-political technologies of power within a particular domain and investigates how can this be constructed from the base level of the human subject. But in another sense, it means that the analyst is not constrained by national boundaries and that there is also an inter-penetration of power from above as well as from below. 'The new democratic state and the cosmopolitan nation are bound up with a much wider political arena that can no longer be treated as merely "external". This cosmopolitan nation implies cosmopolitan democracy, operating on a globalizing scale'.[106] This would suggest, for example, that we will have to identify issues surrounding the hollowing out of the nation state and that due account has to be taken of the prevalent influence of the European Union[107] and of global economic forces in the exercise of any such power.

---

102 P. Vincent-Jones, 'The Regulation of Contractualization in Quasi-Markets for Public Services' [1999] *Public Law* 304, at p. 315.

103 P. Birkinshaw, *Grievances, Remedies and the State* (2nd edn., Sweet & Maxwell, London, 1994), p. 12. In Italy the *Carta dei servizi* has been applied in a number of services e.g., health and electricity supply. See G.L. Vesperini, 'Attuazione della Carta dei Servizi Pubblic in Italia' [1998] *Revista Trimestrale di Diritto Pubblico* 1. For a comparative discussion see L. Lo Schiavo, 'Quality Standards in the Public Sector: Differences between Italy and the UK in the Citizen's Charter Initiative' [2000] *Public Administration* 679. At p. 694 it is noted that 'Despite the relative homogeneity in names, the differences between the two Citizen's Charter initiatives ... are deeply cultural specific and keenly related to the different legal, social and institutional roots of European countries'.

104 J. Morrison, 'The Government-Voluntary Sector Compacts: Governance, Governmentality, and Civil Society' (2000) 27 *Journal of Law and Society* 98, at p. 122. Morrison discusses Foucault's later work on 'governmentalization', and considers how the proper subject of an analysis of contemporary forms of government should be those networks and alliances that exercise 'government at a distance'.

105 Such an approach may appear to have certain affinities with a much earlier concern by Marxist thinkers to recognise the importance of cultural institutions in the distinctive configurations of power in the UK, and to consider the more general conditions of social existence. (See e.g., P. Anderson, 'Origins of the Present Crisis' and 'Problems of Socialist Strategy' in P. Anderson and R. Blackburn (eds.), *Towards Socialism* (Fontana, London, 1965), pp. 44 and 287 respectively. However, Foucault's work has a distinctive conceptualization of power, which sees domination in the 'form of a combination or structure of knowledge and power which is not external to the subject, but still unintelligible from his or her perspective'. According to this view, domination is not in any simple sense caused by subjects. See M. Poster, *Foucault, Marxism & History* (Polity, London, 1984), p. 80.

106 A. Giddens, *The Third Way: The Renewal of Social Democracy* (Polity, London, 1998), p. 138.

107 N. Walker, 'European Constitutionalism and European Integration' [1996] *Public Law* 266.

However, there needs to be particular circumspection when considering the interplay of global forces and their supposed impact. For example, some commentators argue that the world is regressing from interdependence to disorder and chaos, and it has been pointed out that the extent of globalization is often misleadingly reduced to 'a single causal mechanism' namely as an outcome of a new structure of global economic flows, where it might also be argued that 'this also results from the ideas which prominent opinion-formers hold about such flows'.[108] Others, mindful of an economic calamity on at least the scale of 1929, stress that the 'Global laissez-faire is a moment in the history of the emerging world economy, not its endpoint'. It is foreseen not only that the hegemony of the United States may well be superseded by the challenge of newly emerging powers, but also that the solution for the world economy lies in a new era of 'global governance' and not in unbounded markets. Thus, 'the task of transnational organisations should be to fashion a framework of regulation within which diverse market economies can flourish'[109]. Whatever direction these trends actually follow it will be evident that the complex influence of global economic power in a plural world exercised on a supra-national scale will be relevant to any comparison of the structure of government that is undertaken.

5. Conclusion

This chapter suggests developing a method of analysis that is itself determined by a contextual view of public law. Our method seeks to consider not only the institutions and rules by matching and assessing them against models of the state, but also to address aspects of the underlying structure of the institutions and processes that may be revealed as a complex and dynamic social sub-system with a deep historical and cultural dimension. To pursue our mapping metaphor, the respective outline of the nations are approximately outlined by reference to ideal types while the plate tectonics, geological structure and the climatic and atmospheric conditions are assessed by a consideration of the multi-dimensional micro-politics of power. I believe that a refined version of this method has the potential to result in some productive and insightful analysis. However, it will be apparent that there are several problems to overcome. For example, an obvious difficulty that has already been mentioned is that of finding a method for defining and justifying the type and the complexity of the comparative models that are to be adopted in the first place. Another problem is finding a way of containing the study. It is one thing to recognise that power is exercised at many different levels, but quite another to be able to demonstrate the significance of this to the particular question under consideration without going into exhaustive detail. It will be evident that the analyst has to

[108] C. Hay and M. Watson, 'Globalization: "Sceptical" notes on the 1999 Reith Lectures' (1999) 70 *Political Quarterly* 419.

[109] J. Gray, *False Dawn: The Delusions of Global Capitalism* (Granta, London, 1998), pp. 198–199, 235.

constantly balance the discussion of questions at an empirical level with the sophistication of any theoretical approach that is adopted, and in the end, this will always be a question for intuitive judgment.

Chapter 13

COMPARING PUBLIC LAW

*John Bell**

The contributors to this book have broadly two different aims: the pursuit of insights into legal uniformity, and the pursuit of understanding of 'other' legal systems. Bell falls into the latter category, but like most of the contributors of either kind, he takes as starting point the contextual nature of contemporary comparative law; and like Leyland, but to a greater extent than Harding, he sees comparative public law as different in purpose, context, and subject matter from private law, emphasizing the importance of public law's institutional setting, itself influenced, as he indicates, by wider contexts. These contexts now include factors that both limit the autonomy of national legal systems (compare McDonald) and also have the effect, in the age of privatization, of reducing the distinction between public and private law. As against this Bell emphasizes that value-systems (for example regarding freedom of expression, religious tolerance) are also internal to the national public law system.

Readers may wish to consider carefully and comparatively the examples supporting his cogent claim that public law is more influenced by history than private law (compare here Foster, Raffenne, Leyland, Carey-Miller and Harding), is less open to transnational influences, is more connected to politics, and is, moreover, in dialogue 'as much with a nation's past as with the future'. Here, relevant factors discussed include the mode and extent of decentralization and privatization, the nature of public employment, and the role of law itself in administration.

[A. Harding and E. Örücü]

1. Introduction

It is a commonplace of comparative law that one should not simply attempt to compare legal rules, but one should examine the function, which the law is trying to

* Professor of Law, University of Cambridge; British Academy Reader 1999–2001.

A. Harding and E. Örücü (eds.),
Comparative Law in the 21st Century, 235–248.

serve.[1] The suggestion in this article is that generic statements of the functions of law are of limited value. A comparatist has to examine not only rules and functions, but also the context in which they operate and in which legal problems arise. Only by understanding this context or institutional setting can we make effective comparison. The second suggestion in the paper is that public law has a number of institutional features that make it a significantly different activity compared with private law.

In public law, the core function of law is distinctive from private law. Public law is about defining and controlling the powers and activities of government. This is not the function of private law, which exists to provide frameworks within which individuals can undertake voluntarily, and to provide remedies when they exceed the bounds of the acceptable use of private power. Although these functions might be described thus in terms which are applicable to several legal systems, the theme of this paper is that comparison based on similarities at that level of generality are potentially misleading. In order to understand an activity in law, it is necessary to locate it within an institutional setting. It may well be that there is a broadly generic function performed in a number of legal systems, but once one examines this within the different institutional settings, the activities undertaken by the law in the different legal systems become significantly different and difficult to compare.

The particular kind of comparative exercise in which I am engaged is not the search for general principles of law and uniform laws, which has concerned many in recent years. Rather, I am interested in the structure of law and legal systems. Comparison between different legal systems permits one both to understand the dynamics of one's own legal system[2] and to discern whether those dynamics are peculiar to one's own system, or are to be found in a range of other legal systems. The structural analysis proposed in this article provides a building block towards a notion of legal culture.[3]

The core of a structural analysis of legal systems would suggest that an *activity* in law involves both a task or function and a procedure for carrying it out. The *institutional setting* provides a wider context into which the activity fits. The task is defined not only by routine, but also by direct inputs at a national level and more broadly from supra-national legislators. This might be described as the *external environment*. These also affect the institutional setting, but this is also shaped by *history*. The interplay of these features helps to explain the individuality of particular legal systems, but also the specificity of branches of law, among which is public law. While the structural analysis given is not specific to public law and might apply equally to branches of private law, the various elements within the analysis can help to explain why public law is distinctive.

---

1 K. Zweigert and H. Kötz, *An Introduction to Comparative Law* (3rd edn., trans. A. Weir, Oxford University Press, Oxford, 1998), p. 40.

2 H. Collins, 'Methods and Aims of Comparative Contract Law' (1991) 11 *Oxford Journal of Legal Studies* 396 at pp. 400–401.

3 See further J. Bell, *French Legal Cultures* (Butterworths, London, 2001), ch. 1.

1.1. The Activity

Public law serves both to define and control power in the hands of government.[4] In defining the power of government, the law also serves to legitimate the exercise of power, particularly discretionary power in the hands of politicians and officials. By authorizing action, the law sends a signal to society that the actions of certain individuals should be respected and be considered as legitimate in the political society. The law then also sets out the conditions for the control of the power it has legitimated. It may set down procedures before decisions are made, and it may also set out mechanisms and grounds for the review of decisions that are taken.

Now this function of public law in defining and controlling the use of power may seem to be broadly similar to the function of private law. Private law defines the powers of individuals and sets out grounds of control, as well as duties of reparation when powers are exceeded or have unacceptable consequences. But there are important differences. Much private power is not a creature of the state. Within the family, in commerce, in private relationships, private power pre-exists the law. The law is concerned to channel and control the exercise of that power, and uses legal authorization to achieve this purpose. Of course, the law also creates institutions to facilitate individual endeavours and desires, such as the institution of wills or marriage or, more recently, the *Pacte Civile de Solidarité* (a civil union less than marriage).[5] But this does not deny the importance of pre-existing private power.

Among private lawyers, it is more common to talk of social functions as transnational ideas. With some exaggeration, Zweigert and Kötz suggest that the social functions, which have to be performed, and the solutions adopted, are often the same in different legal systems, even if the legal means to achieve them (the norms, concepts and institutions) are different.[6] The legal mechanisms and the way of legal thinking to achieve them are the most important feature of difference between legal systems.[7] Now, to talk at a very high level of abstraction, one can discuss the basic principles of liberal democratic government and the control of abuse of power. This is the kind of discussion you get in works of political philosophers. But if we are going to discuss the role of law, we need to descend into several layers of detail, so the question becomes: how do you govern in a liberal and democratic way in a society divided on linguistic grounds which has a relatively short history of independent government and which has a broadly French tradition of institutions (Belgium), as opposed to how do you govern a long-standing unitary state with religious divisions and with a distinct tradition of governmental institutions (the Netherlands).

In public law, however, the process of lawmaking in democratic societies has been to use the law as a way of defining a broad framework of power. The democratic

---

[4] See J. Bell in K. Hawkins (ed.), *The Uses of Discretion* (Clarendon Press, Oxford, 1992), pp. 107–110.

[5] See J.-J. Lemouland, D 1999 Chr 483.

[6] Zweigert and Kötz, above n. 1, at p. 40.

[7] Ibid., p. 70.

process decides how much power politicians and officials should have and should stipulate the controls exercised over it. The medieval and renaissance monarch had pre-existing or prerogative powers, which the law tried to curb. But to a large extent, the rule of law requires that the law should define the powers of the administration.[8] Prerogative power is relatively confined, and seen as an historical anachronism. Government, in that sense, is a creature of constitutional law and law serves to define the framework of legitimate action. Politics then serves to define the policies that will be implemented in the exercise of the powers, which are permissible through law.

1.2. The External Environment

The similarity of functions between legal systems is reinforced by the character of external inputs into the law. The law consists of a tradition of principles and rules handed down and developed by a caste of lawyers.[9] This body of traditional knowledge has to be updated by lawyers in their practice of the law. This might appear to make it a kind of self-contained system.[10] But this body of law is regularly modified in modern societies by significant inputs from the *national legislator*, consisting of both Parliament and the Executive. The legislator wishes to achieve new objectives and has ideas about how the procedures of the law can be improved and who should be entrusted with particular tasks. Therefore a first feature of the external environment of a legal system is the direct intervention of the national legislator to alter the law. (The picture is complicated in countries like the United Kingdom, Belgium, and Germany by the existence of sub-national legislators. But this does not fundamentally alter the picture of the law being subjected to external inputs.)

In addition, no legal system exists in isolation. People and activities are not confined to national boundaries. We are familiar with the impact of the media and the internet as modern manifestations of such problems when individuals and organisations in one country deliberately seek to affect people in another, as well as of the impact of international law firms.[11] But there are also important indirect impacts, even in public law. The French have had to admit surrounding states as litigants in its administrative courts to deal with issues like the pollution of the Rhine and the siting of nuclear installations on the frontier with Luxembourg.[12] It may be

[8] See J. Bell and J. Rivero in *L'Etat de droit. Mélanges en l'Honneur de Guy Braibant*, Paris 1996, 15–28 and 609–14.

[9] J. Bell, 'Comparative Law and Legal Theory', in W. Krawietz (ed.), *Festschrift for R.S. Summers* (Duncker and Humbolt, Berlin, 1994) 19, at p. 29. See also M. Krygier, 'Law as Tradition' (1986) 5 *Law and Philosophy* 237, at p. 255.

[10] See e.g., N. Luhmann, *A Sociological Theory of Law* (Routledge, London, 1985), pp. 174–183; G. Teubner, *Law as an Autopoietic System* (Blackwell, Oxford, 1993), esp. ch. 3.

[11] On the impact of globalization, see W. Twining, *Globalization and Legal Theory* (Butterworths, London, 2000), pp. 221–238.

[12] See CE 13 Feb. 1987, Actualité Juridique – Droit Administratif 1987, 363.

that public international law deals with the impact of the testing of nuclear weapons, but private international law is invoked for the attraction of investors such as the Disney Corporation to establish themselves in France.[13] The classical conception of public law as being about the relationship between a state and its citizens, or at least those who are found within its territory, tells only part of the story.

The European Union has been an enterprise that has sought to challenge the protection given by public law to the state. In 1988, two French commentators felt able to write that 'if there is one field in which national lawyers should occupy a privileged place, it is in public law, which touches on mechanism which are altogether specific to French society'.[14] Ten years later, Flauss argued that

> Our administrative law, more than any other branch of French law, used to seem strictly Franco-French, practically a pure legal gallicism. However, 'Europeanization' will lead more or less inevitably towards some cross-breeding of French administrative law[15]

Traditional French concepts such as '*service public*' have come under challenge from the framework of European competition law (arguably a private law regime), and new structures have had to be evolved.[16]

The European Convention has also offered external benchmarks against which national law is judged. In terms of procedure, the decision in *Procula v Luxembourg*[17] is seen as a potential threat to the combination of advisory and judicial functions in the *Conseil d'Etat*. Both the Dutch and the Swedes have already had to 'judicialize' their procedures in administrative law matters in the light of judgments of the European Court of Human Rights. *The Osman*, taken with *Factortame*, is likely to alter radically English law rules on the liability of public authorities.[18] There is clearly a reduced autonomy of national legal systems in public law.

The importance of both the European Union and the European Convention is that they eschew a formal distinction between public law and private law. They both set out a number of principles and expect certain results. They are not concerned whether individual states achieve these through mechanisms specific to their public law or their private law, but there must be some equality in the results achieved. But,

13 *Avis* of 6 March 1986, EDCE 1987, 178; B. Pacteau, *Contentieux Administratrifs* (5th edn., Presses Universitaires de France, Paris, 1999), § 126.

14 C.L. Jessua and C. Huglo, Actualité Juridique – Droit Administratif 1988, 127, at p. 129.

15 J.-F. Flauss in J. Schwarze, *Administrative Law under European Influence* (Nomos Verlag, London, 1996), at p. 113.

16 See e.g., J. Bell, 'The Concept of Public Service under Threat from Europe? An Illustration from Energy Law' (1999) 5 *European Public Law* 189; Flauss, above n. 15, pp. 53–62 (public services) and 34–46 (civil service).

17 ECHR 28 September 1995, 22 EHRR 193: for a discussion of its implications, see Pacteau, above n. 13, §§ 46 and 241, and references therein.

18 See P. Craig and D. Fairgrieve, '*Barrett*, Negligence and Discretionary Powers' [1999] *Public Law* 626.

if they do not worry about national classifications of issues as matters of public law or private law, these external legal frameworks do recognise as space for the state as representative of the public interest. It can award state aids under certain conditions within EU law, and it can determine limitations on fundamental rights in the light of its view of the public interest.[19] In other words, the basic issue of the definition and control of the powers of government remains fundamental. But there are aspects of the activity of government that are controlled by mechanisms that are different from those normally adopted by the national legal tradition.

These supra-national sources introduce an element of legal pluralism. No longer are the sources of law simply found within the national legal order either directly or by incorporation into the national legal order. Rather there is a plurality of sources from which legal standards are derived, some national and some supranational.[20] This provides an additional reason for not considering the relationship of the state and its citizens in isolation.

A final and important feature to note is the trend of opinion. If we take but one example, ideas about privatisation have developed through debates in the OECD and then have moved into different countries. For example, state railways have been turned into companies in countries as diverse as New Zealand, Germany, the Netherlands and Sweden. Ideas on how we should be governed, both at a constitutional and a technical level circulate at supranational level and pose challenges to established ways of doing things. The planning state of the post-war period in Europe has given way since the 1980s to the market state, with greater concern for regulation.[21]

The external environment presses us to see similarities in problems, in values and expectations, and thus in solutions that have to be achieved in countries, whatever their particular division between public and private law. This might seem to argue in favour of the idea that there are generic functions that are fundamentally the same from one country to another. If you like, the supranational legal order provides a metalanguage for talking about the specific arrangements in legal system, however these systems may themselves choose to describe them. But this is too simplistic an analysis. Viewed externally, there may be certain general standards that the operations of public law must respect, but the character of the system can only be identified if one takes account also of the institutional setting.

2. Institutional Setting

The distinctiveness of public law in individual countries seems to me to revolve predominantly around *institutions* which arise not only from deliberate design

[19] See ECHR 27 September 1995, *McCann v UK* (1995) 21 EHRR 97.

[20] See F. Ost and M. Van de Kerchove, '*De la Pyramide au Réseau? Vers un Nouveau Mode de Production du Droit?*' (2000) 44 *Revue Interdisciplinaire d'Etudes Juridiques* 1.

[21] See e.g., S. Cassese, *La Nuova Constituzione Economica* (Laterza, Rome, 1995), ch. 6.

(typically from the national legislator or national legal professions), but also from history and underlying social problems such as religious and linguistic diversity.

2.1. The Power of History and Routine

History not only explains the development of legal and governmental institutions, it often provides points of reference for problems with which public law has to deal. I would argue that public law is particularly influenced by historical contingencies.

In terms of history, René David rightly wrote that 'established ways of working' might well constitute barriers to convergence of legal systems.[22] I would not see this as a negative feature, but rather as a recognition that routine is part of the life of any society. In public law, the routine of both law and administrative practice combine to ensure that activities occur in a regular way despite changes in political and administrative personnel.

Take a simple example of David's view that different countries have become used to different institutional ways of dealing with a problem, which they would not seek to alter. Every country needs to ensure that public money is properly spent. Every country therefore has systems in place both for the authorization of public expenditure and the scrutiny of accounts. In the United Kingdom, this process has, for central government expenditure, developed in the form of parliamentary scrutiny through the Comptroller and Auditor General, the National Audit Office, and the Public Accounts Committee. The French system has developed as a *judicial and administrative* process under the *Cour des Comptes*, and the separate civil service corps of the *Inspection Générale des Finances.*[23]

The French idea that there should be a Treasury official in every government department who is the sole person to authorize expenditure would appear bizarre to British administrators. Well-established systems of this kind have become embedded in administrative practice. They will be very hard to shift, and their existence becomes something taken for granted in administrative design and in developing the law.[24]

The impact of history on political institutions is very significant in public law. How many constitutions are written to deal with problems that occurred in the past? Take a very simple example, art. 54 of the 1958 French Constitution provides that the President or the Prime Minister (and now 60 deputies or senators) can refer a treaty to the Constitutional Council for a ruling whether it is compatible with the

[22] *International Encyclopaedia of Comparative Law*, vol. ii (J.C.B. Mohr, Tübingen, 1970), ch. 5, §§ 56–59.

[23] See L.N. Brown and J. Bell, *French Administrative Law* (5th edn., Oxford University Press, Oxford, 1998), pp. 59–60.

[24] E.g, the importance of *ordonnancement* in the procedure for awarding *astreintes* is a barrier to its practical applicability. Under this system, there needs to be an authorization for payment (*ordonnancement*) before a public accountant is able to make a payment. The court order has to be explicitly made in this form, but courts are reluctant to use this power to force public authorities to pay in France.

Constitution before the treaty is ratified. Now this was introduced explicitly because the Gaullists were unhappy about the way in which the Treaty of Rome was ratified in 1957,[25] which they considered to be a breach of national sovereignty. The German Constitution's provisions on the appointment of the Kanzler were an attempt to rectify the problems that occurred in Weimar.[26] Our public institutions in the UK are marked by our own history and experience, which create a distinctiveness in terms of the organisations and procedures which we institute and the resonances which we have. Martin Loughlin captures this well in his comment:

> The journey of finding effective, enlightening and liberating conditions of government is a journey through history and on tracks formed within specific cultural traditions. The maps drawn by societies other than our own are undoubtedly of innate interest – but as guides on the journey they must be treated with circumspection[27]

Public law arrangements are designed as much in dialogue with the past as with the future, and that past is likely to be nationally specific.

A major feature of the history will be the various conquests and state succession. Unitary states are often explained by the power of the sword. Thus France, through Henri IV, Louis XIV, the Revolution of 1789 and Napoleon, developed a centralised country. The UK has undergone a similar gradual process. By contrast, Germany and Italy were much more fragmented and remained so even after unification in the nineteenth century. As a result, we have very different forms of governmental federalism in Germany and Italy. In other countries, notably Belgium and Spain, language plays a significant role. The federalism established in the past 20 years in those countries recognises the importance of linguistic and cultural divisions as part of the identity of social groups. The complexity of the Belgian situation results from a recognition of the underlying social division that has given rise to a range of political parties. By contrast, the French resist any recognition of different social or linguistic groups.[28] Everyone is French and speaks French.

Even the 'multispeed devolution' in the UK builds on many years of administrative and political difference. The prior existence of Scottish legislation with special procedures, a separate Scottish Office administration in Edinburgh, separate courts, a Kirk, and a diverse educational system, pushed towards a particular form of devolved government for the Scots, compared with that offered to the Welsh. Northern Ireland has its own history and that leads to different solutions.

My point is that the institutions of government with which public law is concerned develop in very specific ways. There is not just a generic social function

[25] J. Bell, *French Constitutional Law* (Oxford University Press, Oxford, 1992), p. 31.

[26] D.P. Currie, *The Constitution of the Federal Republic of Germany* (Chicago University Press, Chicago, 1994), pp. 135–140.

[27] 'The Importance of Elsewhere' [1993] *Public Law* 44, at p. 57.

[28] See the language cases, CC decision no. 99–412 DC of 15 June 1999, Rec. 71, which was in line with its decision 94–345 DC of 29 July 1994, *loi Toubon*, Rec. 106.

to be performed. There are specific, national or regional functions, which are involved in governing this country at this time. In consequence, the institutions and processes of government and administration have to be designed and operate to reflect these situations. This regional or national institutional setting provides a context in which the activities or functions of law have to be performed. There are not generic social functions, which the law serves, but there are institutionally situated functions.

2.2. Common Values?

I am probably too wary of accepting common formulations as a statement of common values. In structural terms, attachments to fundamental rights have a different resonance in different legal traditions. In the English common law, rights-talk has traditionally been downplayed. There is a basic right to do anything that the law does not prohibit, but this has not led to positive statements of rights until the Human Rights Act 1998.[29] For all their willingness to state fundamental rights in constitutions and legal texts, the French have traditionally treated them as political ideals, rather than as binding legal norms.[30] By contrast, the Germans have been more willing to treat them as legal norms, especially after the enactment of the Basic Law in 1949.[31] Underlying these differences have been different roles assigned to the judges within institutions of government. But there are also different pre-occupations that shape the understanding of even a single common value. Thus the freedom of expression in art. 11 of the Declaration of the Rights of Man of 1789 is concerned with freedom of publication and dissemination of ideas, especially the refusal of government censorship. The German art. 5 of the Basic Law is concerned with access to a plurality of information and freedom of artistic and scientific opinion. If anything, freedom of expression in the UK has been concerned with the freedom to demonstrate.

Each of the preoccupations reflects a different background and set of issues which freedom of expression is designed to deal with. While there are undoubted similarities and common values, there are important differences, which we should not overlook. A classical notion is that of the 'secular state'. Freedom of religion and tolerance of religious minorities are broadly accepted ideas both in Western Europe and elsewhere; but how this impacts on the role of the state is seen in very divergent ways. In France and the United States, the requirement that the State should not appear to side with any religion is very strong. In France, it has led to serious problems about whether to allow Muslim women to wear headscarves (the *chadour*)

[29] See e.g., the discussion of the right to demonstrate by Charles J. in *R v Cunninghame, Graham & Burns* (1888) 16 Cox CC 421; cf. Jeremy Bentham, 'Anarchical Fallacies', in J. Bowring (ed.), *Works, vol. ii* (Murray, Edinburgh, 1830), p. 573.

[30] Bell, above n. 25, pp. 166–176.

[31] Currie, above n. 26, ch. 4.

in schools or Jewish boys to wear the *kepi*.[32] By contrast, the Germans, British and Belgians, cheerfully subsidize religious schools as part of the state system;[33] the issue of the Muslim headscarves is far less an issue in these countries.

The activity of implementing of common values stated in general terms has to be set in a context of the preoccupations of a particular setting in a particular country. The extent to which the common values have a common impact in different legal systems depends on the institutional settings of the different countries that one is examining.

2.3. Features of the Public Law Institutional Setting

The basic point of this chapter is that the institutional setting for government and administration is not necessarily the same in every country, and comparative law has to take account of this. It is not enough to focus on common rules or on common functions. I would suggest that there are a number of features, which need examining as influences that shape public institutions.

2.3.1. Connection to Politics

Public law is very closely connected to the national political and administrative process. Private commercial and consumer laws are determined to an ever-increasing extent by transnational enterprises, and products and trends in personal relationships transcend national boundaries because of the movements of ideas and also of people. Public law and administration are subjected to international currents of opinion, but are firmly anchored in institutional settings that are national or sub-national. With national electorates to please or with nationally organised civil services, the makers of public law have to focus on the national context, perhaps more than on the international setting. This dynamic is also found in criminal law, social security law and other branches of law akin to public law. But it remains an important part of the institutional setting.

2.3.2. The Decentralization of State Power

The contrast between federal and unitary states is classical. But it is important. If you read the case law of the German Constitutional Court, you will see that many questions presented to it are about the respective competences of the federal and länder governments.[34] The division of competences then gives rise to a divergence in the interlocutors in a debate – one about education, for example. The relative strength of regional government will also affect who is involved in debates and how problems arise. The provision of public services like electricity is in Germany a local

---

32 Brown and Bell, above n. 23, pp. 159–160; J. Bell, 'Religious Observance in Secular Schools: a French Solution' (1990) 2 *Education and the Law* 121.

33 For a comparison, see (1991) *Revue Française de Droit Administratif*, at pp. 56–82.

34 Currie, above n. 26, pp. 35–49.

matter, and this gives rise to different views on the freedom of a market. The whole structure of accountability and participation changes depending on the level at which decisions are taken.

2.3.3. The Provider State

The issue of whether the state provides services itself (for example network services of electricity, gas, transport, and water), or whether it merely regulates to ensure a minimum provision from the market, establishes a major difference in the role of the state. It affects its size, its powers, and its employees. If the state is provider, then a set of responsibilities and expectations arise and these will shape the role law plays in the society. Individuals will be directing their requests and complaints to the supposed provider. By contrast, in a regulatory state, the principal recourse is against the private sector provider with the state as some form of arbitrator and possibly insurer in the background.

2.3.4. Competition

Where competition affects not only the private sector, but also the way in which the public sector performs its tasks, then different issues of accountability and control arise. If the state decides how it performs its tasks, demands are channelled through the political process and access through that process is crucial to determining what is provided, with political power perhaps the greater influence on what is provided. If market testing becomes the key, then the market (and particularly price) are key determinants in what is provided.

2.3.5. The Specificity of Public Employment

There is a European tradition that state employees have a distinct and protected status. But this affects only certain of them, with a number of people being engaged on temporary, contractual tasks. Procedures of recruitment and discipline are distinct in this model. The idea that a civil servant might be made redundant is almost inconceivable. This has created very significant problems for how to conceive of privatisation. By contrast, the English common law has fudged this for a long time and the Deregulation and Contracting Out Act 1994 has finally adopted a contractual solution. The extent of public-sector employment litigation (staff cases), which is very significant in most European administrative law systems, was one of the reasons for the creation of the European Court of First Instance.

2.3.6. The Role of Law in the Governance of the State

There are significantly different traditions in how norms are specified and the legal status that they enjoy. For example, take the status of the principles that have emerged from the Nolan Commission.[35] They have had a significant impact, even

[35] *Standards in Public Life*, Cm 2850, 1995; A.V. Dicey, *An Introduction to the Law of the Constitution*, (10th edn. by E.C.S. Wade, Macmillan, London, 1959), pp. 206–208.

though they have no legislative force. There is a strong parliamentary system, which has incorporated them into constitutional convention and will enforce them through select committees. French controls on political corruption have predominantly arisen in legislative form either in the area of public works or in the funding of political parties, and this experience is shared by other countries, such as Germany. We can all agree on the need for principles, but not on the role of law in achieving these. In further contrast, the Scandinavians place much more emphasis on the ombudsman system of redress than on the courts and the law.[36] In a different vein, the English are more likely to establish *ex gratia* payments systems, rather than to reform legal principles of governmental liability for personal injuries.[37] As I have suggested elsewhere, the English (and to some extent the Scandinavians) operate a system of administrative non-law.[38]

3. CONCLUSION

My suggestion is that public law is the law about the organisation, legitimation and control of government and public administration. It involves sets of principles or values, but these have to be realised through organisational structures and procedures, and through people occupying particular roles. These organisational structures, traditions and values constitute an environment in which common functions, common texts and common social expectations have to be implemented. They also create problems and expectations of their own. As a result, it is necessary to conceive of social functions in this field not simply as activities in themselves, but as part of a social and political context. The activity of providing public transport is situated, for example, in an historical and a current system of regulation and in a setting of expectations from citizens, as well as a political conception of the role of the public sector. If we are going to compare legal systems, then we have to do so in such a setting.

Now, how far is that different from private law? Well, the first point is that the comparators and the similarities of setting which may be appropriate for comparing private law may well not be the same as for public law. Zweigert and Kötz admit as much.[39] They agree that Germany may have more affinity with the United States in constitutional law than in contract law. Now such a criticism of legal families is not confined to branches of public law. One could argue that company law or labour law also operate in different ways from the classical descriptions of legal families centred on the private law of obligations.

[36] See the Danish contribution to Schwarze, above n. 15, pp. 385 et seq.

[37] See M. Brazier, *Medicine, Patients and the Law* (2nd edn., Penguin, London, 1992), pp. 183–185 on contaminated blood, which led to major changes in French administrative liability.

[38] J. Bell, 'Mechanisms for Cross Fertilization of Administrative Law in Europe', ch. 11 of J. Beatson and T. Tridimas (eds.) *New Directions in European Public Law* (Hart Publishing, Oxford, 1998).

[39] Ibid., p. 69

A more fundamental point is the extent to which branches of private law are so constrained by the institutions that exist within a specific society. I can only offer a provisional answer here. I do not think that there are nation-specific forms of civil liability insurance. There are accidents. But there are nation-specific forms of social and private insurance, as well as health care, which could mean that it is right to give tort compensation in one country and to refuse it in another for a similar accident, given the insurance and welfare context in which it occurs. There are not many nation-specific contracts, but there are regimes of public regulation of publicity and redress within which the private contract is set, for example for a consumer. Family and personal life are now very similar (even as to the rates of divorce in European countries), but the redress function of the law often has to take account of different nation-specific institutions, for example the *Pact Civil de Solidarité* for cohabitation. I think labour law and commercial law also have their own institutions. The role of collective agreements and national and local bargaining, as well as employment inspectors, can give rise to different forms of regulation of employment.[40] The different forms of company and regulation of commercial transactions are also important institutional settings.

The suggestion that an institutional setting is important to understanding what a social function really entails seems to me to be an important qualification to the argument of Zweigert and Kötz that there is a similarity of functions between legal systems. Although it may also be true in respect of other branches of law, it is certainly the case that the institutional setting of public law is likely to be distinctive. Public law is anchored firmly in a national setting, whatever wider trends also impinge on it. Public law operates in a constitutional and administrative setting, which dialogues as much with a nation's past as with the future. There are particular dynamics of the system that are specific.

[40] Employment law lies between public law and private law in any case: see M. Freedland, in J. Bell, S. Boyron and S. Whittaker (ed.), *Principles of French Law* (Oxford University Press, Oxford, 1998), ch. 12.

Chapter 14

COMPARATIVE PUBLIC LAW: SOME LESSONS FROM SOUTH EAST ASIA

*Andrew Harding**

Traditional comparative law scholarship in the 20th century concentrated on civil law/common law comparisons, private-law-related topics as the field for comparative law, and normative inquiry. Today this position is challenged. In this chapter, Harding demonstrates this direction, interest and method to be inadequate. A self-confessed 'regionalist comparative public lawyer', he is critical of the relationship of mainstream comparative law both with area studies such as South East Asia, where we have common law, civil law and mixed jurisdictions, and with public law. The so-called 'grand tradition' of comparative law has failed to take seriously public law – seen as an area that lacks comparability; and South East Asia – seen as an extension of civil law and common law, the world being neatly divided between the heirs of Rome and Westminster.

Harding asks the 'millennial' or 'post-modern' comparative law to engage urgently with both. He approaches the two topics and intertwines them effectively to make his point. The chapter looks at public law reform in South East Asia and weighs regional comparative law with traditional comparative law. South East Asia as a region with an abundance of legal traditions, has been neglected to the detriment of comparatists. What are the reasons for this neglect? Does traditional comparative law have a 'universalized grammar of discourse' to deal with this region? Is there a 'global doctrine' to deal with this 'local knowledge'? What should we as comparatists strive for in the 21st century? Answering these questions, Harding finds the comparative law of the 20th century irrelevant to the practical needs of South East Asia, but of great relevance if it can be what it should be in the 21st century.

The first step is to encourage comparative public lawyers to join in the comparative law conversation and the second is to change the topic of the conversation, enhancing it by adding hitherto neglected areas. Comparative law should become a 'joint venture' project.

A wide range of systems, and a wider range of legal issues not hitherto covered, should be considered if comparative law is to have a bearing on the 21st century. It is

* Professor of Law, SOAS Law Department, University of London.

A. Harding and E. Örücü (eds.),
Comparative Law in the 21st Century, 249–266.

time to stop seeing the legal world solely as the domain of Western, private law comparatists.

The message is clear. Comparative public law may have always existed, but as part of public law; now it must become part of comparative law too. Studies in South East Asia have gone on for quite some time, but as an area of interest for historians, anthropologists and regionalists; now these studies must become part of comparative law studies.

This chapter does not discuss public law developments in South East Asia, but the implications of that development for the tools of the comparatist. However, there is also discourse here on 'Asian values', rule of law, democracy, constitutionalism and ASEAN in South East Asia; and, in this context, on the convergence versus divergence debate, seen as 'profoundly political in nature'. The reader will also find here a brief history, a valuable critique and insightful assessment of South East Asian legal scholarship.

Harding's contribution brings to the fore the point that all comparatists are regionalists, the traditional ones being from Europe and America. Therefore the distinction between comparatists and regionalists can no longer be sustained; indeed giving comparative law study a global basis requires that no such distinction be made. Comparatists must understand law as 'a function of humanity'.

The readers should ask themselves, how useful is it to make a distinction between theoretical and applied comparative law? What is the role of western legal assistance and comparative law in public law reform in South East Asia in the new century? Do comparatists actually compare? Must they actually compare to be called comparatists?

[A. Harding and E. Örücü]

In this chapter it is intended to try to disentangle two issues that might at first sight (but misleadingly) seem to deserve quite separate treatment. If the disentanglement succeeds, then the implications for comparative law in the 21st century would be large and obvious. Although one of the restrictions of being a 'regionalist' is that by definition one gets to know little of 'other' regions, much of what is said here could equally be said, at least in general terms, by any other kind of regionalist,[1] such as a Sinologist or an Africanist. I address these issues as one who attempts in his own

[1] For reasons that will be stated, I use the term 'regionalist' as a convenience in this paper. Hopefully I will not have occasion ever to use it again. By 'regionalists' I mean those comparative lawyers (not always regarded as such, as they do not always actually compare) who specialize in 'foreign law' or [legal] 'area studies' of one or more countries.

work[2] to embrace both 'South East Asian legal studies' and 'comparative public law', and in some respects to combine them.

The issues referred to above are these: what is the relationship between the South East Asia 'area studies' tradition of comparative law with the 'mainstream' (or 'grand') tradition of comparative law? What is the relationship of the comparative public law tradition (if one can safely assume that such a tradition exists)[3] and the grand tradition of comparative law? To come clean from the outset, I wish to argue that the grand tradition fell short of the mark in both respects. It failed to take either South East Asia or public law seriously, despite the fact that presumably one of the purposes (or perhaps methods) of comparative law is to test hypotheses across a wide range of empirical data, both geographically/culturally and conceptually. Accordingly, its successor, what we might call 'millennial' or perhaps 'postmodern' comparative law, could be envisaged as engaging with or embracing scholarly traditions that the mainstream would previously have regarded as lying far outside its purview.[4]

There is clearly much complex ground to cover in a short space, and the argument is therefore necessarily somewhat attenuated in places, or not as fully supported as it might be. To be clear, let me begin by sketching the argument in brief.

The chapter begins by arguing that comparative law has unjustifiably neglected South East Asia, and has also unjustifiably neglected public law. It then outlines the context of public law reform in South East Asia, arguing that the rule of law has been and is continuously relevant to discussion of legal development in the region. It proceeds to assess legal scholarship in the field of South East Asian law and relate it to, or contrast it with, the mainstream tradition in comparative law. It concludes by showing that the new comparative law can and should consider both a wider range of legal systems and a wider range of legal issues that arise in them.

---

2 So far this has been mainly on various aspects of public law in Malaysia, Singapore and Thailand, latterly on economic-development law, law and society issues, and environmental law. My teaching entails coverage both of various aspects of law in other SE Asian jurisdictions and the public law of non-SE Asian jurisdictions. See, further, A.J. Harding, 'Comparative Law and Legal Transplantation in South East Asia: Making Sense of the "Nomic Din" ', ch. 9 (pp. 199–222) of D. Nelken and J. Feest (eds.), *Adapting Legal Cultures* (Hart Publishing, Oxford, 2001).

3 See A.J. Harding, 'Comparative Public Law: a Neglected Discipline?', ch. 4 of I.D. Edge (ed.), *Comparative Law in a Global Context* (Transnational, New York, 2000).

4 William Twining ('Comparative Law and Legal Theory: the Country and Western Tradition', ch. 2 of Edge, above n. 3) in a profound analysis of the comparative law literature has defended the 'grand tradition' as I call it (in a conscious reflection of the same term as used in relation to the novel) on the grounds that it liberalized and expanded our horizons, and pursued realizable aims. In criticizing this tradition I do not deny the truth of Twining's defence. To pursue the analogy, there is no reason why a cyberpunk novelist should not admire and learn from Jane Austen; there is equally no reason why he should seek to emulate her. Twining's criticisms of that tradition are I think broadly supported in this chapter. As Örücü and Cotterrell point out in their contributions to this volume, comparative law is now itself a field in which pluralism reigns.

1. South East Asia has been Neglected by Comparative Law

In the main streams of comparative law, as well as in the related field of law and development, virtually no account has been taken of the South East Asian legal experience. Scholars in the field of law in South East Asia have therefore trodden a somewhat lonely path. The neglect of South East Asia is a very unfortunate missed opportunity to experiment in an ideal laboratory. The region has an abundance of legal traditions, practically all of them having been 'received' in one sense or another, and encompassing all of the world's major legal world-views and systems. If the crossroads of legal traditions are 'nodal points where comparatists are to be found',[5] then one ought to be tripping over them in South East Asia;[6] and it is high time that we were able to draw some general wisdom based on region's legal scholarship. The reasons for neglect probably lie in the sheer quantity, spectacular diversity, and strangeness (to the minds of western jurists, at least) of the material; the lack of historical unity of the region;[7] the lack of clearly established definitions of terms such as 'law', and 'legal culture'; and the lack of an already extensive academic legal literature, at least compared with the other 'regions': Africa, the Arab world, India, China, Latin America.[8] These factors make it hard to provide general answers to the kinds of question that the legal disciplines pose. Indeed South East Asian legal scholars have tended (outside London and Leiden, perhaps) to be associated with disciplines other than law, such as anthropology and political science.[9]

Secondly, the conventional approach of comparative law is inadequate to convey South East Asian legal reality; what comparative law lacks, to my mind (as a practitioner who would deeply welcome some off-the-shelf methods and concepts), is a suitably sophisticated and universalized grammar of discourse. Mattei, whom we might see as the representative of current orthodoxy, considers that 'taxonomy is the grammar of legal discourse'. I would argue that taxonomy is mere reductionism: it is

---

5 T. Koopmans, 'Comparative Law and the Courts' (1998) 45 *International and Comparative Law Quarterly* 545.

6 Such is the cultural bias of modern Western education that in Europe there are barely any specialists in SE Asian law, and apart from SOAS, University of London (currently two academics interested in mainland and maritime SE Asia), and Leiden University's Van Vollenhoven Institute (heavy concentration on Indonesia but not on the other SE Asian countries), there are virtually no full-time specialists. Given the importance and population of the region (about 480m in 1998, increasing to about 700m in 2010, and therefore far larger than that of Europe), and the extraordinary growth of law therein, this situation is quite astonishing. If one compares law with economic history of SE Asia, for example, one finds that the latter has probably 10–20 times the number of experts (this is based on informal conversation with economic historians and occasional scanning of the Newsletter of the International Institute of Asian Studies).

7 The term 'South East Asia' was invented by the Royal Navy in World War Two.

8 See, further, Carol G.S. Tan, 'Law and Legal Systems in South East Asia: Three Paths to a Viewpoint', in P.J. Davidson, (ed.), *Trading Arrangements in the Pacific Rim – ASEAN and APEC* (Oceana Publications, New York, 1999), 1.

9 For example, Franz von Benda-Beckmann (anthropology), Daniel Lev (political science).

what we have *instead of* legal discourse.[10] As far as South East Asia is concerned, this is simply the old notion of legal families in new garb.

I have elsewhere attempted to analyse the problems of comparative law research in South East Asia in terms of 'global doctrine' versus 'local knowledge'.[11] By this I mean that we need to understand the function of both the general and the particular and be alive to contexts as well as rules. In essence this entails reversing in every respect the type of comparative law known to the 20th century, in which an expanding notion of 'the other' and her concerns has so far failed to aspire to anything more than a purely conceptual status as far as comparative law is concerned. In my view we cannot make progress in this field unless we can stand behind the individual and try to see the world from her point of view.[12] As I see it, the job of 'regionalists' (juristic or otherwise) in a complex world where tradition and development constitute a potent brew, is to interpret cross-culturally – in both directions simultaneously.

The 20th century view of comparative law is microscopic; euro-centric; rule-based; concerned with private rather than public law; legislative and integrative in purpose. It assumes a degree of commonality and convergence in the objects of the comparison. However, the view which seems to me more useful in relation to South East Asia in the 21st century sees comparative law, on the contrary, as general and inter-disciplinary; pluralistic; context-based; recognising no distinction between public and private law (and in fact being increasingly concerned with public law issues); being intellectual and contrastive in purpose; and assuming differences and probably divergences rather than similarities, even if ultimately there are legislative and integrative purposes as reform processes move forward.

It is, however, a problem of the above narrative of legal scholarship and my attempted *bouleversement* of 'comparative law' that it obscures our lack of real knowledge and understanding of law and society in South East Asia, which results from a comparative lack of empirical socio-legal research. The fundamental problem confronting those working on law in South East Asia is that the conventions of comparative law often prove inadequate, or perhaps irrelevant, to their needs and their experience in trying to fill the gaps in our knowledge and understanding. A complete account of law in South East Asia is thus extremely hard in practice to formulate; one is left with the bare possibility of attempting a kind of 'thick description',[13] which might satisfy the postmodern sensibility better than the generalities of Weber and Maine, whose work seems now descriptive of a world that no longer exists. It could I suppose be seriously questioned whether comparative

[10] U. Mattei, 'Three Patterns of Law: Taxonomy and Change in the World's Legal Systems' (1997) 45 American Journal of Comparative Law 1.

[11] 'Global Doctrine and Local Knowledge: Law in South East Asia', (2002) 51 *International and Comparative Law Quarterly* 35; see, further, Harding, above n. 2.

[12] I am grateful to Professor Jan-Michiel Otto for this insight.

[13] C. Geertz, 'Local Knowledge: Fact and Law in Comparative Perspective' in Geertz, C., *Local Knowledge: Further Essays in the Interpretation of Cultures* (Hutchinson, London, 1975).

work on law in South East Asia could ever actually fit even into the broadest current notions of what comparative law can be expected to do; and by the strictest and most orthodox notions the idea is probably completely unthinkable. Yet globalization and immediate practical problems of, for example, environment, economics, governance, and judiciary, require such work more urgently than ever before. In this sense practical needs have exposed the irrelevance of comparative law as it is, but the great relevance of comparative as it could be. Microscopic accounts are certainly possible and useful in their own way, but they either encounter the same difficulties as macroscopic accounts, or else simply avoid answering the big questions that require to be answered. South East Asian scholars themselves need to engage with socio-legal research in a way in which they have not done so far. Most legal scholarship in South East Asia is still concerned uncritically with expounding doctrine, although this position is starting, slowly, to change. Comparative law in South East Asia in the 21st century will, I imagine, move towards comparative law not as East India Company adventure, but as joint-venture project. Increasingly we will be found working with South East Asian colleagues rather than standing in their shoes.[14]

2. Comparative Public Lawyers Should be Joined in the Comparative Law Conversation

'Public law' is a notoriously difficult concept, which, although recognised by Roman law, emerged rather late in the process of reception of Roman law in Europe, and, having been something like anathema in the common law tradition, finally emerged as a term of art in the common law, and controversially, only in 1983.[15] On the basis that a definition should always reflect some clear purpose, we need not allow the technicalities of the concept to puzzle us unduly. In the context of comparative law we can identify public law as embracing those parts of the law that deal exclusively with the state or with relations between the state and other legal persons. Since the debate over legal transplantation is concerned with 'organic' as well as 'political' laws, we may as well include these in the definition; but I am principally concerned here with constitutional and administrative law. Since, however, one argument in favour of the recognition of comparative public law is that there is in fact no clear or relevant principle on which to draw the dividing line between public and private law, and that in comparative legal research we actually move insensibly over the public/private divide,[16] I do not wish to make much of the precise definition of public law. A moment's reflection on three examples – labour law, revenue law, and environmental law – will illustrate my point.

[14] Compare the approach taken by Leyland in his work on Italy, described in his chapter in this volume.

[15] In *O'Reilly v Mackman* [1983] 2 AC 237, HL.

[16] For a detailed example of this, see Harding, above n. 4, at 110, on the SOAS Access to Environmental Justice Project.

In South East Asia we can pose much more difficult cases: personal law relating to indigenous populations has public law consequences; whether Islamic law is also public law is a very moot question; mixed marriages raise questions relating to the nature of the state; choice of commercial law tells us much about the state and the judiciary; privatisation and the reform of economic law span the public/private divide. The very main reason why public law is being reformed in South East Asia is, one might say, that private law cannot always be very readily distinguished from it in principle; and in practice it would make no sense whatsoever to divide researchers into public and private comparative lawyers. This applies not just to the common law jurisdictions (Malaysia, Singapore, Burma and Brunei); but also to the civil law jurisdictions (Vietnam, Laos, Cambodia, Thailand, Indonesia: Philippines counting as both due to its Spanish-American parentage). As in Europe the civil law/common law distinction is starting to have much less relevance than it once had.[17] Even historically, the regionalists have been concerned with problems of governance: Engel's work on Thailand,[18] and Gullick's on Malaya,[19] for example, are very much concerned with the religious and social nature of sovereignty.

I would argue that comparative public law is increasingly important but is not a new discipline, merely a relatively new or changing subject matter. It enjoys legitimacy as a branch of public law, *and*, these days, of comparative law too.[20] In South East Asia only an holistic view of law and legal development has any chance of engaging with reality, and none of the regionalists of whom I am aware can readily be classified in terms of public or private law specialism: they could not afford such a luxury, since they have to move from one to the other irrespective of their preference in order to deal with practically all of the most important issues. It would clearly follow that comparative public law would not require any *distinct method*, but of course one would have to be sensitized to the institutional/cultural traditions and practices on which it is based. This does not to my mind make it essentially different from private-law studies regionally, where a similar sensitivity needs to be applied. It is difficult to examine and understand one part of a legal system without examining and understanding the whole. To take a fairly typical, random, example, David Linnan[21] writing recently on law reform in Indonesia, embraces various forms of public and private law, and sets out three different ways of analysing the difficulties reform has encountered: a sociological/political science

[17] Take, for example, the fact that between 1986 and 1992, practically all the ASEAN countries reformed their public laws dealing with powers over foreign investment. The fact that the civilian jurisdictions have a 'foreign investment law', and the common-law jurisdictions do not, rather misses the point.

[18] E.g., D.M. Engel, *Law and Kingship in Thailand During the Reign of King Chulalongkorn* (Centre for South and Southeast Asian Studies, University of Michigan, Ann Arbor, 1979).

[19] E.g., J.M. Gullick, *Indigenous Political Systems of Western Malaya* (Rev. edn., London, Athlone Press, 1988).

[20] See, further, Harding, above n. 3.

[21] D.K. Linnan, 'Indonesian Law Reform, or *Once More unto the Breach*: a Brief Institutional History' (1999) 1 *Australian Journal of Asian Law* 1.

approach based on studying the behaviour of elites; a cultural/psychological approach based on Javanese traditions; and an institutional analysis approach based on bureaucratic competition. I have also argued elsewhere that the modernization of law itself in South East Asia was effectively commenced by the abolition of customary marriages.[22]

3. Public Law is Developing Rapidly in South East Asia

It will be appreciated that it is not my purpose here actually to discuss public law developments in South East Asia, but rather to discuss the implications and contexts involved in discussing them, and also to consider the kind of comparatist baggage one brings to such a discussion. However, in order to establish the case, which is that comparative public law research is relevant in South East Asia, some background information and context is clearly necessary.

Public law in South East Asia is undergoing a transition of a similar kind to that taking place in other parts of the developing world. Despite the fact that the region invented the terms 'people power' (Philippines) and '*reformasi*' and 'KKN'[23] (Indonesia), the region has been seen as representing what one might call the Lee-Mahathir notion of 'Asian values': that is, discipline, respect and duty; a notion supposedly antithetical to its assumed opposite, that is, 'Western' values of liberty, democracy and rights.[24] In spite of all the rhetoric, this approach has so far actually failed to obtain general endorsement in South East Asia itself, and it looks as though reform initiatives are steering the region in other directions. The region's public law is characterised by a considerable degree of pluralism, in which democratization, practical and purposeful in Thailand and Philippines, uncertain and hazardous in Indonesia and Cambodia, co-exists with the dominant-party authoritarian democracy of Malaysia and Singapore, the one-party market socialism of Vietnam and Laos, the military dictatorship of Burma, and the absolute monarchy of Brunei. It may be for this reason – the lack of an underlying regional ideological and political matrix – that ASEAN itself has failed significantly in recent years to address environmental, economic and humanitarian crises.

As indices of change it may be noted that between 1986 and 1999 successively Philippines, Indonesia, Thailand and Malaysia have set up Human Rights Commissions; and that Thailand has undergone one of the most ambitious and comprehensive reforms of public law ever undertaken, in the drafting and implementation of its new Constitution of 1997.[25] A comparable process of public

22 Above n. 2.

23 '*Korupsi, kolusi, nepotisme*'.

24 J.R. Bauer, and D.A. Bell, (eds.), *The East Asian Challenge for Human Rights* (Cambridge, Cambridge University Press, 1999); D.A. Bell, *East Meets West: Human Rights and Democracy in East Asia* (Princeton, Princeton University Press, 2000).

25 A.J. Harding, 'May There be Virtue: "New Asian Constitutionalism" in Thailand' (2001) 3 *Australian Journal of Asian Law* 24.

law reform is taking place, albeit in a slower and more piecemeal fashion in Indonesia; and has already taken place in Philippines in 1986–1987 and is now being consolidated. In Indochina new constitutions have been enacted in Laos (1991), Vietnam (1992), and Cambodia (1993, revised 1999).[26] Examples of judicial review and public interest or constitutional litigation, often successful, are starting to proliferate throughout the region, seeking to protect, for example, the environment and indigenous populations, freedom of the press, and other democratic rights; they have not always succeeded, but steady progress is being made in these areas, and most jurisdictions now recognise some form of public-interest litigation. This is an indication of the highly significant advances made by 'civil society' in the last few years. At the very least, courts have (oddly one might think) become a major (one could almost say *the* major) arena for dispute about the nature of the state. The image of the Malaysian former Deputy Prime Minister, Anwar Ibrahim's, famous black eye[27] expresses this idea better than a list of case references. Administrative courts have been set up in Thailand, Vietnam and Indonesia.[28] Judicial and public administration reforms are occurring in many areas; Indonesia is radically devolving its government and allowing more autonomy for its level three (regional) governments,[29] as well as attempting to reform its judiciary and most of its state institutions. The laws relating to state involvement in the economy are also undergoing liberalization throughout the region, reflecting the general move towards privatisation and attraction of foreign investment.[30] Even traumatized Cambodia has made significant progress towards constitutional government, while Westminster-style parliamentary democracy has been generally maintained in Malaysia[31] and Singapore, the latter having nonetheless additionally instituted an elected presidency to act as a check on the government.[32] Of the ASEAN countries only Burma and Brunei remain beyond the pale in terms of the development of public law, but perhaps even then only for the time being.[33] It would therefore be untrue to assert that 'Asian values' have trumped 'public law'; and there is no consensus or evidence

[26] For texts of these constitutions, see <www.charter88.org.uk/politics/links/link_cons.html>.

[27] See Tey Tsun Hang, 'Malaysia: the Fierce Politico-Legal Backlash' (1999) 1 *Singapore Journal of International and Comparative Law* 1.

[28] See, e.g., A. Bedner, *Administrative Courts in Indonesia: a Socio-Legal Study* (Kluwer Law International, The Hague, 2001).

[29] G. Bell, 'The New Indonesian Laws Relating to Regional Autonomy: Good Intentions, Confusing Laws', [2001] 2 Asian-Pacific Law and Policy Journal 1: <www.hawaii.edu/aplpj/2/1.html>.

[30] Indonesia is on the verge of abolishing the distinction between foreign and domestic investment law by enacting a National Investment Law.

[31] A.J. Harding, *Law, Government and the Constitution in Malaysia* (Kluwer Law International, The Hague, 1996).

[32] Kevin Tan Yew Lee and Lam Peng Er (ed.), *Managing Political Change in Singapore: the Elected Presidency* (Routledge, London, 1997).

[33] In Burma a new constitution is supposedly in the process of being drafted; and talks are taking place between the military junta and the opposition.

along the lines that public law can be successfully excluded from the apparently unstoppable progress of general legal reform: the case is in fact quite the reverse.

4. The Rule of Law is not in Decline

There is undoubtedly a sense in which in South East Asia 'the rule-of-law' or 'legality' as understood in the West is 'absent' or is 'in decline' or is 'being challenged', or is 'the tool of authoritarian regimes'.[34] This might tend to make public law research appear somewhat divorced from reality.

I believe this, however, to be at best a half-truth. If there is no rule-of-law in South East Asia, then the region's lawyers, law teachers and students, judges, lawgivers and public servants are making a remarkably good impression of working extremely hard at something completely irrelevant. How would one explain the extraordinary prominence of case law dealing with fundamental issues of government, business, religion, human rights, the family, or the environment; or the burgeoning numbers of law students and practitioners, if the rule-of-law is absent or in decline? There are indeed problems concerning the rule-of-law in all the South East Asian countries, in the sense that strict adherence to law is not an absolute but a *competing* value; and quantity of laws passed does not of course entail enforcement or even relevance to the issue in hand. The big picture, however, is in my view not the decline of the rule-of-law, but rather what Daniel Lev has called 'a struggle for the *rechtsstaat*'.[35] All this has implications for the kind of research we should be undertaking, but not for the relevance of public law research *per se*. Never has the rule-of-law been more relevant than it is today in South East Asia; and never has legal research on law in South East Asia been more needed. The conceptual richness of the rule-of-law will be highly relevant as a basis for future research: it lies at the heart of all the problems relating to law in South East Asia.

There are other factors that offer some encouragement that the rule of law will be embraced in the long-term.

The first is ASEAN. Now comprising ten nations, if ASEAN is to emerge as an economic and strategic bloc of greater importance than it now enjoys, progress in establishing the rule-of-law will be crucial to its consolidation and progress.[36]

Secondly, the emergence of the civil society and a large and ambitious legal profession all over the region give voice to an irrepressible demand for legal reform. It is to be noted that over some years law students have been prominent in most challenges to authority in South East Asia.

---

[34] E.g., K. Jayasuriya, (ed.), *Law, Capitalism and Power in Asia: the Rule of Law and Legal Institutions* (Routledge, London, 1999).

[35] D.S. Lev, 'Judicial Authority and the Quest for an Indonesian *Rechtsstaat*', in Lev, D.S., *Legal Evolution and Political Authority in Indonesia: Selected Essays* (The Hague, Kluwer Law International, 2000).

[36] Apirat Petchsiri et al. (ed.), *Strengthening ASEAN Integration: Lessons for the EU's Rule of Law* (Centre for European Studies, Chulalongkorn University, Bangkok, 2001).

Thirdly, the rule-of-law is a means of bolstering the legitimacy of pluralistic states in times of stress. South East Asia has been successful in state construction as long as economies have prospered; the rule-of-law plays an important part in good decision-making, and in reassuring minorities that they have recourse. It should be remembered that Malaysia, for example, has 178 officially defined ethnic groups, and Indonesia more than 300. Most South East Asian nations are in essence *Pancasila* states: acts of common faith that somehow have worked. The rule-of-law is needed to ensure that social stability continues. Benevolent constitutionalism based on the concept of legality affords a prospect that stability can survive the changing notions of the state and the community.

Here, one might say, lies the dilemma of the comparatist. To argue, as the proponents of 'Asian-values' do, that concepts such as the rule of law and democracy are irrelevant or are differently interpreted in South East Asia, brings into the foreground the notion of cultural difference; this is a position which fits well with the traditions of comparative law,[37] but not with changing reality. To argue that concepts such as the rule-of-law and democracy are one and indivisible denies autonomy and the kind of legal biodiversity which the human race needs – not just as an aspect of 'self-determination' but also as a kind of practical insurance. This is a position that fits ill with the traditions of comparative law and even with a postmodernist approach to the subject. Both positions are fraught with political implications. As comparatists it seems we have to decide individually whether we subscribe to internationalist convergence theories or to cultural divergence theories. Yet to make this decision means to be dragged in two directions, and to take a once-for-all decision that is profoundly political in nature.

In supporting, as I do, a rule-of-law direction for the South East Asian region, I have to be aware how culturally specific this concept is, at least in origin. Europe has taken a thousand years to bring law to a position of primacy in which the union of its nation-states can be based squarely and unquestionably on legality and the rule-of-law. In the meantime the concept of legality itself has become more generalized in international and in non-European legal systems. Law itself in this modern sense is no stranger to the South East Asia of the last century, and it seems as if the region has more or less made its decision on this fundamental question. The next age of constitutionalism in South East Asia can, foreseeably, draw upon reserves of religious and communitarian values to enforce respect for an endogenous version of 'human rights' and 'governance', and provide a framework of political toleration and greater executive accountability to the wider community. Even Malaysia and Singapore, which are seen as having diverged from the original 'Westminster' constitution, have strongly entrenched constitutional principles, which partly preserve the colonial constitutional traditions and partly correspond to the evolving political community. The Malaysian Constitution melds these traditions with the

[37] I mean two things by this: both the grand tradition ('only similar cultures can be compared') and the regional scholars ('Asia is different') would accept the 'Asian values' argument.

entrenchment of an inter-ethnic social contract, which secures social stability but restricts freedom of speech.[38]

This kind of syncretism can be seen emerging all over South East Asia. Informed by a clear commitment to rule-of-law principles, it is possible for the region to make rapid progress in public law reform. I believe that the experience of comparative law in its broader forms is of value in this enterprise, but its theory and method need greater sophistication and flexibility. It seems clear to me that the role of Europe in legal development in South East Asia is by no means over, dubious at it may have been in the past. In the 21st century it is important that comparative law should embrace thoughtful and self-critical legal assistance rather than imperialist design.

For these reasons public law research seems eminently worthwhile and timely. I see no reason why comparative law's remit should not extend to regions such as South East Asia in the next century. Indeed it is already doing so.

4. Regionalists and Comparatists Should Talk to Each Other

It cannot be maintained that all the developments in public law in South East Asia point in one direction or that there are few problems with the reforms in public law. However, my purpose is to use them as an example of the some problems faced by comparative lawyers like myself who concentrate on studying the law in a particular region. Mattei[39] refers to us as 'regionalists' (as though those comparatists who study European or American law are not also regionalists, and regionalists themselves are not also comparatists). However, the point of his referring to us at all is to say that the regionalists and the comparatists should talk more to each other instead of amongst themselves: the W.G.Hart Legal Workshop held at the IALS in London in July 2000[40] was in fact an exercise of that kind. In my view it is the euro-centric nature of comparative law studies in the 20th century that is to blame for their failure to integrate the study of comparative law on a global basis. The distinction between comparatists and regionalists makes no real sense if one perceives the task of comparative law as being that of attempting to understand law simply as a function or creation of humanity.

The problem here is that culture (or rather the perception of culture) renders the study of law opaque and unmanageable. It is I think for this reason that regional legal studies have been placed within the discipline of 'area studies'. There may indeed have been good reasons for this, just as there were good reasons for comparative law concentrating until recently on Europe and North America; law was seen as a cultural artifact, understood through the same processes as any other artifact. This perception failed to understand the technical, professional nature of

[38] Harding, above n. 31, chs. 11, 14; Kevin Tan Yew Lee and Thio Li-Ann, *Constitutional Law in Singapore and Malaysia* (2nd edn., Malayan Law Journal, Singapore, 1997).

[39] Above n. 10.

[40] For which see the Preface.

law as it developed in South East Asia in the last century. It perceived the study of law as entailing the study of custom, and therefore being akin to anthropology and the study of religion. Indeed the modernization of law took regional legal studies in practice almost as far beyond the core of area studies as they were beyond the core of comparative law. Culture remained relevant, but could not explain everything. The regionalists oscillated somewhat between emphasizing culture and emphasizing governance. The cultural emphasis could be accused of implying that 'the other' had to be judged by different (read 'less advanced') rules, while the governance emphasis could be accused of implying that 'the other' had to be brought into line (read 'up to speed with') with European norms.[41]

Clearly Mattei is right, we should talk. The conversation is likely to riddled with misunderstandings, but it has to take place, and I believe it is taking place. What will possibly emerge is that regional legal studies will no longer be marginal but will be central: the periphery emerges as the new core. What my hypothesis really implies is that regional legal studies are an important aspect of comparative law at the millennium. Both are likely to be dramatically changed by this synthesis.

5. Comparative Law is Theory and Practice

So how do we conceive of comparative law once the grand tradition is left behind?

Let us be clear that comparison as such requires no justification. It is unavoidable and necessary, but also stimulating, entertaining, and educational. It entices with possibilities for improvement, and fascinates with the challenge of difference. It is natural to the inquiring mind to compare, and it is only by comparing that we can establish structure, categories, and concepts.[42]

Commentators have generally considered that there are two different meanings of 'comparative law'. One type of meaning sees the subject as an interesting, theoretical discourse about different kinds of laws and legal systems and their structures and traditions;[43] in this sense comparative law is seen as serving purely intellectual ends in rather the same way as legal history, with which I think it has much else in common, to the extent that I see very little distinction between the two (the past is just another country). In my view, if we describe a legal system in terms that are understood by those outside it, this is already in a real sense comparative law, even if

[41] This type of dilemma has been debated for a long time. In the great debates over adat vs. the Civil Code in the Dutch East Indies, the 'culturalists', led by Van Vollenhoven and the adatrecht scholars, both Dutch and Indonesian, won the colonial debate. However, Van Vollenhoven's Indonesian students, returning home and assuming office, found his arguments inspiring but impractical: in practice they preferred the Civil Code: Fasseur, C., 'Colonial Dilemma: Van Vollenhoven and the Struggle Between Adat Law and Western Law in Indonesia', ch. 11 of T. Mommsen and D. de Moor, *European Expansion and Law* (Oxford, New York, Berg, 1992).

[42] Samuel in a recent article argues audaciously that comparative law should be a 'core' subject: G. Samuel, 'Comparative Law as a Core Subject' (2001) 2 Legal Studies 444.

[43] See the chapters by Bell and Leyland in this volume.

there is no overt 'comparison' as such. This would be as true of, say, an Indonesian expert on European law as it would be of a European expert on Indonesian law. The consignment of such experts to an odd discipline called 'foreign law' makes no sense in a globalized world in which law increasingly crosses borders with so much ease that it is hardly noticed to do so; it also appears to make assumptions about what is 'foreign' and what is 'indigenous'/'familiar', and about the way they relate to each other, which look both illogical and prejudiced. In relation to whom is the subject matter of 'foreign law' foreign?[44]

The second kind of meaning sees comparative law as a practical method or tool by which we can decide inter-jurisdictional questions to do with legislation, legal 'transplantation'[45] and legal development or reform, with the possible higher aim of unification or standardization of principles of justice in pursuit of humanistic, economic, environmental, or similar goals.

I would call these 'theoretical comparative law' and 'applied comparative law', respectively (in Goffian language, perhaps the 'hobby' and the 'science' of comparative law[46]). They have been described as being like the two blades of a pair of scissors: the one is useless without the other. Like most regionalists my own concern is with applied comparative law, which might be seen as the business end of the subject, although personally I see the first type of comparison as being both important and useful, in that it creates an indispensable foundation or framework for the second. Regionalists have generally been practitioners of comparative law, and have avoided 'legal theory' as far as they could, stressing instead culture, difference, and relativity.[47] It is important to note here also that the detractors of comparative law or its uses aim their fire at the second rather than the first meaning. Even Kahn-Freund,[48] whose theory of comparative law is now generally rejected (certainly by public lawyers), and who after all held a chair in comparative law, wrote about the value of theoretical comparative law, and was indeed a masterful exponent of it. His objection was not of course to comparative law as such, but rather to the uses or misuses to which it is put, one of which, he considered, was its

44 In Australia the field of study under consideration would be called 'Asian law', even though essentially its character would not be changed if it included, say, Africa and Latin America. This can be explained by political imperatives (now perhaps no longer imperative) in Australia, and the debate about that country's place in the world. 'Asian law' in Australia tends to mean mainly (though not exclusively) SE Asian law (see V. Taylor, (ed.), *Asian Laws Through Australian Eyes* (Sydney, LBC, 1997)); the same term in the United States tends to mean Chinese and Japanese law.

45 I use this term lightly, but see Nelken's discussion of metaphors in this volume.

46 Lord Goff, 'The Future of the Common Law' (1997) 46 *International and Comparative Law Quarterly* 745, at 747–748.

47 They ignore in the process of course the politics of comparative law, and the distributional effects and other uses and misuses of their work, as exposed by Kennedy (conference paper on file, Cambridge, 2000). One of the problems of comparative law is that, as in science, the fact of being observed cannot being ignored; another is that the comparatist himself may become part of what he is observing, his views being useful to one political faction or another.

48 O. Kahn-Freund,'Uses and Misuses of Comparative Law' (1974) *Modern Law Review* 1.

application in public law contexts. To put the matter simply in relation to the kind of research undertaken by what we might for present purposes call 'regionalist comparative public lawyers', what we are trying to do is see what will actually work, given radically different political cultures, processes, problems, and institutions of law and governance. To do so, we need to have some sound intellectual notions about the trade-off between law, politics, economics, and culture (at the very least). We can also learn much from the main practical outcome of 20th century comparative law – the European Union. We can learn both theory and, crucially, *method* from the grand tradition of comparative law.[49] But the tradition itself needs to evolve. No doubt Europe itself has benefited, and therefore so has everyone, at least from the example of integration of European law; but the world has now changed. At a time when public law issues become more prominent,[50] making the private-law-unification objective already somewhat outdated in Europe itself, they are becoming, in the age of 'good governance', more important on other continents too.

6. South East Asian Legal Scholarship: A Brief History of Timelessness

At this point I present a brief history of my discipline that will serve as an example of regional legal studies, and amplify some of the points already made. Looked at from the perspective of South East Asia, a narrative of comparative law scholarship in the last century might run something like this.

The Paris International Congress of Comparative Law in 1900 took no notice of South East Asia. Had it done so, it would have noticed that the modernization of law was already taking place: most of the South East Asian colonial regimes introduced codes of private and criminal law about this time, including Thailand, which was not colonized and which was actually in the throes of fundamental legal reform. As a result all ten countries now forming ASEAN have a legal system with a European-style framework. Even if this is perhaps not even the main fact one needs to know about these legal systems, it is one which should also not be taken for granted or underestimated.

Although notice had been taken, by the likes of Maine and Weber, of 'Asian law', based on religion and cultural difference, little work had been done on South East Asia at that point. Detailed scholarship had already begun in Leiden under the auspices of the *adatrecht* school. A series of scholars did more microscopic research, driven sometimes by the practical requirement of colonial policy to find out about the 'local' law preparatory to, or consequent on, the general reception or imposition of Roman-Dutch law or English common law. These were the likes of Van Vollenhoven and ter Haar in the Dutch East Indies; Taylor and Wilkinson in Malaya; and Quaritch Wales, Lingat and Burnay in Burma and Thailand; they

[49] See Leyland's chapter in this volume.
[50] See Thomas' and McDonald's chapters in this volume.

worked on particular legal cultures or legal history. In so far as they were concerned with public law, they tended to discuss sovereignty and kingship, and in similar terms to those used in relation to personal law. Their approach was essentially anthropological, and they attempted to place law within a frame of reference that dealt with other aspects of local culture. They were also often concerned with the relationship between colonial legislation and the various forms of custom. They described a situation in which the emerging legal systems embraced several kinds of transplanted law: not just European laws (English, Dutch, French, Spanish, German) but also other kinds of Asian law (Chinese, Buddhist, Hindu, Islamic). The anthropologist Clifford Geertz once quipped that 'there is hardly a form of legal sensibility (African perhaps, or Eskimo) to which it [i.e., Java, but it applies to South East Asia as a whole] has not been exposed.'[51]

It is interesting to note here that the scholarship on South East Asian law has not led to its being classified successfully in terms of legal families: no method of classification seems to work or to be helpful. For this reason South East Asia has suffered in terms of scholarship because there is no such entity as a distinctively 'South East Asian' type of law. The region's legal systems have generally been uncomfortably included with 'East Asian' legal systems, and described with mind-boggling inaccuracy as 'customary', 'authoritarian', 'Confucian', or even 'Islamic'. If I might quote from myself on this question:

> The most recent wisdom of the comparatists is contained in an article by Ugo Mattei, in which he laudably attempts to draw the taxonomy of legal systems away from its euro-centric axis.[52] Mattei's world map of law is a triangle with apices representing 'professional lawyers' law', 'the rule of politics', and 'the rule of tradition': all legal systems, he argues, can be placed somewhere on the apices of this triangle. We must be grateful to Mattei for taking the trouble to apply his taxonomy to the South East Asian legal systems: he has expended the entirety of footnote 135 of his article to this awesome task. He says, first, that they are 'not Confucian'; he describes Malaysia and Indonesia as 'Islamic law countries tending towards the rule of politics', and the South East Asian legal systems as 'generally well within the rule of tradition tending towards the rule of politics', adding 'these are personal guesses made under a veil of ignorance.' The truth is that we really have no idea what to say about the legal systems of South East Asia. Mattei has fallen into the trap that all his euro-centric predecessors fell into: the legal-families trap. Legal families tell us nothing about legal systems except as to their general style and method, and the idea makes no sense whatsoever amid the nomic din of South East Asia. To call the South East Asian legal systems any kind of a family or even members of a

[51] Geertz, n. 13 above.
[52] Mattei, n. 10 above.

family is about as accurate and as interesting as calling *rojak* [a spicy Malay salad] a kind of vegetable[53]

The period since 1945 has seen two further phases.[54] The first was the period of decolonization and independence, in which it was assumed that the logic of 'law-and-development' would result in the convergence of Asian legal systems along 'Western' lines, a view that sat easily with the comparative-law orthodoxy of the time. This was the period in which 'new states' would prevail over 'old societies'. It finished with the apparent failure of the law-and-development initiative in the early 1970s, as charted famously by Trubek and Galanter in a *fin-de-siecle* article.[55] In Asia, however, the notion of the 'Asian developmental (or regulatory) state',[56] characterised by social stability, authoritarian governmental structures, and long-term economic planning, is now seen by many as crucial to the understanding of law-and-development in Asia throughout the post-colonial period. Even in this stage, public law was seen as important in that it provided a foundation for development.

A new phase since about 1990 emphasizes 'law-and-governance', and 'globalization-law', which have driven much of legal development in South East Asia. The interesting outcome of this phase and the economic crisis of 1997–8 is a renewed emphasis on culture and society as guides to the analysis and understanding of law, and on legality, legal certainty, or the rule of law, as the way forward beyond the crisis. Thus 'new state: old society' has given way to 'old state: new society'; in this phase it is expected that South East Asian legal systems, propelled by people power and international commerce, will finally reach maturity. Recent discussions concerning development and globalization have highlighted the need for more understanding of the economic, cultural and political influences on the development of law. These discussions seem to me to make assumptions about the role and relevance of law that remain to be tested, and which beg questions we are perhaps not yet in a position to answer. Undoubtedly the significance of public law in South East Asia has changed dramatically in the last ten years due to the changed emphasis of this current phase.

In sum, public law has been continuously relevant to attempts to explain and to reform law in South East Asia. It has never been more relevant than it is at the present time. It is also true that discussion of public law has generally been more

---

53 A.J. Harding, 'Global Doctrine and Local Knowledge: Law in South East Asia' (2002) 51 International and Comparative Law Quarterly, forthcoming. The legal families approach oddly persists in identifying a family called 'Asian law' (see, e.g., M. van Hoecke and M. Warrington, 'Legal Cultures, Legal Paradigms and Legal Doctrine: Towards a New Model for Comparative Law' (1998) 47 *International and Comparative Law Quarterly* 495; in fact it would be extremely difficult according to this type of classification to place any SE Asian legal system within it, if indeed it exists at all.

54 I rely partly here on an excellent analysis by Professor Jan-Michiel Otto in an unpublished paper.

55 D. Trubek and M. Galanter, 'Scholars in Self-estrangement': Some Reflections on the Crisis in Law and Development Studies in the United States' (1974) 4 *Wisconsin Law Review* 1062.

56 See C. Antons, (ed.), *Law and Development in East and South East Asia* (London, Curzon, forthcoming, 2002).

concerned with contexts than rules; although in Philippines, Malaysia and Singapore, public law is somewhat more of a technical subject, given that these jurisdictions have enjoyed a longer period of development.

7. Conclusions

Gutteridge worried about the comparison of legal systems at different levels of development. The illogicality involved in artificially restricting the scope of comparative law, typical of the grand tradition of comparative law, is immediately apparent to anyone who works on South East Asia: how can we even have a concept of legal development without a basis for comparing different levels of it?

In the spirit of this observation, and despite the complexity and the slightly elliptical nature of much of the above argument, my conclusions can I think be simply stated.

Comparative legal scholarship has neglected to consider both public law and regionalist approaches to the study of law. Whether or not these two different kinds of neglect could ever have been justified, they are no longer appropriate as we enter the 21st century. We have to expand the intellectual and geographical scope of comparative law even as we refine its techniques and methods. Even as the lawyers in Paris in 1900 planned the exclusion of South East Asian law and the whole of non-European law from comparative law studies in the 20th century, the Paris public was enthused by South East Asian dance and music, which went on to influence deeply the development of French and other European music. Law, as usual, was far behind society's march. We now have the opportunity to catch up, and complete the project that was misconceived in 1900.

Chapter 15

THE IMPORTATION OF LAW: A NEW COMPARATIVE PERSPECTIVE AND THE HUNGARIAN CONSTITUTIONAL COURT

*Catherine Dupré**

It will be obvious from a number of chapters in this book that the development of comparative law is deeply rooted in the changing circumstances of history. This point is nowhere clearer than from Du Pré's chapter relating to her research on the Hungarian Constitutional Court. The chapter is of course also an example of the new importance of public law in developing legal systems, as is maintained by Harding and Carey-Miller, and acknowledged by van Gerven and Örücü. It addresses a situation that will no doubt become a commonplace of comparative law in the 21st century – namely that of transition from communism to liberalism. This situation raises many new concerns for comparative law. An interesting aspect of Du Pré's chapter is her insistence on reversing the usual perspective of those who look at legal transplantation or imports as she puts it (not exports, please note). Here the cross-border transference of law (with apologies to Nelken for the use of too many terms) is seen from the perspective of the recipient and in the context of the internal factors shaping the development of transitional legal systems. In other words, law is not, in 20th century mode, being transplanted by Western legal systems into a foreign environment, but being seized by legal actors in a developing system for its own purposes. Such circumstances lead to the questioning of assumptions: Du Pré points out that in her research she did not rely on her knowledge of French law or Western constitutional constructs. Her mention of lack of bibliography and having to be 'creative' starts to sound like a familiar theme: similarly her conception of comparative law as having a 'cognitive' rather than 'classifying' role.

So is the provenance of such imported law irrelevant, even to the extent that the donor system does not know or need to know that its law is being used in this way, or that the receiving system does not need to know where its law came from? Specifically – why did the Hungarian court choose German constitutional law for discussion of the

* Lecturer in Law, University of Birmingham. I wish to thank Professor Gordon Woodman for the helpful suggestions and comments he made on this paper. Some of the ideas explored here, in particular those on the definition and methodology of comparative law, represent some initial thoughts about the evolution of legal science.

A. Harding and E. Örücü (eds.),
Comparative Law in the 21st Century, 267–280.

concept of human dignity, and why did differences in approach develop? The answers provided amply justify the reversal-of-perspective approach, because they indicate the importance in the interpretative process of legal actors (here judges) operating in a particular political context (here that of a need for rapid and irreversible transition). The familiarity and prestige of the German legal system and language among Hungarian lawyers explain a good deal: German law was a tool that suited the job. The comparative law literature on legal systems in transition is growing rapidly and contributing much to our understanding of law.

[A. Harding and E. Örücü]

1. Introduction

This paper argues that law importation was one of the strategies adopted by post-communist lawyers in Europe in order to rebuild their legal systems after the collapse of communist rule. Law importation, which is one manifestation of the circulation of rules, law and institutions beyond state borders are considered here in the specific context of constitutional adjudication in Hungary during the very first years of transition from communism (1990–1998). However, I suggest that the phenomenon of law importation also took place in other post-communist countries and that it can help understanding of how the transition from communism to liberalism operated.

This study considers two complementary aspects of the notion of law importation. Firstly, law importation corresponds to a particular perspective of comparison which abandons what is referred here as the exporter's perspective which dominated 20th century comparative legal studies. I argue that this perspective was rooted in Western Europe, from where law was exported to other parts of the world, whose legal systems were studied by reference to Western law. Secondly, law importation corresponds to a particular strategy used by Hungarian constitutional judges in order to develop their case law and, in particular, the right to human dignity (Art. 54 of the Hungarian constitution). I suggest that this phenomenon can be best studied and understood when the comparatist adopts the importer's perspective following, i.e., when the comparatist considers the foreign system in its own term and not by reference to his/her own (Western) system.

2. The 20th Century: the Exporter's Perspective

I propose that the definition and the practice of comparative law in the twentieth century have been influenced by two sorts of factors. The first factor is linked to the very definition of law and comparative law, which led to the exclusion of legal systems considered to be too different from those of Western Europe. The second factor highlights the fact that legal systems, inside and outside Europe, have developed through the exportation of law from Western Europe and that, consequently, their study by comparative lawyers has generally followed this perspective.

I suggest that in 1900, the approach to comparative law was based on two understandings that were so obvious that they were never really spelled out. The first one was that law, as understood in the West, was a sign of civilization. At that time, only civilized societies were considered to have a legal system. The second understanding was that civilization was mainly European (with an extension to America, due to early European emigration and settlement). To make it simple, at the beginning of the twentieth century, civilization was considered as being mainly Western, white and Christian.

These two understandings were as fundamental as they were tacit and arguably, they determined the perception of law as well as its study. Raymond Saleilles at the famous 1901 conference stated the obvious when he associated the comparison of law to the study of legal systems of 'civilized nations'.[1] As a result, the study of comparative law, more precisely the study of foreign legal systems, was limited to those systems that fitted in that geographical and cultural area and that shared a common history. Not surprisingly they also shared common legal features. Societies or, rather, people whose organisation and rules were not reasonably or sufficiently similar to that of Western Europe were not considered as having a proper legal system. Indeed, most of them were not considered as proper civilizations. Consequently, their study did not fall within the scope of law but instead gradually became part of a new discipline, anthropology, which in turn gradually specialized as legal anthropology.[2] As a result of this first understanding of law, comparative law was the study of foreign systems, which by definition were similar to that of the comparatist. Any existing differences were dealt with by the creation of categories, or families, of legal systems.[3] More precisely, these categories were implicitly determined by reference to Western European systems, from which law had been exported.

Later in the century,[4] many of the legal systems in the world developed into legal systems similar to those of European countries. These similarities result from the exportation process through which those legal systems came into existence. In

1 C. Jamin, 'Le Vieux Rêve de Salleilles et Lambert Revisité' (2000) 4 *Revue Internationale de Droit Comparé* 733.

2 It is interesting to note that the very first anthropologists were lawyers by training and occupation. At the early stages, anthropology and law shared a common quest for the 'primitive society'. See A. Kupper, *The Invention of Primitive Society, Transformation of an Illusion* (Routledge, London, 1988).

3 R. David, *Les Grands Systèmes de Droit Contemporain* (9th edn., Dalloz, Paris, 1988).

4 The historical elaboration of legal systems in Europe, and more generally of law, is often and commonly described as the result of the spread of Roman law which in the Middle Ages led to the (mythical and idealised) *ius commune*. See A.-J. Arnaud, *Pour une Pensée Juridique Européenn* (Presses Universitaires de France, Paris, 1991).

particular, colonial powers exported their law that they imposed on their colonies.[5] The Second World War also played a role in that exportation process in that the Allies ensured that the post-nazi countries adopted legal systems that met the requirements of liberal democracies.[6] The World War had a further impact on the development of legal systems in Europe. For the first time, they were divided into two antagonistic ideological families: the liberal or bourgeois democracies on the one hand and the Marxist people's republics on the other. The clash was no longer between civilized and so-called primitive societies. Arguably, it was of a far greater intensity and, in its acute phase, it led to reciprocal animosity and questioning of the validity of each conception and practice of law. It is true that René David included Soviet law in his classification of families of legal systems and that the study of Soviet law was part of that of comparative law. However, in the context of the Cold War the academic approach to Soviet law remained at a general level.[7] Due to the huge and essentially ideological differences of communist systems, their study soon fell within the scope of the new discipline, namely that of Soviet studies.

The Second World War has had an additional and well-known consequence on the development of law in Europe, i.e., the emergence of European institutions and of a European body of law. This has increased the existing similarities of the legal systems of the member states of the European Community in two ways. Firstly, the body of European regulations has hugely expanded and as a result a high proportion of domestic legislation is nowadays enacted in compliance with European requirements. Secondly, the construction of the European Union has brought member states closer together and they have on their own initiative tended to adopt similar legislation. Finally, the Council of Europe and, in particular, the European Convention on Human Rights has also led to the adoption of common standards and rules throughout Europe. Towards the end of the century, this phenomenon has taken on such proportions that it has attracted a lot of academic attention, which has celebrated the emergence of a revived *ius commune* in Europe. As a result, a large number of current comparative studies focus on similarities in an attempt to establish the existence of a common body of law shared by European states, or to develop this *ius commune*.[8]

---

[5] See for instance R.B. Seidman, 'The Reception of English Law in Colonial Africa' in Y. Ghai, R. Luckman and F. Snyder (eds.), *The Political Economy of Law* (Oxford University Press, Oxford, 1987).

[6] On the American influence in the drafting of the post-war Japanese constitution, see L. Henkin and A. Rosenthal (eds.), *Constitutionalism and Rights, the Influence of the United States Constitution Abroad* (Columbia University Press, New York, 1990).

[7] I can only think of a few monographs that presented the communist legal systems. In English, see J.N. Hazard, *Communists and their Law, a Search for a Common Core of Legal Systems of Marxian Socialist States* (University of Chicago Press, Chicago, 1969).

[8] See, among others, M. Cappelletti (ed.), *New Perspectives for a Common Law of Europe* (Sijthof, Leiden/Boston, 1978); and *The Constitutional Heritage of Europe*, Conference organised by the Commission for Democracy through Law, published by the Council of Europe, 1997; A.S. Hartkamp,

This trend peaked after the collapse of communist rule in Eastern Europe in the early 1990s. Liberal democracies and, more generally, the ideology of liberalism were presented as having won the Cold War. As a result, communism and communist law (which had shaped this part of Europe over the last 50 years) were promptly and massively rejected by the post-communist governments. At the same time, the liberal democracies, i.e., European countries and the United States started exporting their expertise, legal rules and institutions to these countries whose legal systems were in need of a speedy and safe reconstruction.[9] The exportation of law followed different channels, such as personal and individual, national and international, governmental and non-governmental, formal and informal. Their general message can be summarised by a few catch phrases that, it was claimed, would metamorphose the failed people's republics into (successful) liberal democracies. The most prominent of these phrases were: 'fundamental rights', 'rule of law', 'separation of powers', 'political pluralism' and 'freedom of expression.

Strictly speaking, most of the expertise and advice provided were not binding. However, the general progress and indeed the success of the democratic transitions were assessed in relation to the ability of individual post-communist countries to adopt the law of liberal countries together with their institutions and to meet their standards. In some cases, compliance with high standards was the requirement for accession to certain institutions, like the Council of Europe, or for being short-listed for subsequent enlargement of the European Union. Consequently, the study of post communist legal systems focused on their similarities with Western law. More precisely, a large part of this study was about trying to fit them into certain categories previously established for liberal legal systems by Western lawyers. When the legal systems developing in post-communist Europe did not fit into the categories, they were deemed to be still in their transitional phase, i.e., not quite yet democratic, nor liberal. In other cases, if these countries did not meet the requirements and criteria set up by the West, for instance, if their legal systems did not achieve the same degree of protection of fundamental rights, they were often described as being 'bad pupils'. The study of these systems and their comparison with Western law has been carried out very much from the perspective of the (Western) exporter of law. Thus and in short, only when their law appeared to take a similar path to ours, were these developments praised and deemed to be satisfactory.

However, not much attention was paid to the differences. Not much time was devoted to trying to appreciate the extent of the differences, their nature and their possible signification. This is, I suggest, because the exporter's perspective does not

---

M. and W. Hesseling, (eds.), *Towards a European Civil Code* (Martinus Nijhoff, Dordrecht, 1994). For an opposite view, see P. Legrand, 'European Systems are not Converging' (1996) 45 *International and Comparative Law Quarterly* 52.

9 A.E.D. Howard, 'How Ideas Travel', in A.E.D. Howard (ed.), *Constitution-making in Eastern Europe* (Woodrow Wilson Press Centre, Washington DC, 1993); and 'Rotunda: Exporting the America Bill of Rights' [1991] *University of Illinois Law Review* 1065; or A. Sajo, 'Universal Rights, Missionaries, Converts and "Local Savages"' [1997] *East European Constitutional Review* 44.

allow a more subtle comparison. Furthermore, it is often conducted at a superficial, i.e., formal and institutional level. Implicitly, the exporter's perspective of comparison ignores the impact that lawyers in post-communist countries can have on the elaboration of their own legal systems. Instead, this perspective generally assumes that these countries (passively) absorb the legal material exported by the West.[10]

3. The 21st Century: The Perspective of Importation

Using the perspective of law importation for the purpose of studying foreign legal systems implies two considerations. The first one is of a methodological nature and it involves reversing our exporter's perspective of comparison. The second dimension of law importation is more specific to the context of post-communist transitions and to Hungary in particular. More precisely, it refers to the process through which Hungarian constitutional judges elaborated their case law by importing significant element of the German case law on human dignity.

3.1. Reversing the Perspective of Comparison[11]

When I started looking at the Hungarian constitutional case law and at human dignity back in 1993, my approach to the Hungarian post-communist system was influenced by the lack of bibliography on this subject. This was due to two main reasons. Firstly, very few Western lawyers had studied Hungarian law during the Cold War. Secondly, these legal systems were so new that little had been published at the time. Moreover, the first publications mostly remained at the level of general introductions directed at an (ignorant) Western audience. Finally, because post-communist transitions were novel and apparently unpredictable, there were not any conceptual tools to understand them.

In response to this novelty, I had to be creative with my own comparative approach. I tried to avoid putting the Hungarian system and in particular the constitutional court into the existing categories (which would have needed some adjustment to take into account the extraordinary circumstances of post-communist

[10] In some earlier cases, the exportation of Western law was opposed by local lawyers. See on this subject: B. Kercher, 'Resistance to Law under Autocracy' (1997) 60 *Modern Law Review* 779; M. Lazarus-Black and S.F. Hirsh (eds.), *Contested States: Law, Hegemony and Resistance* (Routledge, London, 1995) and G. Strauss, *Law, Resistance and the State: the Opposition to Roman Law in Reformation Germany* (Princeton University Press, Princeton, 1986). I suppose here that the notion of 'passive absorption' more accurately refers to foreign law being imposed from outside rather than being sought from the inside.

[11] In this section, I am trying to spell out a few considerations that intuitively guided my Ph.D. research: *L'Importation Juridique et la Cour Constitutionnelle Hongroise; l'Exemple du Droit à la Dignité Humaine (1990–1996)*, (European University Institute, Florence, June 1998). In an attempt to explore this new path, this section lies half way through a summary of my approach and considerations of a more general nature.

transitions). Instead, I decided to concentrate on an empirical case study of just one single right, i.e., the right to human dignity. I deliberately tried not to apply theoretical models or categories to the Hungarian situation that I considered in terms of its own merit and specificity. I did not try to understand this new system in relation to the system I had been educated into. Even less did I try to assess or to judge the Hungarian constitutional case law by reference to my French understanding of constitutional adjudication.[12]

On the contrary, I assumed that the Hungarian system was radically different and that focusing on this essential and admittedly disturbing difference would ultimately help me understand what was going on. In this context, it became clear that reversing the perspective of comparison has meant that differences should not necessarily be interpreted as a sign of failure to achieve a transformation, nor to learn the lessons of the West. Furthermore, learning from the twentieth century and from the work of anthropologists as well as a few open-minded lawyers we have gradually realised that those societies, which are not white, European and Christian, are not inferior to those of the Western comparatists because they are different. With the end of the Cold War, I considered that it was time for our, i.e., the Western, attitude towards post-communist countries to cease to be disdainful of these other legal systems. I considered that our attitude should not become patronizing towards the systems that were in the process of finding their own way and making use of the flood of Western advice.

Furthermore, I realised that in a context of increasing similarity between the various domestic legal systems, differences become more interesting than similarities. The perception of differences naturally depends on the level of comparison. Reversing the perspective of comparison also means opting for a level of comparison that will allow differences to become visible. This implies that comparatists go beyond the mere textual formulation of rules in the foreign legal system studied. This, in turn, means that an actual and explicit comparison between legal systems is undertaken. Comparative law as studied by Western European scholars in the twentieth century essentially meant the study of foreign legal systems and their classification. More recently, it has meant the study of one institution or rule across several countries that are then individually presented in a juxtaposition of chapters in a book. This, arguably, has been a necessary step in the cognitive process of understanding other legal systems. Hopefully, in the twenty-first century we will be able to go beyond this stage and to undertake real comparison between different systems. This implies that we will use comparison as a cognitive (and not only as a classifying) tool for the understanding of other legal systems as well as for the understanding of our own legal systems. Therefore, I suggest that the purpose and the level of comparison have to be made explicit (as far as possible). One way to

[12] This, I admit, was not too difficult to do given the great differences existing between the two systems. The French legal system and the Constitutional Council in particular were not used as a model in Hungarian constitutional adjudication.

achieve this is to set out clearly whether the comparatist aims to focus on similarities or, on the contrary, if she aims to emphasize differences and why. Alternatively, the comparatist has to make clear what her position (as far as she is aware of it) is in relation both to the foreign system and to her own legal system.

Finally and importantly, reversing the perspective implies accepting that the circulation of law and subsequent legal development are not only the result of the exportation of law from Western Europe to outside countries, but that it is also the outcome of law importation. More precisely, reversing the perspective is about realising that these countries (former colonies and post-communist Europe) have deliberately sought to import the law (or at least some of its aspects) from Western Europe in order to suit their own agenda. Indeed, these countries do not passively receive and absorb the law exported from the West: they instrumentalize and transform the imported law in order to meet their own needs.[13] This implies also that the comparative lawyers take into account the role of law importers.

My own research started by observing the interpretation of the right to human dignity by the Hungarian constitutional court during the first years of transition from communism. First, I realised that this interpretation closely followed that developed by the German constitutional court. Not only was the terminology used by the Hungarian court identical to that of the German case law, but the general pattern of interpretation was also very similar and in some cases the whole logic of reasoning was copied from German constitutional case law.[14] However and importantly, German constitutional case law is not legally binding on Hungary. So, why were Hungarian judges using it to develop their own case law?

Following the exporters' perspective, one easy and immediate answer to this question would have emphasized the cultural and historical influence of Germany in this area, which used to be part of *Mitteleuropa*. This reasoning could have been expanded to German law: the historical inclusion of Hungary in the family of

---

[13] In relation to the political structure of Western democracies, the logic of importation developed by non-Western societies was also highlighted by Badie, in B. Badie *L'État Importé, Essai sur l' Occidentalisation de l'Ordre Politique* (Fayard: 1992).

[14] The Leitmotiv of the interpretation of human dignity reads: 'The Constitutional Court regards the right to human dignity as a "general personality right". The Constitutional Court considers the right to human dignity as one of the formulations of the general personality right. Modern constitutions and constitutional case law refer to the general personality right by several of its different aspects, for instance: the right to the free fulfillment of one's personality, the right to self determination, the general freedom of action or the right to a private sphere. The general personality right is a "mother- right", that is, a fundamental subsidiary right that the constitutional court as well as ordinary courts can call upon for the protection of the individual autonomy in instances where none of the named fundamental rights can apply to the facts of the case': Case 8/1990. See my contribution to the collection of studies on *The Principle of Human Dignity* published by the Commission of Democracy Through Law of the Council of Europe, Sept. 1999. Compare this with the paper of C. Walter on human dignity in German constitutional case law, in the same volume. English translations of some of the human dignity cases are to be found in G. Brunner and L. Sólyom (eds.), *Constitutional Judiciary in a New Democracy, the Hungarian Constitutional Court* (University of Michigan Press: 1999).

Germanic legal systems and the current role model played by the German constitutional court in the area of fundamental rights. In addition, the German constitutional court is one of the very few constitutional courts which has developed a substantial case law on human dignity and this is one of its well-known characteristics. Finally, German has long been a widely spoken second language in central Europe and, in particular, it has been a common language among lawyers. Summing up these points, the exporters' perspective would explain the Hungarian case law by the general influence of German law outside Germany.

However, a closer look at both German and Hungarian bodies of case law revealed numerous differences between the two interpretations of human dignity. That is, beyond the superficial and terminological similarities, the two notions differed widely. The differences were such that they could not be attributed to misunderstandings and errors made by Hungarian judges in their reading of German case law. Consequently, the differences in the Hungarian interpretation of human dignity must, I propose, have been deliberate. I started thinking of another and more helpful explanation. At the same time I was puzzled by the extent of the differences that coexisted with clear indications that German case law was the source of inspiration for the interpretation of the Hungarian human dignity provision. I wondered why Hungarian judges had taken so much trouble to imitate the German case law if it was to transform it subsequently. In response to these interrogations, I have developed the notion of law importation, which I argue can explain the elaboration of the Hungarian interpretation of human dignity.

3.2. Law Importation in Hungarian Constitutional Adjudication

Law importation broadly evokes a similar idea, however, in the context of constitutional adjudication it differs from processes such as reception of law, judicial dialogue,[15] imitation or mimicry[16] and legal transplants.[17] Law importation, I propose, corresponds to the deliberate choice of a legal element that is then incorporated into a new legal system. Importers include law students educated abroad and bringing their knowledge back home, scholars, legislators and practising lawyers. Interestingly, judges can import foreign law in support of their own reasoning. In Hungary, law importation played an important role in the development of constitutional adjudication and in constitutional reasoning itself. In this context, the imported legal element ranges from a particular fundamental right to a whole pattern of interpretation or a specific method of reasoning.

15 This phrase has been mainly used to describe the relations between domestic courts and international or European courts. See for instance A.M. Slaughter 'A Typology of Transjudicial Communication' [1994] *University of Richmond Law Review* 99.

16 This terminology seems to reveal a French approach, see Y. Mény (ed.), *Les Politiques du Mimétisme Institutionnel* (L'Harmattan, Paris, 1993).

17 A. Watson, *Legal Transplants, an Approach to Comparative Law* (Scottish Academic Press, Edinburgh, 1974).

In contrast with the reception or incorporation of international law into a domestic legal system, imported law is not legally binding on the court that imports it. In this sense, it cannot be compared with judges' efforts to elaborate their case law in order to comply with higher, i.e., international, norms that are binding on Hungary, such as the European Convention on Human Rights and its body of case law.[18] Furthermore, law importation in constitutional adjudication differs from what some have called 'judicial dialogue'.[19] It is true that law importation can be understood as some sort of communication between courts of different states. However, there is no dialogue at all: the German court has never referred to Hungarian constitutional case law. At most, we could speak of repetition, i.e., we could describe the Hungarian court as trying to repeat or to imitate some elements of German constitutional case law. This, however, is contradicted by the numerous differences that exist between the German and the Hungarian interpretations of human dignity.

Finally and crucially, law importation differs from what A. Watson identified as 'legal transplants' in his seminal book published in 1974. This is because of the differences in focus and perspective. While legal transplants consider the influences that legal systems have had on other legal systems during their historical development, law importation corresponds to the elaboration of current legal systems in a context more complex than that envisaged for 'voluntary legal transplants'. Additionally and essentially, law importation is not connected with the mass movement of a population that would take its law with it.[20] Finally, the perspective of legal transplants, mainly because it is long term and historical, disregards the actors in this process. However, the idea of law importation does not contradict, nor antagonize the perspective developed by A. Watson. In fact, law importation offers a complementary perspective on the elaboration of a legal system that makes it possible to see different elements in this process and which, in particular, highlights the role of the importers of law.

In addition, law importation is part of a strategy carried out by importers, as illustrated by the Hungarian example. A closer reading of Hungarian case law in relation to the wording of the 1989 Hungarian constitution, as well as the wider context in which the court started operating in 1990, reveals that Hungarian judges were faced with several difficulties. First, the Court needed new and clear

18 M. Weller, 'Application of the European Convention on Human Rights in the Hungarian Legal System' [1999] *Acta Juridica Hungarica* 105–108.

19 In particular, see J.H.H. Weiler, 'A quiet Revolution, the European Court of Justice and its Interlocutor' [1994] *Comparative Political Studies* 333.

20 'Voluntary major transplants – that is, when either an entire legal system or a large portion of it is moved to a new sphere – fall into three main categories. First when a people moves into a different territory where there is no comparable civilization, and takes its laws with it. Secondly, when a people moves into a different territory where there is a comparable civilization and takes its law with it. Thirdly, when a people voluntary accepts a large part of the system of another people or peoples.' A. Watson (1974), n. 18 above at pp. 29–30.

constitutional criteria in order to elaborate a conception of law that radically departed from its previous communist basis. Furthermore, in the early 1990s, Hungarian law still contained a number of socialist rules that blatantly contradicted the new, i.e., liberal, conception of law. The Hungarian Court, however, decided to consider these rules on their own merits and not to nullify them simply on the ground that they were adopted under the communist regime. In addition, the Hungarian constitution of 1989 is not a brand new constitution: it is an amendment of the 1949 socialist constitution that endorsed the political compromise reached at the end of the summer of 1989 by the Round Table Talks.[21] It was adopted as being a provisional constitution and the new government was expected to draft a new constitution after the elections of April 1990. The promised new constitution, however, has so far not come into existence. As a result, the Constitutional Court was faced with a constitution which contained many provisions, and in particular those about fundamental rights, inherited from the previous communist regime.

Law importation appeared to have been the response of the Hungarian Court to these difficulties. By importing human dignity from German constitutional case law, the Hungarian Court imported constitutional criteria rather than to mimic the details of a complex body of case law. In other words, the Hungarian Court used human dignity to establish a new conception of fundamental rights that complied with the liberal understanding of rights. More generally, the right to human dignity breaks with the socialist understanding of rights in that it puts individuals in the foreground, as opposed to society under communism.[22] As interpreted by the Hungarian Court, human dignity emphasizes individual autonomy and protects individuals against the state apparatus. More precisely, human dignity is associated with the general personality right and it encompasses the rights to general freedom of action, free development of the personality and the right to individual self-determination. These rights illustrate and embody the new liberal principle according to which individuals have inherent rights that they can oppose to undue state interference with their own lives. On the basis of this understanding of constitutional rights, the Court has nullified many of the controversial and sensitive rules that Hungary had inherited from the communist era. The abolition of the death penalty, the requirement for regulations of legislative ranking for abortion and the nullification of some of the most significant powers of public prosecutors as they were set out under communism can be mentioned as examples of the most prominent cases that were decided on the basis of human dignity.

[21] I. Pogany, 'Human Rights in Hungary' [1992] *International and Comparative Law Quarterly* 676; 'Constitutitonal Reform in Central and Eastern Europe' [1993] *International and Comparative Law Quarterly* 332.

[22] For more detail, see C. Dupré 'Importing German Law: The Interpretation of the Right to Human Dignity by the Hungarian Constitutional Court' (2000) 2 *OsteuropaRecht* 144 and C. Dupré, 'Importing Human Dignity from German Constitutional Case Law' in G. Halmai (ed.) *The Constitution Found? The First Nine Years of Hungarian Constitutional Review on Fundamental Rights* (INDOK, 2000), p. 215.

Such a quasi-systematic nullification of pre-existing principles on the ground of imported human dignity would cause immense political outrage if done by Western courts. It is true that in Hungary, the Constitutional Court was regularly criticised for its activism during the first years of its operation. However, the importation of human dignity from German constitutional case law and, more generally, the importation of constitutional criteria from the West attracted little criticism. It is argued here that this is mainly because Hungarian judges made a strategic use of law importation. This strategy might be described, in a simplified way, as follows. First, judges choose a good model. I suggest that their choice depends on a combination of three factors. Firstly, they can only import law from legal systems with which they have a reasonable familiarity. Legal education, knowledge of languages, personal connections with foreign countries and their lawyers naturally influence their knowledge of foreign legal systems. Secondly, their choice seems to favour foreign legal systems that are both particularly well established and prestigious, such as the German system. Thirdly and crucially, the foreign legal element corresponds to a particular need or purpose of interpretation in the context of Hungarian constitutional adjudication. It helps judges to nullify socialist rules in sensitive and controversial areas. In addition, judges have used it in order to interpret the jurisdiction of the Court in an extensive way.

The transformation of imported law is part of this judicial strategy. To a limited extent, it enabled judges to adjust the foreign element of law to its new constitutional context. More importantly, the specific national origin of imported law is disguised in the general notion of 'modern constitutions'. It is presented as being a general standard of constitutionality shared by all 'modern constitutions', i.e., respectable and good constitutions. In this sense, it can be compared to a modern version of natural law. As a result, when Hungarian constitutional judges nullified rules on the ground of human dignity, they did not simply destroy a part of Hungarian law. The Court emphasized the fact that this contributed to the transformation of the Hungarian constitution into a 'modern constitution'.

4. Conclusion

The first years of constitutional adjudication in Hungary took place in a very unusual and extreme legal and political context: a massive and speedy revolution in the conception of law, a constitutional court with an amended and provisory constitution, the inability to predict the near future in the early 1990s, the fear that the Soviet Union might try to curb this process and the corresponding effort to safeguard as quickly as possible and as many as possible of the liberal principles and conceptions that would make a complete return of communist rule impossible. As a result of these particular features, the strategy set out by the Hungarian Constitutional Court is probably an extreme example of law importation in constitutional adjudication (and thus particularly visible) due to these extreme circumstances. Indeed, after most of the first judges left the court in 1998 and were replaced by new judges, the 'new' Constitutional Court seems to have adopted a much lower profile and it has developed a more formal and strict approach.

However, Hungary has shared a fate similar to that of its neighbouring post-communist countries. The need to reconstruct an entire legal system on a radically different basis, the extent and the speed of this process, the need for quick and almost ready-made solutions, the pressures of the West for a rapid transformation and settlement of the situation and the involvement of Western lawyers eager to propose their 'constitutional kit for a successful transformation' were features common to post-communist transitions. As a result, the perspective of law importation arguably provides a valuable insight into this phenomenon, which no one apparently expected. Without being a strictly theoretical model that would explain the details of this complex phenomenon, the perspective of law importation reflects the logic of constitutional transitions from communism.

In Great Britain the constitutional situation greatly differs from that of post-communist countries. However, the vast transformation that the British constitution is currently undergoing is likely to lead to law importation. Indeed, academics and lawmakers are looking at foreign legal systems from which they could draw some inspiration for the constitutional changes. Probably more than ever before, British lawyers are looking abroad for solutions and inspirations to modernize the British constitution. This is affecting the nature and the definition of comparison of law. More precisely, lawyers are increasingly looking at other systems from a very specific perspective, namely from the perspective of importation. For the time being, this is not yet visible at the level of judicial reasoning.[23] However, British academic comparatists have been looking at a wide range of foreign systems in search of inspiration for the current constitutional reforms, in particular in the area of fundamental rights.[24] In so doing, lawyers are no longer purely academic comparatists; they are also part of this importation process. As a result, the twenty-first century challenge for comparative lawyers will be to try to do both at the same time, while still being able to distinguish between the process of understanding a foreign system and that of importing some of its elements for particular purposes.

[23] We can note here that other Western courts are already and increasingly referring to foreign law in their reasoning. See for instance: J.M. McIntyre, 'The Use of American Cases in Canadian Courts' [1996] *University of British Columbia Law Review* 478; P. Pescatore, '*Le Recours dans la Jurisprudence de la CJCE à des Normes Déduites de la Comparison des Droits des États Membres*' [1980] *Revue Internationale de Droit Comparé* 337; J.H.H. Weiler, 'A quiet Revolution, the European Court of Justice and its Interlocutor' [1994] *Comparative Political Studies* 333.

[24] Among others, J. Craig and N. Nolte, 'Privacy and Free Speech in Germany and Canada: Lessons for an English Privacy Tort' [1998] *European Human Rights Law Review*; or G.A. Anderson (ed.), *Rights and Democracy: Essays in UK-Canadian Constitutionalism* (Blackstone, Oxford, 1999); I. Loveland (ed.), *Importing the First Amendment* (Hart Publishing, Oxford, 1998).

Chapter 16

SOUTH AFRICA: A WORLD IN ONE COUNTRY ON THE LONG ROAD TO REALITY

*David Carey-Miller**

Here is a system, transplanted from various sources, which has in the past ignored the indigenous. Now, still transplanting but aware of its own social and historical elements, it is settled as to its internal values but still embraces western values. This is a case study, with some strong theoretical analysis. This piece is firstly descriptive, with an analytical section on history. The illustrative subject area is property law. The piece also assesses the role of transmigration of ideas in the new South Africa, where there is now a critical approach to foreign materials. Certain aspects of the South African Constitution are also assessed. Present and possible future developments are put in the context of the past.

Carey-Miller takes issue with recent scholarship on South Africa, criticizing the particular private-law specialists' world-view of regarding a 'mixed jurisdiction' through a technical legal historical evaluation, 'rather than one that identifies the system in terms of its socio/normative focus'. He himself does not take a narrow technical perspective, but assesses the implications of the Westminster model for the pre-reform South Africa and in dealing with the 1996 Constitution. He sees the pre-1990s system as 'a positivist system with an active discriminatory normative basis'. This aspect of his chapter reflects also the concerns of Harding.

The transmigrations and transfers in the pre-reform era, which the author designates as being 'open to ideas but alert to differences', are looked at through the example of property law. Trust here is singled out as an example of adaptation and assimilation of an English idea, in an interesting comparator to the piece by Rafenne above. The actors of the system displayed a capacity 'to understand the technical difference between English property law and (their) own civilian form', even if not initially. However, the system 'functioned on the basis of the method and system of English law.' Also the adjectival law that developed has more affinity to English law than for example, it has

* Professor of Property Law, Centre for the Study of the Civil Law Tradition, School of Law, University of Aberdeen. Professor C.G. van der Merwe, Professor of Civil Law at the University of Aberdeen, formerly Professor of Roman and Private Law at the University of Stellenbosch, kindly read and commented on a draft of my W.G. Hart Workshop 2000 paper on which this chapter is based; I, however, am alone responsible for the form and substance of the present version.

A. Harding and E. Örücü (eds.),
Comparative Law in the 21st Century, 281–304.

in Scots law, another mixed jurisdiction. The same English influence is seen in administrative law.

Carey-Miller, by looking at the past transfers, illustrates how the 'perspective factor' can affect the assessment of the nature and character of a given system. By looking at the active normative character of the reformed system, he demonstrates the passage from 'a monolithic system dominated by a legislature giving effect to minority interest in the name of community interest'. The new order's response is 'to equip the system to function to protect and develop human rights within the context of articulated social norms.' The role of the Constitution and the Constitutional Court here is clearly indispensable.

Does comparative law have a suitable role in this new environment? Although the Constitution provides for the consideration of foreign law in the interpretation of its provisions, we are told that the peculiar socio-cultural needs of the country may bar this activity. Thus the place of transplant now is limited and delicate handling is needed. There are examples of the Constitutional Court using foreign law and foreign opinion, for example, in the abolishment of the death penalty. However, in the interpretation of the property clause, the use of foreign material can be questioned, although extensive use has been made of German developments and those in common law jurisdictions. Nevertheless, foreign law may not offer a safe guide to interpretation and due regard has to be paid to the legal system, its history and its circumstances. The chapter then tests this position in the context of land reform.

Is the Bill of Rights a carte blanche for comparative law, as South African law 'is clearly open to external influence to a greater extent than it formerly was'? Notions of universality may indicate active comparison and adherence to common themes in the area of human rights. Nevertheless, the 'indigenous African factor', 'involving considerations of "hearts and minds"', must now have greater weight than ever before. It is obvious that the particular domestic circumstances of the country must be addressed as a priority. This offers only limited scope for the application of foreign law. We are reminded that the comparative approach has certain limits.

So what of transmigration and transferability in the 21st century South Africa? In Bill of Rights matters, there is strong interest in foreign solutions and the courts have the tradition and capacity to assimilate foreign material in a discerning manner. They have been able to resolve clashes between English common law and Roman Dutch law since 1910. The critical approach is apparent here and this is a healthy development. There will be difficulties, but the future for discerning transfers and for South African law, with its demonstrable capacity for originality, seems bright. 'Arguably, the mixed factor in South African law becomes potentially more prominent'. Carey-Miller tells us that, with a wholly revised 'value norm agenda', 'the system will assimilate by reference to its own development and traditions'. There is strong contrast here with the situation in Hungary presented by Dupré and a comparison with the work of McDonald.

[A. Harding and E. Örücü]

1. Introduction

It could hardly be controversial to observe that the nature and emphasis of South African law is significantly different at the start of the twenty-first century from the relatively static form that dominated until the landmark political changes of the 1990s. But to what extent does the 'transmigration and transfer of legal ideas and institutions' feature in this sea change? The answer involves both the factors and forces that led to the new shape of South African law and an early assessment of how external influence will contribute to the development of the reformed system. The paper's emphasis on identifying the trends of present and possible future development must be put in the context of the past because the 1990s transition reflects a strong continuity factor.[1]

2. Essential Positivist and Historical Character of the Pre-reform System

In another variation of the colonial factor, the circumstances of history brought into existence, a mixed, but predominantly European, system of law in South Africa.[2] The initial period of an extended colonial epoch, from the mid-seventeenth century, was dominated by Roman-Dutch law – specifically the variant of Holland, the provincial jurisdiction of the Dutch East India Company, which effected the settlement at the Cape.[3] In the late eighteenth/early nineteenth century, following the Napoleonic Wars, Britain acquired control of the Cape and was a dominant force in the destiny of the developing state for at least a century. But while the administration of justice came to acquire a form and substance which reflected features of English law, the standard British colonial policy position, enunciated in an eighteenth century decision[4] left in place the established system of Roman-Dutch substantive law.

Despite a population structure in which people of European descent are a small minority, the customary law of Africa has had only a peripheral role,[5] of limited

1 See H. Corder, 'Towards a South African Constitution' (1994) 57 *Modern Law Review* 491, 522–523.

2 See R. Zimmermann and D. Visser (eds.), *Southern Cross: Civil Law and Common Law in South Africa* (Clarendon Press, Oxford, 1996), the introduction and chs. 1–4.

3 For the most up-to-date and authoritative view on an issue which has been long debated in South African case law see *Du Plessis NO v Strauss* 1988 (2) SA 105 (A). In this case, Corbett JA (at p. 150) concluded that 'the South African case law should not be permitted to override the law of Holland'. See also R. Zimmermann, 'Roman Law in a Mixed Legal System – the South African Experience', in R. Evans-Jones (ed.) *The Civil Law Tradition in Scotland* (Stair Society, Edinburgh, 1995), pp. 68–69.

4 See *Chambell v Hall* (1774) 1 Cowp 204 (98 ER 1045).

5 See, generally, T.W. Bennett, *The Application of Customary Law in Southern Africa: the Conflict of Personal Laws* (Juta, Cape Town, 1985). See also Professor Bennett's preface comment in T.W. Bennett, *Sourcebook of African Customary Law for Southern Africa* (Juta, Cape Town, 1991), v: 'In comparison with other branches of the South African legal system customary law is small game. It

significance in the picture of mainstream legal development.[6] While customary law is recognised in the Constitution[7] and given effect to in legislation,[8] its role is circumscribed by the 'Bill of Rights factor'. Differentiation of provision, seeking to give effect to a customary factor, may well fail to pass muster under the new dispensation.[9]

In the twentieth century, the Roman-Dutch based private law of South Africa developed strongly with a definite emphasis upon the retention of its civilian identity. This was partly associated with the rise to power of the Afrikaner national group and a perception of Roman-Dutch law as an aspect of European cultural heritage. Not without some justification, a purist mentality tended to see English law influence as potentially damaging to the integrity of an established ius commune form of private law, but this attitude did not go unchallenged.[10] For present purposes it is significant that, for much of the first three-quarters of the twentieth century – in a context of legal development driven by minority self-interest, on one view reflecting Dworkin's 'community morality' notion[11] – informed legal debate was largely preoccupied with a concept of law as the positivist product of history.

---

would be generous to attribute the want of attention to unconscious neglect; it is more probably the result of a deliberate policy to exclude Africans from full participation in the South African legal system'.

6 Zimmermann and Visser, above n. 2, pp. 12–15 characterise African customary law as 'the third Grace' of South African law, with the common law and civil law component features; the learned authors write (at p. 15): 'The three Graces of the South African legal system are civil law, common law and customary law. The free spirit of the third Grace makes it difficult for her to join in the circle'. This choice of image seems to be off the mark, given that the dominant social, economic and political development of South Africa left no room for customary law in any more than an ethnic factor role.

7 In ch. 12 ('Traditional Leaders') under the sub-heading 'Recognition', s. 211(3) provides that 'The courts must apply customary law when that law is applicable, subject to the Constitution and any legislation that specifically deals with customary law'.

8 See the Recognition of Customary Marriages Act 120 of 1998.

9 In *Zondi v President of the Republic of South Africa and Others* 2000 (2) SA 49, 52; after noting that '[p]lainly in terms of our new Constitution ... the various systems of indigenous law fall to be recognised and respected... ', Levinsohn J went on to declare a statutory provision providing for the application of customary law in an African matrimonial property/succession context as unconstitutional. On this entire issue, see now C. Himonga and C. Bosch, 'The Application of African Customary Law under the Constitution of South Africa' (2000) 117 *South African Law Journal* 306.

10 On this '*bellum juridicum*' see H.R. Hahlo and E. Kahn, *The South African Legal System and its Background* (Juta, Cape Town, 1968), pp. 578–596; see also '[o]f purists and pollutionists' in Zimmermann and Visser, above n. 2, pp. 22–24.

11 See R. Dworkin, *Taking Rights Seriously* (Duckworth, London, 1977), p. 126. Dworkin's concept of 'community morality' was evoked by R. Wacks in his inaugural lecture call for the resignation of South African judges. The hundred-year-old *South African Law Journal* carried the debate on this issue: see R. Wacks, 'Judges and Injustice' (1984) 101 *South African Law Journal* 266; J. Dugard, 'Should Judges Resign?' (1984) 101 *South African Law Journal* 286; R. Wacks, 'Judging Judges: a Brief Rejoinder to Professor Dugard' (1984) 101 *South African Law Journal* 295; J.M. Didcott, 'Address to the Graduation Ceremony at the University of Natal' (1984) 3 *South African Journal of Human Rights* 23, 26.

For present purposes, the relevant starting point is the constitution of the post Boer War union of 1910, which created modern South Africa and chartered its essential course until the early 1990s. From a legal development perspective, the critical feature of the Act of Union was its replication in South Africa of a British Westminster system of government and constitution.[12] The tendency of much of twentieth century South African juristic writing to preoccupation with the law as civilian or mixed represented a sectional perspective that the majority of the population would not have shared. This potential for polarity of perspective is reflected in a relative failure to recognise the significance of the Westminster factor in the pre-reform South African legal development. As I have commented elsewhere,[13] to neglect the significance of the adoption in 1910 of a Westminster form of government is to deny the factor of the impact of the law upon the majority of the South African population. One need hardly say that decades of apartheid legislation – which the 'norm-neutral' Westminster system allowed – is the historical hallmark of twentieth century South African law rather than its mixed civilian/common law character. The publication of *Southern Cross*[14] is testimony to the emphasis upon the development of private law in South Africa. While there cannot be the slightest quarrel with this work as a valuable exercise in comparative private law, it may be seen as reflecting the particular world-view of South African private law specialists who apply a definition of 'mixed system', with the emphasis upon a technical legal historical evaluation rather than one which identifies the system in terms of its socio/normative focus. The disparate definitions of 'mixed system' are, of course, equally legitimate in the sense of having the potential to serve different purposes of legal investigation. The point for present purposes is that it should be recognised that the prevalent concept of 'mixed system', applied to the pre-reform South African legal development by private law specialists, tends to represent a narrow technical perspective. This emphasis largely ignores the negative institutional factors of the

[12] *In Pharmaceutical Mnfrs of SA: in re ex parte President of the RSA* 2000 (2) SA 674 (CC) 692–695 the President of the Constitutional Court identified a certain continuity in the root and branch constitutional development from the South Africa Act, 1909 to the present position of a written constitution incorporating a Bill of Rights. As the learned President noted, while '[s]ubstantive constitutional law principles governing the relationship between the various arms of government … were not expressly included' in the 1909 Act the common-law constitutional principles – most importantly the rule of law, the supremacy of Parliament and the prerogative – prevailed. While the concept of the rule of law incorporated a substantive as well as a procedural dimension, which gave rise to a notion of fundamental rights because of 'the countervailing constitutional principle of the supremacy of Parliament, the fundamental rights could be, and frequently were, eroded or excluded by legislation', in contrast, the new constitutional order, as the learned President observed 'expressly rejects the doctrine of the supremacy of Parliament, but incorporates other common-law constitutional principles and gives them greater substance than they previously had'.

[13] D.L. Carey Miller, 'South Africa: a mixed system subject to transcending forces', in E. Örücü, E. Attwooll and S. Coyle (eds.), *Studies in Legal Systems: Mixed and Mixing* (Kluwer Law International, London, 1996), pp. 173–174.

[14] Zimmermann and Visser, n. 2 above.

prevailing Westminster model, with all its implications for the system of lawmaking in a joint legislative and judicial process. Any characterisation of the post-reform South African law will reflect a complex mixed system with the positive features of the 1996 Constitution – and, in particular, its Bill of Rights – in a prominent role.

A perception of 'mixed system' more relevant to the single most striking feature of pre-1990s South African law – a positivist system with an active discriminatory normative basis – should emphasise the two British derived features of the supremacy of an unfettered parliament and a judiciary functioning upon the premise of a narrowly defined interpretive role. Two cases, respectively from the early and late stages of apartheid – can be taken to demonstrate these features.

In *Minister of Post and Telegraphs v Rasool*[15] decided in 1934, the introduction of segregated national post office facilities was challenged as illegal on the basis of inherent inequality of treatment. But, in the absence of any form of prescriptive norm directed towards the fair and equal treatment of all racial groups, the highest court's decision reflected the prevailing community *mores* of the minority ruling class.[16]

Some forty years later, Didcott J[17] commented from the bench on the role of South African judges in interpreting unjust legislation. The 'draconian effect' of section 6 of the Terrorism Act 83 of 1967 had to be seen in the context of the courts being contained in a system with limited scope for resort to norms concerned with fairness, freedom and individual liberty. The tradition of preference for a route of interpretation which achieved the 'least amount of interference with the liberty of the individual' existed only 'as a normal part of the process of interpretation', and not 'because the Courts have or claim the authority to supervise statute law'. The basic position, Didcott J noted, was that 'stringent enactments' intended by Parliament, must be given effect to 'however offensive to conventional legal standards they may be'.[18]

15 1934 AD 167.

16 See B.A. Hepple, 'Economic and Racial Legislation', in H.R. Hahlo and E. Kahn (eds.), *The Union of South Africa* (Juta, Cape Town, 1960), p. 813: '[t]he judgements rendered are a microcosm of the varying attitudes of white South Africans to race and colour'. The majority of the Court, expressing views consistent with the prevailing politically controlling value system, saw racial segregation as not unreasonable; the dissenting judge alone applied the universal principle of equality before the law.

17 One of only three from the old Supreme Court to be appointed to the eleven judge inaugural Constitutional Court. For details of the process of appointment, candidates and appointees to the Constitutional Court see B. Dickson, 'South Africa's Constitutional Court' [1995] *New Law Journal* 246.

18 *Nxasana v Minister of Justice and Another* 1976(3) SA 745(D) 747–748. While this statement might be seen to be at odds with the British inspired judicial ethos of a-political detachment, it also reflects the independence factor that leaves room for different interpretations of the judicial role by members of the bench. The late Didcott J was very much representative of the 'judge as active reformer' model. With regard to differences in the conduct of the judicial role see the articles cited in n. 11 above. See also M. Lobban, *White Man's Justice* (Clarendon Press, Oxford, 1996).

3. Transmigrations and Transfers in the Pre-reform Era

3.1. Open to Ideas but Alert to Differences: the Property Example

From a comparative law perspective the primary feature of pre-reform South African law is an interplay between the civilian Roman-Dutch system and English law, which came to have a role through the early nineteenth century British acquisition of the Cape. This composite development feature is reflected in the subtitle 'Civil Law and Common Law in South Africa' of *Southern Cross*,[19] a major new work which seeks to demonstrate 'how civil law and common law came to be accommodated within one legal system'.[20] This, of course, produced the 'mixed system' that, largely from the perspective of private law, was recognised by the late Professor Sir Thomas Smith to have aspects in common with the development of the similarly derived mixed system of Scots law.[21]

While one cannot generalize about a development that varied between subject areas,[22] the fact that South African control over the shape of developing legal rules is a prominent, if not the overriding, feature. This is well illustrated in relation to the law of property.

In the property context, the system is markedly civilian and to this extent, very much distinguishable from English law.[23] The greater complexity of English property law – particularly land law – was a factor in the recommendation of a commission, appointed in 1826 by Cape Governor Lord Charles Somerset, that the Roman-Dutch law of property be retained.[24]

Despite the historical proximity factor, South African property law has avoided direct substantive influence from the English system, but, at the same time, some

19 Zimmermann and Visser, n. 2 above.

20 Ibid., flyleaf.

21 Most of Sir Thomas Smith's relevant writing can be found in T. Smith, *Studies Critical and Comparative* (W. Green, Edinburgh, 1962). The presently flourishing links between South African and Scots private law specialists (seven South Africans are represented in the thirty writers who contributed to the book: K. Reid and R. Zimmermann (eds.), *A History of Private Law in Scotland* (Oxford University Press, Oxford, 2000) also stems from Sir Thomas Smith's endeavours: see D.L. Carey Miller and D.W. Meyers (eds.), *Comparative and Historical Essays in Scots Law: a Tribute to Professor Sir Thomas Smith QC* (Butterworths, Edinburgh, 1992), p. 13.

22 The best single source covering the various aspects of this civilian/common law development is Zimmermann and Visser, above n. 2.

23 Reflecting the far-reaching structural and conceptual differences identified in W.W. Buckland, MacNair and D. Arnold, *Roman Law and Common Law* (2nd edn., (Lawson, F.H.), Cambridge University Press, Cambridge, 1952) pp. 60–126.

24 See B. Beinart, 'The English Legal Contribution in South Africa: the Interaction of Civil and Common Law' (1981) 7 *Acta Juridica* 30. The dominant position of Roman-Dutch common law is reflected in the fact that the controlling land title legislation, the Deeds Registries Act 47 of 1937, is derived, via earlier legislation, from the law and practice of 18th century Holland. The essence of conveyancing as a formal act of execution by a conveyancer attested by the Registrar of Deeds reflects the common law requirement of an act of delivery to bring a real right into being. On this see D.L. Carey Miller and A. Pope, *Land Title in South Africa* (Juta, Cape Town, 2000), pp. 45–48, 63–65.

reception of English ideas has almost certainly been assimilated into an essentially civilian landscape. The conclusion of Hamlyn lecturer O.D. Schreiner, a distinguished Judge of Appeal (1940–1960), that '[o]ur law of property owes little to English law'[25] is true to the extent that South African Roman-Dutch property law has hardly been touched by English law. However, this is not to deny the influence of English legal thinking in the wider context of property, even if not in the technical aspects of the law.

The English law form of trust is probably the prime example of the adaptation and assimilation of an English idea. It is not a device that fits the civilian property structure; indeed, on a strict civil law basis, it might not even be classified as a creature of property law,[26] even though its role in the property context is a significant one. While South African law has studiously avoided the English law dichotomy of a separation between law and equity,[27] it would appear that trust has been adopted as a self-contained device.[28] This means that its more formal and restricted application does not include access to English law's flexible constructive trust device, which is open to application in a range of situations on the basis of the concept of an equitable or beneficial interest as a form of ownership.[29] While it may be impossible to explain the trust in terms of the well-understood dogmatism of South African property law, the self-contained nature of its exceptionality causes no real difficulty.

Under British nineteenth century administration, a system of freehold land-ownership developed from the dominant earlier pattern of limited, if not precarious, forms of land-holding;[30] but, the British influence involved in this change did not bring with it a shift to English property law. This said, one would not deny that the combined effect of a British inspired motivation for freehold and a Roman-Dutch capacity to provide the necessary legal form were probably the primary ingredients in the development of the property regime which came to exist. The legal form was, of course, the critical factor from the point of view of legal development; in the Roman-Dutch form, ownership was the ultimate legal right, both distinguishable in kind from possession, and unitary in nature (but, of course, not absolute). In a quite

[25] *The Contribution of English Law to South African Law; and the Rule of Law in South Africa*, Hamlyn Lectures (Stevens, London, 1967), p. 40.

[26] See Buckland et al., above n. 23, pp, 176–179.

[27] See H.R. Hahlo, 'The Trust in South African Law' (1961) 78 *South African Law Journal* 95: 'Among the fundamental civil law concepts which South African law has retained in its pure form, perhaps the most important one is the Roman *dominium*. There cannot be two ownerships or two kinds of ownership in one and the same thing at one and the same time, with the result that the English form of trust is ruled out'.

[28] See, generally, T. Honoré and E. Cameron, *Honoré's South African Law of Trusts* (4th edn., Juta, Cape Town, 1993). See also T. Honoré, 'Trusts' in Zimmermann and Visser, above n. 2, pp. 849–872.

[29] See *Estate Kemp v MacDonald's Trustee* 1914 CPD 1084; *Verseput v De Gruchy* 1977 (4) SA 440 (W). Note also the comment of Honoré (1996), n. 28 above, p. 858: 'Constructive and resulting trusts have not in fact taken root in South African soil'. See now also E. Cameron, 'Constructive trusts in South African Law: the Legacy Refused' (1999) 3 *Edinburgh Law Review* 341.

[30] See J.L.R. Milton, 'Ownership' in Zimmermann and Visser (1996), n. 2 above, pp. 664, 670.

different form and structure, English ownership is determined as a matter of right to possession with distinct and sometimes competing legal and equitable forms.[31] The development of rights and obligations pertaining to ownership in South African law has proceeded on the basis of this Roman-Dutch form, even where ideas as to what the end result should be have been borrowed from English law. The development of the law of nuisance – on the basis of the importation of 'the right to personal welfare and comfort as an incident of land ownership'[32] – is an example of this.[33]

South African law has, by and large, demonstrated a capacity to understand the technical differences between English property law and its own civilian form – if not initially, at least over the course of a particular development. Professor C.G. van der Merwe has shown how the English law concept of 'adverse user' came to have a role in the context of acquisitive prescription but was eventually recognised to be superfluous.[34] Another example is the adaptation of the English law doctrine of 'attornment' in the commercially important matter of the delivery of goods held by a third party for and on behalf of the owner.[35]

In South Africa, English property influence is almost non-existent at the technical substantive level, because the incompatibility problem has been recognised and because the development of the law has been with a view to an effective Roman-Dutch based system. However, the thinking of English law – the thinking of England – has influenced the development of certain aspects of property, largely in terms of ends rather than means. In being conversant with its history, and therefore with its identity, South African law has been in a position to embark on development with confidence.[36] The system's capacity in this respect now faces the challenge of a

---

31 Buckland et al., n. 23 above, pp. 55–76; 176–178.

32 See Milton, above n. 30, p. 678.

33 The extent of this particular influence was noted by D. Van der Merwe, 'Neighbour Law' in Zimmermann and Visser, above n. 2, p. 760: '[j]udicial definitions of nuisance in English law were adopted and applied by South African judges and English case law was a constant and comprehensive source of inspiration'.

34 'Original Acquisition of Ownership' in Zimmerman and Visser, above n. 2, pp. 702–714.

35 See D.L. Carey Miller, 'Transfer of Ownership' in Zimmermann and Visser, above n. 2, pp. 745–747. In *Caledon & SWD Eksekuteurskamer Bpk v Wentzel* 1972(1) SA 270 (A) the Chief Justice observed that there had to be a limit to this doctrine because in South African law, unlike English law, ownership could not pass by mere agreement; see also D.L. Carey Miller, *The Acquisition and Protection of Ownership* (Juta, Cape Town, 1986) pp. 152–157.

36 The major land reform developments of the 1990s support this; see D.L. Carey Miller, 'A New Property?' (1999) 116 *South African Law Journal* 749; D.L. Carey Miller and A. Pope, 'South African Land Reform' (2000) 44 *Journal of African Law* 167. 1990s land reform law concepts – initial ownership and beneficial occupation – might be taken to presage the possible adoption of a divided concept of ownership along the lines of English law. It seems likely, however, that the courts will seek to interpret these concepts in accordance with established principles. The new forms make the South African concept of ownership more complex, but they do not necessarily signal a shift to the technical structure of English property law.

new social order in which a focus on the delivery of rights will override any preoccupying concern with doctrinal compatibility.[37]

3.2. Significance of English Law Methodology

A consideration sometimes neglected in accounts of South Africa's civilian based 'mixed system' is that it functions on the basis of the method and system of English law.[38] One consequence of this is that the controlling approach in any development involving the assimilation of a new concept tends to be Anglo-American rather than civilian.[39] The inductive approach, very much a feature of English common law methodology, has facilitated a development of Roman-Dutch substantive common law through judicial pronouncement. The absence of controlling code provisions and the dominant 'judicial role factor' gives scope for the development of the law, limited by practical compatibility rather than doctrinal boundaries. This has tended to give an overall development resembling the unstructured common law, in which perceived need drives instrumentality – in contrast to a more predetermined form of legal evolution represented by the modern codified civilian systems. It is significant that English lawyers who – language difficulties aside – face a 'comprehension' barrier in seeking access to codified civil law systems, do not have any real difficulty with South African law; Scots lawyers, equally comfortable with the system and method, but also familiar with much of the underlying substantive civil law, increasingly see the system as kindred.[40]

The foundation influence of an English model of administration of justice in the formative period of South African legal development has produced an adjectival law, which has more in common with modern English law than with the distinctive procedural forms of Scots law. A consequence of this affinity is that in its development, South African procedure has borrowed freely from English law[41]

[37] Testifying to a new order is the fact that the definitive text on the 1996 Bill of Rights is already in its third edition: see J. De Waal, I. Currie and G. Erasmus, *The Bill of Rights Handbook* (Juta, Cape Town, 2000).

[38] For an acknowledgement of this see the comment of Professor Duard Kleyn in Zimmermann and Visser, above n. 2, p. 842, that the protection of possession on the basis of the *mandament van spolie* 'like other remedies received from Roman and Roman-Dutch law, functions within a system of civil procedure, which is predominantly based on English law'.

[39] See H.J. Erasmus, 'The Interaction of Substantive Law and Procedure' in Zimmermann and Visser, above n. 2, p. 141; see also the same author's 'Roman and Common Law in Southern Africa: Past and Future' in J.E. Spruit, W.J. Kamba and M.O. Hinz (eds.), *Roman Law at the Crossroads* (Juta, Cape Town, 2000) pp. 43, 45–48.

[40] That a number of South African specialists contributed to the new history of Scots private law (Reid and Zimmermann, n. 21 above) indicates a perception of proximity between the two systems, even though the Scottish motive may be a voyage of civil law discovery. In a related project, launched at an Edinburgh University Conference in December 2000, aspects of Scots and South African law were considered in chapters researched and written jointly by experts representing the two systems.

[41] See, e.g., *Rhino Hotel & Resort (Pty) Ltd v Forbes and Others* 2000 (1) SA 1180.

where, because of the prominence of legal remedies and the volume of litigation, the growth of adjectival law has flourished.

As a contrast to the approach in respect of property the largely unrestricted influence of English administrative law may be mentioned. South African law's ready capacity to adopt and assimilate English law is no better demonstrated than in the development in this field,[42] a development which had a highly important positive effect in making the executive accountable to the courts in the administration of discriminatory and suppressive legislation during the long years of apartheid government.[43] English law material continues to have a role in decisions on administrative law.[44]

This aspect of the South African mixed system illustrates the point that a 'perspective factor' may affect an assessment of the nature and character of a given system. In this regard, there is a risk that agenda priorities may lead to a selective view of what is central, and the possible neglect of some significant aspect with detriment to depicting the true overall character.[45]

4. Active Normative Character of Reformed System

The 1990s saw the transformation of South African law moving from a monolithic system dominated by a legislature giving effect to minority interest in the name of community interest. Under the 'old order', the law functioned on a positivist basis to the extent that scope for judicial activism was limited to technical rather than normative control;[46] although, even between opponents of the system, there were

---

42 A development no better exemplified than in the groundbreaking text of L. Baxter, *Administrative Law* (Juta, Cape Town, 1984).

43 See my comments in Örücü et al., above n. 13, pp. 182–183.

44 In the *Pharmaceutical Mnfrs* case (above n. 12) Constitutional Court President Chaskalson observed (at p. 694) that 'the development of administrative law in South Africa was much influenced by the developments in England. As a result our Courts have frequently sought guidance from English law on this subject'. See also *Dusani v Minister of Correctional Services and another* 1999 (1) SA 1020 (Tk HC) 1024–1025, where Madlanga J makes use of W. Wade and C. Forsyth, *Administrative Law* (Clarendon Press, Oxford, 1994).

45 It is somewhat surprising that Zimmermann and Visser, above n. 2, pp. 58–59, makes only the barest mention of administrative law as a subject 'largely derived from English law'.

46 As in the development of the protection of possession against title in circumstances which frequently arose in the context of segregation policy evictions; see, e.g., *Fredericks v Stellenbosch Divisional Council* 1977 (3) SA 113 (C) (Kleyn, n. 38 above, pp. 821–822, cites this case as one in which the courts 'have protected mala fide possession even in circumstances where they were fully aware of the mala fides'); other relevant cases are cited in Carey Miller and Pope, above n. 24, p. 599. In contrast, the protection of possession is now on a normative basis: see *Despatch Municipality v Sunridge Estate and Development Corp* 1997 (4) SA 596 (SEC); see also A.J. Van der Walt and A.J. Squatting, 'Spoliation and the New Constitutional Order' (1997) 60 *Tydskrift vir Heedendaagse Romeins-Hollandse Reg* 522.

different views as to the scope for judicial activism.[47] The weak position of lawyers in terms of capacity to initiate and advance change is reflected in their relatively limited contribution to the demise of the old order – represented by isolated and impotent judicial *dicta*[48] and unrepresentative – but sometimes significant – academic criticism of the prevailing system.[49] The 'positivist mentality factor' was identified by Professor A.S. Mathews as an important part of the answer to the question why lawyers 'who ought to have known and done better, failed to retain the rule of law, if not as a living institution, even as an ideal for official behaviour'.[50]

The more complex system, substituted in the politically inspired and driven reform process is dominated by a comprehensive prescribed normative agenda, deriving from a democratic premise – albeit one which, in the socio-political context of South Africa, translates into political reality via an allegiance to 'leadership factor'.

The new order's response to the law's former role as an instrument of oppression has not been to clip its wings – *a la* revolutionary France – but, rather, to equip it in order to function to protect and develop human rights within a context of articulated social norms. Reversing these two priorities, one might say that the new order sets out to achieve social reform in a context and climate of the development of a culture of human rights – including the protection of the rights and interests of minority groups.[51] From an institutional point of view, the Constitution and the Constitutional Court are the key elements; on one interpretation, this is controlling to the extent that, while the role of lawyers has changed from a passive to an active function, this has happened on the basis of a prescribed, if not prescriptive, agenda.

5. Role of Comparative Law in the Reformed System

The Constitution provides that in the interpretation of a provision of the Bill of Rights, 'a court, tribunal or forum ... must consider international law; and ... may consider foreign law'.[52] Other sections in the Constitution deal with international law – specifically: international agreements, customary international law and the

---

47 See above n. 11; see also D.L. Carey Miller, 'South African judges as Natural Lawyers – a Roman-Dutch Basis?' (1973) 90 *South African Law Journal* 86, and Professor John Dugard's reply printed immediately following my comment.

48 See, e.g., Didcott J in *Nxasana*, above n. 18.

49 The most sustained work came from Professor A.S. Mathews of the University of Natal and Professor John Dugard of the University of Witwatersrand; see my comments in Örücü et al., above n. 13, p. 182. One may also note, in this regard, the founding of the *South African Journal on Human Rights*: (1985) 1 *South African Journal on Human Rights* 1.

50 A.S. Mathews, *Freedom State Security and the Rule of Law* (Juta, Cape Town, 1986), p. 297.

51 The work of the Truth and Reconciliation Commission under the Promotion of National Unity and Reconciliation Act 34 of 1995 shows the aim to draw a line under the past and proceed on the basis of an entirely new value system. See J. Sarkin, 'The Trials and Tribulations of South Africa's Truth and Reconciliation Commission' (1996) 12 *South African Journal of Human Rights* 617.

52 S. 39(1)(b) & (c).

application of international law[53] – in provisions which reflect the apparent intention of the framers that South African law should conform with and operate according to international law and standards.

From the point of view of comparative law, the option to consider foreign law is relevant. In developing bill of right jurisprudence concerned with fundamental human rights or universal values, there is scope for consideration of relevant foreign material. The decision of the Constitutional Court abolishing the death penalty, on the basis of the interim Constitution, shows foreign law and legal opinion in this role.[54] Scope for recourse to foreign material also exists in matters of pure constitutional law. In this regard, while formerly, precedents applicable to the Westminster model would have tended to dominate, the shift to a new constitutional order gives scope for a wider ambit of potentially relevant authority.[55]

A perception of the relevance of foreign provisions and precedents in the interpretation of the property clause has motivated some significant academic work. Professor A.J. van der Walt, in a monograph on the constitutional property clause, has argued that in 'interpreting and applying the South African property clause ... one may (and should) make extensive use of examples from a wide range of foreign law'.[56] In coming to this conclusion the learned writer observes that:

> ... differences in the phraseology and structure of a property clause, and even larger structural differences such as between the common-law and civil-law traditions, are often less influential in the interpretation of the property clause than one might expect. Very often the problems which arise and some of the possible solutions are not so much the result of the phraseology, structure or background of the property clause, but rather a function of the role assigned to a constitutional property clause in its social, political and legal context in a specific society[57]

There may well be room for interpretation on a comparative basis at the level of general functioning of the property clause, for example, with regard to what

---

53 See ss. 231–233.

54 *S v Makwanyane* 1995 (3) SA 391(CC); see also *S v Williams* 1995(3) SA 632 (CC) declaring unconstitutional the corporal punishment of juveniles. In *S v Baboyi (Minister of Justice and Another Intervening)* 2000 (2) SA 425, concerned with the reverse onus, the Constitutional Court made extensive reference to North American material in dealing with 'the novel and complex task of establishing the appropriate balance between the state's constitutional duty to provide effective remedies against domestic violence and its simultaneous obligation to respect the constitutional rights of a fair trial of those who might be affected by the measures taken' (at 428).

55 In President of the *RSA v South African Rugby Football Union* 2000 (1) SA 1(CC) the Constitutional Court, concerned with the constitutional role of the President vis-a-vis the administration of civil justice, considered a wide range of authority including material from the law of Canada, German, New Zealand and the United States.

56 A.J. Van der Walt, *The Constitutional Property Clause* (Juta, Cape Town, 1997), pp. 5–6.

57 Ibid., p. 5.

constitutes property for the purposes of protection against deprivation.[58] In this, and on other aspects of the entire issue, the South African literature has paid close attention to German developments[59] as well as to those in common law jurisdictions.[60] This will be considered more fully in the following section.

It would appear that the comparative approach is subject to certain limits. In the critical function of the interpretation of scope-defining provisions that reflect particular domestic policy priorities, it is difficult to see significant room for recourse to foreign material. In this regard, it may be noted that the Bill of Rights interpretation provision, which contains the invitation to have recourse to foreign law, is immediately followed by a subsection confirming that interpretations 'must promote the spirit, purpose and objects of the 'Bill of Rights'.[61] A dictum of the President of the Constitutional Court in the death penalty case is relevant authority on this issue:

> Comparative 'Bills of Rights' jurisprudence will no doubt be of importance, particularly in the early stages of the transition when there is no developed indigenous jurisprudence on which to draw. Although we are told by s. 35(1) that we 'may' have regard to foreign case law, it is important to appreciate that this will not necessarily offer a safe guide to the interpretation of chap. 3 of our Constitution[62]

This is a reference to the interim Constitution, but the sentiments expressed would, it is submitted, hold true in respect of the counterpart chapter 2 (the Bill of Rights chapter) of the final Constitution of 1996. The learned President went on to observe that:

> [i]n dealing with comparative law we must bear in mind that we are required to construe the South African Constitution, and not an international instrument or the constitution of some foreign country, and this has to be done with due regard to our legal system, our history and circumstances, and the structure and language of our own Constitution[63]

---

58 For a summary see Carey Miller and Pope, above n. 24, pp. 294–298.

59 See, e.g., D.G. Kleyn, 'The Constitutional Protection of Property: a Comparison between the German and the South African Approach' (1996) 11 *South African Public Law* 402; see also the strongly comparative discussion and detailed citation of foreign authority in Van der Walt, above n. 56, pp. 30–71. See also H. Mostert, 'The Relevance of Constitutional Protection and Regulation of Property for the Private Law of Ownership in South Africa and Germany' Doctor of Laws Dissertation, University of Stellenbosch, 2000.

60 See, e.g., M. Chaskalson, 'The Problem with Property: Thoughts on the Constitutional Protection of Property in the US and Commonwealth' (1993) 9 *South African Journal of Human Rights* 388.

61 S. 39(2).

62 *S v Makwanyane* 1995 (3) SA 391(CC) para. 39.

63 Ibid. See also now the dictum of Davis J in *City of Cape Town v AD Outpost (Pty) Ltd and Others* 2000 (2) SA 733 (CPD) 746 regarding the apparent similarity between counterpart provisions in the German basic law and the new South African constitution on the issue of freedom of trade and expression in a billboard case: 'There is always a great danger in the uncritical employment of foreign law in the

6. The Land Reform Context

The intense 1990s South Africa debate as to the need for[64] and the appropriate formulation of a property clause[65] made it inevitable that the decision, when it eventually came, reflected a policy choice intended to be given effect to as a matter of clear mandate.[66] What is significant in the South African context is the extent to which the property clause represents the African National Congress' (ANC) land reform agenda, formulated and argued for over an extended period.[67] It would appear that this does more than confirm the legitimacy of the property clause. Arguably, it supports the case for interpretation informed by domestic history rather than by reference to external considerations.

The need for interpretation attuned primarily to the particular policy position of the Constitution was recognised in the Constitutional Court's first relevant decision on the land restitution legislation. At issue, as a deprivation of property, was the system, under which the official publication of notice of a claim has the effect of limiting a landowner's normal rights of use and enjoyment. In *Transvaal Agricultural Union v Minister of Land Affairs*[68] the Constitutional Court rejected the applicant's claim to a right of direct access under the Court's rules and, accordingly, no definitive decision was required on constitutionality. However, in indicating that the Court did not perceive the relevant provisions as infringing the right to property, President Chaskalson observed as follows:

> The restitution of land rights is a complex process in which the rights of registered owners and other persons must be balanced against the constitutional injunctions to ensure that restitution be made where this is just and

---

process of domestic constitutional interpretation. Notwithstanding that art. 12 and s. 22 are similar in wording, the latter must be interpreted in the context of the South African constitutional text and its own pedigree'.

64 See A.J. Van der Walt, 'Property Rights, Land Rights and Environmental Rights' in D.H. van Wyk et al. (ed.), *Rights and Constitutionalism: the New South African Legal Order* (Juta, Cape Town, 1994), pp. 455, 461, 479. As Van der Walt, above n. 56, at p. 2, n. 6 points out, the views expressed in opposition to the inclusion of a property clause were largely driven by reference to the Canadian decision to exclude a property clause from the 1982 *Charter of Rights and Freedoms*.

65 The essentially neutral formulation in s. 28 of the interim Constitution stimulated political and academic debate (see Van der Walt, n. 56 above, at p. 3, n. 9, for references) and a completely different form reflecting the land reform agenda was adopted in s. 25 of the Constitution; for the essential differences see Carey Miller and Pope, above n. 24, pp. 285–309.

66 As the Constitutional Court pointed out in the First Certification Case, 'no universally recognised formulation of the right to property exists'; see in re: *Certification of the Constitution of the Republic of South Africa* 1996 (4) SA 744 (CC), paras. 71–74.

67 Not long after the British negotiated South African union of 1910, African leaders brought their land tenure grievances to Britain. Sol Plaatjie, representing the South African National Native Congress (later the ANC), led a delegation to an official audience with Prime Minister Lloyd George in 1919; see B. Willan, *Sol Plaatjie: Selected Writings* (Witwatersrand University Press, Johannesburg, 1996), pp. 257–264.

68 1997(2) SA 621 (CC) 633.

> equitable. Parliament is given a discretion by the Constitution to decide how this process is to be carried out. Provisions in such legislation that are designed to protect claimants and maintain the status quo pending determination of a claim serve a legitimate purpose

Subject to the Bill of Rights property clause text being controlling, there remains scope for comparative law, in working out an appropriate balance between a protected right of property, and the possible entitlement of a claimant on the basis of the land reform agenda.[69]

A Transvaal High Court Full Bench decision shows the tension in land reform matters between the traditional thinking of the Roman-Dutch common law – in which the right of private ownership has primacy – and revised priorities in terms of the new order. While the majority opinions in this case reflect traditional thinking, a dissenting judgment looks to African sources on the basis of the issue being a matter of African values.[70] The minority approach may seem unexceptional in an African jurisdiction, but, of course, South African legal development is represented by jurisprudence informed by Europe rather than by Africa.

At a more specific level, there is clearly scope for invoking the comparative law approach of 'concept borrowing' in a process of interpretation or implementation of aspects of the land reform agenda. As indicated, South African legal practice and adjectival law has been very much subject to the influence of English law in its development.[71] For this reason it is not surprising to find the Land Claims Court adopting a conceptual device from a decision of the House of Lords. In *Chief Nchabeleng v Chief Phasha*,[72] and in *Van der Walt & others v Lang & others*,[73] the Court applied the 'balance of convenience' approach developed in *American Cyanamid Co v Ethicon Ltd*[74] with regard to the issue of interim relief by way of interdict (injunction) pending the final outcome of a land reform claim.

The land reform context also shows room for a perspective that, while not amounting to an actual invocation of foreign law, reflects a position or conclusion developed in the context of a comparative study or survey. In *Farjas (Pty) Ltd v*

69 See, e.g., E. De Wet, *The Constitutional Enforceability of Economic and Social Rights: the Meaning of the German Constitutional Model for South Africa* (Butterworth, Durban, 1996), pp. 135–137 and, generally, Mostert, above n. 59.

70 *Burmann v Nkosi and Another* 2000 (1) SA 1145 (TPD) 1160; on the issue whether a land reform statute (the Extension of Security of Tenure Act 62 of 1997) could be interpreted to provide for a right of burial, Ngoepe JP invoked, inter alia, the African Charter on Human and Peoples' Rights (1981) in contending for an interpretation of the right of 'freedom of religion, belief and opinion', accorded by the Act on the basis of the Bill of Rights, in arriving at his minority decision that the right existed.

71 See Erasmus, above n. 39.

72 1998 (3) SA 578 (LCC).

73 1999 (1) SA 189 (LCC).

74 [1975] 1 All ER 504 (HL).

Land Claims Commissioner, KwaZulu-Natal[75] comparative work on expropriation[76] is cited in support of an observation by Judge President Bam of the Land Claims Court that in apartheid South Africa expropriation, apparently for public purpose, was in fact frequently in pursuance of racial discrimination.

7. The Bill of Rights – a Carte Blanche for Comparative Law?

South African law is clearly open to external influence to a greater extent than it formerly was. It has joined an international club of jurisdictions in which the normative position of the law is subject to overall control, on a basis intended to reflect appropriate social and cultural values. Notions of universality lead to active comparison of laws and legal processes by reference to common themes expressed in bills of rights, or other constitutional documents.

An initial observation is that South Africa's legal dispensation has, indeed, not changed, in that it continues to order its existence by reference to Western European values. As already observed, the pre-reform law, usurping any significant 'indigenous African factor', largely reflected a civilian substantive position functioning according to English system and method. The new form represents a continuation of this orientation, now consolidated by a constitution and seeking guidance on evaluating criteria. The apparent imperative, of economic viability in the context of a unitary state, involves an implicit acknowledgement of the prerequisite of consolidation, and so appears to rule out any fundamental reorientation to African values. Some writers,[77] however, urge more holistic[78] approach.

That the position or the interpretation of the Constitution does not match the public priority on a particular issue is, of course, a position held in common with some Western democratic states. With regard to capital punishment, it should be noted that the protection of the right to life in South Africa differs from the norm in being unqualified.[79] This would appear to underline the question whether the

75 1998 (2) SA 900 (LCC) 937.

76 The Oxford D. Phil thesis of G.M. Erasmus, *Comparative Compensation Systems for Eminent Domain, Compulsory Purchase and Expropriation* (1991); see also G.M. Erasmus (ed.), *Compensation for Expropriation: a Comparative Study* (UKNCCL Series, London, 1991).

77 See, e.g., G.J. Van Niekerk, 'A common law for Southern Africa: Roman law or indigenous African law?' in Spruit et al., above n. 39, p. 83.

78 A word coined by South African General J.C. Smuts: see W.K. Hancock, *Smuts: the Sanguine Years 1870–1919* (Cambridge University Press, Cambridge, 1962), pp. 304–306; and possibly indicative of his thinking in respect of colonized Africa.

79 The South African Constitution in s. 11 simply provides that '[e]veryone has the right to life'. See De Waal et al., above n. 37, p. 215 where it is also pointed out that in the South African death penalty case (above n. 62) the unqualified character of the right to life was seen as significant. The learned writers observe that 'the absence of qualification indicated that the drafters of the interim Constitution intended the Constitutional Court – and not Parliament – to decide' this difficult question and, as they note: 'This gave the Court, in a political sense, the "authority" to decide the issue and to invalidate the death sentence, despite strong public opinion in favour of its retention'.

transplantation of a moral position, involving considerations of 'hearts and minds', will be successful in the circumstances of far-reaching socio-cultural differences between donor and host.

The Constitutional Courts 'gay rights' decision illustrates a confident position in the application of foreign material to the development of the law. In *National Coalition for Gay and Lesbian Equality v Minister of Justice*,[80] the Court surveyed the repeal of sodomy laws in Western democratic states as a prelude to dealing with the American Supreme Court decision in *Bowers v Hardwick*,[81] in which, in the words of Ackermann J, 'a sharply divided Court, by a majority of five to four, declared itself unpersuaded that the sodomy laws of some 25 states should be invalidated'.[82] After noting the 'sustained criticism' of this decision in the United States, Ackermann J proceeded to deal with the implications of the American position:

> For the purposes of the present case I consider it unnecessary to consider such criticism nor what the present standing of Bowers is in the United States. Our 1996 Constitution differs so substantially, as far as the present issue is concerned, from that of the United States of America that the majority judgment in Bowers can really offer us no assistance in the construction and application of our own Constitution. The 1996 Constitution contains express privacy and dignity guarantees[83] as well as an express prohibition of unfair discrimination on the ground of sexual orientation, which the United States Constitution does not. Nor does our Constitution or jurisprudence require us, in the way that the United States Constitution requires of its Supreme Court, in the case of '... rights not readily identifiable in the Constitution's text', to '... identify the nature of the rights qualifying for heightened judicial protection'[84]

---

80 1999 (1) SA 6 (CC).

81 478 US 186 (1986).

82 See above n. 80, para. 53.

83 Ss. 14 and 10 respectively.

84 See above n. 80, para 55; in the final sentence citing Justice White in Bowers, above n. 81, at pp. 191–192. See also *National Coalition for Gay and Lesbian Equality v Minister of Home Affairs* 2000 (2) SA 1 (CC) 30–31; in ruling on the constitutionality of immigration legislation providing for the rights of 'spouses' from the point of view of the possible equal rights of 'same-sex partners', Ackermann J set out the basis for a comparative survey of jurisprudence dealing with the equality issue from the highest courts of Canada, Israel, the UK and the USA. While noting the different nature of 'their histories, legal systems and constitutional contexts' the learned judge observed that 'these judgments give expression to norms and values in other open and democratic societies based on human dignity, equality and freedom which, in my view, gives clear expression to the growing concern for, understanding of, and sensitivity towards human diversity in general and to gays and lesbians in their relationships in particular'. With reference to s. 39(1)(a) of the Constitution providing for interpretation of the Bill of Rights so as to 'promote the values that underlie an open and democratic society based on human dignity, equality and freedom', the court noted that the foreign jurisprudence was 'an important source from which to illuminate our understanding of the Constitution and the promotion of its informing norms'.

In addition to the clarity of the constitutional position, an underlying reason for the confident approach shown in the South African gay rights case was the relatively well-developed domestic literature. In particular, the Court made use of a *South African Law Journal* article[85] concerned with sexual orientation as a constitutional right – '[i]n what follows I rely heavily on an influential article written by Prof Edwin Cameron'.[86] In a subsequent part of his judgement Ackermann J refers approvingly to an example from the article of the 'absurdly discriminatory'[87] purpose of a particular statutory provision.[88]

The proportionality consideration has arisen,[89] and will continue to arise in the process of adjustment of the existing law to an overriding Bill of Rights. The open nature of the issue of proportionality means that, in any given matter, a wide range of sources is likely to be potentially applicable.[90]

The advent of a new constitution in South Africa has, of course, brought scope for comparative law in the purely constitutional sense of issues of form and procedure, as well as in the potentially vast normative sphere arising from the Bill of Rights.[91]

It would hardly seem open to counter argument that, in terms of the future of South Africa, the most important areas of the Constitution – directed to social and economic reform for the benefit of the majority of the population deprived by a long history of discrimination – are concerned with particular domestic circumstances and conditions, and so, offer limited scope for the application of foreign law. The land reform legislation falls into this category.[92]

---

85 E. Cameron, 'Sexual Orientation and the Constitution: a Test Case for Human Rights' (1993) 110 *South African Law Journal* 450; see citation in the gay rights case, above n. 80, para. 20.

86 See n. 80 above, para. 20.

87 Ibid., para. 75.

88 S. 20A of the Sexual Offences Act 23 of 1957, under which a kissing gay couple would be guilty of an offence, while kissing lesbians and heterosexuals would not, in the hypothetical situation, of the three groups being represented at the same social function.

89 See *Makwanyane*, above n. 62, p. 436, per Chaskalson P, noting that the limitation of rights on the basis of necessary and reasonable considerations in a democratic society ultimately required the balancing of competing interests by 'an assessment based on proportionality'.

90 *In S v Manamela (Director-General of Justice Intervening)* 2000 (3) SA 1, 34 & 43 O'Regan J and Cameron AJ, in their dissenting judgment, adopted arguments made by T. Honoré in *Responsibility and Fault* (Hart Publishing, Oxford, 1999).

91 *Ex parte President of the RSA: Constitutionality of the Liquor Bill* 2000 (1) SA 732 (CC) addressed the issue of the general powers of the Constitutional Court in the context of the President's referral of a Bill on a specific issue of constitutionality. In deciding the matter, reference was made (at 740–741) to the procedure in the 'comparable systems' of the USA, the UK, Australia, New Zealand and Germany, but also to systems in which '[c]omparable procedures' exist ('though none is quite like our own') in Ireland, France, Canada and India.

92 In a comprehensive decision covering many aspects of the law relevant to the application of the Restitution of Land Rights Act 22 of 1994 the Land Claims Court cites exclusively South African authority and opinion; see *In re Kranspoort Community* 2000 (2) SA 124 (LCC). See also *In re Former Highlands Residents: Sonny v Dept of Land Affairs* 2000 (2) SA 351 (LCC) 360–361 in which Gildenhuys J considers the thinking behind and purpose of restitution in terms of the relevant

8. Conclusion – 'Transmigration and Transferability' in Twenty-first Century South Africa

Despite the limitation noted in the previous section, the new circumstances of South African law have increased its appetite for foreign material in terms of both range and volume. A perusal of the law reports of the post-reform era shows that this tendency is especially strong in relation to Bill of Rights matters.[93] The diversity of South Africa's mixed system and the longstanding tendency of lawyers to study abroad are factors in this, both in terms of demand and supply.

A factor in the judicial control of the development of the law in terms of the Constitution is the strength of an established tradition, which has come to mean that the law has a well-developed capacity to assimilate foreign material. South African case law began to develop this capability from the mid-nineteenth century, when the courts had quite frequently to deal with situations involving a tension between the Roman-Dutch common law and potentially influential aspects of English law which, not infrequently, were incompatible on a fundamental basis.[94] The viability of domestic jurisprudence, developed over an extended period, is an important factor in South African law being sufficiently well equipped and resourceful to control the assimilation of foreign material.[95] The practice of the courts to look for guidance in

constitutional provisions and legislation. While the learned judge makes reference to German restitution and to views expressed by South African academic writers as to the basis and purpose of restitution his conclusion is that the process should be seen from the 'perspective of what was taken away' and 'being the purge of a wrong committed through the dispossession of land for racist purposes'. This approach – rightly, it is submitted – puts the emphasis on the relevant domestic history over and above a notionally analogous basis.

93 In *Jooste v Botha* 2000 (2) SA 199, concerned with the legal duty of the father of an illegitimate child to afford him or her love, attention and affection, Van Dijkhorst J considered a wide range of authority including a doctrinal thesis in Afrikaans cited both for its argument and as a secondary source of foreign material.

94 An obvious example is the tension between the civilian *justa causa* and the English consideration as the basis of contract that was worked through in late nineteenth century early twentieth century case law; see D. Hutchison, 'Contract Formation' in Zimmermann and Visser, above n. 2, pp. 166–173.

95 Factors in this regard are: the early reception and development of the idea of a literary tradition associated with the *ius commune* heritage of Roman-Dutch law – on this now see M.L. Hewett, 'The Roman Law in Roman-Dutch Law – Weft or Woof?', in Spruit et al., above n. 39, p. 53. This literary tradition is shown, for example, in the translation of Roman-Dutch works for local use – something consolidated in modern law under the auspices of the Law Revision Committee established in 1949: see H.R. Hahlo and E. Kahn, *The Union of South Africa* (Juta, Cape Town, 1960), pp. 291–292. For an example of the domination of South African sources in relation to issues of pure private law see *Frankel Pollak Vinderine Inc v Stanton NO* 2000 (1) SA 425.

domestic decisions or writings is likely to play a part when some aspect of foreign law is borrowed or adapted.[96]

Another aspect of what might be identified as a critical approach to foreign material by South African courts is to apply the perspective of the donor jurisdiction. Where the standing of a device or interpretation is open to doubt, or has somehow suffered a loss of credibility at home, its value for transfer purposes must come into question. The Constitutional Court's treatment of the US Supreme Court decision in *Bowers*[97] is a recent example. In earlier works, reference has been made to the adoption and subsequent rejection of *Liversidge*[98] in the (so-labelled) 'security legislation' context.[99] This, of course, was not driven by revised English thinking as a precedent *per se*, but rather by what was perceived to be appropriate for South Africa.[100]

The time-warp appearance of pre-1990s South African law reflected its static normative basis and positivist context – both kept firmly in place by a controlling state. The unrepresentative system bred lawyers of legalistic mentality.[101] But, in the areas of life not directly affected by the apartheid state's socio-political agenda, legal development flourished. The development of the protection of the individual's private sphere is an example. On the basis of the Roman *actio iniuriarum*, the courts, over a period, have developed a comprehensive protection of privacy as part of the development of the protection of interests of personality.[102] Significantly, the development – described by Professor Jonathan M. Burchell as 'one of the most impressive and enduring legacies of Roman law'[103] – owes very little to the contemporary, and accessible, North American developments, and reflects a striking

[96] See, e.g., *Ex parte Griffin Shipping Holdings Ltd* 1999 (1) SA 754 (D & CLD) 762–3 where Levinsohn J, having cited relevant dicta of Lindley LJ in *In re English, Scottish and Australian Chartered Bank* [1893] 3 Ch. 385 (CA) 409, notes that Broome J (as he then was) expressed a view to the same effect in *Mahomed v Kazi's Agencies (Pty) Ltd and others* 1949 (1) SA 1162 (N) 1171.

[97] See above n. 81.

[98] *Liversidge v Anderson & Anor* [1942] AC 206.

[99] See Örücü et al., above n. 13, p. 179.

[100] In this context it may be noted that the lists of foreign cases referred to which are published in the South African Law Reports indicate that South African judges continue to refer to the case law of England to a greater extent than to that of any other jurisdiction. In this, the South African and Scottish mixed systems have something in common; a recent study has shown more or less total domination of English case law as external material referred to in Scotland: see E. Örücü, 'Comparative Law as a Tool of Construction in Scottish Courts' (2000) 112 *Juridical Review* 27.

[101] See Mathews, above n. 50, pp. 296–302. See also Lobban, above n. 18, pp. 249–264.

[102] See, generally, J. Neethling, J.M. Potgieter and P.J. Visser, *Neethling's Law of Personality* (Butterworth, Durban, 1996).

[103] See Zimmermann and Visser, above n. 2, at p. 650.

contrast to the failure of English[104] and Scots[105] law to find a solution. The capacity for innovative development of the South African common law may become an even more prominent feature, given the factor of the Bill of Rights and its implications for the interpretation of a rich heritage of common law rules.[106]

The view of South African law as a self-confident system does not necessarily mean that the new, and unfamiliar, role of the South African courts in giving effect to newly entrenched values and rights will proceed without any difficulty. The point is simply that the approach of South African law to foreign authority is likely to be on the basis of assimilation with domestic material, rather than by way of out and out transplantation. That said, the risk of an unsuitable or distorted outcome clearly remains. This could arise from misunderstanding, or misinterpretation of the new legislation or of foreign material brought in as an aid to interpretation. Even at the preliminary, purely domestic stage, difficulties of interpretation can arise. The problem of conflicting interpretations of the definition of 'labour tenant' for the purposes of the Land Reform (Labour Tenants) Act 3 of 1996 – critical in terms of the definition of a revised correlative right position – has been resolved, but illustrates the inherent difficulty involved in establishing the meaning of a complex statutory provision in terms of the priorities of broadly expressed constitutional norms.[107]

The introduction of the novel statutory concepts of 'initial ownership' and 'beneficial occupation', mentioned above,[108] shows a capacity for originality in post-reform South African lawmaking, which goes to structure.[109] Any concern that an interpreting court might think in terms of the structurally incompatible concept of equitable ownership of English law in the interpretation of the concept of 'beneficial occupation' can only be on the basis of acknowledging the possibility of an

104 See, e.g., *Malone v Metropolitan Police Commissioner* [1979] 1 Ch. 344; some 15 years later, one may note the preface comment 'still no legal protection against the gratuitous exposure of private lives by the press'; See R. Wacks, *Privacy and Press Freedom* (Blackstone Press, London, 1995), vii. Only the advent of the European Convention on Human Rights has provided a clear basis for the protection of privacy.

105 The argument that Scots law could also develop protection on the basis of the *actio iniuriarum* has come to nothing. Regarding this possibility see 'Confidential Information' Scottish Law Commission Memorandum no. 40, April 1977, paras. 48–58; D.L. Carey Miller, 'Privacy: Interception of communications' [1980] *Scots Law Times (News)* 209.

106 In *Janse van Rensburg v Grieve Trust CC* 2000 (1) SA 315 (CPD) 326 Van Zyl J supported his conclusion that an extension of the Roman aedilitian actions relevant to sale was appropriate as a matter of private law on the basis of being 'consonant with the spirit and values contained in the Bill of Rights'; the development being consistent with a recognition of 'the adaptability of our common law and of the need to adopt a flexible approach in applying ancient principles to modern legal issues, particularly in the rapidly developing commercial world'.

107 On this see Carey Miller and Pope, above n. 24, pp. 528–532.

108 As to how these new forms fit the existing property system see Carey Miller, above n. 36, pp. 752–758.

109 Rather than being restricted to the normative, which was largely the case with apartheid legislation; see Carey Miller, above n. 35, pp. 191–192.

aberration factor.[110] As a practical observation, it may be noted that the likelihood of this happening in the Constitutional Court is higher than in the Supreme Court of Appeal, given the expertise in private law in the latter.

In the South African context, there would appear to be a limit to any counterpart to the notion of 'shared foundations underpinning European private law making it possible to import a doctrine created by a foreign court and typical of a different legal system'.[111] But the denial or control of a possible import would be likely to be a position open to South African law to a greater extent than it might be to a jurisdiction in the context of modern Europe, where institutional factors may be at work in the promotion of uniformity. Arguably, the 'mixed factor' in South African law becomes potentially more prominent in a context in which the fundamental norms are neutral, in the sense of deriving from the Constitution. In these circumstances, there is no longer any real need to think in terms of the ethos of the *ius commune* as being necessarily prevailing.

While there is clearly scope, and indeed an active appetite,[112] for recourse to relevant foreign material in the development of South African law in its newly found reformist mode, my conclusion is that the system will, by and large, assimilate by reference to its own development and traditions[113] but, of course, informed by a wholly revised value norm agenda. The *ius commune* background includes familiarity with a diverse choice of solutions, sometimes conflicting. To this extent, South African lawyers – perhaps in common with the lawyers of Scotland – should not be subject to the problem of 'how do they England know, who only England know'. While South African law undergoes a sea-change in terms of its normative position on a vast range of issues, it will represent a continuity in a certain important sense. This final point is well illustrated by a Cape High Court Full Bench decision, on an extradition matter.[114] In a judgment unanimously concurred in by his brother judges

---

110 See Carey Miller and Pope, n. 24 above, p. 584.

111 A. Vaquer, 'Importing Foreign Doctrines: yet Another Approach to the Unification of European Private Law? Incorporation of the *Verwirkung* doctrine into Spanish Case Law' (2000) 6 *Zeitschrift für Europäisches Privatrecht* 301.

112 The list of foreign cases (followed; applied; considered; distinguished; dictum or dicta (cited); referred to) compiled in monthly parts of the South African Law Reports demonstrates this; *The Bill of Rights Handbook*, above n. 37, illustrates the extent of recourse to foreign material in the constitutional context.

113 Which, as shown in this paper, includes a readiness and capacity to access the vast resource of relevant English case law; see, e.g., Farlam AJA's application of a House of Lords precedent in *National Director of Public Prosecutions v Carolus and Others* 2000 (1) SA 1127 (SCA) 1144.

114 *S v Harksen* 2000 (1) SA 1185 (C); an appeal to the Constitutional Court failed: see 2000 (2) SA 825 (CC).

the learned judge (Van Zyl J) cites Digest passages from Ulpian and Papinian in Latin and provides his own translation.[115]

South African law has embarked on a new era. Without abandoning its established substantive and methodological base, it has adopted a comprehensive set of norms which revise priorities and control evolution. From a comparative law position, the changes make legal development open to a wider set of influences more likely to emanate from the Bill of Rights than the *ius commune*.

115 Ibid., at 1200. See also *Director of Public Prosecutions: Cape of Good Hope v Bathgate* 2000 (2) SA 535 (CPD) 561 where on the issue of proportionality applied to the problem of provisions directed against crime via the proceeds of crime, Van Zyl J cited the historical acknowledgement of a need to constrain the use of criminally acquired benefits implicit in texts of Ulpian and Paul.

A SHORT BIBLIOGRAPHY OF COMPARATIVE LAW

This bibliography is compiled from the contributions to this book, and is to that extent limited: it does not purport to be comprehensive. However, the reader will find here most of the works in comparative law considered by the contributors to be general and significant. It is hoped this will serve as a convenient tool for those who wish to study or teach comparative law in the 21st century. Individual chapters in collections on comparative law have not all been included.

[A. Harding and E. Örücü]

1. Ajani, G., 'By Chance and Prestige: Legal Transplants in Russia and Eastern Europe' (1995) 43 *American Journal of Comparative Law* 93
2. Allison, J.W.F., *A Continental Distinction in the Common Law* (Oxford University Press, Oxford, 1996)
3. *American Journal of Comparative Law* Special Issue (Symposium: 'New Directions in Comparative Law') (1998) vol. 46(4)
4. Ault, H.J. and Glendon, M.A., 'The Importance of Comparative Law in Legal Education: United States – Goals and Methods of Legal Comparison', in Hazard, J.N. and Wagner, W.J. (eds.), *Law in the USA in Social and Technological Revolution* (Bruylant, Brussels, 1974)
5. Banakas, E.K., 'Some Thoughts on the Method of Comparative Law: The Concept of Law Revisited' (1981) LXVII *Archiv fur Rechts- und Sozialphilosophie* 289
6. Banakas, E.K., 'The Method of Comparative Law and the Question of Legal Culture Today' (1994) 3 *Tilburg Foreign Law Review* 113
7. Bauer, J.R. and Bell, D.A., (eds.), *The East Asian Challenge for Human Rights* (Cambridge, Cambridge University Press, 1999)
8. Bell, D.A., *East Meets West: Human Rights and Democracy in East Asia* (Princeton, Princeton University Press, 2000)
9. Bell, J.S., 'Comparative Law and Legal Theory', in W. Krawietz et al. (ed.), *Prescriptive Formality and Normative Rationality in Modern Legal Systems: Festschrift for Robert Summers* (Duncker and Humblot, Berlin, 1995)
10. Bingham, T., '"There Is a World Elsewhere": Changing Perspectives on English Law' (1992) 41 *International Comparative Law Quarterly* 513
11. Bogdan, M., *Comparative Law* (Kluwer Tano, Göteborg, 1994)
12. Bradley, D., 'Convergence in Family Law: Mirrors, Transplants and Political Economy' (1999) 6 *Maastricht Journal of European and Comparative Law* 127
13. Buckland, W.W., et al., *Roman Law and Common Law* (2nd edn., Cambridge University Press, Cambridge, 1952)
14. Bussani, M. and Mattei, U. 'The Common Core Approach to European Private Law' [1997–1998] *Columbia Journal of European Law* 339
15. Beinart, A., 'The English Legal Contribution in South Africa: the Interaction of Civil and Common Law' (1981) 7 *Acta Juridica* 30

A. Harding and E. Örücü (eds.),
Comparative Law in the 21st Century, 305–312.

16. Cappelletti, M., (ed.), *New Perspectives for a Common Law of Europe* (Sijthof, Leiden/ Boston, 1978)
17. Collins, H., 'Methods and Aims of Comparative Contract Law' (1991) 11 *Oxford Journal of Legal Studies* 396
18. Constantinesco, L.J., *Traité de Droit Comparé: La Méthode Comparative*, Tom II, (Libraire Générale de Droit et de Jurisprudence, Paris, 1974)
19. Cotterrell, R., 'A Legal Concept of Community' (1997) 12 *Canadian Journal of Law and Society* 75
20. Cotterrell, R., 'Law and Community: A New Relationship?' (1998) 51 *Current Legal Problems* 367
21. Cotterrell, R., 'Why Must Legal Ideas Be Interpreted Sociologically?' (1998) 25 *Journal of Law and Society* 171
22. Curran, V.G., 'Cultural Immersion, Difference and Categories in US Comparative Law' (1998) 46 *American Journal of Comparative Law* 43
23. Curran, V.G., 'Dealing in Difference: Comparative Law's Potential for Broadening Legal Perspective' (1998) 46 *American Journal of Comparative Law* 657
24. David, R. and Brierley, J.E.C., *Major Legal Systems in the World Today*, (3rd edn., Stevens, London, 1985)
25. David, R., *Les Grands Systèmes de Droit Contemporain* (9th edn., Dalloz, Paris, 1988).
26. de Cruz, P., *Comparative Law in a Changing World* (2nd edn., Cavendish, London, 1999)
27. Demleitner, N.V., 'Challenge, Opportunity and Risk: An Era of Change in Comparative Law' (1998) 46 *American Journal of Comparative Law* 647
28. Dezalay, Y. and Garth, B., *Dealing in Virtue: International Commercial Arbitration and the Construction of a Transnational Legal Order* (University of Chicago Press, Chicago, 1996)
29. Edge, I.D., (ed.), *Comparative Law in a Global Context* (Transnational, New York, 2000)
30. Emiliou, N., *The Principle of Proportionality in European Law: A Comparative Study* (Kluwer Law International, London, 1996)
31. Evans-Jones, R., 'Receptions of Law, Mixed Legal Systems and the Myth of the Genius of Scots Private Law' (1998) 114 *Law Quarterly Review* 228
32. Evans-Jones, R., 'Roman Law in Scotland and England and the Development of one Law for Britain' (1999) 115 *Law Quarterly Review 1999* 605
33. Ewald, W., 'Comparative Jurisprudence I: What was it Like to Try a Rat?' (1995) 143 *Pennsylvania Law Review* 1889
34. Ewald, W., 'Comparative Jurisprudence II: The Logic of Legal Transplants' (1995) 43 *American Journal of Comparative Law* 489
35. Feest, J. and Gessner, V., (eds.), *The Proceedings of the 2nd Onati Workshop on Changing Legal Cultures* (Onati Institute, Spain, 1998)
36. Fletcher, G.P., 'Comparative Law as a Subversive Discipline' (1998) 46 *American Journal of Comparative Law* 683
37. Friedman, L., 'Borders: On the Emerging Sociology of Transnational Law' (1996) 32 *Stanford Journal of International Law* 65
38. Friedman, L.M., *Law and Society: an Introduction* (Englewood Cliffs, NJ, Prentice Hall, 1977)
39. Friedman, L., 'Is there a Modern Legal Culture?' [1994] *Ratio Juris* 117
40. Glenn, H.P., *Legal Traditions of the World* (Oxford University Press, Oxford, 2000)
41. Lord Goff, 'The Future of the Common Law' (1997) 46 *International and Comparative Law Quarterly* 745
42. Gordley, J., 'Is Comparative Law a Distinct Discipline?' (1998) 46 *American Journal of Comparative Law* 607
43. Grossfeld, B., *The Strength and Weakness of Comparative Law* (Clarendon Press, Oxford, 1990)
44. Graveson, R.H., *One Law: On Jurisprudence and the Unification of Law: Selected Essays Volume II.* (North-Holland, Amsterdam, 1977)
45. Gutteridge, H.C., *Comparative Law* (2nd edn., Cambridge University Press, London, 1949; reprint, Wildy & Sons, London, 1974)
46. Hall, J., *Comparative Law and Social Theory* (Louisiana State University Press, Baton Rouge, 1963)

47. Hahlo, H.R. and Kahn, E., *The South African Legal System and its Background* (Juta, Cape Town, 1968)
48. Harding, A.J., 'Comparative Public Law: a Neglected Discipline?', in Edge, I.D., (ed.), *Comparative Law in Global Perspective* (Transnational, New York, 2000)
49. Harding, A.J., 'Comparative Law and Legal Transplantation in South East Asia: Making Sense of the "Nomic Din"', in Nelken, D. and Feest, J., (eds.), *Adapting Legal Cultures* (Oxford, Hart Publishing, 2001)
50. Harding, A.J., 'Global Doctrine and Local Knowledge: Law in South East Asia' (2002) 51 *International and Comparative Law Quarterly* 35
51. *Hastings International and Comparative Law Review* Special Issue (Symposium: 'New Directions in Comparative Law') (1998) 21(4)
52. Hazard, J.N., *Communists and their Law, a Search for a Common Core of Legal Systems of Marxian Socialist States* (University of Chicago Press, Chicago, 1969)
53. Henkin, L. and Rosenthal, A., (eds.), *Constitutionalism and Rights, the Influence of the United States Constitution Abroad* (Columbia University Press, New York, 1990).
54. Huxley, A., (ed.), *Religion, Law and Tradition: Comparative Studies in Religious Law* (Curzon, Richmond, 2002)
55. Hyland, R., "Comparative Law", in Patterson, D., (ed.), *A Companion to Philosophy of Law and Legal Theory* (Blackwell, London, 1996)
56. Ibbetson, D.J., 'A Reply to Professor Zimmermann' in C. Jamin, 'Le Vieux Rêve de Saleilles et Lambert Revisité' (2000) 4 *Revue Internationale de Droit Comparé* 733.
57. Jagtenberg, R., Örücü, E. and De Roo, A., (eds.), *Transfrontier Mobility of Law* (Kluwer Law International, The Hague, 1995)
58. Jayasuriya, K., (ed.), *Law, Capitalism and Power in Asia: the Rule of Law and Legal Institutions* (Routledge, London, 1999)
59. Joerges, C., "The Impact of European Integration on Private Law: Reductionist Perceptions, True Conflicts and a new Constitutional Perspective" in Gerstenberg, O. and Joerges, C., (eds.), *Private Governance, Democratic Constitutionalism and Supranationalism* (European Commission, Brussels, 1998)
60. Kahn-Freund, O., 'Comparative Law as an Academic Subject' (1966) 82 *Law Quarterly Review* 40
61. Kahn-Freund, O., 'Uses and Misuses of Comparative Law' (1974) *Modern Law Review* 1
62. Kamba, W.J., 'Comparative Law: A Theoretical Framework' (1976) 23 *International Comparative Law Quarterly* 494
63. Koopmans, T., "Sources of Law: the New Pluralism", in *Festskrift til Ole Due* (Liber Amicorum, GEC Gads Forlag, Copenhagen, 1994)
64. Koopmans, T., 'Comparative Law and the Courts' (1998) 45 *International and Comparative Law Quarterly* 545
65. Kozyris, P.G., 'Comparative Law for the 21st Century: New Horizons and New Technologies' (1994) 69 *Tulane Law Review* 165
66. Lawson, F.H., 'The Field of Comparative Law' (1949) LXI *Juridical Review* 16
67. Lawson, F.H., *The Comparison: Selected Essays, Volume II.* (North-Holland, Amsterdam, 1977)
68. Legrand, P., 'How to Compare Now?' (1996) 16 *Legal Studies* 232
69. Legrand, P., 'The Impossibility of Legal Transplants' (1997) 4 *Maastricht Journal of European and Comparative Law* 111
70. Legrand, P., 'Against a European Civil Code' (1997) 60 *Modern Law Review* 44
71. Legrand, P. and Merryman, J.H., 'Comparative Legal Studies: A Dialogue' (1999) 47 *American Journal of Comparative Law* 201
72. Legrand, P. and Munday, R., (ed.), *Comparative Legal Studies: Traditions and Transitions* (Cambridge, Cambridge University Press, 2002)
73. Legrand, P., *Fragments on Law as Culture* (Tjeenk Willink, Deventer, 1999)

74. Levy, E., 'The Reception of Highly Developed Legal Systems by Peoples of Different Cultures' (1950) 25 *Washington Law Review* 233
75. Markesinis, B.S., 'Comparative Law: a Subject in Search of an Audience' (1990) 53 *Modern Law Review* 1
76. Markesinis, B.S., (ed.), *The Gradual Convergence* (Clarendon Press, Oxford, 1994)
77. Markesinis, B.S., *Foreign Law and Comparative Methodology* (Hart Publishing, Oxford, 1998)
78. Markesinis, B.S., (ed.), *The Clifford Chance Millennium Lectures: The Coming Together of the Common Law and the Civil Law* (Hart Publishing, Oxford, 2000)
79. Mattei, U., 'Efficiency in Legal Transplants: An Essay in Comparative Law and Economics' (1994) 14 *International Review of Law and Economics* 3
80. Mattei, U., 'Three Patterns of Law: Taxonomy and Change in the World's Legal Systems' (1997) 45 *American Journal of Comparative Law* 5
81. Mattei, U. and Reimann, M., 'Introduction' (1998) 46 *American Journal of Comparative Law* 597
82. Mattei, U., 'An Opportunity Not to be Missed: The Future of Comparative Law in the United States' (1998) 46 *American Journal of Comparative Law* 709
83. Menski, W.F., *Comparative Law in a Global Context: the Legal Systems of Asia and Africa* (Platinium, London, 2000)
84. Moccia, L., 'Historical Overview on the Origins and Attitudes of Comparative Law' in De Witte, B. and Forder, C., (eds.), *The Common Law of Europe and the Future of Legal Education* (Metro, Kluwer Law International, Deventer, 1992)
85. Monateri, P.G., '"Everybody's Talking": The Future of Comparative Law' (1996) 21 *Hastings International and Comparative Law Review* 825
86. Monateri, P.G., 'The "Weak" Law: Contaminations and Legal Cultures', in *Italian National Reports for the XVth International Congress of Comparative Law, Bristol 1998*, (Guiffre editore, Milano, 1998)
87. Müller-Graff, P.C., 'Common Private Law in the European Community' in De Witte, B. and Forder, C., (eds.), *The Common Law of Europe and the Future of Legal Education* (Metro, Kluwer Law International, Deventer, 1992)
88. Nelken, D., "Disclosing/ Invoking Legal Culture" in D. Nelken (ed.), *Social and Legal Studies, Special Issue: Legal Culture, Diversity and Globalisation* (1995) 4:4, 435
89. Nelken D.,(ed.), *Comparing Legal Cultures* (Dartmouth, Aldershot, 1997)
90. Nelken, D., "Studying Criminal Justice Comparatively" in Maguire, M., Morgan, R. and Reiner, R., (eds.), *The Oxford Handbook of Criminology* (2nd edn., Oxford University Press, Oxford, 1997)
91. Nelken D.,(ed.), *Contrasting Criminal Justice*, (Dartmouth, Aldershot, 2000)
92. Nelken D. and Feest, J., (eds.), *Adapting Legal Cultures* (Hart Publishing, Oxford, 2001)
93. Nelken, D., "Beyond the Metaphor of Legal Transplants? Some Consequences of *Autopoiesis* Theory for the Study of Cross Cultural Legal Adaptation" in Priban, J. and Nelken, D., (eds.), *The Consequences of Autopoeisis* (Dartmouth, Aldershot, 2001)
94. Obiora, L.A., 'Toward an Auspicious Reconciliation of International and Comparative Analyses' (1998) 46 *American Journal of Comparative Law* 669
95. Örücü, E., *Symbiosis between Comparative Law and Theory of law – Limitations of Legal Methodology*, (Erasmus Universiteit Rotterdam, Mededelingen van het Juridisch Instituut Nr. 16, Rotterdam, 1982)
96. Örücü, E., 'A Theoretical Framework for Transfrontier Mobility of Law' in Jagtenberg, R., Örücü, E. and De Roo, A., (eds.), *Transfrontier Mobility of Law* (Kluwer Law International, The Hague, 1995)
97. Örücü, E., Attwooll, E. and Coyle, S., (eds.), *Studies in Legal Systems: Mixed and Mixing* (Kluwer Law International, London, 1996)
98. Örücü, E., 'Mixed and Mixing Systems: A Conceptual Search' in Örücü, E., Attwool, E. and Coyle, S., (eds.), *Studies in Legal Systems: Mixed and Mixing* (Kluwer Law International, London, 1996)
99. Örücü, E., 'Shifting Horizons for Comparative Law in the New Century' (2000) 8 *Asia Pacific Law Review* 115

100. Örücü, E., *Critical Comparative Law: Considering Paradoxes for Legal Systems in Transition* (Kluwer Law International, Deventer, 1999)
101. Örücü, E., 'Critical Comparative Law: Considering Paradoxes for Legal Systems in Transition' (2000) 4 *Electronic Journal of Comparative Law* 2
102. Örücü, E., 'Law as Transposition' (2002) 51 *International Comparative Law Quarterly* 205
103. Péteri, Z., "Some Aspects of the Sociological Approach in Comparative Law" in Péteri, Z., (ed.), *Hungarian Law – Comparative Law: Essays for the 8th International Congress of Comparative Law* (Académiai Kiadó, Budapest, 1970)
104. Puchalska-Tych, B. and Salter, M., 'Comparing Legal Cultures of Europe: the Need for a Dialectical Analysis' (1996) 16 *Legal Studies* 157
105. Reimann, M., 'Stepping Out of the European Shadow: Why Comparative Law in the United States Must Develop Its Own Agenda' (1998) 46 *American Journal of Comparative Law* 637
106. Reimann, M., (ed.), *The Reception of Continental Ideas in the Common Law World 1820–1920* (Duncker and Humblot, Berlin, 1993)
107. Reitz, J.C., 'How to do Comparative Law' (1998) 46 *American Journal of Comparative Law* 597
108. Rheinstein, M., 'Types of Reception' (1956) 6 *Annales de la Faculté de Droit d'Istanbul* 34
109. Riles, A., (ed.), *Rethinking the Masters of Comparative Law* (Hart Publishing, Oxford, 2001)
110. Roebuck, D., 'The Past is Another Country: Legal History as Comparative Law' (1994) 2 *Asia Pacific Law Review (Special Issue)*
111. Sacco, R., 'Legal Formants: a Dynamic Approach to Comparative Law' (1991) 39 *American Journal of Comparative Law* 1 and 343
112. Samuel, G., 'Comparative Law and Jurisprudence' (1998) 47 *International and Comparative Law Quarterly* 817
113. Samuel, G., 'Comparative Law as a Core Subject' (2001) 21 *Legal Studies* 444
114. Schmid, C.U., 'The Emergence of a Transnational Legal Science in European Private Law' (1999) 10 *Oxford Journal of Legal Studies* 673
115. Schwarze, J., (ed.), *Administrative Law under European Influence* (Sweet and Maxwell, London, 1996)
116. Seidman, A. and Seidman, R.B., *State and Law in the Development Process: Problem Solving and Institutional Change in the Third World* (Macmillan, Basingstoke, 1994)
117. Seidman, R.B., 'Administrative Law and Legitimacy in Anglophonic Africa: A Problem in the Reception of Foreign Law' (1970) 5 *Law and Society Review* 161
118. Seidman, R.B., "The Reception of English Law in Colonial Africa" in Ghai, Y., Luckman, R. and Snyder, F., (eds.), *The Political Economy of Law* (Oxford University Press, Oxford, 1987)
119. Schlesinger, R.B., (ed.), *Formation of Contracts: a Study on the Common Core of Legal Systems* (Oceana, Dobbs Ferry, Vol. I, 1968)
120. Schlesinger, R.B., 'The Past and Future of Comparative Law' (1995) 43 *American Journal of Comparative Law* 477
121. Smits, J.M., 'A European Private Law as a Mixed System' (1998) 5 *Maastricht Journal of European and Comparative Law* 328
122. Smits, J.M., 'How to Take the Road Untravelled? European Private Law in the Making: A Review Essay' (1999) 6 *Maastricht Journal of European and Comparative Law* 25
123. Smits, J.M., "Multiculturalisme in Europees privaatrecht: een pleidooi" in *Nederlands Tijdschrift voor Burgerlijk Recht* (2000) p. 289
124. Smits, J.M., *The Good Samaritan in European Private Law; on the Perils of Principles without a Programme and a Programme for the Future* (Kluwer, Deventer, 2000)
125. Smits, J.M., 'A European Private Law as a Mixed Legal System' (1998) 5 *Maastricht Journal of European and Comparative Law* 328
126. Smits, J.M., *Europees Privaatrecht in Wording* (Intersentia, Antwerpen-Apeldoorn-Oxford, 1999)
127. Taylor, V., (ed.), *Asian Laws Through Australian Eyes* (Sydney, LBC, 1997)
128. Teubner, G., 'Legal Irritants: Good Faith in British Law or How Unifying Law Ends Up in New Divergences' (1998) 61 *Modern Law Review* 11

129. *Tulane Law Review*, Special Issue ('Centennial World Congress on Comparative Law', New Orleans 2000) [2001]
130. Twining, W., 'Globalization and Comparative Law' (1999) 6 *Maastricht Journal of European and Comparative Law* 217
131. Twining, W., 'Comparative Law and Legal Theory: the Country and Western Tradition' in Edge, I.D., (ed.), *Comparative Law in Global Context* (Transnational, New York, 2000)
132. Twining, W., *Globalization and Legal Theory* (Butterworths, London, 2000)
133. van Caenegem, R.C., *Judges, Legislatures and Professors* (Cambridge, 1987)
134. van Caenegem, R.C., *An Historical Introduction to Western Constitutional Law* (Cambridge University Press, Cambridge, 1995)
135. van Gerven, W., 'Casebooks for a Common Law of Europe' (1996) 4 *European Review of Private Law* 67
136. van Gerven, W., 'A Common Law for Europe: the Future Meeting the Past' (2000) 8 *European Review of Private Law* (forthcoming)
137. van Gerven, W., "Comparative Law in a Texture of Communitarization of National Laws and Europeanization of Community Law" in *Liber Amicorum* in honour of Lord Slynn of Hadley, Vol. I, O'Keeffe, D., (ed.), *Judicial Review in European Community Law* (Kluwer Law International, The Hague, 2000)
138. van Hoecke, M. and Warrington, M., 'Legal Cultures and Legal Paradigms: Towards a New model for Comparative Law' (1998) 47 *International and Comparative Law Quarterly* 495
139. van Hoecke, M. and Ost, F., 'Legal doctrine in crisis: towards a European legal science' (1998) 18 *Legal Studies* 197
140. van Hoecke, M., "The Harmonization of Private Law in Europe: Some Misunderstandings", in van Hoecke, M. and Ost, F. (eds.), *The Harmonization of European Private Law* (Hart Publishing, Oxford, 2000)
141. Walker, N., 'European Constitutionalism and European Integration' [1996] *Public Law* 266
142. Ward, I., 'The Limits of Comparativism: Lessons from UK-EC Integration' (1995) 2 *Maastricht Journal of European and Comparative Law* 23
143. Watkin, T.G., *The Italian Legal Tradition*, (Dartmouth, Ashgate, 1997)
144. Watkin, T.G., (ed.), *The Europeanization of Law* (UKNCCL, London, 1998)
145. Watson, A., *Legal Transplants: An Approach to Comparative Law* (Scottish Academic Press, Edinburgh, 1974)
146. Watson, A., 'Legal Transplants and Law Reform' (1976) 92 *Law Quarterly Review* 79
147. Watson, A., *Social and Legal Change* (Scottish Academic Press, Edinburgh, 1977)
148. Watson, A., 'Legal Change: Sources of Law and Legal Culture' (1983) 131 *University of Pennsylvania Law Review* 1121
149. Watson, A., *The Evolution of Law* (Blackwell, Oxford, 1985)
150. Watson, A., *Roman Law and Comparative Law* (University of Georgia Press, Athens, Georgia, 1991)
151. Watson, A., *Legal Origins and Legal Change* (Hambledon Press, London, 1991)
152. Watson, A., *Legal Transplants: An Approach to Comparative Law* (2nd edn., University of Georgia Press, Athens, Georgia, 1993)
153. Watson, A., 'Aspects of Reception of Law' (1996) 44 *American Journal of Comparative Law* 345
154. Watson, A., *Legal Transplants Again*, Ius Commune Lectures on European Private Law (Research School Ius Commune, Maastricht, 2000)
155. Watson, A., *Law out of Context* (University of Georgia Press, Athens, Georgia, 2000)
156. Watson, A., 'Legal Transplants and European Private Law' (December 2000) 4 *Electronic Journal of Comparative Law* 9
157. White, A., 'Some Problems of a Hybrid Legal System: A Case Study of St. Lucia' (1981) 30 *International Comparative Law Quarterly* 879
158. Wiegand, W., 'The Reception of American Law in Europe' (1991) 39 *American Journal of Comparative Law* 229

159. Wiener, J., *Globalization and the Harmonization of Law* (Pinter, London, 1999)
160. Wise, E., 'The Transplant of Legal Patterns' (1990) 38 (Supplement) *American Journal of Comparative Law* 1
161. Lord Woolf, '*Droit Public*-English Style' [1995] *Public Law* 57
162. Yntema, H., 'Comparative Legal Research – Some Remarks on Looking out of the Cave' (1956) 54 *Michigan Law Review* 902
163. Yntema, H., 'The American Journal of Comparative Law' (1952) 15 *American Journal of Comparative Law* 1
164. Zimmermann, R., "Roman Law in a Mixed Legal System – the South African Experience", in Evans-Jones, R., (ed.), *The Civil Law Tradition in Scotland* (Stair Society, Edinburgh, 1995)
165. Zimmermann, R., "Roman Law and European Legal Unity" in Hartkamp, A., (ed.), *Towards a European Civil Code* (2nd ed., Kluwer Law International, 1998)
166. Zimmermann, R. and Visser, D., (eds.), *Southern Cross; Civil Law and Common Law in South Africa* (Clarendon Press, Oxford, 1996)
167. Zweigert, K. and Kötz, H., *An Introduction to Comparative Law* (3rd. edn., trans. Weir, A., Clarendon Press, Oxford, 1998)
168. Zweigert, K., "Quelques Réflexions sur les Relations entre la Sociologie Juridique et le Droit Comparé", in Cassin, et al., R., *Aspects Nouveau de la Pensée Juridique: Recueil d'Etudes en Hommage à Marc Ancel* (Pedone, Paris, 1975)

INDEX

W.G. Hart Legal Workshop Series

Volume 1
Property Problems from Genes to Pension Funds, 1998.
(Editor J.W. Harris)
ISBN 90-411-9643-9

Volume 2
Law Making in the European Union, 1998.
(Editors Paul Craig and Carol Harlow)
ISBN 90-411-9683-8

Volume 3
Legal Regulation of the Employment Relation, 2000.
(Editors Hugh Collins, Paul Davies and Roger Rideout)
ISBN 90-411-9812-1

Volume 4
Comparative Law in the 21st Century, 2002.
(Editors Andrew Harding and Esin Örücü)
ISBN 90-411-9875-X

www.ingramcontent.com/pod-product-compliance
Lightning Source LLC
LaVergne TN
LVHW020644300926
849161LV00004B/801
* 9 7 8 9 0 4 1 1 9 8 7 5 4 *